Finance for Non-Financial Managers

An Active-Learning Approach

A.H. Millichamp
B.A., M Soc.Sc., F.C.A., F.C.C.A., A.T.I.I.

Alan Millichamp is a former lecturer at the University of Wolverhampton. He has many years experience in teaching accounting to student accountants and to managers. His current activities include tutoring managers in accounting at the Open University Business School.

DP Publications Ltd
Aldine Place
London W12 8AW
1992

Acknowledgements

A CIP catalogue record for this book can be obtained from the British Library

ISBN 1 873981 06 6

Copyright A.H. Millichamp © 1992

Typeset by
DP Publications Ltd

Printed in Great Britain by
The Guernsey Press Co Ltd

Preface

Aim

The aim of this book is to provide an activity- based approach to *Finance for non- financial managers*. It will be found most useful on those courses where students are encouraged to be active participants in the learning process.

Typical courses on which it can be used include:

D.M.S., M.B.A., BTEC Higher National, Certified Diploma in Accounting and Finance, Degree Courses in which Accounting and Finance is a part and all courses (eg engineering, personnel, sales, purchasing, catering, tourism etc) on which students need an understanding of accountancy in order to communicate with accountants and implement necessary financial controls and plans as part of their management role.

Approach

The book has a practical approach and is carefully structured to support and encourage the students to discover and to learn by doing.

There are three main sections:

Section 1

This section traces the rapid growth of a company from *inception* through its first *ten years*. The owner of the company is *not* an accountant but has to learn to *understand* and *use* financial accounts, management accounts and financial management techniques in order to successfully manage his company.

You are presented with the problems as seen through the eyes of the owner of the company and via tackling and solving the problems, discover, as he does, the accountancy and financial knowledge and skills required of non-accountant managers.

Section 2: The Information Bank

This section provides a concise but well illustrated summary of Financial Accounting, Management Accounting and Financial Management principles and practice.

Students consult the Information Bank to carry out the Tasks in Section 1. The Tasks are fully referenced to the Information Bank.

Section 3: Developing knowledge and skills

A mixture of Exercises, Case Studies and Assignments enables the student to gain practice and develop understanding and practical skills. In addition, some subjects are pursued in more depth and further examples and problems given.

The section can be used as directed by lecturers, as a diagnostic tool by students or as revision.

Brief answers are provided in the appendix to some of the questions.

Note for lecturers

This book may be used in a variety of ways. For example as a classroom workbook, as a basis of directed but unsupervised learning, as a conventional textbook, as a follow up of formal teaching or a mixture of the above. Plenty of examples are included for classroom teaching and as homework and assignments.

Lecturers' supplement

A comprehensive Lecturers' Supplement is available free to lecturers adopting this book as a course text.

The supplement contains:

❐ Answers for all tasks in Section 1

❐ Answers and Guidance notes for all the exercises, case studies and assignments in Section 3

❐ Suggestions for role play, group work, further reading etc.

Appendices

There are appendices:

a. Answers to some of the exercises in Section 3;

b. A Glossary of Accounting Terms.

Suggestions and criticisms

In the preparation of this book, I have drawn on long experience in teaching full-time, part-time and distance learning students in the classroom and on the telephone and in marking many thousands of scripts and assignments. I have received many helpful suggestions from students, managers and colleagues. I would welcome many more.

Alan Millichamp
August 1992

Contents

Section 3: Developing knowledge and skills

Section 1

Discovering finance

This section consists of fifteen Units, each containing several single story line scenarios. Each Unit illustrates some managerial problem or need or practice from which you can discover a part of the theory and practice of Financial Accounting, Management Accounting or Financial Management.

Each Unit has:

❏   Scenarios

❏   Quick answer questions (QAQs)

❏   Tasks.

Scenarios

The scenarios describe the experiences of Martin who has set up a business initially to wholesale padlocks. He is faced with the problems of cash flow forecasting, understanding Profit and Loss Accounts and Balance Sheets, budgeting, pricing his products, investment appraisal and many others.

We follow his experiences over ten years as he expands, moves into manufacturing, takes over other businesses, and finally contemplates floating his company on the Stock Exchange.

Quick answer questions

These are questions which draw your attention to key features of the Scenarios. *Always* make some attempt at the Quick answer questions *before* looking at the answers. The answers will always be on the *next left hand* page.

Tasks

There are several Tasks within each Unit. These define the core knowledge, understanding and skills which practical managers need in accounting. To deal with them you will most likely need to study the Information Bank in Section 2; each Task is referenced to a specific part of the Information Bank. There are also Extension tasks in some units which enable those of you with Spreadsheet experience to develop themes on your computers.

Discovery and learning

The Quick answer questions and the Tasks are vital parts of the discovery and learning process. They should not be ignored or skimped.

The Units and Scenarios have been arranged in a sequence which progressively develops your knowledge, understanding and skills. They should be worked on in sequence and not in a haphazard fashion.

Happy learning!

Section 1 Units: Discovering finance

Unit 1: Starting a new business

Introduction

The objective of this first unit is to introduce three of the financial matters found on starting a new business. These are the provision of **capital**, **cash flow forecasting** *and the acquisition of* **fixed assets**.

Scenario 1

Martin is a production control manager of a department of Stubbykey plc a large firm manufacturing padlocks. Stubbykey are suffering from a reduction in demand for their products and, in a cost reduction exercise, Martin is made redundant. He is given some £10,000 severance pay which he invests in a deposit account at the Mudland Bank. He is unable to get a new well-paid job and determines instead to start a business buying or making padlocks and selling them to small hardware and security shops.

He talks over his intentions with his friend Ted, a manufacturers' agent who tells him the main problem with new businesses is the need for *capital*. Martin considers his private affairs and realises that, in addition to his severance pay, he has some £5,000 of savings invested in the Impeccable Building Society.

Quick answer questions 1a

1. *How much capital has Martin got?*

2. *In what form does Martin hold his capital?*

3. *Why does Martin's new business need capital?*

Scenario 2

Martin decides to go ahead with starting the business but takes advice from Anne whom he appoints as his accountant and auditor. Anne suggests that he forms a *company* to operate the business and agrees to form it for him. The company is to be called *Martin Padlocks Limited*. She suggests that he should begin by preparing a cash flow forecast as it will be necessary to make arrangements to open a bank account – and bank managers need a cash flow forecast.

To this end he thinks hard, makes some informed guesses and estimates and sets out the following set of facts about the company's first six months: (the company will begin on January 1st 19x1).

a. He can sell his padlocks at cost + 50%. He reckons that the market will allow him to make sales at this price.

b. He should be able to make sales as follows:

	Jan	Feb	Mar	Apr	May	Jun
Sales in £'000	6	9	15	15	18	18

His customers will on average pay in the second month following delivery. For example sales in January will result in the receipt of cash in March.

c. He will need to acquire an immediate *stock* to cost £8,000 and increase this by £1,000 every month, beginning in February, till the end of June as he will need a good stock to be able to satisfy customers' needs. In addition he will need to buy in each month sufficient stock to meet the following month's sales.

Thus in February he will need to buy £1,000 + £10,000 (because £10,000 + 50% = £15,000, the estimated sales for the following month) = £11,000 of stock. He will pay for his stock purchases in the month following each purchase.

d. Anne will charge him £500 for forming the company, preparing the cash flow forecast and general advice. This will be paid in March

e. He will need a computer (£1,000), a second hand van (£5,000) and some stacking equipment (£3,000). These sums need to be paid in January.

f. He needs to pay for a small workshop: 6 month's rent in advance payable in January £2,000; Rates £750 for the period to September payable in May; electricity £220 payable in April; stationery payable in January £240; Advertising payable in March and June £600 each.

g. Van running expenses payable as incurred at £200 a month.

h. Wages to his two assistants will be payable monthly and will be £900 a month to Lucy and Tom £600.

i. A salary to himself £700 a month which is low but he wants to keep his *drawings* low to start with in order to build up the business.

j. He will put his £15,000 into the company in January and will be issued with £1 *shares* in exchange.

 Tasks 1.1

1. *What would you expect his cash flow forecast for the first six months to look like?*

   Note that you can prepare a cash flow forecast:

   i. On any piece of paper

   ii. Using a form supplied for this purpose by any branch of a high street bank

   iii. Using a *spreadsheet* programme on a computer.

Section 2 – Information Bank Topic 15 Cash Flow Forecasting, page 182

A

Quick answer questions 1a: *Answers and comments*

1. Martin has a total capital of £15,000. He may well have other possessions (accountants usually call possessions assets) such as a house on mortgage but all we know about is £15,000.

2. His capital of £15,000 is held in the form of

		£
Assets:	Impeccable Building Society	5,000
	Deposit Account Mudland Bank	10,000
Capital:		15,000

   You will note that you can consider capital in two ways:

   the total amount

   the detailed way that the capital is held.

   Accountants frequently look at capital in this dual way.

3. We will look at this again later but two points may give you an indication:

   a. He will need to acquire some equipment to store his stock of padlocks and also he will need to buy a van and a computer to keep records on.

   b. He will need to pay for some padlocks to put into stock so that he can sell them. He will have to pay for these padlocks. In addition when he has sold them it may be some time before the customers actually pay for them.

   So, before the business receives any money it will have to make some payments. The amount needed will be put into the business by Martin as the initial capital of the business.

Scenario 3

The cash flow forecast that was actually prepared looked like this:

Martin Padlocks Ltd Cash Flow Forecast for the six months to June 19x1

	Jan £	Feb £	Mar £	Apr £	May £	Jun £	Total £
Receipts:							
Customers			6,000	9,000	15,000	15,000	45,000
Capital	15,000						
Total	15,000		6,000	9,000	15,000	15,000	60,000
Payments:							
Suppliers		14,000	11,000	11,000	13,000	13,000	62,000
Anne			500				500
Computer	1,000						1,000
Van	5,000						5,000
Equipment	3,000						3,000
Rent	2,000						2,000
Rates					750		750
Electricity				220			220
Stationery	240						240
Advertising			600			600	1,200
Van Expenses	200	200	200	200	200	200	1,200
Wages	1,500	1,500	1,500	1,500	1,500	1,500	9,000
Martin	700	700	700	700	700	700	4,200
Total	13,640	16,400	14,500	13,620	16,150	16,000	90,310
B/F (a)	0	1,360	−15,040	−23,540	−28,160	−29,310	0
C/F (b)	1,360	−15,040	−23,540	−28,160	−29,310	−30,310	−30,310
	(c)	(d)					(e)

Note:

a) B/F stands for *Brought Forward* and indicates the balance at the beginning of the month which is nil at the 1st January 19x1.

b) C/F stands for *Carried Forward* and indicates the balance at the end of the month.

c) At the end of January the balance in the bank will be *Receipts* £15,000 less *Payments* £13,640.

d) At the end of February the Balance will be £1,360 − £16,400 = £15,040 overdrawn. All the overdrawn balances have a minus sign −.

e) The total column forms a check on the detail columns.

As this was the first Task, I have given the answer but future tasks will not have answers.

After preparing the cash flow forecast Martin and Anne sit down to review it. They find that the balances at the bank at the end of each month are likely to be:

	Jan £	Feb £	Mar £	Apr £	May £	Jun
In the bank	1,360					
Overdrawn		15,040	23,540	28,160	29,310	30,310

Martin is horrified to realise that, despite putting £15,000 of his capital into the company, a large overdraft would be necessary.

Quick answer questions 1b

1. *Summarise the principal reasons why payments will greatly exceed receipts in the first six months of trading.*

2. *What would happen if Martin wanted to make payments and the bank overdraft was at or over its limit?*

Scenario 4

Martin arranges an appointment with the manager of his local branch of the Mudland Bank plc and takes Anne with him. The manager agrees to grant the company an *overdraft facility* of £15,000 as he does not wish to invest more in the company than Martin. This is insufficient as £30,000 is needed but Anne suggests some ways that the extra can be found. These are:

a. agreeing with his suppliers that he will receive two months credit instead of one month for a period of six months;

b. *leasing* the van for £200 a month instead of paying for it outright.

The bank manager also suggests that the *capital expenditure* might be financed separately. Martin is not quite sure what capital expenditure is and asks Anne to explain it to him after the meeting.

Anne explains that capital expenditure is expenditure on the acquisition of fixed assets which leaves Martin still in the dark.

 Tasks 1.2

1. Recast the cash flow forecast to take into account the changes suggested by Anne but not those suggested by the bank manager

 | Section 2 – Information Bank Topic 15 Cash Flow Forecasting, page 178-183

2. List the fixed assets which Martin's company intend to buy and discuss how businesses distinguish capital expenditure from *revenue expenditure* like rent, electricity and wages.

 | Section 2 – Information Bank Topic Depreciation 3.1 and 3.2, page 116

Quick answer questions 1b: *Answers and comments*

1. The principal reasons why payments are greater than receipts in the first six months are:

    a. Martin will need to pay for some items as soon as he starts. These include the computer, the Van, the Equipment and Anne's fee.

    b. The company will need to build up a stock which has to be paid for before it is sold.

    c. The company will trade on credit. This means it will buy goods in one month and pay for them at an agreed later date. Most suppliers expect payment in the month following the purchase but frequently find that customers take longer to pay than the agreed time allowed. Similarly Martin has to give credit to his customers. The problem arises as Martin gives more credit to his customers than his suppliers give to him.

2. He would have to delay making them until money came in from customers but by then other payments may be due. Ultimately being unable to make payments when they fall due can cause a business to go into receivership or liquidation or, in a word, go bust.

Extension tasks

1. Continue the cash flow forecast for the second six months on the assumptions:
   - ❏ Sales will stabilise at £18,000 a month
   - ❏ Stock will stabilise at the end of June
   - ❏ Rent will be £2,000 payable in July and rates will be £500 in October
   - ❏ Electricity will be £300 in July and £300 in October
   - ❏ Stationery will be £200 in August
   - ❏ Advertising will be £600 in September and December
   - ❏ Wages and Martin's salary will continue at the same amount.
2. Explain why the overdraft steadily diminishes.
3. Put the forecast on a spreadsheet.

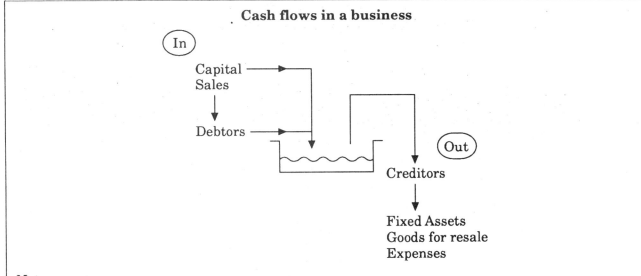

Cash flows in a business

Note:

1. The supply of fixed assets, goods for resale and expenses can be maintained without payment as long as *credit* can be obtained from suppliers of these things.

2. Sales do not immediately lead to an inflow of cash as sales are on credit.

3. The trick is to collect debts as fast as possible while keeping *creditors* waiting a reasonable time.

Summary of Unit 1

1. Starting a new business usually involves finding some capital to put into the business.

2. Before beginning to trade a new business needs to seek advice from an accountant.

3. Some businesses just begin with no formalities. Some are formed as limited companies as is Martin Padlocks Ltd. A limited company has to be registered with the Registrar of Companies. Formation can be performed by accountants, lawyers or on a do-it-yourself basis using company formation agents who advertise in the business press.

4. It is essential to forecast cash flows for at least the first six months of a new business. Accountants often assist in this process. The cash flow forecast often shows that the business will need more money than the initial capital invested. The most common source of this extra cash is a bank overdraft.

5. A cash flow forecast enables changes to be made to receipts and payments to keep the overdraft within agreed limits.

6. Cash flow difficulties arise when receipts are less than forecast or payments are more than forecast.

7. Trading on credit allows customers to delay payment and while delaying payment to suppliers can compensate, it can cause problems with the supplier – like the supplier cutting off supplies or putting in the bailiffs.

Developing knowledge and skills

You are now in a position to tackle questions 1a and 2a in Section 3.15, page 300.

Unit 2: The end of the first year – the profit and loss account

Introduction

The objective of this chapter is to introduce one of the two principal financial statements – the Profit and Loss Account. The other is the Balance Sheet which is dealt with in Unit 3. We will see how the Profit and Loss Account measures the profit made by the business over a period (usually one year). The conventions used in constructing it will be discovered and some of these may surprise you!

Scenario 1

Martin's company has just completed its first year and Martin has asked Anne to prepare and audit the Accounts which he understands have to be produced. She spends some two weeks on this and finally presents Martin with what she calls the draft Profit and Loss Account. This is it:

Martin Padlocks Ltd
Trading and Profit and Loss Account for the year ending 31 December 19x1

		£
Sales		212,400
Less: Cost of Goods Sold:		
Opening Stock	–	
Purchases	160,730	
Less Closing Stock	14,730	146,000
Gross Profit		66,400
Less: Expenses		
Rent	4,000	
Rates	1,120	
Electricity	900	
Printing and Stationery	630	
Advertising	1,180	
Van Expenses	2,712	
Wages	18,000	
Director's Remuneration	9,600	
Employers' National Insurance	2,542	
Company Formation	250	
Audit and Accountancy	1,300	
Sundries	764	
Lease on van	2,400	
Bank Interest and Charges	2,990	
Depreciation	1,100	49,488
Net Profit		16,912

Quick answer questions 2a

Compare these figures with those you produced in your Cash Flow Forecast (Extended task 1 in Unit 1).

1. *Are the figures as expected?*

2. *Are there any expenses not forecast?*

3. *Is the stock as expected?*

Scenario 2

Martin is pleased with the profit shown but Anne tells him that an important expense – depreciation – has been included on a provisional basis. He agrees to wait for Unit 4 before going into detail on depreciation in the final profit and loss account. However we make a start on it in Scenario 3 later in this unit.

In the meantime he has a host of questions to ask Anne about the Profit and Loss Account.

 Tasks 2.1

These are the questions. How would you answer them?

1. Why are the words *"Trading* and" included in the heading ?

> You may find it helpful to read through Information Bank 1: The Profit and Loss Account, to help with these tasks. For the first task the section to look at is Section 1:4, page 107.

2. The business sold a parcel of padlocks on credit to Hubert on 31 December. These were invoiced at £620 and delivered all on that date. Hubert has not yet paid for them but he will do so eventually. Is this sale included in the figure of *sales*?

> Information Bank 1: 7d, page 108.

3. Why is there no opening stock?

> No help needed for this task!

4. The company bought a consignment of padlocks from Brassbits Ltd on December 28th and this arrived on that date together with the invoice for £405. Martin has not yet paid for these. Are these included in the figure for purchases? Also does *"Purchases"* include the purchase of stationery £28 in March?

> Information Bank 1: 7g, page 108

Quick answer questions 2a: *Answers and comments*

1. Sales are more than forecast.

    Rent, Electricity, Stationery, Van running, Wages and Director's Remuneration are more or less as forecast.

    Rates are a little more and Advertising less than forecast.

2. Employers' National Insurance Contributions were not forecast. Remember that it cost more to employ people than the gross wages. The audit fee was not forecast but part of it was included in the preliminary costs. Bank Interest is a significant item but is hard to forecast as rates vary and the borrowing is up and down.

3. Stock is less than expected. Perhaps Martin found that a large stock was not necessary.

5. Martin was asked to count his stock at 31 December and to value it at the prices at which the company had been invoiced. This had been done and the final result included as *closing stock* £14,730. Why was the stock valued at the cost to the company?

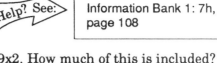

Information Bank 1: 7h, page 108

6. The company paid rates £740 for the half year to 31 March 19x2. How much of this is included?

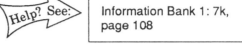

Information Bank 1: 7k, page 108

7. The company paid £1,200 for the computer. Why is this not included?

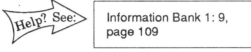

Information Bank 1: 9, page 109

8. The company sells its padlocks at cost + 50%. The *gross profit* does not seem to agree with this. Why might this be?

Information Bank 1: 7h, page 108

9. The company finished the year with a large overdraft. If it made a *profit* of £16,912 surely we should find cash in the bank of £16,912 somewhere. Why is this not so?

Information Bank 1: 11, page 110

10. In what ways is the Profit and Loss Account subject to accounting *conventions*. You should discuss the *entity*, *periodicity*, *money measurement*, *realisation*, *cost* and *accruals* conventions.

See Section 2 Information Bank Topic 1 Profit and Loss Account section 1:7d (page 108),7k (page 108) and Topic 7 Accounting Conventions 7:8, page 136.

Scenario 3

Anne then asks him how long he thinks his fixed assets will last. He thinks and then replies:

The Computer – two years

the Stacking Equipment – 5 years

In that case, Anne says, I have computed the depreciation correctly for each year as:

Computer   £500

Equipment   £600

and so we put depreciation in the Profit and Loss account as an expense at £1,100.

Martin is quite excited at understanding how a profit and loss is constructed and decides to plan his second year by *forecasting* the profit and loss account for 19x2 in the same way.

He makes a note of all the necessary data:

a. Sales should be £290,000

b. Goods will be sold at cost + 45% on average

c. Stock at the end of the year will be about one tenth of total annual purchases. As this is uncertain Martin thinks this should be rounded to the nearest £'000.

d. Rent will be as in 19x1

e. Rates will be as already paid for the first quarter and the rates for the year to 31 March 19x3 should be £2,000

f. Electricity, printing and stationery, and advertising will be as 19x1 but plus 20%, as will van expenses.

g. Wages will be as 19x1 but plus 30% but the *director's remuneration* will double. We can assume that the employer's *national insurance* will be 10% of the employees' and director's remuneration.

h. Audit and Accountancy will be £1,600 and Sundries about £1,000.

i. Bank Interest and charges may well be only half of that in 19x1.

j. Redecoration of the premises will occur in the last month of 19x2 at a cost of £2,500 and Martin will pay half of this in 19x2 and half in February 19x3.

k. Depreciation will be as in 19x1.

Tasks 2.2

1. Prepare a forecast profit and loss account for the year 19x2.

 Help? See: Information Bank Topic 1 Profit and Loss Account, page 107

2. Prepare a memo for Martin on the following topics:

a. Why the sales will include all sales made in 19x2 even though the cash was not received for some of them in 19x2.

 Help? See: Information Bank 1: 7d, page 108

b. The treatment of some padlocks which Martin expects to be ordered and paid for by an overseas customer in December 19x2 in the sum of £800. These will be delivered in January 19x3. Martin thinks they should be excluded from stock as he will have packed them by December 31st although he will not have sent them off. They cost £550 to make.

 Help? See: Information Bank 1: 7h, page 108

c. Why the profit and cash flows in the year are not the same.

 Help? See: Information Bank 1: 11, page 110

d. How the realisation and accruals conventions apply to this account.

 Help? See: Information Bank 1: 7d and k, page 108

3. Martin is considering buying a second hand lathe in 19x2 for £5,000. It would last about 10 years. If he buys it how would the profit be affected?

Information Bank 1: 9, page 109

4. Explore the effect on profit of:

    buying £2,000 more goods in the year and still having them in stock at the year end.

    selling his goods at an average mark up of 50%.

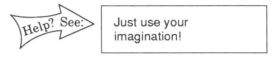

Information Bank 1: 7i, page 108

5. If the forecast 19x2 profit is insufficient, suggest feasible ways in which the profit might be improved.

    Help? See: Just use your imagination!

Extension tasks

Set up the Profit and Loss Account on a spreadsheet and explore the effects on profit of changes such as:

❐   a 5% change in sales (but with the same *mark-up*)

❐   a 5% change in mark-up (eg from 45% to 42.75%)

❐   a 5% change in wages.

Scenario 4

Finally, Martin discusses the profit with Anne and comes to realise that he has earned £9,600 from the business in 19x1 and that the business has earned £16,000 or so on top of that. He has really made more than £25,000 which compares well with his earnings when he worked with Stubbykey PLC. However there are differences:

a. All his earnings were paid to him by Stubbykey albeit after deducting PAYE and National Insurance.

b. He has actually been paid only £9,600 by his own company and Tax and Insurance have been deducted from that.

c. The profits made by the company belong to him but are *retained* in the company. Martin is richer in that the company has made a profit and has gained value but being richer has not resulted in any extra spending money for Martin.

d. The company will have to pay some *Corporation Tax* on the profits in due course.

Accounting conventions and the profit and loss account			
Entity convention	**Martin Padlocks Ltd**		
Periodicity convention	Profit and Loss Account for the year ending 31 December 19xx		
Money measurement			£
Realisation convention	Sales		210,000
	Less: Cost of Sales:		
	Opening stock	–	
	Purchases	160,730	
		160,730	
Cost convention	Less: Closing Stock	14,730	146,000
	Gross profit		64,000
Accruals convention	Expenses		45,988
	Net Profit		18,012

Summary of Unit 2

1. At the end of each financial year, the profit (or loss) is measured for every business. This is done by preparing a formal document or financial statement called a Profit and Loss Account.

2. If the company trades in goods or is a manufacturer, the financial statement is usually headed a Trading and Profit and Loss Account.

3. The heading should indicate the title of the business, title of the document and period concerned.

4. The Trading and Profit and Loss Account contains the following sections:

The Trading Account:	Sales	x
	Cost of goods sold	x
	Gross Profit	x
The Profit and Loss Account:	Gross Profit	x
	Itemised Expenses	x
	Net Profit	x

5. If the business does not trade in goods (eg a *service industry*) then the format may be:

Sales (or other form of *revenue* eg fees or fares)	x
Itemised expenses	x
Net Profit	x

6. In most businesses the profit depends on a measurement of stocks (raw materials, goods for resale and work in progress). This is valued at the *input cost* to the business (or sometimes less).

7. Sales include all sales made even if the cash is received in another period (the realisation convention).

8. Expenses include the precise cost of the resources or services consumed whether or not the items have been paid for in the period. (the accruals convention).

9. Expenses also include depreciation of fixed assets and we will deal with this later.

10. Business managers often see the profit and loss account as a *model* of the business and producing forecast profit and loss accounts is a useful adjunct to the *planning* and *budgeting* process.

Developing knowledge and skills

You are now in a position to tackle questions 1.1 to 1.7 in Section 3.1, pages 207 and 208.

Unit 3: The end of the first year – the balance sheet

Introduction

*The objective of this Unit is to introduce the second of the two principal financial statements – the **Balance Sheet**. We will see that this document presents a list of the **assets** employed in the business at the period end and a list also of what is owed (**liabilities**) by the business. Each of the assets and liabilities is assigned a (sometimes surprising) monetary value and the total of assets less liabilities is shown as the **net assets**. The sources of the funds required to acquire the net assets are shown as the **capital and reserves**.*

Scenario 1

Anne produces what she calls a draft balance sheet as at 31 December 19x1. This is it:

Martin Padlocks Ltd
Balance Sheet as at 31 December 19x1

Fixed Assets	Cost	Depreciation	£ Net Book Value
Computer	1,000	500	500
Stacking Equipment	3,000	600	2,400
	4,000	1,100	2,900
Current Assets			
Stock		14,730	
Debtors		51,200	
Prepayments		1,230	
		67,160	
Creditors: amounts falling due within one year			
Creditors		25,900	
Bank Overdraft		7,248	
		33,148	
Net Current Assets			34,012
Total assets less current liabilities			36,912
Creditors: amounts falling due after more than one year			
Loan at 10%			5,000
			31,912
Capital and Reserves			
Share Capital			15,000
Profit and Loss Account			16,912
			31,912

Martin thinks he can make some sense of the balance sheet but has a number of questions.

Quick answer questions 3a

1. *At what date is this list of assets and liabilities made up?*

2. *Which items do you recognise from the cash flow forecast?*

3. *Comment on the Net Profit shown in the Profit and Loss Account, page 9 and the Profit and Loss Account shown in the Balance Sheet.*

4. *Which items are assets and which are liabilities?*

5. *What do you see as the essential differences between the Profit and Loss Account and the Balance Sheet?*

Scenario 2

Martin feels that he has got the basic idea of the Balance Sheet in that he knows the assets from the liabilities but is still mystified by a great deal of it and he sits down with Anne to try and sort out the detail.

 **Tasks 3.1**

1. What are the distinguishing features of the two sorts of assets – *fixed* and *current* ?

    Information Bank 2:6 (c,d,e,g), page 113.

2. Does the *net book value* of the fixed assets mean that I could get back these amounts if I sold them?

    Information Bank 2: 7-8, page 114.

3. Who or what are *debtors*?

    Information Bank 2:6 (i), page 113.

4. What are *prepayments*?

    Information Bank 2:6 (j), page 113.

5. Who or what are *creditors*?

    Information Bank 2:6 (m), page 114.

6. Explain the phrase *net current assets*?

   See Information Bank 2:6 (p), page 114.

7. Why is the bank overdraft in amongst the creditors which fall due in less than one year?

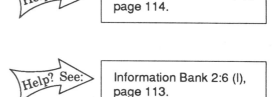

Help? See: Information Bank 2:6 (n), page 114.

8. What are current liabilities?

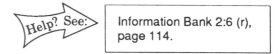

Help? See: Information Bank 2:6 (l), page 113.

9. What is the meaning of "at 10%" ?

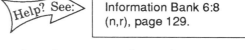

Help? See: Information Bank 2:6 (r), page 114.

10. What are *reserves* ?

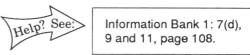

Help? See: Information Bank 6:8 (n,r), page 129.

11. Does the existence of "profit and loss account £16,912" mean that the company have that amount of cash somewhere?

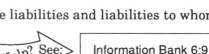

Help? See: Information Bank 1: 7(d), 9 and 11, page 108.

12. How is it that Share Capital and Profit and Loss Account are liabilities and liabilities to whom?

Help? See: Information Bank 6:9 (n,r,s), pages 130-131.

Scenario 3

Anne explains that the balance sheet in paragraph 3 is at a draft stage which means that she will make some alterations to it before it can be finalised and typed up as the audited balance sheet. When it is finalised it will be sent to the company's *shareholders* (in fact only Martin and his wife are shareholders) and to the *Registrar of Companies* where it will be filed and can be seen by members of the public.

Before finalising the balance sheet Anne asks Martin a series of questions:

a. The stock is valued at cost but are there any items which are slow moving, damaged, obsolete etc which can only be sold for an amount below cost? Martin remembers that there is a case of RT padlocks imported from Italy which he is having much difficulty in selling. They cost him £1,200 and he thinks he will get only about £800 for them.

b. Are all the debtors collectable? Martin replies that yes they are except perhaps one. Dodgy Ltd owed £880 at the year end and have not paid. He understands that the company have appointed a *receiver* and the creditors will receive nothing.

c. Have I included all the prepayments? Martin looks through the list and then points out that there is nothing for advertising. He paid £600 for advertising in the Padlock Users' Monthly in October 19x1 and this was for six monthly insertions beginning with the November issue.

d. Are all the creditors included? Martin could only think of one that had been omitted. A consignment of padlocks had been received from a supplier in Tipton on 29 December 19x1 and taken into stock and counted in the stocktake at 31 December. Martin had queried the invoice and it had only been entered in the books when the dispute had been resolved last week. **The agreed amount is £520.**

e. The loan of £5,000 was received from Martin's father on 31 July 19x1 and I have not included any interest in the profit and loss account as I understand that *interest* does not start straightaway. That is true. The loan is repayable in five years time and interest starts to accrue only from 1 October 19x1.

Quick answer questions 3b

Would you expect the adjustments to the Balance Sheet needed would also affect the Profit and Loss Account?

 Tasks 3.2

1. Prepare the finalised Profit and Loss Account and Balance Sheet for Martin Padlocks Ltd taking into account the adjustments required in the scenario. Remember that the profit and loss account balance in the capital and reserves will be affected by the adjustments.

 Help? See:

> Information Bank 7:8 (conservatism), page 138 and 1:6 (k), page 107.

Quick answer questions 3a: *Answers and comments*

1. 31 December 19x1. Balance sheets are lists of assets and liabilities at a particular date which in this case is 31 December 19x1.

2. You may have recognised:

    ❐ the Fixed Assets: the Computer and the Stacking Equipment. You may recall the cost of these from the cash flow forecast and the depreciation from the profit and loss account.

    ❐ the Stock

    ❐ the Bank Overdraft. Well, at least you knew that the company had a bank overdraft. The balance is different from the forecast but forecasts are never quite right.

    ❐ the Share Capital: you know that Martin put £15,000 into the company.

    ❐ the Profit and Loss Account: you know that the company made a profit of this amount but it may surprise you to see it on the Balance Sheet.

3. You will see that these show the same amount. The figure in the Profit and Loss Account shows the profit made in the year and this results in an increase in net assets at the end of the year compared with the beginning. The figure in the Balance Sheet shows the source of the increase in net assets measured in the Balance Sheet.

4. The Fixed Assets and all the Current Assets are assets. The creditors: amounts falling due within one year and the Loan are all liabilities.

    You should have got these right but you may be surprised to know that the Share Capital and the Profit and Loss Account are also liabilities. They are liabilities to the shareholders.

5. The Profit and Loss Account measures the profit earned over a period of time – one year in this case.

    The Balance Sheet shows the assets and liabilities at the year end.

Scenario 4

The revised Profit and Loss Account and the revised Balance Sheet will look like this:

Martin Padlocks Ltd
Trading and Profit and Loss Account for the year ending 31 December 19x1

	£	£
Sales		212,400
Less: Cost of Goods Sold:		
Opening Stock		
Purchases	161,250	
Less Closing Stock	14,330	146,920
Gross Profit		65,480
Less: Expenses		
Rent	4,000	
Rates	1,120	
Electricity	900	
Printing and Stationery	630	
Advertising	780	
Van Expenses	2,712	
Wages	18,000	
Director's Remuneration	9,600	
Employers' National Insurance	2,542	
Company Formation	250	
Audit and Accountancy	1,300	
Sundries	764	
Lease on van	2,400	
Bad Debt	880	
Bank Interest and Charges	2,990	
Depreciation	1,100	49,968
Net Profit		15,512

Balance Sheet as at 31 December 19x1

Fixed Assets	Cost	Depreciation	Net Book Value £
Computer	1,000	500	500
Stacking Equipment	3,000	600	2,400
	4,000	1,100	2,900

Current Assets		
Stock	14,330	
Debtors	50,320	
Prepayments	1,630	
	66,280	
Creditors: amounts falling due within one year		
Creditors	26,420	
Bank Overdraft	7,248	
	33,668	
Net Current Assets		32,612
Total assets less current liabilities		35,512
Creditors: amounts falling due after more than one year		
Loan at 10%		5,000
		30,512
Capital and Reserves		
Share Capital		15,000
Profit and Loss Account		15,512
		30,512

Notes:

a. The conservatism convention requires that the stock be valued at the lower of cost and net realisable value and as the realisable value of the RT padlocks at £800 is lower than the cost, £800 will be their value in the accounts. This means lowering the stock in the Profit and Loss Account by £400 thus lowering the gross and net profit and lowering the stock in the Balance Sheet.

b. Common sense (as well as the conservatism convention) tells us that it is no good including a debt on the Balance Sheet when it will not be paid. The bad debt is a loss to the firm so it also has to be included in the expenses in the Profit and Loss Account

c. The advertising was paid for in 19x1. But it is for adverts in six issues of the magazine – two in 19x1 and four in 19x2. This means that it is £200 as an expense of 19x1 and £400 as an expense of 19x2. £400 is a prepayment in the Balance Sheet.

d. Purchases must include all the purchases in the year and so the £520 must be included in purchases in 19x1 in the Profit and Loss Account and in creditors in the Balance Sheet. In practice getting all the creditors in the accounts presents many possibilities for error and accountants spend much time getting the cut-off right.

e. The Balance Sheet balanced before these adjustments (balanced means the total of the net assets equals the total of capital and reserves) and as each adjustment changed figures in both financial statements, the Balance Sheet balances after the adjustments.

Quick answer questions 3b: *Answers and comments*

Yes – most adjustments to the Profit and Loss Account will also affect the Balance Sheet and vice versa. If a liability had been omitted – say a van repair of £50, then:

❏ van expenses in the Profit and Loss Account would go up by £50 and consequently the net profit would go down.

❏ the creditors would go up by £50 in the Balance Sheet and consequently the assets less liabilities would go down by £50.

❏ the capital and reserves would go down by £50 as the Profit and Loss Account figure in the Balance Sheet would go down and consequently the capital and reserves total would still be the same as the net assets.

Tasks 3.3

Martin remembered some other things which he thought might affect the accounts.

1. Consider the following items. State whether each would be included in or excluded from the Balance Sheet giving reasons:

   a. An invoice for £300 for padlocks sold to Rich a customer on 31 December 19x1. Rich paid on 12 February 19x2.

 Information Bank 1.6d, page 107 and 2.4i, page 112.

   b. Martin considers that the *goodwill* of the business must have been worth at least £10,000 at 31 December 19x1.

 Information Bank 2.7, page 114.

c. Martin bought £200 worth of Padlocks in November from Brown, a supplier, on a *sale or return* basis. In fact Martin could not sell them and they were returned to Brown in January 19x2

d. Martin's van knocked over the gatepost of Lowe, a customer in December 19x1 and after much argument he has agreed to pay £600 of damages to Lowe. The company are insured but have to pay the first £250 of any claim.

Information Bank 7.8 (accruals and conservatism), page 138.

Scenario 5

Martin shows his Balance Sheet to his father who is not an accountant and they discuss what it all means. His father says that the Balance Sheet shows *net assets* of £30,512 and the company is divided into 15,000 shares and therefore the *value* of each share is £2.034. Martin agrees that that is how he understands it. His father then says that must mean that Martin would be able to sell each share for £2.034. And that if the assets were sold they would fetch £69,180 and after paying off the liabilities of £38,668 there would be a surplus of £30,512 which could be paid out to the shareholders so that the holder of one share would receive £2.034.

Tasks 3.4

Write a report on these ideas, concluding with a concise comment on the *informational* content of a company balance sheet.

Information Bank 2. 7 to 2.10, pages 114-115.

Extension task

A way to become familiar with the ideas in Balance Sheets and Profit and Loss Accounts is to use a spreadsheet, so:

1. Update the Profit and Loss Account which you put onto a spreadsheet in Unit 2.

2. Add the Balance Sheet to the Profit and Loss Account on the spreadsheet in Unit 2.

3. Explore the relationships between the two financial statements by adding some transactions, for example:

a. Sell on credit a padlock in stock which had cost £20 for £30. This will change:

Stock	− 20
Sales	+ 30
Debtors	+ 30

b. Pay £70 for some advertising so that £30 is an expense and £40 is a prepayment. This will change:

Advertising	+ 30
Prepayment	+ 40
Overdraft	+ 70

c. Incurring a bad debt of £500.

Note that the utility of spreadsheets of Profit and Loss Accounts and Balance Sheet can be greatly improved if the spreadsheet can automatically do the additions. For example the cell showing gross profit can use a formula subtracting the cost of goods sold cell from the sales cell and the cell showing the net current assets can be a formula deducting creditors falling due within one year from the current assets. Also the Profit and Loss Account can be related to the Balance Sheet by having the cell for stock in the Balance Sheet being the same as the cell for stock in the Profit and Loss Account.

The two parts of a balance sheet

Capital	=	Cash	The beginning of a company – shareholders invest cash
Capital	=	Net Assets	The investors cash is turned into a set of assets less liabilities
Capital Reserves*	=	Net Assets	A Profit is made so net assets are more

* = Profit and Loss Account

Note:

1. The two parts of the Balance Sheet must always be the same monetary amount.
2. Any increase or decrease in net assets must be reflected in a similar increase or decrease in Capital and Reserves.
3. The Net Assets show what assets the business has and what liabilities it has to others.
4. The Capital and Reserves explain how the Net Assets were financed.

Summary of Unit 3

1. At the end of each financial year a balance sheet is drawn up for all businesses showing the financial position as at the balance sheet date.

2. A balance sheet lists the assets of the business under suitable categories. The usual *categories* are fixed assets and current assets with subcategories of each. Current assets usually include stocks, debtors,prepayments (often not shown separately but included in debtors), cash at bank (unless there is an overdraft) and in hand.

3. Asset values do not reflect possible resale values but are at or derived from input costs.

4. A balance sheet also includes liabilities distinguishing between those payable within one year from those payable after more than one year.

5. The total of net current assets is given and also the total of net assets.

6. The *source* of finance for the net assets is shown in the capital and reserves section of the balance sheet and this has at least two subheadings – share capital which is the funds originally obtained from the shareholders and profit and loss account which is the amount of funds obtained from retained profits.

7. A balance sheet is a classified summary of the assets employed in a business entity, its liabilities and the sources of its net assets.

8. Profit can be defined as an endogenous (= from within) increase in net assets.

Developing knowledge and skills

You are now in a position to tackle questions 1 and 2 in Section 3.2, page 211.

Unit 4: Depreciation

Introduction

The objective of this Unit is to introduce the idea of depreciation of fixed assets. We will find out how depreciation is calculated and how it affects the annual profit and the values of fixed assets on the balance sheet.

Scenario 1

When the final typed accounts arrive from Anne's office, Martin spends some time going through them. One of the areas he is not at all sure about is fixed assets and the depreciation.

The accounts show:

On the balance sheet:

Fixed Assets

	Cost £	Depreciation £	Value £
Computer	1,000	500	500
Stacking Equipment	3,000	600	2,400
	4,000	1,100	2,900

and in the profit and loss account among the expenses:

Depreciation £1,100

> **Quick answer questions 4a**
>
> 1. What are fixed assets?
>
> 2. What does "cost" mean?
>
> 3. What is the amount of the depreciation?
>
> 4. Would it have been different if three years instead of five had been chosen as the life of the stacking equipment?
>
> 5. Would the profit then have been different?
>
> 6. Does the depreciation in the Balance Sheet agree with the amount of depreciation which is an expense in the profit and loss account?
>
> 7. What is the total value of the fixed assets according to the balance sheet?
>
> 8. Do you think that this means that the company could sell the fixed assets for £2,900?

Scenario 2

Martin thinks he understands what depreciation means and how it has affected his profit and the figures on the balance sheet. However he now wonders if he was not too quick in answering Anne's questions about the fixed assets. He rings her up and asks her what assumptions have been made in calculating the depreciation.

She tells him:

Asset:	Computer	Stacking
Estimated useful life	2 years	5 years
Salvage value	nil	nil
Depreciation policy	Straight Line	Straight Line

She also tells him that she had thought of using *reducing balance* depreciation.

Martin thinks about these assumptions and says to Anne:

"Suppose the assumptions were different, would that make the profit and balance sheet values different?".

"Yes". Says Anne.

Firstly, he makes sure that he understands the terms *Salvage Value, Depreciation Policy,* and *Straight Line,* then he suggests that it would be more accurate to change the assumptions to:

Asset:	Computer	Stacking
Estimated useful life	3 years	3 years
Salvage value	£125	£300
Depreciation policy	Reducing Balance	Straight Line

Quick answer questions 4a: *Answers and comments*

1. Fixed Assets are long lasting and relatively valuable assets. They are owned to be used in the business to help make a profit. They are not expected to be sold except when they are no longer needed.

2. Cost means simply what they cost the company when they were bought. The idea of cost is simple but students often wonder whether the original or *historical cost* is relevant or useful information.

3. £1,100. This is based on the information which Martin gave to Anne about the useful economic lives of the fixed assets.

4. If three years had been chosen then the depreciation on the Stacking Equipment would have been £1,000 and the total depreciation would have been £1,500.

5. Yes. The profit would have been £400 less as depreciation directly affects the measurement of profit.

6. Yes. This year the assets have depreciated by £1,100 and this "loss in value" is regarded as an *expense* and so the profit is reduced by this amount.

7. and 8.

   £2,900. This is called the net book value or sometimes the written down value. It is simply the original cost less the depreciation so far. It does not mean that the assets can be sold for this amount. Students wonder what it does mean and accountants usually say it represents the value of the assets *to the business* and not the value to some hypothetical buyer.

Tasks 4.1

1. What did Anne mean by the terms: salvage value, depreciation policy, straight line and reducing balance?

Help? See: Before beginning the tasks in this unit you should read through Information Bank Topic 3: Depreciation. For this particular task the section is 3: 5,6 and 12, pages 116-119.

Quick answer questions 4b

Calculate the depreciation to go in the Profit and Loss account and the figures for the Fixed Assets in the Balance Sheet based on the new assumptions. Reducing instalment rates for the computer are 50%.

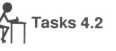 **Tasks 4.2**

1. He has a choice of depreciation policy of straight line or reducing balance. What thinking lies behind his choice of reducing balance for the computer.

Information Bank 3:6 and 8, pages 117-118.

2. Which method should he choose if:

   i. He wants to report as high a profit as possible to the bank.

   ii. He wants to be absolutely *objective* about the measurement of his profit?

Help? You can puzzle this out for yourself.

Scenario 3

In the second year Martin intends to continue to lease the van but to buy an additional van for £7,000. He also intends to buy a skin-packing machine for £3,000. He reckons appropriate estimates for these are:

	Van	Machine
Cost	£7,000	£3,000
Salvage value	£2,400	£1,000
Life	3 years	5 years
Depreciation Policy	Reducing Balance	Straight Line

 **Tasks 4.3**

1. Show the Depreciation total in the Profit and Loss Account for all four Fixed Assets for the second year assuming that the new assets receive a full year's depreciation in their first year.

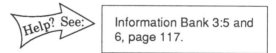

Information Bank 3:5 and 6, page 117.

2. Show the Fixed Assets section in the second year's Balance Sheet in the form:

   Fixed Assets

	Cost	Accumulated Depreciation	Net Book Value
Computer	x	x	x
Stacking Equipment	x	x	x
Van	x	x	x
Skin-Packing Machine	x	x	x
	x	x	x

Information Bank 4:8 and 10, pages 121 and 122.

3. Explain why the Company will have spent £10,000 on new Fixed Assets in year 2 but the Profit of that year will be reduced by only £2,500 as a consequence.

Information Bank 3:4, page 116.

Scenario 4

Martin is talking at the Golf Club to his friend Carlo who has had a haulage business for several years. Carlo confides that he does not really understand the accounts his accountant produces for him and confesses that the fixed assets and depreciation mystify him especially.

Martin is full of his new found understanding of this subject and offers to explain Carlo's accounts to him. Carlo produces these and Martin sees:

Balance Sheet

Fixed Assets

	Cost £	Accumulated Depreciation £	Net Book Value £
Land	30,000	–	30,000
Buildings	185,000	68,200	116,800
Lorries	243,000	102,000	141,000
Plant and Equipment	84,000	53,400	30,600
	542,000	223,600	318,400

Profit and Loss Account:

Depreciation:

Buildings	4,625	
Lorries	43,600	
Plant and Equipment	7,600	
Loss on Sale of Lorry	2,180	58,005

They manage to find a section in the accounts called "accounting policies" and in it find:

Depreciation:

"Depreciation is calculated so as to write off the cost of an asset by the straight line method over the period of its useful life as follows:

Freehold Buildings	40 years
Lorries	5 years
Plant and Equipment	10 years"

Martin recognises many of the words but is unclear about some of the others. He resolves to ask Anne for further enlightenment.

Quick answer questions 4b: *Answers and comments*

		£
The computer: Cost		1,000
	50% year 1	500
		500
	50% year 2	250
		250
	50% year 3	125
Salvage value at end of year 3		£125

Stacking Equipment: The cost was £3,000 and the salvage value is estimated at £300 so the expected loss is £2,700. Using the straight line method and assuming a three year life depreciation will be:

$$\frac{2,700}{3} = £900 \text{ a year.}$$

The Balance Sheet values will be £2,100 at the end of year 1, £1,200 at the end of year 2 and £300 at the end of year three.

Tasks 4.4

Write a memo as from Anne explaining:

a. *Accumulated Depreciation* and why this is different from the depreciation in the profit and loss account.

| Information Bank 3:10, page 118. |

b. Why land is not depreciated.

| Information Bank 3:11, page 118. |

c. Martin works out that the cost of the buildings (£185,000) divided by 40 gives £4,625 which he can see in the Profit and Loss Account. However he is not clear why the accumulated depreciation on the buildings is not an exact multiple of £4,625.

| Help: try to puzzle this out for yourself. |

d. Explain what is meant by "*loss on sale* of lorry" and how it was calculated.

| Information Bank 3:14, page 119. |

e. Carlo reckons that the premises are worth about £500,000 and wonders why the property is valued at only £146,800.

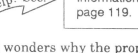

| Information Bank 3:8 and 11, page 118. |

f. Carlo also reckons that the plant and equipment is old and would only fetch about £5,000 at auction.

| Information Bank 3:8 and 9, page 118. |

Scenario 5

Martin is a member of an old established and exclusive Golf Club with 1,000 members and has just received the annual accounts. The Club is a company by guarantee. He does not normally read these but decides to do so in order to see what happens about Fixed Assets and Depreciation. He sees:

Fixed Assets

	Cost £	Accumulated Depreciation £	Book Value £
Freehold Golf Course	240,000	nil	240,000
Club House	90,000	54,000	36,000

The accounting *policies* state:

❏ the Freehold Golf Course is not depreciated

❏ the Club House is depreciated over 50 years.

The directors' report contains a paragraph to the effect that the Freehold Golf Course may be worth significantly more than its *historical cost* but that the directors decline to put a value upon it as there is no intention to sell it.

Quick answer questions 4c

1. *How can Martin calculate the age of the Club House?*

2. *Why do you think the Freehold Golf Course is not depreciated?*

Scenario 6

Martin knows that planning permission might be obtained to build houses on the Golf Course as it is in the middle of a residential area. Planning permission may also be obtainable to build a new Golf Course in the nearby countryside on what is now farming land.

Martin thinks that he would give more *relevant* information than the *limited* and *historical* nature of the *information* given in the Annual Accounts.

 **Tasks 4.5**

Write a criticism of the Golf Club's depreciation policies and suggest alternatives that might be more informative.

Extension task

Set up Martin's two fixed assets and the depreciation on them on a spreadsheet and explore different depreciation policies and assumptions on the Balance Sheet and Profit and Loss Account.

Depreciation calculations

Cost	– Known
Useful Economic life	– Estimate
Salvage Value	– Estimate
Method – Straight Line	
– Reducing Balance	
– Other	– Policy

Depreciation and financial statments

Profit and Loss Account

     – Annual Depreciation

     – Losses/Profits on Sale

Balance Sheet

     – Fixed Assets at Cost

less – Accumulated Depreciation

= – Net Book Value

Notes

1. Some fixed assets (Land and Buildings usually) can be included at a valuation. But then depreciation is applied to the valuation.

2. Land is not usually depreciated.

3. When assets are revalued upwards, the net assets are of course increased. The Capital and Reserves have therefore also to be increased and this is done by including an amount headed Revaluation reserve.

Summary of Unit 4

1. Fixed Assets appear in the balance sheet under a small number of convenient headings such as land, buildings, plant, equipment, vehicles etc. A value is also shown which has three components: cost, accumulated depreciation and net book value.

2. Annual Depreciation is calculated by reference to the cost, the salvage value and the estimated useful life of the asset.

3. There are two common (and many less common) methods of calculating depreciation: straight line and reducing balance.

4. Each firm has to select one of the methods for depreciation. That is then its depreciation policy and it is then usually adhered to for all years.

5. Salvage value is the amount expected to be recovered from the sale of the asset at the end of its life. This is often regarded as nil.

6. Net book value is also known as written down value or *carrying value*. It is simply cost less accumulated depreciation. It has no economic meaning except that it might be considered the value of the asset to the business or the value in use. There is always an assumption that the net book value (which is the undepreciated portion of the original cost) can be recovered by charging it as an expense in the profit and loss account over the remaining life of the asset.

7. Each fixed asset owned is depreciated each year and the total depreciation suffered over the years is called the accumulated depreciation. It is this which appears in the balance sheet.

8. When a fixed asset is sold, or otherwise disposed of, the difference between the book value and the disposal proceeds is either a *loss or a profit on sale*. This loss or profit appears in the profit and loss account.

9. The depreciation undergone each year by the fixed assets is an expense which appears in the profit and loss account.

10. This expense depends on the assumptions made (estimated life and estimated salvage value) and the depreciation policy selected. Consequently the measurement of profit is much affected by depreciation.

11. Land is not depreciated but buildings are. The value of premises in the sense of what the premises can be sold for can be estimated. It is usually very different from the book value.

12. Depreciation represents a fairly subjective area of accounting but has a significant effect on the Profit and Loss Account and the Balance Sheet.

13 Depreciation shows the limitations on the informational value of Annual Accounts. The amount of information given is strictly limited by the accounting conventions and is historical in nature

Quick answer questions 4c: *Answers and comments*

1. As the Club House is depreciated over 50 years the annual depreciation will be $\frac{£90,000}{50} = £1,800$.

    Since the accumulated depreciation is now £54,000 Martin can assume that the Club House has been depreciated for $\frac{54,000}{£1,800} = 30$ years.

2. The Golf Course is land and usually land is not depreciated. The reason is that land is assumed to have an infinite life. The Golf Club may also think, that as the Course has appreciated rather than depreciated in value, no depreciation is necessary. However *appreciation* in value is not considered a valid reason for not depreciating an asset with limited life.

Developing knowledge and skills

You are now in a position to tackle questions 1 and 2 in Section 3:3, page 217.

Unit 5: Costing and pricing a product

Introduction

*The objectives of this Unit are to introduce some **costing** terminology (costing terminology can be rather confusing) and to see how the costs of manufacture of a product can be measured and the information used in fixing a selling price for the product. Finally we shall see how costing information can be used in some simple **decision making** situations and we shall also look at a **breakeven chart.***

Scenario 1

Martin finds that his business of buying in complete padlock sets and selling them to his customers has worked well in the first two years. However in the third year he has difficulty in finding a sufficiently low priced padlock called the SP. He feels that he could manufacture the product himself from bought in parts and at the same time add some features which would help its saleability. He decides to set up a small assembly plant in a small factory unit near his warehouse.

Before he does so he contacts his accountant who advises him to carefully forecast all his costs. This he does and the following is the result:

Capital expenditure – machinery (life 5 years, salvage value £3,000, straight line depreciation)	£15,000
Rent, rates, insurance, repairs etc	£10,000
Other overheads	£1,500
Electricity	£3,000
Foreman/Supervisor	£10,500

The above revenue costs are for one year.

Labour costs – Piecework rates (adjusted for national insurance, holiday and sick pay) 30p a padlock

Material costs 50p a padlock

Martin estimates that the factory will be able to produce about 60,000 padlocks a year.

Quick answer questions 5a

1. What is the annual depreciation on the machine?

2. What will be the *total cost* of manufacturing the 60,000 items?

3. What will be the *cost per unit*?

Scenario 2

Martin takes the cost list to his accountant and they discuss the costs and how Martin might fix a selling price for the product.

 **Tasks 5.1**

1. Calculate and produce a formal statement showing the manufacturing cost for each padlock SP, showing the *direct costs*, the *prime cost*, the *manufacturing overheads* and the total manufacturing cost.

 Help? See:

Information Bank Topic 10: Total Absorption Costing paragraphs 1 to 10, page 157.

2. Calculate a selling price based on the idea that the selling price should be manufacturing cost + 30%. The 30% is necessary to cover *non-manufacturing overheads* as well as giving a profit. Martin thinks that 30% should be enough.

 Help? See:

Help ? See Information Bank 10:11, page 157.

Quick answer questions 5a: *Answers and comments*

1. Annual Depreciation is $\dfrac{£15,000 - £3,000}{5}$ = £2,400

2.

	£
Depreciation	2,400
Rent etc	10,000
Other overheads	1,500
Electricity	3,000
Foreman	10,500
Labour 60,000 x 30p	18,000
Materials 60,000 x 50p	30,000
Total	75,400

3. $\dfrac{£75,400}{60,000}$ = £1.26

You will see that the cost of manufacture of one unit of a product depends on how many are made.

Scenario 3

Martin is in regular contact with all his customers and he considers that the price asked will affect the number of units of SP that he can sell.

He feels he can draw up a table of probable sales in units against selling price:

Selling price	£1.80	£1.75	£1.69	£1.65	£1.55
Sales in 1,000 units	40	50	60	70	90

Quick answer questions 5b

1. Explain why more than twice as many of the product can be sold if the price is reduced from £1.80 to £1.55.

2. How certain do you think Martin is that the sales will be achieved at the suggested prices?

3. What is the constraint on output mentioned in the first scenario?

4. How do you think that the level of output will affect each of the costs listed in scenario 1.

Scenario 4

Martin has to decide the level of output and sales which will bring him in the greatest profit. To make the decision on price and hence on output he has gathered together some more data:

❑ He cannot get a smaller factory unit but he can get a larger one. The larger one would enable output to rise to 90,000 units but would cost annually £15,000 in rent rates etc.

❑ more machinery would be needed and as he would lease these the annual leasing charge would be £12,000.

❑ Electricity would cost £900 at either factory + a cost would which would *vary linearly with output* of 3.5p a padlock.

❑ the Foreman/Supervisor would need to have better qualifications at the larger factory and would cost £13,500 a year.

 **Tasks 5.2**

1. Which selling price should Martin choose to maximise his profit?

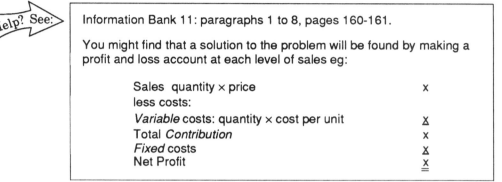

Help? See: Information Bank 11: paragraphs 1 to 8, pages 160-161.

You might find that a solution to the problem will be found by making a profit and loss account at each level of sales eg:

Sales quantity × price	x
less costs:	
Variable costs: quantity × cost per unit	X
Total *Contribution*	x
Fixed costs	X
Net Profit	x

 Quick answer question 5c

What considerations, other than the maximisation of profit, might Martin take into account in making his decision?

 **Tasks 5.3**

1. How might the third year cash flow forecast be changed as a result of Martin's decision to go ahead with manufacturing?

Help? See: Information Bank 15, pages 178-182

Scenario 5

Martin decides to go ahead with the original (maximum output 60,000 units) small factory plan and price his product at £1.70. He is not at all certain that 60,000 units can be sold and worries that a loss will be incurred if he fails to sell enough. He organizes a sales conference with the two agents who sell his padlocks and confides his need to sell enough of the SP to avoid making a loss. He is technologically minded and shows them an overhead projector slide illustrating the need to sell sufficient SP.

Tasks 5.4

Prepare a breakeven chart based on data as:

Sales Price	£1.70
Variable costs	£0.80
Fixed costs	£27,400

Help? See: Information Bank 11: 9 to 11, pages 161 to 162.

Quick answer questions 5b: *Answers and comments*

1. We all have a tendency to prefer a product which is cheaper so more will be sold if the price is lowered. The relationship between sales quantity and price is very difficult to estimate in practice. Economists talk about *elasticity of demand* by which they mean that sales of some products are more *sensitive* to price differences than others.

2. Not certain at all. Management accounting is about what to do in the future and the future is simply uncertain. Bear in mind that the sophisticated techniques used in management accounting usually work on very uncertain forecasts!

3. We said that the factory could only produce 60,000 units in a year. If more can be sold Martin will have to buy them from another manufacturer or enlarge his own factory.

4. The cost of a single unit of output is:

Labour and Materials	80p
The rest of the costs divided	
by 60,000:	
$\frac{27,400}{60,000}$	46p
	126p

   If the £27,400 was divided by a different output (say 40,000 units) then the cost per unit would be more:

Labour and Materials	80p
$\frac{27,400}{40,000}$	68p
	148p

   We canot make more than 60,000 a year so we will have to calculate the costs of a higher output later.

Quick answer questions 5c: *Answers and comments*

Considerations that Martin might take into account include:

- ☐ some pricing strategies may be more *risky*
- ☐ the larger factory unit will be greater burden if things do not work out well – risk again
- ☐ a higher turnover may require more of Martin's time
- ☐ a higher turnover will involve a greater investment of cash and he may have other priorities for this *scarce resource*.

Scenario 6

Martin has categorised his costs as fixed and variable:

Variable:	Materials	
	Labour	
Fixed:	Rent	
	Rates	
	Insurance	
	Repairs	
	Electricity	
	Foreman	

He is not sure if all of these costs are truly fixed or truly variable even in the *relevant range* of up to 60,000 padlocks produced.

 **Tasks 5.5**

1. Discuss each cost and decide how it would *behave* at different levels of output comparing say 40,000 units with 60,000 units.

 Help? See: | Information Bank 11: 1 to 6, pages 160 to 161.

Cost categorisations

1.

Direct	**– traceable to individual products**
Indirect	**– overheads – shared by products**

Use: In Total Absorption Costing to find:

– cost for fixing selling prices

– valuing stock for Accounts purposes

Fixed – remains the same at different activity levels
Variable – changes as activity changes

Use: In marginal costing in making decisions eg:
– making or buying in a product
– output levels
– choosing between production methods
– what to make when resources are
– limited

There are other categorisations eg:

a. Materials: Labour: Services
b. Manufacturing: Administration: Selling and Distribution
c. Controllable: Non-controllable

Use: we shall see uses for these in later chapters

Summary of Unit 5

1. Costs can be categorized in several different ways.

2. One categorisation is into direct and indirect costs. The Direct cost of a product are those costs which are traceable uniquely to that product. Indirect costs are those costs which are shared by more than one product. This distinction is especially important when we consider multi-product firms.

3. The total absorption cost of a product is the sum of the direct costs traced to that product + its share of the indirect costs.

4. Total absorption cost is the preferred method for valuing year end stocks of finished goods for the purpose of preparing a Profit and Loss Account and a Balance Sheet.

5. Total absorption cost is often used in selling price decisions.

6. Most other decisions are based on another categorisation of costs – into fixed and variable costs.

7. Decisions can be made on pricing and output based on this categorisation. This method of costing is usually known as marginal costing.

8. A breakeven chart is a useful way of demonstrating the effect of different output levels on profit.

Developing knowledge and skills

You are now in a position to tackle questions 1 to 5 in Section 3.10 and questions 1 to 8 in Section 3.11, pages 264-265 and 271-273.

Unit 6: Future strategy

Introduction

*This Unit introduces the need to **budget** and the uses of **marginal costing** in **decision** making.*

Scenario 1

Towards the end of his third year, Martin is reviewing his progress so far and considering what to do in the fourth year. He has achieved a turnover of £600,000 in his wholesaling business and £100,000 in the SP product which he is making in his small factory unit. He is confident that the company is now well established in the market and he can double his wholesale turnover and more than double his sales of the SP product in the coming year. There are also several other products that he could manufacture profitably. He decides that he must contemplate several alternative strategies:

a. Stay in his present premises

b. Retain the wholesaling in his original unit and move the manufacturing to larger premises.

c. Retain the original manufacturing unit and move the wholesaling into larger premises.

d. Move both activities into separate larger premises.

e. Move into larger premises and operate both activities under one roof.

If he decides to move either or both premises he can either buy or rent.

Quick answer questions 6a

1. *From your reading so far, what essential actions must Martin take in order to make a choice?*

2. *What might be the consequences of a wrong choice? You should consider each choice.*

Scenario 2

Martin decides to keep the two activities apart but to move both activities into separate new premises which will be large enough to accommodate expansion for several years. He decides to rent both sets of premises. He sets about producing a set of budgets for each activity. We will concentrate on the manufacture of the SP padlock. He has decided to concentrate his own time on the wholesaling and appoint a manager to run the manufacturing. Information he has collected includes:

(all data are for one year)

The SP Padlock:

Sales 150,000 units at £2.00 each
Material costs 60p a unit
Labour cost 40p a unit
Manager's salary £20,000
Rent £12,000
Rates £7,000
Other factory overheads £40,000
Capital expenditure £60,000 (he will buy the equipment)

Quick answer questions 6a: *Answers and comments*

1. Martin must prepare a summary of the *financial* effects of each alternative. This should be in the form of forecast profit and loss accounts and balance sheets. In order to do this he will need to assess the costs of each alternative, the prices of property etc. He will also need to produce a *cash flow forecast* for each alternative to see what finance may be required. He will then have to determine if the finance will be available and what it will cost.

2. Consequence of a wrong choice:

    a. Loss of opportunity to make money, provide employment etc

    b. Loss of opportunity in wholesaling but risk of failure if the manufacturing does not turn out as planned.

    c. Loss of opportunity in manufacturing and risk of failure if wholesaling does not work out as planned.

    d. Risk of failure due to either activity failing. Loss of control by Martin as he cannot be in two places at once and more activity will require more of his limited time.

    e. Risk of failure if either activity fails.

    Purchasing will involve taking a mortgage and if the business fails and property prices fall then the company may fail.

    Renting usually involves taking on a commitment to pay rent for a defined period of years. Failure of the business will still leave this requirement.

Quick answer questions 6b

1. *Which of these costs are fixed and which are variable?*

2. *What is the prime cost of one SP padlock?*

Scenario 3

He will carry no stock of finished goods as finished goods will be shipped on completion to the customers.

The equipment will last about five years and have a salvage value of about £5,000.
Ignore interest.

**Tasks 6.1**

1. What is the *principal budget factor* here?

Information Bank Topic 13: Budgeting. For this task, see Information Bank 13: 3, pages 168-172.

2. Prepare a budgeted profit and loss account for the SP Padlock for the fourth year for the SP padlock.

Information Bank 13:4, pages 168-172.

3. Prepare a budgeted balance sheet as at the end of the year. You can assume:

   Opening capital is £28,500

   Creditors will be equal to two months purchases

   Debtors will be equal to two months sales

   The balance sheet will be balanced by including a figure for bank overdraft.

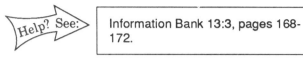

| Help? See: | Information Bank 13:3, pages 168-172. |

4. The newly appointed manager has been asked to prepare *subsidiary budgets*. List the budgets that will be required and explain the contents of each. What action will be necessary as a result of each budget.

| Help? See: | Information Bank 13:4, pages 168-172. |

5. Explain how the budgets will be useful to Martin under the headings:

   Coordination, Communication, Motivation, Control, Evaluation and Delegation.

| Help? See: | Information Bank 13:3, pages 168-172. |

Scenario 4

In the factory the fourth year gets under way as budgeted. In March, Martin finds a customer who wants to buy a product with a particular use. Martin designs a suitable padlock and asks the Manager (Janet) to determine costs etc.

Janet finds that it is possible to *have the product made* in Taiwan for £2.50 each but Martin would have to pay for some special tools which would cost £6,000. Transport of the products to the UK would cost £100 for each batch of 500. Martin's factory would need to box the products at a cost of £1,000 for a machine and 30p each for labour and parts. The special tools would have no salvage value and would last for 5 years. The machine in the factory would last four years and have a salvage value of £200.

Alternatively Janet could *make the product in the factory*. This would necessitate the purchase of machinery costing £20,000 which would last five years and have a salvage value of £2,000. Materials would cost £1.00 a padlock and labour would cost 70p a unit. It would be necessary to hire a supervisor to oversee the production at a cost of £12,000 a year. Extra overheads including insurance, power and stationery would come to about £3,000 a year.

Martin reckons that the selling price will be £4.

 **Tasks 6.2**

1. What is the *breakeven* sales volume (numbers of padlocks to be sold) if:

   i.   The padlock is purchased in Taiwan

   ii. The padlock is made in the company's own factory?

| Help? See: | For these tasks you should read through Information Bank Topic 12: Uses of marginal costing, pages 164-168. |

2. Sales are forecast at 20,000 units a year. Should the company make the padlocks themselves or buy it in Taiwan?

Information Bank, pages 164-168.

3. At what turnover would buying and making be equally profitable?

Information Bank, pages 164-168.

4. Discuss the merits and demerits of the two choices in addition to purely financial considerations.

Information Bank, pages 164-168.

Quick answer question 6b: *Answers and comments*

1. Material and labour costs are variable. The remaining costs are fixed. However it is possible that some of the other factory overheads may be variable.

2.
Material cost	60p
Labour cost	40p
Prime cost	100p

Scenario 5

Martin sells the type ER2 padlock to wholesalers in the UK. He imports these for £2.00 each and sells them at £4.20. He has received an enquiry from a French company who want the ER2 but with a modification. The modification will involve design expenditure of £3,000. In addition modifying the padlocks will cost £0.50 in labour and materials and transporting them to the customer will cost £100 a case. A case contains 500 padlocks.

The French firm are willing to give a firm order for 5,000 a year for two years and they may require more in future years. They are looking at a price of £2.50 but Martin knows that that is negotiable.

Tasks 6.3

1. What is the *minimum price* that Martin can accept from the French company that will just allow him to break even on the deal?

Information Bank, pages 164-168.

2. What would be the minimum price if the acceptance of the order enabled Martin to negotiate a reduction in price from his supplier to £1.80 each? Currently he buys 60,000 padlocks a year.

Information Bank, pages 164-168.

3. What might be the advantages and disadvantages of accepting the order at a price which was *less than the normal price* of £4.20 but which was profitable to Martin.

Information Bank, pages 164-168.

Scenario 6

During the year the factory added two new products – the AM and the PM. These require machining by a neighbouring firm and this firm is the only one that the company can find to do the machining at a reasonable price. The costs of manufacture of the new products are:

	AM £	PM £
Labour	2.40	3.10
Materials	3.10	3.90
Machining	2.00	4.00
Sales Price is	11.00	15.00

Martin expects sales of the two products to be 6,000 AMs and 9,000 PMs in the next six months.

The machining firm charges £12 an hour for machining and can supply an absolute maximum of 3,400 hours in the next six months.

Martin eventually finds another firm that will do the machining but they want to charge £30 an hour. He knows this is negotiable.

 **Tasks 6.4**

1. Assuming that output should not exceed expected sales and that the company wish to maximise profit, how many AMs and how many PMs should be made?

 Information Bank, pages 164-168.

2. What is the maximum price that Martin can pay per hour for machining to make up the shortfall at a profit?

 Information Bank, pages 164-168.

Budgeting

Negotiation   Participation

Master Budget   Communication

Subsidiary Budgets   Motivation

Budgets

Coordination   Control

Anticipation   Evaluation

Delegation   Flexible Behaviour

Rigidity

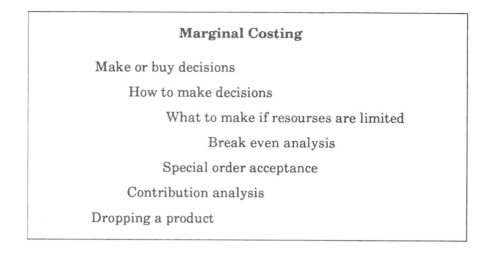

Marginal Costing

Make or buy decisions

How to make decisions

What to make if resourses are limited

Break even analysis

Special order acceptance

Contribution analysis

Dropping a product

Summary of Unit 6

1. Determining the costs and profitability of alternative courses of action is essential in choosing between options.

2. Budgeting has several objectives and benefits including anticipating potential difficulties before they arise, coordination of the different parts of an enterprise, communication with staff at all levels, motivation, control, evaluation and delegation.

3. The master budget will be in the form of a forecast Profit and Loss Account and Balance Sheet but these will be supported by detailed subsidiary budgets.

4. Financial considerations are essential in planning the future both in the long term in terms of major decisions such as moving premises but also in shorter term decision making.

5. Marginal costing is especially useful in decision making and can be used in such decisions as:

    i.   whether to make or buy a product

    ii. whether to sell a product in a different market at a price below the usual price

    iii. What to make if output is restricted by a necessary input which is in limited supply.

6. Calculation of breakeven points is valuable in negotiating both prices of inputs and sales prices.

Development of knowledge and skills

You are now in a position to tackle questions 1 to 5 of Section 3.13 and questions 1 to 18 of Section 3:12, pages 284-285 and 275-280.

Unit 7: Working capital

Introduction

*This unit introduces the idea of **working capital**, the problems it causes and how to manage it.*

Working Capital can be defined as:

Stocks + Debtors – Creditors – Overdraft

Most firms find that *stocks* have a tendency to increase even without an increase in business and that customers have a tendency to take ever longer to pay for the goods supplied to them. When customers do not pay on time, money becomes tight and the firm tend to want to take longer before paying suppliers. Not unnaturally suppliers do not take kindly to this. Paying suppliers on time when customers do not pay on time, may require an increase in overdraft and unless this is agreed by the bank trouble may ensue. In any case a large overdraft costs a great deal in interest. Slow payment is a major problem in the UK and the larger firms are especially slow and cause much anguish among the small firms that supply them.

Scenario 1

At the end of the fourth year, Martin Padlocks Ltd shows the following figures in part of its balance sheet:

Current Assets		
Stocks:		
Goods for resale		£84,000
Raw Materials and components		£35,000
Debtors		£187,000
Creditors: amounts falling due within one year		
Trade creditors		£80,000
Bank Overdraft		£109,000

Martin knows that the goods for resale are in stock in the wholesale warehouse and that the raw materials and components are in the factory.

The debtors and creditors are not distinguished between the two parts of the company.

Quick answer questions 7a

1. *How are the stocks valued?*
2. *What is the working capital?*

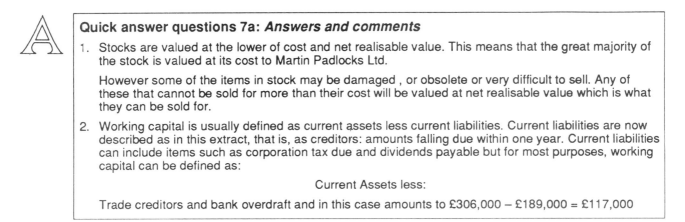

Quick answer questions 7a: *Answers and comments*

1. Stocks are valued at the lower of cost and net realisable value. This means that the great majority of the stock is valued at its cost to Martin Padlocks Ltd.

    However some of the items in stock may be damaged , or obsolete or very difficult to sell. Any of these that cannot be sold for more than their cost will be valued at net realisable value which is what they can be sold for.

2. Working capital is usually defined as current assets less current liabilities. Current liabilities are now described as in this extract, that is, as creditors: amounts falling due within one year. Current liabilities can include items such as corporation tax due and dividends payable but for most purposes, working capital can be defined as:

    Current Assets less:

    Trade creditors and bank overdraft and in this case amounts to £306,000 – £189,000 = £117,000

Scenario 2

Martin is worried about the size of the overdraft and the interest it is costing. The Bank have agreed an overdraft limit or facility of £120,000. Nonetheless Martin would much like to reduce the overdraft. In order to find a way to reduce it he asks for an analysis of the figures from his bookkeeper who manages to produce the following data:

	June to September	October	November	December	Total
Debtors (customers):					
Owing from	13,000	31,000	61,000	82,000	187,000
Sales	251,000	73,000	76,000	84,000	484,000
Creditors (suppliers):					
Owing from		2,000	27,000	51,000	80,000
Purchases		46,000	54,000	51,000	151,000
Stocks on hand for resale:					
Date Purchased	8,000	18,000	22,000	36,000	84,000
Stocks of raw materials and components:					
Date Purchased	6,000	9,000	7,000	13,000	35,000

The bookkeeper warns Martin that the information on stocks is approximate and that some of the items labelled as purchased in the period June to September were actually purchased before June.

Quick answer questions 7b

1. *The top right hand figure of £187,000 is the total amount owed as per the Balance Sheet extract. What do you make of the £82,000 figure immediately to the left?*

2. *Immediately below the £187,000 is the sum of £484,000. What is this total? And what is the figure of £84,000 (immediately to its left) in relation to it?*

3. *What is the relationship between the £82,000 figure in 1 and the £84,000 figure in 2?*

Note that the total sales and purchases figures are given to put the debtors, creditors and stocks into perspective.

Scenario 3

Martin wants to make sense of all this information and tries to see what messages for him are contained in it.

Quick answer questions 7c

1. *What proportion of the customers pay:*
   - ❐ *in the month after the sale*
   - ❐ *in the month after that*
   - ❐ *in the third month or more after the sale?*
2. *When does Martin pay his suppliers?*
3. *What would happen to the overdraft if:*
   - ❐ *all customers paid in the month after the sale?*
   - ❐ *goods spent a shorter time in stock before being sold or used?*
   - ❐ *the suppliers were paid more slowly?*

Scenario 4

Martin is distracted by other matters and does nothing about his working capital problem until July when his bookkeeper reports that he cannot pay any of the June accounts as the overdraft is on the limit. He presents a summary as at the end of June similar to the one produced for the end of December:

	January to March	April	May	June
Debtors:				
Owing from	33,000	48,000	71,000	94,000
Sales	320,000	102,000	96,000	94,000
Creditors:				
Owing from		6,000	59,000	67,000
Purchases		72,000	59,000	67,000
Stocks for resale:				
Date Purchased	14,000	29,000	32,000	48,000
Stocks of raw materials and components:				
Date Purchased	9,000	7,000	9,000	17,000

Martin remembers that he had agreed to increase the overdraft limit to £130,000 and that the working capital had increased because of the profitable trading in the first six months of the year. The overdraft now stands at £131,000.

Tasks 7.1

> Help? See: | Before tackling these tasks, you should read through Information Bank 18: Working Capital, pages 193-197.

1. Analyse the data at 30th June in the same way as the data at 31 December and comment on the differences shown.
2. Analyse the differences in sales, purchases and stocks between the two half years and explain the difference this will make to working capital and the bank overdraft.

3. Make suggestions to Martin as to how he can:
    i.   Reduce the average credit period taken by his customers
    ii. Reduce his stock of goods for resale while retaining a good service to his customers.
    iii. Reduce the stock of raw materials and components in the factory.

 Help? See: | Information Bank 18 paragraphs 1 to 4, pages 193-196.

Quick answer questions 7b: *Answers and Comments*

1. Some customers pay quickly and some take several months. In fact some customers still owe for goods sold in this period June to September. £82,000 is for goods sold in December and not paid for at the end of December.

2. £484,000 is the total amount of sales made and invoiced in the seven months June to December. Of the total sales in this period £187,000 is still owing so £297,000 was paid by December 31st. £84,000 is the total sales made and invoiced in December.

3. £84,000 is the total sales made in December. Of these sales, £82,000 was still unpaid at 31 December. So, £2,000 only must have been paid in December.

Quick answer questions 7c: *Answers and Comments*

1. Debtors:

    Within one Month after sale $\frac{76,000 - 61,000}{76,000} * 100 = 20\%$

    Within two months after sale $\frac{73,000 - 31,000}{73,000} * 100 = 57\%$

    We can deduce from this that 37% (57% – 20%) is paid in the second month after the sale.
    Three months or more (balance)   43%

    This is a sample only and other month ends may yield a different view.
    However it is probably a good indication.

2. Creditors:

Month after sale	approx	50%
Month after that	approx	50%

    You will recall (see Chapter 1) that Martin intended to pay in the month following the purchase. He does not do this but does pay half of his suppliers in the following month and the other half in the month after that. Presumably keeping to monthly payment would push his overdraft over the limit.

3. Debtors paying more quickly would reduce the overdraft
    Lower stocks would also reduce the overdraft
    Paying creditors more quickly would increase the overdraft.

Scenario 5

Martin's bookkeeper reports that as a result of the working capital problem he cannot now take *settlement discounts* from some of the suppliers who offer them. For example Amalgamated Padlocks Ltd offer 5% for payment within 5 days of invoice date.

He suggests that if Martin offered similar discounts to his customers, the customers would pay more quickly and the company could then take advantage of the discounts offered by suppliers.

The bookkeeper also says that suppliers are ringing up and asking for their money. Should he say to them that the company is having temporary working capital or cash flow problems and will pay very soon or should he make some other excuses?

Tasks 7.2

1. Evaluate the suggestion of the bookkeeper that settlement discounts should be offered to customers.

    > Help? See: Information Bank 18:4, page 195.

2. What excuses could the bookkeeper make to suppliers for non-payment?

    > Help? See: Information Bank 18:1, page 193.

3. Martin's bookkeeper says that, in his previous firm, he used to manage the creditors by paying some quickly and some after a long interval. Explain how managing creditors may help to finance Martin's business and the problems that might be encountered

    > Help? See: Information Bank 18.5 and 18.7, pages 196-197.

4. Martin hopes to increase his turnover rapidly. What financial problems might this cause?

    > Help? See: Information Bank 18.6, page 196

Scenario 6

Martin has an old house and the central heating system is now very old and decrepit. He decides to have a brand new system installed and obtains tenders from a number of suppliers. One of these is from Ted whose tender is the lowest by 25% but as Ted has a good reputation locally Martin commissions him to install the new system at a price of £5,100 to be paid when the system is complete and working satisfactorily.

On August 5th Ted appears with an apprentice in an ancient van and does three days work. He then disappears for a week and when he returns Martin irately asks him where he has been. Ted is apologetic and says that he has been completing another job. He then works for a further four days before not appearing again. During this work period, the boiler and all the radiators are delivered to Martin's house from a local plumbers merchant.

Ted and his apprentice work intermittently until early December when Martin finally insists on completion before Christmas. Ted then starts to work very hard during the day, in the evenings and at the weekend. On December 15th he asks Martin for an advance payment of part of the sum due as he is being pressed by his suppliers. Martin agrees to pay £1,000 as he is worried that Ted will go bust and not complete the contract.

Finally the system is completed on Christmas Eve and works perfectly but Ted does not present his bill until January 5th as he is snowed under with work.

 **Tasks 7.3**

Ted clearly has both *profitability* problems and *liquidity* problems but is not short of work.

Analyse his problems and suggest ways in which he can improve his business.

 Help? See:

Information Bank 18: paragraphs 3 and 4, pages 194 to 195.

Scenario 7

Martin orders 500 type RP padlocks from his usual supplier as the company is out of stock and he has an order from a customer. The supplier is very apologetic but they have run out and their manufacturer in the Far East cannot supply for another three weeks. The supplier's salesperson is especially upset as her company have invested in a state of the art computer system incorporating EOQ and Automatic Ordering when Re-order levels are reached. She cannot understand what has gone wrong. Martin is upset at having to disappoint his customer and cannot understand what the salesperson is talking about.

Tasks 7.4

Explain to Martin what the salesperson means by EOQ and Reorder levels and what may have gone wrong.

Help? See:

Information Bank 18: 3, page 194.

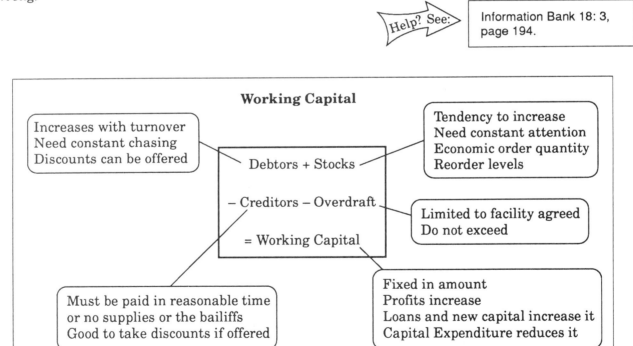

Working Capital

Increases with turnover
Need constant chasing
Discounts can be offered

Tendency to increase
Need constant attention
Economic order quantity
Reorder levels

Debtors + Stocks

– Creditors – Overdraft

= Working Capital

Limited to facility agreed
Do not exceed

Must be paid in reasonable time
or no supplies or the bailiffs
Good to take discounts if offered

Fixed in amount
Profits increase
Loans and new capital increase it
Capital Expenditure reduces it

Summary of Unit 7

1. Stocks have a tendency to increase even without an increase in business

2. Customers have a tendency not to pay unless pressed

3. Banks give firms finite overdraft limits

4. A firms working capital is limited

5. The above phenomena tend to cause difficulty in paying suppliers.

6. This is called a working capital problem or is said to cause cash flow difficulties

7. A monthly analysis of debtors showing how long accounts have been outstanding is helpful in highlighting the problem and in suggesting solutions.

8. An analysis of the age of stocks is also very useful

9. Firms should constantly review all stocks and try to sell off or use old, slow moving and obsolete items

10. The Buying function is very important but is often seen as much less critical than sales, production and other activities.

11. Taking settlement discounts is highly desirable but offering settlement discounts is very expensive

12. Contracting firms are advised to tender realistically, to obtain stage payments and to complete work in as short a time as possible

13. All firms who manufacture whether on sites or in a factory are advised to complete work in as short a time as possible

14. Invoicing promptly and chasing payment vigorously is an essential for all firms

15. Stock control using EOQs and Re-order levels is good policy but often goes wrong.

Developing knowledge and skills

You are now in a position to tackle questions 1 to 10 of Section 3:18, pages 318-321

Unit 8: Investment appraisal

Introduction

*Firms do not stand still but continually make changes. Most changes involve new capital expenditure on fixed assets. Such **capital expenditure** may be for replacement assets or for more efficient assets or in connection with new products, production methods, factories, branches etc. The acquisition of an entire business or company as in **takeover** situations can also be regarded as capital expenditure.*

*Clearly decisions on such capital expenditure should not be made without thought and the processes by which possible capital expenditure is considered is called **capital budgeting** or **capital investment appraisal.** There are various techniques for considering such capital expenditure and this unit is about them.*

Scenario 1

Martin has discovered that there is a market for a new type of lock which he calls the Zitron. His manager is asked to design the lock and a production system in detail and consider the feasibility of setting up a production line for it. Martin commissions his local College marketing department to determine the likely demand at various price levels.

The College charge him £1,000 and tell him that demand over the next few years is likely to be:

	Units
year	
1	10,000
2	20,000
3	20,000
4	15,000
5	10,000
6	5,000

Price should be about £10 each.

The manager has spent £4,000 on designing the lock and the production system and is ready to go ahead with obtaining firm prices for the production system from suppliers if Martin gives the go ahead.

He estimates that costs will be:

Capital costs:

Market survey (see above)	£1,000
Design (see above)	£4,000
Machinery	£80,000
Working capital	£35,000

Production costs:

Variable:	Labour	£2 a lock
	Material	£4 a lock
	Energy	£0.50 a lock
	Consumables	£0.30 a lock
Fixed:	Labour	£15,000 a year
	Other costs	£6,000

He expects that the machinery will fetch a salvage value of about £10,000 whenever it is sold.

The working capital would reduce as sales fell off in years 4 and 5 but it is reasonable to simplify the calculations to say that the original investment in the working capital will be returned at the end of the project.

Quick answer questions 8a

1. *Before considering whether to go ahead with the project, Martin has already spent £5,000. Do you think that in deciding whether or not to go ahead Martin should take the £5,000 into account?*

2. *Why do you think sales of the product will decline towards the end of the project?*

3. *What is meant by an investment in working capital? Why will it be returned at the end of the project?*

4. *What will be the contribution from the sale of one lock?*

5. *Will it be worthwhile making and selling just 5,000 locks in year 6?*

Scenario 2

Martin is wondering how to appraise the project when he remembers a course he once attended. He recovers the notes and makes himself familiar again with the techniques.

Firstly he has to make some decisions. These are:

a. He will assume that the project will last five years as year 6 promises to be unprofitable. He will of course continue into year 6 and beyond if sales are still keeping up.

b. He has talked about *cost of capital* to Anne and has calculated it at 16%.

c. He reckons that he requires that any project should *pay off* within four years.

**Tasks 8.1**

 Before tackling these tasks you should read through Information Bank Topic 16: Investment appraisal, pages 183-187.

1. Appraise the project by:

    a. Calculating the *payback* period

     Information Bank 16: 4, page 183.

    b. Calculating the net present value and profitability index.

     Information Bank 16:5, page 184.

    c. Calculating the *accounting rate of return* using average capital investment over the life of the project.

     Information Bank 16:7, page 186.

2. Write a report to martin arguing out the correct decision on the project. You should bring in any non-financial arguments you can think of, stating any assumptions you may care to make.

     Information Bank 16.8, page 187.

 **Extension tasks**

1. Set up the problem on a spreadsheet

2. Test the model for *sensitivity* to changes in the data. Changes may be in the initial cost, the discount rate, the time horizon, the volume of sales, the sales price, the input costs etc.

Information Bank 16, page 183.

Scenario 3

Martin lives on a main road and is talking one day to a neighbour who tells him that she supplies replacement windows. Martin agrees to consider any quotation that she makes for his house. Being familiar with capital appraisal techniques, he writes down all the relevant data:

Estimate for all front facing windows: £6,000

Savings from reduced energy loss: £900 a year

Addition to value of house (estimated) £4,000

Cost of Capital: 12%

Time Horizon: 5 years

Note:

a. He has worked out the saving in energy from data supplied by his neighbour.

b. The addition to the value of his house was estimated by a friend who is an estate agent. He will realise the extra money only when he sells the house.

c. The cost of capital is the rate he can borrow at.

d. The time horizon is just a guess. He arrived at it by thinking that he would move when his last child left home which will be in five years time.

Quick answer questions 8a: *Answers and comments*

1. No! Martin has already spent the £5,000. Cost accountants call this a *sunk* or *dead* cost. What is done cannot be undone. In making decisions only the *future* costs and revenues should be considered.

2. Most products have a limited life. When a firm develop a new product which is good then, for a time, it will do very well. However good products inspire competition and probably the college think that by year 6 the competition may make it unprofitable for Martin's company.

3. Martin will have to build a stock of raw materials for manufacture and also maintain a stock of finished goods. This will cost money. In addition the money spent on finished goods will not be recovered immediately on sales but will have to await payment from the customer. Some mitigation of this will come as Martin will take credit from his suppliers. At the end of the project, money will come in as stocks are sold off without replacement and debtors pay without further debtors being created.

4. The Contribution is Sales price less marginal costs:

    £10.00 – £6.80 = £3.20.

5. No! 5,000 units sold will give a contribution of:

    5,000 x £3.20 = £16,000 but fixed costs will be £21,000 so a loss would be made.

Tasks 8.2

1. Calculate the net present value of this project.

> Help? See: Information Bank 16:5, page 184.

2. Suggest and discuss any factors other than the purely financial that Martin may care to take into account.

3. Advise him on whether to accept or reject the project.

4. Consider how accurate each of the figures are. How variable do you think each of them might be?

5. What addition to the value of the house would make the project exactly viable, that is, have a net present value of zero?

> Help? See: Information Bank 16:5, page 184.

Capital budgeting	
Uses	– Adding to fixed Assets
	– Replacing Fixed Assets
	– New Products
	– New Branches
	– New Methods
	– Acquisition of businesses
	– Acquisition of companies
	– Investing in Financial Assets
Appraisal Methods	– Payback
	– Net Present Value
	– Internal Rate of Return
	– Accounting Rate of Return
Net Present value	– Initial cost
	– Cash Flows
	– Working Capital
	– Disposal of assets/working capital
	– Discount Rate/ Cost of Capital
	– Profitability Index
	– Time Horizon

Summary of Unit 8

1. All firms engage in capital expenditure

2. All capital expenditure should be subject to capital budgeting or capital investment appraisal

3. Capital investment appraisal techniques include: payback period, discounted cash flow (net present value), internal rate of return, accounting rate of return.

4. All figures used are forecasts and estimates. These are not necessarily reliable.

5. Estimates required include the initial capital outlay, working capital requirement, salvage value, cash flows for sales or savings, cash flows of costs, cost of capital and time horizon.

Development of knowledge and skills

You are now in a position to tackle questions 1 to 5 of Section 3:16, pages 305-306.

Unit 9: Sources of finance

Introduction

As we saw in Unit 1, starting a business requires some initial **capital**. Starting a business as small as a window cleaning round may require money to buy ladders, buckets etc and perhaps even a van. Starting a motor car factory would require hundreds of millions of pounds.

Most people start a business with their **savings**. If more is required then money can be obtained from relatives and friends and money can be **borrowed** from the Bank. The high street banks are the primary source of capital to the small business. However there are many other sources and we shall look at the main ones in this Unit.

All sources of money have a **cost**. This cost is the **interest** payable and the rate varies from source to source. The actual interest **rate** is not always made explicit but today lenders are required by the Consumer Credit Act 1974 to state the **Annualised Percentage Rate (APR)** which is the true rate of interest charged.

Scenario 1

Martin Padlocks Ltd has now concluded six years in business and has reached a turnover of £2,000,000. The balance sheet at the end of year six can be summarised as:

Fixed Assets			
Cost			300,450
Less Depreciation			128,300
			172,150
Current Assets			
Stocks		330,000	
Debtors		304,000	
		634,000	
Creditors: amounts falling due within one year			
Trade Creditors		248,000	
Bank Overdraft		201,000	
Corporation Tax		35,000	
Taxes and Social Security		189,000	
Dividend		20,000	
		693,000	
Net Current Liabilities			(59,000)
Total Assets less current Liabilities			113,150
Capital and Reserves			
Share Capital			15,000
Profit and Loss Account			98,150
			113,150

Quick answer questions 9a

1. *The company has total assets of £172,150 + £634,000 = £806,150. Explain how these have been financed.*

2. *Financing can be considered to be from external sources and from internal sources. Which of the sources in this balance sheet are internal and which are external?*

Scenario 2

Martin understands his balance sheet and its implications and is explaining it to his son who is studying business at school. His son is having difficulty in seeing how Profit and Loss Account is a source of finance.

Martin consults Anne and comes up with this explanation:

- profit enables the company to pay a dividend up to the amount of the profit.

- imagine that the company paid the full dividend by writing cheques to the shareholders.

- at the same time the company need finance from the shareholders so the shareholders are prevailed upon to write cheques of the same amounts as the dividends in favour of the company.

- all the cheques are torn up.

In practice, most companies find that *retained profits* are insufficient for their desired expansion and Martin Padlocks is no exception.

Martin is still attempting to expand the business and he realises that involves the acquisition of new assets and that involves finding some money.

Among the assets he wants to finance are:

a. The factory has been rented up to now but the landlord has offered to sell it to the company for £200,000.

b. The company need three new large vans. The vans will cost about £20,000 each.

c. An increase in turnover of 30% will require an increase in stock, debtors and trade creditors of the same percentage.

d. The company needs some additional machinery which will cost £75,000.

He talks to Anne and to his bank manager and finds out some sources of finance. These include:

- *Hire Purchase* is available on most fixed assets over three or four years. He is quoted 24% APR.

- The Bank will offer *mortgage loans* over ten or fifteen years at a negotiable fixed rate of $1\frac{1}{2}$% over base rate.

- The Bank will be willing to increase the *overdraft* by £50,000 at a cost of 4% over *base rate*. The overdraft is already *secured* by a *floating charge*.

- A *factoring* company are willing to factor up to 50% of approved debts at a rate of 4% over base rate + a $1\frac{1}{2}$% service charge.

❑ A cousin of Martin has just won a large sum on the football pools and is willing to offer a long term loan of up to £50,000 at 12% with *convertibility* after a few years into ordinary shares.

❑ A *venture capital* company is willing to offer an investment of up to £100,000 of which half would be in *equity* and the loan rate would be long term at 3% over base rate.

Martin finds that the current base rate for most banks is 10.5%.

Tasks 9.1

Martin decides to investigate the alternatives. Set out the results of his investigation in the form of a report:

1. Summarising the amount of finance needed.

2. Suggesting which sources of finance might be suitable for each new investment. You should summarise the advantages and disadvantages of each.

3. Suggesting some sources of finance not reviewed in the scenario.

 Help? See:> | Information Bank Topic 17 : Sources of Finance, pages 188-192.

Scenario 3

Martin is interested in buying a small second hand cruising boat. The price is £12,000 and Martin would need to borrow all but £3,000 of this. The boat yard tell him that they are willing to lend him the money at 10% interest and that they are willing to offer this low rate as a concession in order to make the sale. Martin asks for a written quote and takes it to Anne for appraisal. The terms are:

The loan is for 3 years

The loan is repaid in 3 equal instalments, together with interest, on the anniversary of the loan.

The annual interest is 10% on the whole £9,000.

(Thus each instalment will be £3,900.)

Tasks 9.2

Calculate the approximate APR of this loan. It can be calculated as the internal rate of return of the arrangement.

Help? See:> | Information Bank 16:6, page 186.

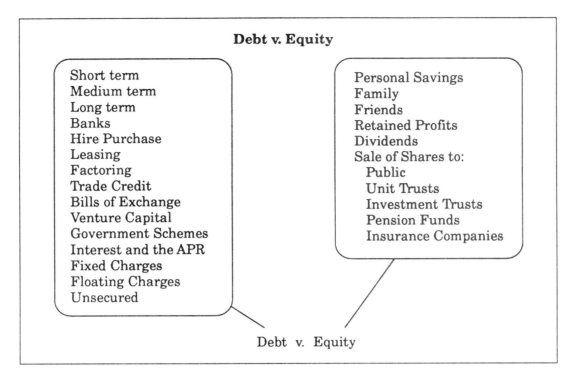

Debt v. Equity

Short term
Medium term
Long term
Banks
Hire Purchase
Leasing
Factoring
Trade Credit
Bills of Exchange
Venture Capital
Government Schemes
Interest and the APR
Fixed Charges
Floating Charges
Unsecured

Personal Savings
Family
Friends
Retained Profits
Dividends
Sale of Shares to:
    Public
    Unit Trusts
    Investment Trusts
    Pension Funds
    Insurance Companies

Debt v. Equity

Summary of Unit 9

1. Expansion usually involves the acquisition of assets.

2. Acquisition of assets usually means obtaining finance.

3. Sources of finance can be internal. This means the owners putting up the money either from their private sources (if any) or from retained earnings.

4. Other sources are external. These include relatives, friends, banks, HP companies, leasing companies, factoring companies, suppliers and venture capital companies.

5. Some forms of finance are secured by fixed or floating charges or by operation of law (as HP).

6. Interest rates vary from source to source depending on security and term.

7. Interest rates may be fixed at the outset of the loan or vary during the period of the loan according to prevailing market rates.

8. Repayment periods can be short, medium term or long term.

9. Interest rates quoted can be misleading and it is important to recognize the APR.

Development of knowledge and skills

You are now in a position to tackle questions 1 to 3 in Section 3:17, pages 312-314.

Unit 10: Stock valuation, manufacturing accounts and multiproduct costing

Introduction

*This unit begins with the valuation of stock. You will recall from Units 2 and 3 that it is necessary to value stocks for the purposes of preparing Trading and Profit and Loss Accounts and Balance Sheets. This is not a difficult procedure for the stocks of retailers and wholesalers but we will look at the problems of **fungible stocks** and **net realisable values.***

The stocks of finished goods (and also work in progress) held by manufacturers are conceptually harder to value and in addition to the need for valuing stocks for inclusion in Profit and Loss Accounts and Balance Sheets, it is necessary to find the cost of manufacture of goods manufactured for sale in order to ensure that the selling price is above cost.

*The Profit and Loss Accounts of **manufacturing** enterprises need to be enlarged from the simple Trading and Profit and Loss Accounts of retailers and wholesalers by the creation of a **Manufacturing Account** and we deal with this next.*

*Finally the cost of manufacture of items made for sale by a **multiproduct** firm will be explored and the techniques of **total absorption costing** discovered.*

Scenario 1

Martin is well aware that stocks of the goods he buys from his suppliers are assessed in the annual *stocktake* at the year end. He himself organizes the stock take and makes quite sure that:

- ❐ each type of stock is separately identified and counted;
- ❐ each type of stock is counted twice by separate people;
- ❐ the state of each item in stock is assessed for condition and saleability. Any items that are old, slow to sell, obsolete or damaged are noted;
- ❐ all this information is recorded in stock sheets which are numbered on issue and the return of each sheet is carefully recorded;
- ❐ any items not belonging to Martin Padlocks Ltd are not recorded;
- ❐ any items belonging to the company but not physically present (perhaps because they are in transit) are included;
- ❐ *cut-off* is correct. Cut-off means making sure that any goods which are included in purchases in a year are also included in stock if not sold and any goods sold in the year are not included in stock at the year end.

Martin hands the stocksheets to the accountant who takes each item, puts on a price, multiplies the price by the quantity to find the value of each category, adds the individual values to find the grand total and puts this in the Profit and Loss Account and Balance Sheet.

However Martin has not concerned himself with the price to be attached to each category other than knowing that it is the cost price to the company and not the selling out price. Several difficulties present themselves to him and he asks Anne to explain how these items would be valued.

The following categories of stock present special difficulties with valuation:

i. Padlock type G276 is imported from Taiwan at £2 each. Martin imports so many that the supplier gives him a trade discount of 20% off the £2 price. Martin pays the shipping cost of £200 a 1,000 units. On arrival at the works, Martin pays June £6 a 100 units to rebox and label them. the boxes cost 3p a unit and the labels 4p a unit. There were 860 in stock at the December 31st stocktake.

ii. Lock type G726 costs £48 a dozen from a local supplier and by special agreement **Martin pays** the day after each delivery and receives a 5% cash (another word is settlement) **discount for** doing so. He has 2,760 in stock.

iii. Lock type G627 contains a component made from a rare mineral which has a cost **which varies** from week to week. Consequently the price to Martin varies and so he buys from **his supplier in** small quantities. There were none in stock three months before the stocktake. **There has been** the following movements in the last three months:

October	14 Bought 500 at £4.90 each
	21 Sold 200 at £7.00 each
	28 Sold 250 at £6.70 each
November	3 Bought 400 at £3.60 each
	8 Bought 600 at £3.20 each
	15 Sold 350 at £6.00 each
	24 Sold 240 at £6.20 each
December	7 Sold 100 at £7.00 each
	15 Bought 200 at £4.25 each
	21 Sold 350 at £7.50 each

Martin Padlocks value stocks on the *FIFO* principle.

iv. Lock G400 was bought in July in a job lot of 2,000 for £1.50 each. Since then 200 have been sold but Martin knows that further sales will be made only at a low price as the locks are too flimsy. He has decided to sell off the remaining 1,800 at £1.60 each. Before selling them he will have to fit a replacement part at a cost to each lock of 20p for the part and 5p for labour. He will also have to pay a 10% commission on the sale to his representative.

 **Tasks 10.1**

1. Show how each of these items of stock should be valued.

> Help? See:
>
> You should read Information Bank Topic 4 Stocks before tackling these tasks. Paragraph 4: 5 for items i. and ii., 4:8 for the fungible items iii., 4:7 for item iv, pages 120-122.

2. Explain the effect on profit of 19x2 and 19x3 of the following errors in stocktaking **and valuation** in the stock at 31 December 19x2:

i. 35 H13s were counted as 30.

ii. 43 H14s were included in the stocksheets as 34.

iii. 100 H15s were omitted altogether.

iv. 130 H16s were counted and entered twice.

v. 60 H17s were sold and invoiced on 29th December. However they were **collected by the** carrier on Jan 2nd only and so were counted in the stocktake.

vi. 45 H18s were priced at selling price instead of cost price.

vii. 20 H19s were priced at cost but they are damaged and net realisable value is **below cost.**

viii. 100 H20s were valued on LIFO principles instead of FIFO. The price of H20s has **been** rising.

ix. Stock sheet 18 was not handed in and the items on it excluded from the final total.

x. an H21 was in the warehouse for a warranty repair. The stocktaker did not know this and included it in the stocktake.

Help? See:	Information Bank 4 (Stocks, page 120) and a little logical thinking!

Scenario 2

Martin is familiar with the accounts of his own company but has relied on Anne going through the Manufacturing Account section with him to really understand what the words and figures mean. He would like to expand his manufacturing and knows that he can do this by building up manufacturing in his own business or perhaps by buying an already existing business. He is approached by a fellow member of the Chamber of Commerce who suggests Martin might be interested in buying her business as she makes a complementary range of products. Before making a decision he asks for a copy of the accounts and is supplied with a copy of the two most recent sets of figures. Here they are:

Bukkeyball Lock Manufacturing Company

Manufacturing, Trading and Profit and Loss Account
For the year ending 31 December

	19x1		19x2	
	(£'000)			
Raw materials				
Opening Stock	23		17	
Purchases	223		195	
	246		212	
Less Closing Stock	17		16	
Consumed		229		196
Direct labour		431		420
Other Direct Costs		20		18
Prime Costs		680		634
Production Overheads		145		152
Factory Inputs in the year		825		786
Opening Work in Progress		13		17
		838		803
Less Closing Work in Progress		17		45
Works Cost of Finished Goods Output		821		758
Opening Stock of Finished Goods		105		68
		924		826
Less Closing Stock of Finished Goods		68		143
Cost of Finished Goods Sold		856		683
Sales		1,050		840
Gross Profit		194		157
Administration Costs	94		82	
Repair to roof	80		–	
Selling and Distribution Costs	89		75	
Financial Charges	12	275	18	175
Net Loss		81		18

Tasks 10.2

Martin wants to form a general impression of the company and its performance over the last two years. Comment on the following matters which Martin thought about:

a. Does the company carry much raw material in stock?

b. How has the relative proportions of the three elements of prime cost changed over the two years?

c. Is Bukkeyball a hi-tech company or a rather old-fashioned manufacturer?

d. The size of work in progress at the year ends.

e. The stock of finished goods at the year end.

f. The trend in sales.

g. Gross Profit as a percentage of sales.

h. Containment of overhead costs.

i. Why repairs to roof is shown separately.

j. Financial charges.

k. Depreciation of machinery, the computer and the delivery van must be included under headings somewhere. Which headings?

l. The accounts have been typed in a hurry and it is possible that they contain an error. Can you find one?

m. Martin understands that the accounts have been drawn up using the usual conventions including going concern, accruals, prudence, materiality and consistency. Explain how these conventions have been used in the Accounts and discuss why the going concern convention may not be appropriate.

Help? See:> | Help: see Information Bank Topic 5 Manufacturing Accounts. and Topic 7 Accounting Conventions, pages 123 and 136.

Scenario 3

Martin is aware that finished goods stocks are valued at the lower of cost and net realisable value in his own and Bukkeyball's Accounts but has not had time to research in depth how his accounting staff and Anne have measured cost bearing in mind that both businesses make a range of products – they are multiproduct firms. He has also accepted their estimates of production costs when fixing selling prices. He now thinks it is time he investigated this area more fully.

Some costs, known as *direct* costs, are *traceable* to particular products but some costs, known as *indirect* costs, are *shared* by more than one product. You will remember the concept of direct and indirect costs from Unit 5. In building up the cost of a product it is relatively easy to find the direct costs which relate to it. This will primarily be the materials and components which compose it and also labour where a worker spends time exclusively on the product. However the rent and rates of the factory are equally costs of manufacture with some portion of them having to be included in pricing decisions and stock valuation.

Martin markets a special lock which he has made by pieceworkers in a part of his factory. His costs of manufacture for this product are:

For each lock:	Materials and components	£2.80
	Labour of worker (piecework)	£1.40
Overall annual costs relating to the lock:		
	Supervisor	£12,000
	Licence to use patent process	£4,000
	Rent and Rates	£3,000

Quick answer questions 10a

1. *Divide these costs into:*

   a. Material, labour, services

   b. Fixed, Variable

   c. Direct, Indirect

2. *Calculate the total cost and the cost per unit if*

   a. Total output is 5,000 units

   or b. Total output is 10,000 units

Scenario 4

Martin has developed a range of special locks which he is making in a bay of his factory. He has estimated the costs attached to the bay which is divided into three shops: machining, assembly, and, packing. The overheads for a year of the whole bay are:

	£
Rent	8,800
Rates	3,700
Fire Insurance	1,200
Supervision	15,800
Repairs to machinery	3,000

In addition the overheads which can be *allocated* to specific shops are:

	Machining	Assembly	Packing
Depreciation of Machinery	13,000	1,500	2,400
Energy	2,600	350	600
Labour on fixed rates	12,200	9,150	–

Some information about the three shops is:

Area in square metres	40	30	40
Number of employees	5	6	5

Martin recognises that the principal activity in the Machining shop is machining and that activity can be measured in *machine hours*. He reckons that output will be large enough in the next twelve months to require 10,000 hours. In the Assembly shop, *labour hours* are the important factor and that output will require 12,000 hours. In the Packing shop also, labour hours are the relevant output and that production will require 8,000 hours.

Quick answer questions 10a: *Answers and comments*

1. a. Materials: Materials and Components

    Labour: Outworkers and the supervisor

    Services: Licence, rent and rates

    b. Variable: Materials and components and the outworkers

    Fixed: Supervisor, Licence and rent and rates

    c. In this case, all the costs can be seen as direct in that they are all traceable to the particular product. On the other hand, the supervisor, licence and rent and rates are shared by all the output and so they are overheads in that they are shared by each individual lock.

2. a. Total cost = 5,000 * 4.20 + 19,000 = £40,000

    Cost per unit $\frac{40,000}{5,000}$ = £8

    b. Total cost = 10,000 * 4.20 + 19,000 = £61,000

    Cost per unit $\frac{61,000}{10,000}$ = £6.10

This example illustrates the point that costs per unit are lower if the fixed costs are shared among a larger number of products.

It also raises the point that in valuing a product it is necessary to specify the output. "What is the cost of making this product?" does not have a simple unequivocal answer!

Tasks 10.3

1. Produce an overhead summary allocating and apportioning the expense items to the three shops and derive a total overhead cost for each shop.

> Help? See: | You should read through Information Bank Topic 10 Total Absorption Costing before tackling this task. Paragraph 13 applies specifically to this task. Pages 157-159.

2. Suggest absorption rates for each department.

> Help? See: | Information Bank 10:14, page 158.

Scenario 5

Martin has two products, the VX and the WY, which he can sell at prices which are restricted by competition. They are made in the factory bay discussed above and he needs to know what it would cost to make them.

He reckons the costs will be:

	VX	WY
Materials and components	£2.40	£2.60
Piecework Labour	£1.80	£3.30
Machine time (Machining)	20 mins	30 mins
Labour Time (Assembly)	15 mins	10 mins
Labour Time (Packing)	25 mins	20 mins

Tasks 10.4

1. Calculate the total cost of manufacture of each item.

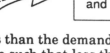 Help? See:

| Information Bank 10:13 and 10:14, page 158. |

2. Martin is worried that demand for the products may be less than the demand used in the estimates above (for example he thinks that demand may be such that less than 10,000 hours will be worked in the Machine shop). He suspects that output will be only sufficient to require 75% of the hours stated for the three shops.

   Recalculate the costs for the two products on the 75% assumption.

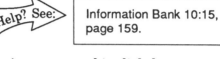 Help? See:

| Information Bank 10:13 to 10:15, pages 158-159. |

3. Discuss the relationship between the costs obtained under tasks 1 and 2.

Help? See:

| Information Bank 10:15, page 159. |

4. Martin deliberately arranged to pay most of the workers on piece rates and is slightly put out when he realises that the cost of production is still partly dependent on the time taken to make an item. Explain why this is so.

Help? See:

| Information Bank 10:15, page 159. |

5. Martin has assumed that all the machines in the machine shop are the same but actually there are three different machines of different sizes. Clearly product costs will be differ depending on the machine used. How can this be handled in the cost accumulation process?

Help? See:

| Information Bank 10:13, page 158. |

6. Martin feels that if the calculated costs of production of the products manufactured in the three shops are less than the selling prices he must make a profit. Anne explains that there are several reasons why that is not so. Explain what Anne means.

Help? See:

| Information Bank 10:15, page 159. |

Scenario 6

Martin estimates that in his factory as a whole the relative magnitudes of overheads will be:

Manufacturing Overheads	3
Administrative Overheads	1
Selling and Distribution Overheads	1

He has calculated the cost of making a lock called the TU at:

	£
Direct Costs	1.60
Manufacturing Overhead Absorbed	1.20
Total Manufacturing Cost	2.80

Martin aims to sell that product at a price which will cover all costs (Manufacturing **and non-** manufacturing) and give a profit of 10% of the selling price.

Tasks 10.5

1. Calculate the selling price required.

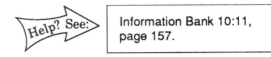

2. Explain why Martin may actually set the price either higher or lower than the price you have calculated.

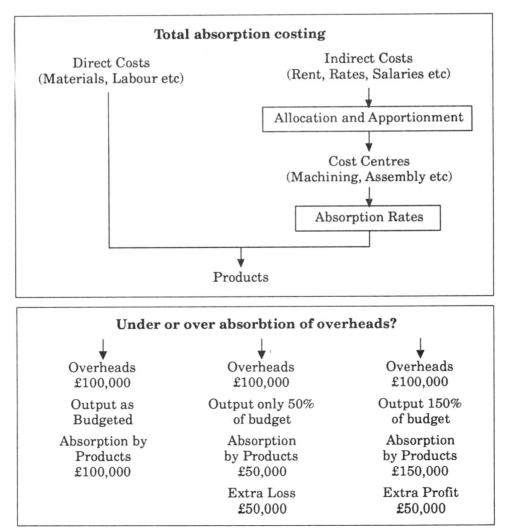

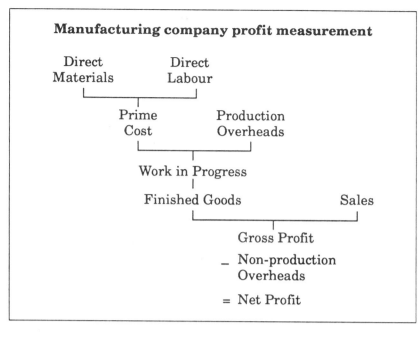

Summary of Unit 10

1. Stocks are valued at the lower of cost and net realisable value in the Profit and Loss Account and Balance Sheet.

2. Cost is defined as the cost of bringing the item in stock to its present location and condition. The definition can be extended to the cost of purchase + the cost of conversion.

3. Cost includes the purchase price including import duties, transport and handling costs and any other directly attributable costs less trade discounts and subsidies if any.

4. If the actual cost of a stock item cannot be identified because they are fungible items then valuation can be FIFO or AVCO or LIFO. LIFO is not generally used in the UK. Do not confuse valuation method with actual sequence of use. A shop may value its stock of pork pies on a LIFO basis but I hope it does not sell them on that basis.

5. Net realisable value is the selling price less any necessary expenditure before or as a consequence of sale.

6. Errors in counting, recording and valuing stock are easy to make. Watch out especially for cut-off errors.

7. Profit in a manufacturing business is measured by:

Sales		x
Less:		
Manufacturing cost	x	
Administrative cost	x	
Selling and Distribution cost	x̲	x̲
Net Profit		x

8. The total cost of manufacturing a product is called the total absorption cost.

9. Costs can be direct or indirect

10. It is relatively easy in building up the cost of a product to measure its direct costs

11. Indirect or overhead costs are more difficult to ascribe to particular products as they are shared by more than one product in a multi-product firm

12. Indirect costs are first allocated or apportioned to cost centres.

13. A product which uses a cost centre absorbs some of the overheads of that cost centre based on some measure of use such as a machine hour rate or labour hour rate

14. A labour hour rate is an absorption method for overheads. It is in addition to the wages paid to the workers.

15. An absorption rate is based on a budgeted output estimate such as machine hours required in a period. Any shortfall in machine hours will mean an under-recovery of overheads

16. Selling prices must be sufficient to cover all three types of cost. Of course, some products will have inadequate selling prices but be compensated by other above averagely profitable products.

17. In measuring the cost of a product it is usual to include only manufacturing costs. Selling prices have to be high enough to cover both the manufacturing cost and some part of the other overheads and to give a profit.

18. Product costing was developed for manufacturing but can be applied to service industries also.

19. The addition of overheads to direct costs is sometimes called the oncost and sometimes the burden. I personally like oncost but it is considered very old fashioned! Burden is American.

Development of knowledge and skills

You are now in a position to tackle questions 6 to 8 in Section 3:10 (pages 265-267) and 1 to 5 in Section 3:4 (pages 222-223) and question 1 of Section 3.5 (page 226).

Unit 11: Standard costing

*The objective of this Unit is to introduce **Standard Costing**. Firms can examine the cost of a product and establish a **standard cost** for it. The **actual cost** of making the product can then be compared with the standard and any difference noted. The difference can be broken down into separate causes known as **variances**.*

Thus management have an objective standard against which actual costs can be compared and can take action to investigate variances and correct any adverse cost movements.

Scenario 1

Martin is worried about the costs of manufacture of a range of keys which are made in a corner of his factory called the key department. These keys are made by stamping them out of sheets of metal. They are then polished and packed. An investigation of the annual cost of the department reveals:

	£
Materials:	20,000
Labour: Stamper	8,000
Polisher	10,200
Packer	7,500
Energy and consumables	3,800
Depreciation of Machines	18,000
Apportionment of rent etc	9,000

Quick answer questions 11a

Which of these costs are likely to be:

Direct

Indirect

Fixed

Variable?

Scenario 2

Martin asks his general manager to measure a standard cost for a *batch* of type 433 keys made in the department.

The manager comes up with the following:

Standard Cost of one batch of type 433 Keys

	£
Materials:	
10 Kilos of Metal at £5.20 a kilo	52.00
Packaging	2.00
Labour :	
Stamper : 3 hours at £4.00 an hour	12.00
Polisher: 3 hours at £5.00 an hour	15.00
Packer : 3.5 hours at £3.90 an hour	13.65
Variable Overheads : 6 hours at £1.50 per Stamper and Polisher hour	9.00
Fixed Overheads : 9.5 hours at £6 a direct labour hour	57.00
Total	160.65

Martin is perplexed by the way that the variable and fixed overheads are expressed.

The manager explains that the amount of electricity and consumables like lubricating oil that are used depends on how long the machines are used. Since the machines are used by the Stamper and

Polisher, the amount of variable overhead will depend on how many hours they operate the machines. It is the stamper and polisher which *drive* the variable overheads.

He also explains that the fixed overheads of the department have to be divided over the output of the department. The department do not make a single type of key but a range. It is thus necessary to express the output in some common form. The method chosen is to take a view that the department provides a quantity of direct labour hours in a year. Production can then be expressed in terms of direct labour hours. Thus it is possible to say that output in a period is n *thousand standard labour hours*. Suppose that Lock 555 should take under standard conditions 5 hours and lock 666 should take 7 hours then total output is two locks but can also said to be 12 standard hours of output.

In this case the fixed costs were budgeted as:

Depreciation of Machines	£18,000
Apportionment of rent etc	£9,000
	£27,000

The total direct labour hours budgeted are 4,500.

So the fixed costs are $\dfrac{27,000}{4,500}$ = £6 per direct labour hour. A batch of type 433 keys should take 9.5 hours of direct labour. Therefore it will absorb 9.5 × 6 = £57 of fixed overheads.

Quick answer questions 11b

What would you expect the standard cost of type 501 keys using the following data:

Materials:

6 Kilos of Metal at £4 a kilo

Packaging £3.00

Labour : Stamper : 2 hours at £4.00 an hour

Polisher: 2.5 hours at £5.00 an hour

Packer :2 hours at £3.90 an hour

Quick answer questions 11a: *Answers and comments*

Direct:	Materials and Labour
Indirect:	The rest
Variable:	Materials , labour and energy
Fixed:	Depreciation and rent etc

Energy is clearly a variable cost as more energy will be used if more keys are made. However measuring the cost of energy for a batch of each type of key made is not economically feasible and so energy is regarded as a variable overhead.

Scenario 3

Martin now understands that he has a standard cost for type 433 keys and can similarly find a standard cost for all the keys produced in the department. He still wonders whether this will be useful to him and the manager gives him several possible uses:

a. In *pricing*. Suppose a selling price was required for a job that included a batch of type 433 keys. He has at least a cost for the keys which he can incorporate in his estimate.

b. In *monthly accounting*. If Martin wished to prepare a profit and loss account and balance sheet monthly, he would be put off by the labour of finding the costs of items in stock. However if he counts up 4 batches of type 433 keys in stock, he can use the standard cost. For the annual accounts however he should not use standard costs as these may not coincide with actual costs which are required for accounts prepared under the requirements of the Companies Act.

c.   In *variance analysis* which we explore later in the Unit.

Some months later, Martin picked out a batch of type 433 keys and enquired what the actual cost of making them was:

Records had been carefully kept and the costs were collected as:

Materials:	11 Kilos at £6 a kilo
	Packaging £2.60
Labour:	Stamper : 3.25 hours at £3.60 an hour
	Polisher: 2.75 hours at £6.00 an hour
	Packer : 4 hours at £4.20 an hour

Quick answer questions 11c

Why do you think the actual costs of overheads were not recorded for the batch Martin picked out so that we can compare them with the actual costs?

Tasks 11.1

1.   Calculate *material* and *labour* variances.

2.   Suggest reasons for the variances

Help? See:> You should read through Information Bank Topic 14 Standard Costing before tackling this task. The specific paragraphs relevant to this task are numbers 4 and 5, pages 173-177.

Scenario 4

Martin is very interested in the schedule of variances and seeks an explanation for them from the manager. After due enquiry the manager produces a schedule of reasons as:

Materials:

Metal:	Price – the price has gone up from the supplier as the price of the metal has increased on world markets.
	Usage – the stamper is newly appointed and has not yet mastered the knack of getting the maximum number of keys from a sheet.
Packaging:	the price has gone up and on this batch some materials were torn during use and had to be replaced. Martin finds that splitting the cost of packing into price and usage variances would cost more than any benefit.

Labour:

Stamper:	Rate – the stamper is new and is paid less than the old stamper
	Efficiency – she takes a little longer than the old one
Polisher:	Rate – a wage increase was given above the normal rate as he now supervises the others as well as doing his own work.
	Efficiency – this varies from batch to batch and he was on form in this batch.
Packer:	Rate – she has been given the usual annual wage increase.
	Efficiency – she had a bad cold on that day and took a little longer.

Tasks 11.2

1. Suggest which variances are *planning* variances and which are *operating* variances.

Help? See: Information Bank 14.4 and 14.5, pages 173-174.

2. What actions might Martin take as a result of investigating the variances?

Help? See: Information Bank 14.4 and 14.5, pages 173-174.

Quick answer questions 11b: *Answers and comments*

1. Standard Cost of one batch of type 501 Keys

				£
Materials:				
	6 Kilos of Metal at £4 a kilo			24.00
	Packaging			3.00
Labour:	Stamper:	2 hours at £4.00 an hour		8.00
	Polisher:	2.5 hours at £5.00 an hour		12.50
	Packer:	2 hours at £3.90 an hour		7.80
Variable Overheads:				
	6.5 hours at £1.50 per Stamper and Polisher hour			13.00
Fixed Overheads:				
	6.5 hours at £6 a direct labour hour			39.00
Total				107.30

Quick answer questions 11c: *Answers and comments*

The material and labour costs are direct costs and variances are extracted for specific products or batches of single products. It is useful to know if the actual costs of making a product or a batch are as standard or more or less.

Overhead variances are shared by all products and driven by the total output for variable overheads and by time for fixed overheads. So overhead variances are extracted for total output and periods of time.

Scenario 5

After a month designated as operating period 5, Martin enquired about overhead variances. He was told that budgeted standard direct labour hours (the measure of output) were 375. Actual output was measured as 340 hours only. This output included 110 hours of Stamping, 125 hours of Polishing and 115 hours of Packing.

Expenditure was:

	Budgeted	Actual
Variable		£402
Fixed :		
Depreciation	£1,500	£1,500
Rent etc	£750	£800

The hours spent on production were:

Stamper	125
Polisher	130
Packer	105

Tasks 11.3

1. Calculate overhead variances.

2. Suggest reasons for the variances

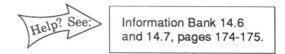

Help? See: Information Bank 14.6 and 14.7, pages 174-175.

Scenario 6

Martin reads the schedule of variances and asks for investigations to be made. The reasons brought out were:

Variable:

> *Efficiency*: the temperature in the department had been unseasonably hot in the month and as the department was always too hot anyway output had been even lower than normal as a consequence.

> *Expenditure*: Electricity prices had risen.

Fixed:

> *Expenditure*: this was nothing to do with the department as it was an apportionment of the fixed costs of the factory as a whole.

> *Efficiency*: see under variable above.

> *Volume*: both of the machines had broken down and production was lost as a result.

As a result of these explanations, Martin dug deeper and found that the temperature of the department varied considerably but that it was usually too hot and that efficiency suffered as a consequence. He agreed to investigate ways of maintaining a more comfortable temperature. He also found that the machines often broke down and that output was lost. He agreed to look at the possibility of new machines or a programme of preventative maintenance.

Martin feels that standard costing and variance analysis have a lot to offer and decides to extend his experiment.

The company have an agent in Canada who sells just one type of lock – the AZ500. The standard cost of this was worked out at £20 each and the Canadian agent is expected to sell them at £30 each. In fact the price he gets depends on the prices charged for a similar lock sold by a competitor. In addition the sales in Canada are in Canadian Dollars.

For month 9, Martin has set a budget for Canadian sales as:

Number of units to sell	2,000
Selling Price	62 Dollars
Exchange rate	2.1 Dollars to the pound sterling

The actual sales in the month were:

Sales	2,200 units
Selling Price	58 dollars
Exchange rate	2.05 dollars to the pound

Tasks 11.4

1. Calculate suitable *sales variances*.

2. Write a report explaining precisely what the variances mean.

Help? See:	Information Bank 14.8, page 176.

Standard costing

Standard Costs Established			Actual Costs
	Compare Variances		
Material	Labour	Variable Overheads	Fixed Overheads
Price Usage	Rate Efficiency	Efficiency Expenditure	Expenditure Volume

---

Summary of Unit 11

1. Standard product costs can be established for any product where it is worth the effort of doing so. To be worth doing it, the product must be repeatedly produced in a similar format.

2. These standards are usually regarded as attainable in efficient but not perfect operating conditions.

3. Once established it is possible to compare actual costs with standards.

4. Standard costs can be used in pricing products and in measuring profit for internal reporting purposes.

5. By comparing actual with standard costs, variances can be calculated.

6. Variances which are more than trivial can be investigated.

7. Causes of variances can be planning. In such cases the standards need amending. Causes can also be operational. In these cases it may be that action should be taken to correct any fault.

8. The objectives of variances is not to find fault or to apportion blame but to initiate action.

Development of knowledge and skills

You are now in a position to tackle questions 1 to 11 in Section 3:14, pages 291-293.

Unit 12: Company accounting

Introduction

The Accounts of limited companies (including Public Limited Companies – PLCs) are not easy to understand and are full of an amazing amount of detail. As a result even accountants find the Annual Report and Accounts of a PLC somewhat formidable. They are considered very important by the financial community and are highly regulated by the Companies Act 1985 and the Accounting Standards Board.

This Unit gives an overview of published accounts and of some of the detail. It is designed to assist my readers in understanding the accounts of their own companies and of companies that they come in contact with as customers, suppliers, investors etc.

Scenario 1

An informal approach has been made to Martin by a *director* of a local *Public Limited Company* suggesting that the PLC might be interested in taking over Martin Padlocks Ltd. She explains that they are interested because Martin's company would fit well into their current business plans and that they would like to have Martin on the Main *Board* of their company as an executive director. Martin is not really interested but is intrigued to find out that the director seems to know quite a lot about Martin Padlocks Ltd and its accounts.

She explains that her company have searched the file on Martin Padlocks Ltd at Companies House in Cardiff.

Martin feels he would like to know more about the public company and finds that his uncle is a shareholder and has a copy of the latest Annual Report and Accounts.

Below is the Profit and Loss Account and Balance Sheet of the company which is called XYZ Manufacturing and Trading PLC at 31 December 19x8:

Profit and Loss Account
For the year ending 31 December 19x8

		£'000
Turnover		10,500
Cost of Sales		6,900
Gross Profit		3,600
Distribution Costs	1,280	
Administration Expenses	1,450	2,730
Operating Profit		870
Interest Payable		220
Profit on Ordinary activities before taxation		650
Taxation		250
Profit on ordinary activities after taxation		400
Extraordinary items		280
Profit of the year		120
Dividends		100
Retained profit for the year		20
Earnings per share	4p	

Group Balance sheet as at 31 December 19x8

	£'000 19x8	19x7
Fixed Assets		
Tangible assets	4,360	2,190
Investments		500
		2,690
Current Assets		
Stocks	1,300	970
Debtors	2,200	1,684
	3,500	2,654
Creditors:amounts falling due within one year		
Creditors	1,100	838
Bank Overdrafts	350	202
Taxation and Social Security	102	102
Corporation Tax	250	164
Dividends	40	40
	1,842	1,346
Net Current Assets	1,658	1,308
Total Assets less Current Liabilities	6,018	3,998
Creditors: amounts falling due after more than one year		
14% Debentures 1998-1999	1,200	840
	4,818	3,158
Capital and Reserves		
Issued Share Capital (in 10p shares)	1,000	500
Share Premium	380	
Revaluation Reserve	760	
Profit and Loss Account	2,678	2,658
Shareholders Funds	4,818	3,158

Quick answer questions 12a

1. *How many words do you recognize from Units 2 and 3?*

2. *How do you think the fixed assets will have been valued?*

3. *What is the working capital?*

Scenario 2

Martin has many questions about these Accounts and asks Anne to help him understand them. Can you help him with the questions?

Tasks 12.1

Before and while tackling the tasks you should read Information Bank Topic 6 Company Accounts (pages 126-135).

1. What is *turnover* and what items will be included in this figure?

2. What is calculated by Turnover less Cost of Sales?

3. Below are seven expense headings:
   - ❑ settlement discounts given to customers;
   - ❑ the managing director's salary;
   - ❑ public relations costs;
   - ❑ goods purchased for resale;
   - ❑ the auditor's fee;
   - ❑ depreciation on a computer system;
   - ❑ repairs to forklift trucks.

   In which of the following three general expense headings may each be included:

   Cost of Sales, Distribution Costs, Administration Expenses?

4. In how many lines of the Profit and Loss Account does the word "profit" occur?

5. Interest in the Profit and Loss Account relates to which items in the Balance Sheet?

6. To which item in the Balance Sheet does the Taxation item in the Profit and Loss Account relate?

7. Are the *extraordinary items* profits or losses?

8. How many shares have the company issued?

9. What is the *dividend* per share using the Profit and Loss Account figure for dividends?

10. Why is the dividend in the Profit and Loss Account different from that shown in the Balance Sheet?

11. How were the *Earnings per Share* calculated?

12. What are *tangible* assets?

13. What types of fixed asset would this company probably have?

14. What does the expression "Taxation and Social Security" mean in the Balance Sheet?

15. What rate of interest is paid on the debentures and when are they *redeemable?*

16. What is the significance of the term *"Share Premium"*?

17. Why was the line "Revaluation Reserve" included?

18. Does the word "Reserve" in *"Revaluation Reserve"* mean that the company has some money cached away somewhere?

19. How are the Retained Profits in the Profit and Loss Account related to the Profit and Loss Account figure in the Balance Sheet?

20. If all the assets were sold off at their book values and all the liabilities paid off at the amount of their book values, how much money would be left for the shareholders?

21. According to the newspaper city page, one share in XYZ can be purchased for 80p. How does this figure square up with the answer you calculated for question 20?

Scenario 3

Martin now feels he understands the overall view given by the Accounts and he is now interested in some details.

The first thing he wants to know about is the Board of Directors. He looks at the notes and finds several bits of data:

Directors		Beneficial Shareholdings	
		31.12.19x8	31.12.19x7
Joseph Smith	(1)	600,000	800,000
Edward Crippen	(2)	1,000	1,000
Amanda Burke		30,000	2,000
William Hare	(3)	140,000	50,000
Jean Palmer		6,000	6,000
Paul Pilate	(3)	14,500	4,000
Lord Pott	(3)	5,000	5,000
Jane Ripper		2,300	2,300

(1) – the Chairman
(2) – the Chief Executive
(3) – non-executive

Directors Remuneration

Aggregate *emoluments* of Directors including pension contributions:

	19x8	19x7
Fees	£5,000	£5,000
Other emoluments	£300,500	£260,000
Chairman's Emoluments	£20,000	£18,000
Highest Paid Director's Emoluments	£85,000	£60,000

All directors:

			19x8	19x7
£0 –	£5,000		3	3
£15,001 –	£20,000		1	1
£55,001 –	£60,000		1	4
£60,001 –	£65,000		2	
£80,001 –	£85,000		1	

Quick answer questions 12b

1. What can you conclude from this data about:

    a. *Directors' shareholdings*

    b. *The ownership of the company*

    c. *The roles of particular directors*

    d. *The remuneration paid to directors*

Quick answer questions 12a: *Answers and comments*

1. You should recognize some of the following:

    Gross Profit, Profit, Interest, Fixed Assets, Current Assets, Stocks, Debtors, Creditors, Bank Overdrafts, Capital, Share Capital, Profit and Loss Account.

    You may well know some of the other words.

2. Fixed Assets are usually valued at cost less accumulated depreciation. However land is usually valued just at cost. In this case some of the fixed assets have been valued at a valuation above cost but we will look at this later.

3. Working capital is defined differently by different people but you have probably included Stock , Debtors , Creditors and the Overdraft.

Scenario 4

As he really is not very sure about the revaluation reserve Martin looks at those parts of the Annual Report and Accounts which set out details of the property and other fixed assets. He discovers the following:

Accounting Policies:

Fixed Assets are stated at valuation, for property, and cost for plant. The provision for depreciation of fixed assets is on a straight line basis at rates estimated to be sufficient to write off the assets over the terms of their working lives under normal conditions. The rates of depreciation are:

Land	– nil
Buildings	– 2%
Plant etc	– 12.5%

Tangible Fixed Assets: (all figures in £'000)

	Premises	Plant etc
Cost at 31 December 19x1	1,500	2,200
Additions	1,222	600
Revaluation	440	
at 31 December 19x2	3,162	2,800
Depreciation		
at 31 December 19x1	320	1,190
Charge for year	62	350
Revaluation Adjustment	(320)	
at 31 December 19x2	62	1,540
Net Book Value 31 December 19x2	3,100	1,260
Net Book Value 31 December 19x1	1,180	1,010

Revaluation

In November 19x2, the premises were independently valued by Slick, Sharp & Co, Chartered Surveyors at open market value. They had previously been carried at cost less depreciation.

 ## Tasks 12.2

1. Comment on the movements in fixed assets
2. How much of the value of the premises is in the land?

 | Information Bank Topic 3 Depreciation and Topic 6 Company Accounting and in particular paragraph 9q, page 131.

Scenario 5

Martin now turns his attention to the extraordinary item. He finds in the notes that it is described as

"Loss on disposal of investment"

In the Directors' Report he finds that the company had divested itself of a 15% holding in a steel foundry company which had begun to make losses.

Tasks 12.3

Why do you think that this loss is put *"below the line"*. What is the effect of doing so on earnings per share?

What impact might the information on this loss have on any decision you might make to invest in this company?

 | Information Bank 6:5n and 6:9o, pages 127 and 130.

Scenario 6

Finally Martin turns to a financial statement in the Report and Accounts labelled: Cash Flow Statement.

This is it:

Cash Flow Statement for the year ending 31 December19x8

	(£'000)	
Net Cash Inflow from operating activities		698
Returns on Investments and servicing of finance:		
Interest paid	(220)	
Dividends paid	(100)	(320)
Taxation		
Corporation tax paid		(164)
Investing activities		
Payments to acquire fixed assets	(1,822)	
Receipts from sale of investment	220	(1,602)
Net Cash outflow before financing		(1,388)
Financing		
Issue of ordinary share capital	880	
Issue of Debentures	360	1,240
Decrease in cash		(148)

Notes to the cash flow statement

1. Reconciliation of operating profit to net cash inflow from operating activities.

Operating Profit	870
Depreciation Charges	412
Increase in stocks	(330)
Increase in Debtors	(516)
Increase in Creditors	262
	698

Tasks 12.4

1. Compare the two Balance Sheets at 19x1 and 19x2 line by line and explain how the cash flow statement relates to them.

2. The company have increased working capital due to an increase in turnover. Is the cash flow from operating activities net of tax, dividends and interest sufficient to finance this?

3. The company have invested heavily in new premises and plant. How has this been financed?

 Help? See:

> Information Bank Topic 9 Cash Flow Statements, pages 151-156.

Contents of a company annual report and accounts

Chairman's Statement

Directors   Balance Sheets

Directors' Report   Accounting Policies

Profit and Loss Account   Auditors' Report

Notice of Meeting   Financial Calendar

Principal Companies   Financial Summary

Cash Flow Statement   Notes to the Accounts

Divisions   Share Data

Profit and loss account

Turnover

     Cost Of Sales

       Gross Profit

         Operating Expenses

        Trading Profit

         Interest

           Profit on ordinary
           activities before tax

           Tax

             Profit on ordinary
             activities after tax

           Extraordinary items

         Profit for the
       financial year

       Dividends

      Retained Profits

    for year

   Retained Profits *
   from previous years

*Profit and Loss Account
figure in Balance Sheet

Note:

1. * these items are usually shown in the notes to the Accounts
2. The final line is the Earnings per Share
3. The previous year's figures are also included so that a comparison can be made.

Balance sheet

Fixed Assets	– Tangible
	– Intangible
	– Investments
+ Current Assets	– Stocks
	– Debtors
	– Cash and Bank
– Creditors: amounts falling due within one year	– Trade Creditors
	– Overdrafts
	– Tax and social security
	– Corporation Tax
	– Dividends
	– etc
– Creditors: amounts falling due after more than one year	– Loans
	– Debentures
	– Provisions for liabilities and charges*
= Capital and Reserves	– Share Capital
	– Share Premium
	– Revaluation Reserve
	– Profit and Loss Account

Notes:

1. * these are rather technical. Only accountants understand them.

2. Four balance sheets are usually given. Only the two labelled Group are of any real interest.

Summary of Unit 12

1. Company Accounts are very complex documents with a very large amount of detail.

2. Basic information is as in the simple accounts introduced in Chapters 1 to 4 but simple messages are often obscured by a mass of detail and unfamiliar language.

3. The relationship between Profit and Loss Account items and Balance Sheet items can often be followed through.

4. Information on any particular topic can often be found in more than one document in the Annual Report and Accounts.

5. For such information, search may be made in the Balance Sheet, Profit and Loss Account, notes to accounts, accounting policies, directors report and yet others.

6. The Profit and Loss Account shows several different figures for "profit". These are not usually difficult to understand but in discussion it is important to ensure that all parties are talking about the same profit.

7. The capital and reserves section of the Balance Sheet is not easily understood. The total is more important than the detail and represents the assets less the external liabilities.

8. The net asset value of one share is usually rather different from the stock exchange quotation.

9. Information about the directors is copious but strangely woolly. It always follows the requirements of the Companies Act 1985.

10. Extraordinary items are an interesting area to look at in company accounts. Treatment is still subject to much debate in accounting circles.

11. As the corresponding figures for the previous years are also given, changes between the years can be explored.

Development of knowledge and skills

You are now able to tackle questions 1 to 3 of Section 3.6 (pages 232-233) and questions 1 and 2 of Section 3.9 (page 256).

Unit 13: More company accounting

Introduction

*This Unit continues the study of company accounting and introduces Martin to a number of issues which he is curious about. Two of these – **auditing** and **annual general meetings** – affect his own company and three – **rights issues**, **bonus issues** and **creative accounting** – he has encountered in his reading of the financial pages.*

Scenario 1

Martin has invested some of his savings in shares in a local *listed* company – Soopertek Manufacturing PLC. He wanted to see how a listed company went about things because he felt he might seek a listing for his own company eventually and because the whole subject of company accounting and finance had begun to fascinate him. He also thought he might make a profit!

He has just received the glossy Annual Report and Accounts for the year ending 31 December 19x8 and eagerly looks for the things he thinks he might understand. Firstly he looks at the notice of the Annual General Meeting:

Notice is hereby given that the annual general meeting of the shareholders will be held at the Hotel Colossal, Birmingham on Tuesday 11 June 19x9 at 12 noon.

Agenda

1. To approve the Report of the Directors and the Accounts for the year ended 31 December 19x8.

2. To approve the final dividend of 10p a share for the year ended 31 December 19x8.

3. To re-elect as directors:

   Thomas Gilbert
   Andrea Sullivan

4. To re-appoint Puce, Mauve & Co. as auditors and authorise the directors to determine their remuneration.

5. To consider and if thought fit, pass the following resolution:

That the directors are authorised to allot new ordinary shares of 50p each in the company to shareholders who elect to receive such an allotment as a scrip issue in lieu of all or part of the interim and final dividends for the year ending 31 December 19x9.

By order of the Board
A Smith, Secretary 12 May 19x9.

Quick answer questions 13a

1. *Martin knows the company have some 25,000 shareholders. Why do you think the AGM can be held in a hotel?*

2. *Do you think that Martin will miss his lunch if he attends the AGM?*

3. *In the Chairman's review he sees that Mr Gilbert was appointed a director by the Board on 4th December 19x8 and that Ms Sullivan retires by rotation but is available for re-election. Do you think that these elections are democratically made by the shareholders?*

Scenario 2

Martin realises that as a shareholder he can receive the dividend mentioned in resolution 2 but that he can receive new shares instead as a consequence of resolution 5.

He has 500 shares in the company.

The offer is to receive the dividend or 25 new ordinary shares which are currently quoted at £2 each.

**Tasks 13.1**

1. Evaluate the two alternatives from Martin's point of view. Martin has a high salary from his company and is adding to his savings all the time.

2. Evaluate the offer from the point of view of the Incompetent Assurance Co PLC which owns 4% of Soopertek.

3. Some of the shareholders accept shares and some the cash. Explain how the balance of power among the shareholders is changed by this. Explain how in a normal bonus issue the balance of power is not affected.

Help? See: Information Bank Topic 6.11, page 133.

Scenario 3

Martin is interested in the auditors and manages to find in the notes to the Accounts that their remuneration was £250,000. This seems to him to be a large amount and he wonders what they do for this sum. He is also puzzled by Resolution 4 which seems to make the auditors somewhat less independent as the directors are able to fix the audit fee. He thought that the auditors were completely independent of the company and acted in the interests of the shareholders. He discusses this matter with Anne who tells him that auditors are supposed to be completely independent from the company but in practice:

a. auditors are appointed by the Board although the fiction that they are appointed by the shareholders is maintained in the resolution.

b. the Board fix the auditors' remuneration although this is normally a matter of negotiation between the directors and the auditors.

c. the auditors do work other than auditing for the company and are specially interested in lucrative management consultancy contracts.

d. Boards of directors do shop around for cheaper or more amenable firms of auditors.

This makes Martin think that the auditors are beholden to the directors when they should be taking an entirely objective view of the Accounts. Anne points out that all is not what it seems as:

a. audit firms are very tightly regulated by their professional bodies.

b. failure to perform an audit properly may lead to claims of negligence against the auditors and in many recorded instances auditors (or rather their insurers) have had to pay very large sums to aggrieved persons.

c. If the Board wish to remove an auditor because he goes against their wishes (for example, by insisting on the company revealing full details of directors remuneration as required by the Companies Act when the Board wish to keep some matters secret) the Companies Act gives the auditor extensive powers of publicity.

d. the whole issue of auditor independence is very contentious and EEC inspired legislation on the subject in the Companies Act 1989 is still being absorbed. Further legislation is expected in the next few years.

Martin finds the auditors report and sees that it is actually very short:

Auditors' report to the members of Soopertek Manufacturing PLC.

We have audited the accounts on pages 30 to 48 in accordance with Auditing Standards.

In our opinion the accounts give a true and fair view of the state of affairs of the company and the group at 31 December 19x4 and of the profit and cash flow of the group for the year then ended and have been properly prepared in accordance with the Companies Act 1985.

Puce, Mauve & Co Birmingham

> **Quick answer questions 13a:** *Answers and comments*
>
> 1. Only a small number of shareholders attend Annual General Meetings so that the hotel will be able to accommodate the hundred or so who will turn up.
>
> 2. AGMs take very little time and most are called for 12 noon so that those present can enjoy a lunch at the expense of the company.
>
> 3. In theory the Board of Directors of public companies are elected by the shareholders. In practice vacancies on the Board are filled by the Board and the new appointment ratified at the next AGM as in this case. One or more directors are required to resign each year but they are usually re-elected. On rare occasions a group of shareholders may attempt to unseat a director but these efforts are seldom successful. Shareholder democracy only really becomes a reality when a takeover bid is made for the company.

 **Tasks 13.2**

1. Discuss why is it essential that an annual Report and Accounts is produced for every company.

2. Discuss why it is essential that readers of the Accounts should have confidence in the truth and fairness of the Accounts.

3. Describe the role of the auditor in making the Accounts credible.

4. Discuss what the auditor does if she considers that the Accounts fail to show a true and fair view in some particular or do not comply with the requirements of the Companies Act in some way.

Help? See: Information Bank 6.12, page 134.

Scenario 4

In the Chairman's statement Martin reads that the company have acquired two other companies in the year and that this has involved the company in borrowing substantial sums from the bank to the extent that the company is *overgeared*. In order to reduce the gearing the company intend to make a *rights issue* later in the year. This will probably be an issue of 2 new shares for every 5 held at a price of 40p.

 **Tasks 13.3**

1. Discuss what is meant by overgearing and how this can come about. How can a rights issue reduce gearing?

Help? See: Information Bank 8.8 and 6.11, pages 145 and 133.

2. Martin intends to take up his rights. How much will he have to pay? What will be the value of his total holding after the rights issue?

Help? See: Information Bank 6.11, page 133.

Scenario 5

Martin has heard that profits can be increased by creative accounting and wonders if Soopertek have increased their profits in this way. He discusses the matter with Anne who tells him that creative accounting means selecting accounting policies that maximised profits rather than policies that did not. Generally in creative accounting policies are created which are unexpected or not generally accepted. Creative accounting has been almost eliminated by the *Statements of Standard Accounting Practice* and the new *Accounting Standards Board*. New ideas in creative accounting did come up from time to time in the City but these would usually be rapidly defeated by the *Urgent Issues Task Force* which is a subsidiary body of the Accounting Standards Board. Most "creative accounting" ideas are highly technical and not understood even by other accountants.

Anne urged Martin to forget creative accounting and to concentrate instead on *comparability* in accounting. She mentioned two issues specifically – Depreciation of property and Goodwill. Martin resolves to do this and looks up what Soopertek have done in this area and what two similar companies – Veni Manufacturing PLC and Vidi Manufacturing PLC, have done.

He finds:

Premises Depreciation:

	Soopertek	**Veni**	**Vidi**
Land values	cost	revalued two years earlier	revalued this year

None of the companies depreciate land

Buildings values			
	writing off over 50 years	writing off over 25 years	Not * depreciated

* on the grounds that the company spend large sums on maintaining the buildings in order to extend their economic lives indefinitely.

Goodwill

Written off against reserves immediately	amortised over five years	amortised over twenty years

---

Quick answer questions 13b

1. *What is the effect of depreciation (amortisation is another word for the same thing) on profit and the carrying values of assets in the Balance Sheet?*

2. *What is the effect on annual profit and the balance sheet of an immediate write-off of goodwill to reserves?*

Scenario 6

Extracts from Statement of Standard Accounting Practice 12 – Accounting for depreciation show:

para 15   Provision for depreciation of fixed assets having a finite useful economic life should be made by allocating the cost (or revalued amount) less estimated residual value of the assets as fairly as possible to periods expected to benefit from their use.

para 17   It is essential that assets lives are estimated on a realistic basis.

para 24   Buildings are no different from other fixed assets in that they have a limited useful economic life, albeit usually significantly longer than that of other types of assets. They should, therefore, be depreciated having regard to the same criteria.

An extract from Statement of Standard Accounting Practice 22 – Accounting for Goodwill says:

para 35   No amount should be attributed to non-purchased goodwill in the balance sheets of companies or groups (Note that all of the three companies comply with this)

para 39   Purchased goodwill should normally be eliminated from the accounts immediately against reserves ("immediate write-off")

para 41   Purchased goodwill may be eliminated from the accounts by amortisation through the profit and loss account in arriving at profit or loss on ordinary activities on a systematic basis over its useful economic life ("amortisation")

Quick answer questions 13b: *Answers and comments*

1. The depreciation for a year reduces profit of the year and also reduces the carrying value of assets in the Balance Sheet. Remember that the carrying value (= net book value or written down value) is the cost (or revaluation) less accumulated depreciation.

2. Imagine a company with a balance sheet as:

(all figures in '000)

Fixed Assets	1,200	
Current Assets	900	
	2,100	
Current Liabilities	800	Detail
	1,300	
Debentures	500	
	800	
Capital	200	
Profit and Loss Account	600	Total
	800	

Note that the "Reserves" in this case is the profit and loss account.

The company buys another company for £300,000 and borrows the money short term from the bank. The cost of the company £180,000 for net physical assets and £120,000 for goodwill.

The effect on the Balance Sheet is:

Fixed Assets (Investments)	+ £180,000
Current Liabilities (borrowing)	+ £300,000
Profit and Loss Account	– £120,000

So the Balance Sheet after acquisition is:

Fixed Assets	1,380	
Current Assets	900	
	2,280	
Current Liabilities	1,100	Detail
	1,180	
Debentures	500	
	680	
Capital	200	
Profit and Loss Account	480	Total
	680	

There will be no effect on the annual profit.

**Tasks 13.4**

Write a report on the comparability of the annual profit measurements and the net assets in the balance sheets of these three companies.

Bonus, rights and other share issues

Bonus Issues:

Shareholders receive free new shares
Company receive no new resources
In the balance sheet:
Share Capital   – up
Share Premium or
Profit and Loss Account   – down
Total value remains the same
on the stock exchange but each share
is worth less as there are more of
them

Rights Issues

Shareholders buy new shares from
the company
The company receives new resources
Bank   – up
Share Capital   – up
Share Premium   – up
Stock Exchange value of a share is
weighted average of previous value
and issue price

Issue of shares in Exchange for a
company (a takeover)

Shareholders of taken over company
become shareholders in taking over
company
Victim company becomes asset
(investment) of predator company
Goodwill element written off
Net Assets   – up
Share Capital   – up
Share Premium   – up
     but then: as goodwill is written off:
Net Assets   – down
Reserves   – down

Summary of Unit 13

1. All companies hold an Annual general meeting of Shareholders. Few shareholders attend and the meetings are short. Most of the resolutions rubber stamp the actions of the directors.

2. A bonus issue is a free issue of shares to all shareholders pro rata to their existing holdings.

3. Many companies allow shareholders to take a cash dividend or to have a bonus issue of shares in lieu.

4. Auditors have a vital role in validating the credibility of Accounts.

5. The independence of auditors from a company and its directors is currently a contentious issue.

6. A company can make a rights issue which means that further monies are invested in the company by existing shareholders. Rights can be sold so that the buyer of the rights takes up the new shares and some change occurs in the shareholding.

7. Creative accounting is largely a myth now but was more prevalent in the past.

8. companies can keep within the Statements of Standard Accounting Practice and yet have different accounting policies. This means that comparing the performance of a company with other companies requires careful consideration of what policies have been adopted.

Development of knowledge and skill

You should now be able to tackle questions 4 and 5 of Section 3.6., pages 234-235

Unit 14: Ratio analysis

Introduction

The objective of this Unit is to introduce **ratio analysis** *of Accounts. It is possible to evaluate a company's* **performance** *by comparing the Accounts with those of* **previous years**, **budgets** *and the Accounts of* **other companies**. *Definitive conclusions cannot be drawn because:*

❑   *circumstances change over time*
❑   *actual conditions are always different from those forecast in budgets*
❑   *other companies operate in different conditions and use different accounting policies*

Ratio analysis does nonetheless assist the management, shareholder or other interested party in asking the **right questions**.

We shall examine the use of ratio analysis by looking at a part of Martin's company over time and as part of an inter firm comparison scheme.

Scenario 1

Martin is concerned about the performance of a particular division of his company which is run from a separate factory in Darlaston which is rented. In fact Martin Padlocks bought the business as a going concern and it is still run by its original general manager and it still exercises autonomous decision making and has a separate sales organisation. The Accounts for the last two years show:

Manufacturing, Trading and Profit and Loss Accounts

(All figures in £'000)

	19x6		19x7		IFC%	
Raw Materials:						
Opening stock	82		105		4.6	
Purchases	270		340		14.7	
	352		445		19.3	
Closing Stock	105	*247	132	315	4.6	14.7
Direct Labour		360		400		22.4
		*607		715		37.1
Works Overheads						
Rent, rates, insurance	130		145		8.6	
Plant Depreciation	34		62		3.6	
Energy	190		252		10.2	
Staff Salaries	87		93		5.2	
Other overheads	102	543	132	684	6.4	34.0
		*1,150		1,399		71.1
Opening Work in Progress		127		163		5.4
		1,277		1,562		76.5
Closing Work in Progress		163		140		5.4
		*1,114		1,422		71.1
Opening Finished Goods Stock		245		280		11.1
		1,359		1,702		82.2
Closing Finished Goods Stock		280		231		11.2
		*1,079		1,471		71.0
Sales		1,758		1,930		100.0
		*679		459		29.0
Administration Costs	182		154		5.1	
Selling Costs	264		296		9.2	
Distribution Costs	82	528	63	513	1.1	15.4
Net Profit		151		(64)		13.6

Balance Sheet

Fixed Assets			
Plant + Vehicles			
Cost at beginning	180	190	17.4
Additions in year	<u>10</u>	<u>160</u>	<u>6.2</u>
	*190	350	23.6
Depreciation at start	123	157	11.1
Depreciation in year	<u>34</u>	<u>62</u>	<u>3.6</u>
	157	219	14.7
	* 33	131	8.9
Current Assets			
Stock	548	503	21.1
Debtors	<u>420</u>	<u>477</u>	21.0
	968	980	
Less Current Liabilities			
Creditors – Materials	65	92	3.3
– Overheads	<u>54</u>	<u>68</u>	2.4
	119	160	
	*849	820	
Net Assets	882	951	

We have omitted the capital section as it is not relevant to our analysis on this occasion.

The final columns, headed IFC%, are from an interfirm comparison We will look at them later.

Quick answer questions 14a

1. *There are six lines in the Profit and Loss Account and three in the Balance Sheet which are marked with an asterisk*. Suggest suitable descriptions for these lines.*

2. *Has there been an increase / decrease from 19x6 to 19x7 in:*

   Work in progress, turnover, other overheads, capital expenditure, stocks?

3. *Relate the stocks in the Balance Sheet to those in the Profit and Loss Account.*

4. *Relate the depreciation in the Balance Sheet to that in the Profit and Loss Account.*

Scenario 2

Martin is disappointed in the results as a loss is shown in 19x7 after a profit in 19x6. He decides to review the two years accounts without calculating any ratios and discovers:

- ❐ Turnover is up (but is it up greater than inflation?)
- ❐ Gross Profit is down
- ❐ Both administration costs and distribution costs are down but selling costs are up. The net effect is a reduction in non-manufacturing overheads.
- ❐ a net profit of £151,000 has become a loss of £64,000.
- ❐ there has been capital expenditure of £160,000 in the year 19x7 as against only £10,000 in 19x6.
- ❐ Stocks are down but debtors are up.
- ❐ Creditors are also up.
- ❐ Net assets are up by £69,000.

Martin knows that the last point means that in 19x7 he has invested £133,000 from the rest of Martin Padlocks Ltd. The actual calculation is:

(all figures in £'000)

Capital at end of 19x6	882
less Loss in 19x7	64
	818
New capital invested	133
Capital at end of 19x7	951

Martin considers that the division has spent large sums on new plant and has increased its turnover and yet has managed to make a loss. This clearly needs some investigation and to assist him in the investigation he needs a benchmark or standard which will enable him to compare the division's performance against.

To do this he has enrolled at some expense in an interfirm comparison which is run by the National Association. The division has a narrow range of products and there are many other firms in the Industry. Many of these subscribe to the Interfirm comparison and the results are now available to Martin.

The process is:

i.   Each firm completes a set of accounts in standard form. This is necessary as different accounting policies are used by different firms and it is necessary to standardise these. In addition two other major differences between firms exist:

   a.   Some own their own property and some rent. This difference has been eliminated by assuming that all rent and making notional adjustments to accounts of owning firms.

   b.   Financing can be from equity or from borrowings. The interfirm comparison figures used have eliminated all borrowings and interest charges. Financing figures are available but we have ignored them.

ii.   The sets of accounts are set out in the form of percentages of turnover. The mean (average) of these percentages are circulated to subscribing members.

This enables ratio comparisons to be made. For example:

The gross profit to sales ratio for the Industry is 29% but for our division the ratio is:

$$19x6 \ \frac{679}{1,758} \times 100 = 38\%$$

$$19x7 \ \frac{459}{1,930} \times 100 = 24\%$$

The rate was very good in 19x6 but has become very poor in 19x7. To find the reason it is necessary to explore the make up of costs.

 Tasks 14.1

1.   Calculate suitable ratios for both years and compare them with the Industry averages. Do not confine yourself to the ratios in Information Bank 8 but calculate any ratio that seems relevant.

2.   Write a report on the divisions performance detailing:

   ❑   where the division's performance has changed between the two years.

   ❑   where the division's performance is different from the Industry average.

   ❑   which items need attention.

Help? See:> | Information Bank 8, pages 143-150.

Quick answer questions 14a: *Answers and comments*

1. Raw Materials consumed, Prime Cost, Factory inputs in the year, Works cost of finished goods output, Cost of goods sold, Gross Profit.

    Cost of Fixed Assets held at the year end, Net book value or written down value, Net current assets.

2. Increase for turnover and capital expenditure (up from £10,000 to £160,000)

    Decrease for work in progress, other overheads, and stocks.

3. Stocks in the Balance Sheet are at the end of 19x6 £548,000 consisting of materials £105,000, work in progress £163,000 and finished goods £280,000.

4. Depreciation in the Profit and Loss Account for 19x6 is £34,000 and in the Balance Sheet the same amount. I have charged all the depreciation to works overheads but as fixed assets are both plant and vehicles, depreciation should be split between works overheads and probably distribution costs. We will keep the problem simple!

Scenario 3

Martin's company has never dealt with Stade Ltd, a wholesaler of locks in Northumberland. However Stade have now asked Martin to supply them with a significant quantity of locks on credit. Martin suspects that Stade may have difficulty in paying their existing suppliers and that they are asking Martin for goods as existing suppliers have restricted deliveries. Before agreeing to grant credit, he asks for a recent set of accounts. To his surprise Stade supplies these and Martin is able look at them. Here they are:

Profit and Loss Account

(all figures in £'000)

	19x7		19x8	
Sales		2,400		2,950
Opening stock	230		254	
Purchases	1,560		1,930	
	1,790		2,184	
Closing Stock	254	1,536	287	1,897
		*864		1,053
Overheads		624		785
		*240		268
Corporation Tax		65		74
		*175		194
Dividends		100		105
		* 75		89

Balance Sheets
Fixed Assets

	19x7		19x8	
Cost		462		730
Depreciation		280		345
		182		385
Current Assets				
Stock	254		287	
Debtors	660		740	
	914		1,027	

Current Liabilities			
Creditors			
Purchases	410	580	
Expenses	67	91	
Overdraft	340	359	
Tax	65	74	
Dividends	70	75	
	952	1,179	
	*(38)	(152)	
Net Assets	144	233	
Capital and Reserves			
Share Capital (£1 shares)	50	50	
Profit and Loss Account	94	183	
	144	233	

The notes indicate:

❏ that the fixed assets are equipment and vehicles. The company rent its premises.

❏ the bank overdraft is secured by a floating charge on all the assets.

Quick Answer Questions 14b

1. *Give a title to the items marked with an asterisk**

2. *What is the dividend per share?*

3. *Relate the Profit and Loss Account to the Balance Sheet.*

Scenario 4

Martin feels that the company seems healthy in that it has increased its turnover, made profits and paid dividends. However he notes that the overdraft seems high and has got even higher in 19x8.

Tasks 14.2

1. Write a report on the events of 19x8 compared with the events of 19x7.

2. Calculate ratios of interest when assessing liquidity.

3. Explain the liquidity problem and how it arose.

4. Give a justified opinion on whether Martin should grant credit.

Information Bank 8, pages 143-150.

Quick answer questions 14b: *Answers and comments*

1. Gross Profit

    Net Profit before tax

    Net Profit after tax

    Retained Proft for the year

    Net Current Liabilities

2. The dividend per share is £2 in 19x7 and £2.10 in 19x8.

    Of this 60p in each year was an interim and the remainder are the final dividends.

3. The retained Profits for 19x8 are £89,000 and the Profit and Loss Account in the Balance Sheet has increased by that amount from £94,000 to £183,000.

Ratio analysis

Gross profit to Sales

Gross Profit to Cost of Sales (Mark up)

Overheads to sales in detail and in total

Net Profit to Sales

Annual Sales growth

Costs or Sales per square metre

Costs or Sales per employee

Asset Utilisation Ratio

Return on Capital Employed

Return on Shareholder funds

Stock Turnover

Debtors Average Payment Time

Creditors Average Payment Time

Operating Cycle

Dividend Cover

Dividend Yield

Earnings per Share

Price Earnings Ratio

Gearing ratio

Notes:

1. Your author does not include the current ratio or the acid test ratio as he does not consider that these have any diagnostic value.

2. Some writers distinguish some ratios as performance indicators and some ratios as liquidity indicators. For example, stock turnover is often regarded as a liquidity ratio. In fact it really does say something about management's ability to manage stocks and it does have an effect on liquidity in that a worsening stock turnover will tie up money. However it does not say anything to answer the questions of a loan or trade creditor: will I be paid and, if so, when?

3. The ratios which are of interest to loan and trade creditors on liquidity are the creditors average credit time and the gearing ratios.

4. Each Industry and indeed each firm has ratios which are not included above but which are very useful. For example:

    Sales returns to Sales in a foundry

    Cost per mile in a Railway.

    Hotel Costs per patient/day in a private hospital

Summary of Unit 14

1. Accounts can be appraised without using ratios and much useful analysis can be done without them

2. Ratios can add greatly to the analysis and comparison of Accounts. Comparisons can be made with:
   previous years
   budgets
   other companies
   industry averages

3. A company can often highlight particular areas that require attention.

4. Appraisal of accounts can assist a company in granting or refusing credit.

5. There are many standard ratios but each firm and Industry will have useful ratios peculiar to it.

Development of knowledge and skills

You are now in a position to tackle questions 1 to 12 in Section 3.8, pages 249-253.

Unit 15: The Stock Exchange

Introduction

The **Stock Exchange** is a **market** where **Investors** can buy and sell shares in companies and trade in other **financial assets**. It is essentially a **second hand market**. However companies can use the Exchange to raise money for development by selling new shares to investors but investors will only be willing to buy these shares when they know that a **secondary** (= second hand) market exists and that they can sell the shares again later to other investors.

This Unit is about the Stock Exchange and the advantages and disadvantages for a company of having its shares listed or quoted there. The Stock Exchange is important to Martin because of personal investment in quoted securities and because he is contemplating having his company **listed**. My readers may note that much information is available on listed companies. A reader may work for a listed company and will no doubt have business contact with many listed companies.

Scenario 1

After ten years Martin Padlocks has become a relatively large company but Martin still has ambitions and sees many opportunities for further expansion. These include:

- ❐ Updating his plant, machinery and vehicles

- ❐ Buying premises where he currently rents

- ❐ Increasing sales of his current products

- ❐ Introducing new products and production lines

- ❐ Opening branches

- ❐ Increasing exports

- ❐ Acquiring existing businesses in order to:
  complement his own products
  eliminate competition
  acquire suppliers
  acquire customers

Martin realises that all of this will require lots of money and that at the present time the company is short on money. He looks at his balance sheet:

(all figures in £'000)		
Fixed Assets		4,400
Current Assets		
Stock	3,580	
Debtors	<u>2,560</u>	
	<u>6,140</u>	
Creditors: amount falling due within one year		
Creditors	2,790	
Bank Overdraft	1,450	
Obligations under finance leases	450	
Factoring Companies	410	
Hire Purchase Commitments	120	
Corporation Tax	280	
Dividends	50	
Bills Payable	<u>240</u>	
	<u>5,790</u>	
Net Current Assets		<u>250</u>
Total assets less current liabilities		4,650

**Creditors : amounts falling due
after more than one year**

Bank Loans	700	
Mortgage Debenture		
Impressionable Assurance	800	1,500
		3,150

Capital and Reserves

Share Capital (£1)	400
Share Premium	280
Profit and Loss Account	2,470
	3,150

Martin thinks about his Balance Sheet and remembers that:

- ❐ the fixed assets include property at a carrying value of £1,900,000 which is probably worth over £4 million.

- ❐ Martin and his wife and children own most of the shares but 50,000 shares are owned by an uncle who would like to sell them in order to buy a farm in Wales.

- ❐ The Mortgage is secured on a property and all the bank lending is secured by a floating charge on the assets

Quick Answer Questions 15a

1. *Identify the forms of finance so far used by the company.*

2. *Calculate the net assets value of one ordinary share. One share is certainly worth much more than this. Explain why.*

3. *What privileges are available to the secured creditors?*

Scenario 2

Martin reckons his shares must be worth at least £5 million and probably much more. However he feels that although he lives well and has some private assets he is unable to enjoy the fruits of his ten years hard work in building up the company. He has taken out of the company reasonable directors' remuneration and some dividends but much of the profit earned has been retained in the company.

He would like to:

- ❐ realise some of the capital which is tied up the company in order to buy a country estate he knows of that is going cheap.

- ❐ allow his uncle to buy the farm in Wales.

The company cannot give him or his uncle any cash as the company needs cash for expansion.

Anne mentions that flotation of his company on the stock exchange may allow all of these things to be done.

**Tasks 15.1**

Write a report on the ways that flotation may enable Martin to achieve all the ends that have been mentioned so far in this chapter.

Information Bank Topic 19 The Stock Exchange, pages 197-203.

Quick answer questions 15a: *Answers and comments*

1. Forms of finance used include:

   Trade credit, Bank Overdraft, Leasing, Factoring, Hire Purchase, Bills of Exchange, Longer term bank loans, Mortgage loans from an insurance company, Shares sold to shareholders, Retained Profits.

2. $$\frac{£3,150,000}{400,000} = £7.875$$

   A share is worth more than this for many reasons including:

   ☐ The assets are valued by reference to cost and they include an asset (property) which is worth substantially more than book value.

   ☐ A principal asset of the company – goodwill – is omitted entirely from the Balance Sheet.

   In practice share valuation is very difficult and depends on whether a minority or majority holding is being valued, the profits of the company and many other factors.

3. A creditor secured on a fixed charge has first access to the proceeds of sale of the property on which the loan is secured so he cannot lose if the property is sold for more than the loan.

   A creditor secured by a floating charge has first access to the proceeds of sale of all the assets (but ranks behind the fixed charge creditors) and so cannot lose if the assets are sold for more than the amount of the loans. Note that in practice there are some creditors (including staff) who take preference over floating charge creditors.

Scenario 3

Martin consults a member of the Stock Exchange who tells him that she could arrange a flotation on the unlisted securities market. A vital consideration would of course be the price at which the shares could be sold to investors.

The broker suggests that the price would mostly depend on the profits earned by the company and perhaps by the dividends paid.

Martin looks up a number of companies quoted on the USM and finds that PE ratios in his sector average about 12 and that dividend yields average about 4%.

He notes that his Profit and Loss Account shows:

Net Profit after tax	£650,000
Dividends (interim and final)	£70,000
Retained	£580,000

Quick answer questions 15b

1. *What is the company worth if it can be sold at a Price Earnings Ratio of 12?*

2. *What is the company worth if the company is valued by reference to the dividend yield?*

3. *Can you account for the discrepancy between the two values?*

Scenario 4

Martin feels that he would like to float the company and with this in mind a procedure like this is proposed:

i.   Split the 400,000 £1 shares into 4,000,000 shares of 10p each.

ii. Create 2,000,000 new 10p shares

iii. Sell to the public 3,000,000 shares at £1.80 each

The shares to be sold will be:

> The 2,000,000 new shares
> The 400,000 shares owned by Martin's uncle
> 600,000 shares owned by Martin

 **Tasks 15.2**

1. Calculate:

    a. How much money the offer for sale to the public will raise if all the shares are sold.

    b. How much money will go to the company.

    c. How much money will go to Martin.

    d. How much money will go to his uncle.

    e. What proportion of the shares will remain in the hands of the original shareholders.

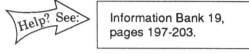

Help? See:	Information Bank 19, pages 197-203.

2. Describe the benefits that the company will enjoy as a listed company.

Help? See:	Information Bank 1, pages 197-203.

3. Describe the disadvantages that a listing will bring to:

    a. Martin

    b. the company.

Help? See:	Information Bank 1, pages 197-203.

4. Who would buy the shares in Martin Padlocks PLC?

Scenario 5

Martin successfully floats his company and the shares settle down at a price fluctuating around £2. Martin is introduced to the principal shareholder, Gordon Oldee, in a private company Goldee Locks Ltd and he agrees that Martin Padlocks PLC will takeover the company for a consideration of £600,000. This agreement was made of course after due investigation by Anne and other professionals.

The problem that arises is the nature of the consideration. Three possibilities are considered:

1. Cash

2. 300,000 new shares in Martin Padlocks PLC

3. £600,000 convertible loan stock.

Cash is undesirable as it will involve Oldee in paying lots of capital gains tax.

The convertible loan stock will carry a coupon of 8% and be redeemable at a premium of 10% in 10 years time. The stock will be convertible at a rate of 40 shares for each £100 of stock at any time after 5 years from the date of issue.

Tasks 15.3

1. Discuss the advantages and disadvantages to Oldee of selling his company and of each form of consideration. He will be given a one year contract as an adviser after the sale at a reasonable salary and thereafter will leave the group.

2. Discuss the effect on Martin personally if Martin Padlocks PLC took over the private company of Ted Keen of which Ted owns 98% of the shares. The consideration is £15,000,000 to be settled entirely in ordinary shares in Martin Padlocks PLC.

Information Bank 19, pages 197-203.

Quick answer questions 15b: *Answers and comments*

1. The value, using PE, would be 12 x £650,000 = £7,800,000

2. A 4% yield means that the company is worth 25 $\left(\frac{100}{4}\right)$ times the dividend =

    25 x £70,000 = £1,875,000.

3. The profits are what the company earns. They are the best the company can do and are objectively measured. The dividend is a matter of policy. Martin pays a small dividend (small as a proportion of profits) in order to expand the company. Most of the dividend comes to him and he prefers to pay himself very little. If the company were floated a much larger dividend would need to be paid to satisfy the investors need for a 4% yield on a price calculated by reference to earnings.

Scenario 6

Martin finds that he has received a very large amount of money from the flotation of his company. He has firstly to pay some capital gains tax but then realises that he needs to invest the rest. His income is large so he is mainly interested in capital gains to preserve and enhance his estate which will descend to his children and grandchildren.

Tasks 15.4

List possible investments and evaluate each from the point of view of capital growth in preference to income.

Help: see Information Bank 19, pages 197-203.

Scenario 7

Some of the shares in Martin Padlock were bought by the company's general sales manager Harold Sligh. Sligh is an excellent salesman and is able to secure a megadeal selling secure door locks to 5 motor car manufacturers at a very good price. Before telling the Board the good news he rings his maiden aunt Mary and asks her to buy, in her name, 200,000 shares in Martin Padlocks PLC. As soon as the Board hear of the deal they make a public announcement of the deal through the Stock Exchange and the price of the shares rises from £2 to £2.40.

Tasks 15.5

Comment on this scenario.

| Help? See: | Information Bank 19.19, page 202.

Scenario 8

Martin has come a long way from starting a small business with a few pounds to being the boss of a public company and a millionaire. Not all new businesses go this way but, as Napoleon said, every soldier has a Field Marshal's baton in his knapsack.

Where might Martin go from here? His company may grow larger and larger by internal growth or acquisition. His company may be taken over, Martin given a seat on the Board of the larger company and he eventually becomes boss once again. He may get a knighthood.

But of course his company may go bust. As Napoleon also said "it is only one step from the sublime to the ridiculous".

Summary of Unit 15

1. The Stock Exchange is a second hand market for shares and other securities. It is also a market where companies can raise money from investors who know they can sell the new shares to other investors because there is a secondary market.

2. Expansion as a private company is limited by limitations in finance availability

3. Flotation as a listed company makes finance available to a company and also makes money available to individual shareholders.

4. The value of a private company can be assessed in many ways including by reference to its net assets value, its earnings and its dividends. The most usable data in a flotation is an assessment of future earnings.

5. Being a listed company gives advantages including access to capital and the ability to offer shares as a consideration in a takeover.

6. Disadvantages include being in the public eye, having to maintain profits and dividends, and fear of takeover.

7. Consideration in takeovers can be cash, shares or convertible loans or a combination of these.

8. Insider trading is common, immoral and illegal. It is sometimes called a victimless crime and may have economic justification in bringing about a true and fair value for the share.

9. Individual investors have an immense choice for investing their savings. Each type of investment can be characterised by the risks attached and the returns expected.

Developing knowledge and skills

You are now in a position to tackle questions 1 to 8 in Section 3.19, pages 324-325.

Section 2

The Information Bank

Introduction

This section is divided into nineteen Topics each explaining a part of Financial Accounting , Management Accounting or Financial Management. It provides a succinct explanation with numerous examples of the principles, techniques and knowledge required to carry out the Tasks in Section 1. It is not intended that you read the Section through from beginning to end but rather that you concentrate on the Topics to which you are directed from Section 1.

By the time you have worked through the whole of Section 1, you will also have worked through all of Section 2.

Also, when doing Section 3: Developing knowledge and skills, you may need to come to this Section if you have difficulty with any of the Exercises, Cases or Assignments.

Contents

1 The profit and loss account

1. At the end of each financial year, all businesses (and other enterprises like local government, clubs and societies) produce financial statements to report their activities in the year in financial terms. One of these financial statements is the *profit and loss account*.

2. The profit and loss account measures and demonstrates the profit or loss achieved during the year. A year is the usual period as it is required by statute for organisations such as limited companies and building societies and for all enterprises for tax purposes. Many enterprises also produce profit and loss accounts for shorter periods.

3. The *year end date* chosen is at the choice of the enterprise. Nearly all choose a month end which may be the calendar year end or the government's year end (31 March) or the month end nearest the date of formation of the business or it may be a date which is convenient for stocktaking. Once selected most businesses stay with the same year end but it can be changed.

4. For retailing, wholesaling and manufacturing enterprises the full statement is usually called the *trading and profit and loss account*.

5. Financial statements are always *formal documents* with proper *headings* and *formats* which conform to accepted practice although several formats can be regarded as acceptable.

6. For retail and wholesale enterprises the format might be:

a)	**Evelyn Babel – builders' merchant**		
b)	**Trading and profit and loss account**		
c)	**For the year ending 31 January 19x2**		
			£
d)	Sales		872,000
e)	Less cost of goods sold:		
f)	Opening stock	54,300	
g)	Purchases	571,000	
		625,300	
h)	Less closing stock	63,900	561,400
i)	Gross profit		310,600
j)	Less expenses:		
k)	Rent	30,000	
	Rates	26,500	
	Insurances	7,800	
l)	Wages and salaries	104,500	
m)	Sundry other expenses	72,000	
n)	Depreciation	23,000	263,800
o)	Net profit		46,800

You will see that profit is measured by beginning with the total sales or *turnover* achieved in the period. From this figure, successive deductions are made. The first deduction is the *cost of the goods sold* and this is derived by a calculation. A builders' merchant makes a profit by selling goods at a price which is greater than the price at which they were purchased. The difference between sales and the cost of the goods sold is called the *gross profit* and the whole section (d) to (i) is called the trading account.

Having measured the gross profit, deductions from it are made to derive the net profit. These further deductions are the *expenses* incurred in running the business. These may be called the *overhead expenses*.

7. I will now comment in detail on the content of the trading and profit and loss account:

a) The name of the enterprise must always be given.

b) The title of the financial statement must be given in full.

c) The period of time must be made clear.

d) Sales is the total amount of sales invoiced in the period. It is also termed the turnover. Note that it does not include VAT.

   If a sale has been made in the period then it will be included in this figure even if the cash relating to the sale is received in another period. For example if Babel made a sale of bricks on 28 January 19x2 on credit to Aztecan Pyramids Ltd £200 then the £200 is included in the sales for the year ending 31 January 19x2. This is so despite the fact that Aztecan did not pay until 14th April 19x2, that is in the following financial year.

   This idea that all sales are included in a year if they are made in that year, irrespective of the date of payment, is called the *realisation convention*. It is discussed further In Information Bank Topic 7.

e) The sales made are of specific goods and the cost of these specific goods is matched against the sales to determine the gross profit. The idea is that each sale generates a profit which equals the sale price less the input cost. The total gross Profit for the year is the total of such profits. This cost is not usually measured directly but is implied by the calculation (f) to (h).

f) Firstly the stock of goods for sale at the beginning of the period viz at 1st February 19x1 is considered. This total will have been arrived at by counting the goods and valuing them at *input cost* (this can be modified but is a complication we will ignore for the moment).

g) Then the total amount of goods for resale purchased in the year is added. All such goods purchased in the year are included irrespective of the date of payment.

   This gives the total of goods in stock at the beginning and of goods added to stock in the year (£625,000). This is the total input cost of goods which could be sold in the year.

h) However not all such goods were sold and the unsold ones are counted and valued at input cost and deducted from the goods that could be sold to give the cost of the goods that actually were sold in the year. It should be noted that some goods will be included that were not sold. They may have been lost through other causes – theft, breakage, evaporation, mice etc. They are still included under the heading cost of goods sold although strictly speaking they were not sold. They do of course diminish profit.

i) The *gross profit* represents the profits made (that is sale price less input cost) on all sales made in the period. It is much used as an indicator of achievement both by itself and as a *ratio to sales*. This is discussed In Information Bank Topic 8.

j) Clearly all businesses have overhead expenses and these are explored next. The expenses are listed by suitable *categories* and the amounts expended in the year are calculated. The categorisation is according to taste. Some businesses may have a dozen categories and some may use more and some may use less.

k) Rent is a common expense. The rent for the year will be in accordance with the lease and the amount included reflects the exact period not the amounts paid in the period. For example:

   Rent was £28,000 a year up to 31 July 19x1 and was increased to £32,000 from that date. Rent is supposed to be paid quarterly in advance.

   In fact payments were:

Jan 29	19x1	– for the quarter to 30.4.19x2	£7,000
May 6	19x1	– for the quarter to 31.7.19x1	£7,000
Aug 3	19x1	– for the quarter to 31.10.19x1	£8,000
Nov 25	19x1	– for the quarter to 31.1.19x2	£8,000
			£30,000
Jan 29	19x2	– for the quarter to 30.4.19x2	£8,000

You will see that the true cost of rent for the year is £30,000 and that is the amount which is regarded as the expense for the year ending 31 January 19x2.

Part of this was paid in the previous year (on Jan 29 19x1) and a payment for the following year (on Jan 29 19x2) was made in the year. However accountants go to some trouble to measure the cost of the resource (eg occupation of the premises) actually consumed in the period. Dates of payment are irrelevant.

This measurement of the cost of the resource actually consumed is called the *accruals convention* and will be explored more fully In Information Bank Topic 7.

l) Wages and Salaries includes the wage and salary cost of employing the staff in the year. It is usually calculated as gross remuneration payable + employer's national insurance and pension contributions. Like the rent and all other expenses placing expenditure in the right year is important. For example if the firm pay a week in arrear such that the wages (£2,040) for the week ending 31 January 19x2 are paid on 7 February 19x2 then the £2,040 would be included in the total for the year ending 31 January 19x2 ignoring the date of actual payment.

m) I have included a bulk expense to avoid cluttering the profit and loss account with more categories. In practice there would be more categories. All would be calculated in accordance with the accruals convention.

n) *Depreciation* on *fixed assets* is dealt with In Information Bank Topic 3.

o) Finally the net profit (or loss) in the period is calculated. You may hear talk of *'the bottom line'* meaning the profit.

8. Students often have difficulty in appreciating why two money columns are used. Note that the extreme right column is a summary:

Sales less cost of goods sold = gross profit which less expenses = net profit.

The left hand of the two columns is used for detail.

9. Some items are *not* included in the profit and loss account. These include:

i) *Drawings*. Babel may take cash (or goods) out of the business for her private purposes. This is why people have businesses – so that they may draw money etc from the business to spend on their private purposes. The reason why the business can stand money being drawn from it is that it makes a profit. Clearly, in the long term, a business where drawings exceed profits is going to go bust. It makes sense therefore for the business profit to be measured to enable the proprietor to see how much he can draw. Some proprietors talk about their 'wages' from the business. These are drawings and not wages in the profit and loss account sense.

ii) *Capital expenditure*. Capital expenditure is expenditure on the acquisition of fixed assets. Fixed Assets are things (eg plant, machinery, vehicles etc) which last a long time and cost more than a trivial amount. Buying a new machine for £10,000 in the year ending 31 January 1991 does not reduce the profit for that year by £10,000 but does reduce the profit for the whole five years (say) in which the machine will be in use. Thus there is a reduction of profit in the year:

$$\left(\frac{£10,000}{5} = £2,000 \right)$$

which is known as depreciation. More of this In Information Bank Topic 3.

iii) *Receipt* and *repayment of loans*. These do not affect profit. However any interest will do so.

10. *Service industries* such as transport, professional services etc also produce profit and loss accounts but omit the gross profit stage. As an example:

Example

K.Nain – veterinary surgeon
profit and loss account
For the year ending 28 February 19x4

	£	£
Fees receivable		62,000
Drugs etc:		
Opening stock	890	
Purchases	4,320	
	5,210	
Less closing stock	770	
	4,440	
Wages	12,810	
Rent and rates	4,900	
Accountant's fee	1,000	
Bank interest and charges	2,480	
Advertising	1,300	
Depreciation	5,600	
Other overheads	12,200	44,730
Net profit		17,270

It is not possible to calculate a gross profit since the fees (= sales in a trading business) are for the supply of drugs *and* the supply of professional services such as consultations, inspections, surgical operations etc.

Profit and cash

11. People usually think that if a business has made a profit as measured in the Profit and Loss Account then the business will have cash somewhere of the amount of the profit. Surprisingly this is not so. The reason is that a Profit and Loss Account measures the profit and profit is not cash.

To see that profit made in a period is not equivalent to net cash receipts in a year, consider:

a) Sales are included when invoiced and not when the cash was received

b) Purchases are included when the invoiced and not when the cash was paid

c) Expenses are exactly related to the time of consumption and not to the time of payment.

d) Payments for fixed assets are excluded from the Profit and Loss Account although part will be included in depreciation

e) Payments for drawings and dividends are excluded

As profit is not cash then what is it?

This is not easy to answer. It can be described, not as an increase in cash, but as an increase in net assets. Net assets are assets less liabilities. Understanding the concept of profit is difficult and you will take a little while before you fully grasp it.

 **Key principle summary**

○ Financial statements are produced for all businesses for each financial year.

○ One of the financial statements is the profit and loss account which measures and demonstrates the profit or loss earned during the period.

○ The profit and loss account may also be called the trading and profit and loss account in which case a gross profit will be calculated as well as a net profit.

○ The trading and profit and loss account will have the format:

Sales	X
Less cost of goods sold	X
Gross profit	X
Less overhead expenses	X
Net profit	X

○ Sales will include all sales invoiced in the period irrespective of year of payment by the customers.

○ Cost of goods sold should be the cost of goods actually sold in the year + the cost of goods lost due to other causes such as theft and destruction.

○ Overhead expenses will include the exact cost of the resource consumed in the year, again irrespective of year of payment.

○ Overheads will include depreciation but will exclude drawings, capital expenditure and loan receipts and repayments.

○ Service industries omit the gross profit calculation

○ The essence of profit computation is the placing of revenues (eg sales) and expenses in the right year.

○ Profit is not cash.

2 | The balance sheet

1. Every business produces a profit and loss account measuring and demonstrating the profit or loss achieved in the year. All but the smallest also produce an additional financial statement – the *balance sheet*.

2. The balance sheet is simply a list of the *assets* and *liabilities* of the business at a specified *date*. The date will normally be the year end. Thus the profit and loss account shows the profit (loss) earned over the period and the balance sheet shows the position at the *end* of that period.

3. In addition to the summarised list of assets and liabilities the balance sheet also gives values. The methods of valuation, particularly of assets, may seem odd to non-accountants. There is however a logic to them. They are based on *historical input cost* to the business. If a business bought an asset (say a motor van) for £3,000 six years ago. Then the historical input cost is £3,000 and the value placed upon it will be *derived* from that figure.

4. A balance sheet is a formal document and the format is important. Several formats are possible but a common one today is:

Evelyn Babel – builders' merchant
Balance Sheet as at 31 January 19x2

		Cost	Depreciation	Net book value
a)				
b)				
c)	Fixed assets			
d)				
e)	Plant and equipment	98,000	56,000	42,000
	Vehicles	41,000	17,000	24,000
f)		139,000	73,000	66,000
g)	Current assets			
h)	Stock		63,900	
i)	Debtors		164,200	
j)	Prepayments		1,800	
k)			229,900	
l)	Less creditors: amounts falling due within one year:			
m)	Creditors		95,400	
n)	Bank overdraft		102,700	
o)			198,100	
p)	Net current assets			31,800
q)	Total assets less current liabilities			97,800
r)	Creditors: amount falling due after more than one year			
	Loan at 12% from Tom			2,000
s)				95,800
t)	Capital			
u)	as at 31 January 19x1			86,100
v)	Net profit for the year			46,800
w)				132,900
x)	Less drawings			37,100
y)	As at 31 January 19x2			95,800

5. You will notice that the balance sheet comes in several sections:

   i) *Fixed assets* are assets which have a long life (more than one year) and have more than a trivial value. Examples are land and buildings (none here as Babel rents her premises), plant, machinery, equipment, vehicles.

   ii) *Current assets* are those which change frequently. The normal *categories* are those included in this balance sheet.

   iii) 'Creditors: falling due within one year' are liabilities which need to be paid before 31 January 19x3.

   Some balance sheets including this one have in addition 'Creditors: amounts falling due after more than one year' which are longer term liabilities like mortgages.

   iv) Having calculated the assets less the liabilities to external persons (£95,800) there is an additional section which causes more difficulty in understanding. Lines (c) to (s) list the assets and liabilities in detail. Lines (t) to (y) consider the assets less liabilities as a single sum and how that single sum has changed from the end of the previous year to the end of this. The explanation is that the total assets less liabilities were *increased* by a *profit* and *reduced* by the *drawings* of cash and goods taken from the business by the owner in the year. The total assets less liabilities is a useful statistic in that it tells the proprietor how much *resources* she has tied up in the business. Another way of looking at it is to regard the capital as a liability of the business (seen as a separate entity) to the owner so that the assets in total equal the liabilities in total:

$$\text{Assets} = \text{Liabilities} + \text{Capital}$$

6. Considering the balance sheet line by line:

   a) The name of the business should be made clear.

   b) The title of the financial statement should be given and the date make explicit.

   c) Fixed assets are considered in more detail In Information Bank Topic 3.

   d) It is usual to show three figures for each category of fixed asset:

      ❑ the *original cost* to the business

      ❑ the total amount by which the asset has *depreciated* since its acquisition.

      ❑ the difference which is called the *net book value* or *written down value*. This value is cost derived and will probably bear no resemblance at all to the possible amount for which the assets might be sold. This usually surprises people new to accounting!

   e) Two categories of fixed assets are included here. Sometimes there are more such as land and buildings.

   f) Totals are given. We can see the total 'value' of the fixed assets.

   g) Current assets are more ephemeral and the categories are the usual ones. This business, like many, has a bank overdraft but some have cash at the bank and this would then be included as a current asset.

   h) Stock is as counted at 31 January 19x2 and valued at input cost not selling price. Some items may be valued at less than cost and this will be considered In Information Bank Topic 4. You will note that this item also appears in the profit and loss account. Calculation of stock quantity and value is time consuming and the problem of stock determination is the main reason why financial statements are not produced more frequently than annually (some businesses do produce monthly or quarterly or half yearly accounts).

   i) Some businesses sell goods and receive payment at the same time. When I buy groceries at the supermarket I pay cash at the check out. However many businesses sell goods *on credit*. This means that on a sale, the sale is evidenced by the sending of an invoice to the customer setting out the goods sold and the amount due. Most invoices also state that payment is due at some specified time. Often this is 30 days after the sale. In practice customers often ignore this and pay anything up to several months after the date of supply of the goods. This whole business of credit is a major problem to many companies. Since Evelyn sells on credit there will always be some customers who have had goods and not yet paid for them. These customers are called *debtors* and at each year end the total amount of sales invoiced for which payment has not been received will be assessed and included in the assets as debtors.

   j) This item is rarely significant and is often included with the debtors in a global sum. When expenses such as fire insurance or rent are paid the payment is often for a period in advance. For example fire insurance for the calendar year 19x3 £600 may be paid on 1st January that year. This means that on the year end date 31st January, 11 months fire insurance cover has been paid for and is still to be enjoyed. This is $\frac{11}{12} \times £600 = £550$ and would be included in the assets as a prepayment.

   k) The total of the three kinds of current assets is demonstrated. There can be other categories of current assets. A great number have cash in the bank. Manufacturing businesses will have work in progress. Some will have various kinds of short term investments such as bank deposits.

   l) Liabilities are usually shown in two separate sections. Short term liabilities which are those for which payment is due soon after (in fact up to one year after the year end) the year end and long term liabilities which are those such as loans which will be settled more than one year after the year end. Not all businesses have long term liabilities.

m) Just as Evelyn offers credit to her customers so she takes credit from her suppliers. At balance sheet date it is necessary to count up the amount she owes for goods and services which she has received but for which payment had not been made.

n) Many businesses borrow money from their bankers on overdraft. In fact the principal source of income to the high street banks is interest charged to business customers and the principal source of money to business is the bank loan or overdraft. Overdrafts are forms of borrowing in which the amount borrowed changes continually as money is paid in and cheques are drawn. For most businesses an overdraft once taken out is constantly renewed and is a form of long term liability. However as it is technically repayable on demand, an overdraft is normally included among the short term liabilities.

o) The total of the short term liabilities is shown. Note that in the past short term liabilities were always called *current liabilities* but that the modern term in balance sheets is 'creditors: amounts falling due within one year,

p) A single figure for current assets less the short term liabilities is normally shown, This total is sometimes called the *working capital* which is the subject of Information Bank Topic 18.

r) Liabilities such as mortgages and loans which have a repayment requirement more than one year away are included here. Evelyn has only one which is a loan from Tom. The actual repayment date is the end of 19x9 but this is not shown. Usually the *interest rate* is shown. The 12% means that Evelyn must pay Tom 12% of the sum outstanding (ie 12% × £1,000 = £120) every year as long as the £1,000 remains outstanding.

s) The total assets less liabilities is then shown as a single figure. Most people can understand a balance sheet up to this point. However the capital part always follows.

t) Capital is the assets less liabilities of the business expressed as a total sum. Some writers describe it as the *net worth*. Just as a person might add up his fortune by valuing his assets (house, car, money in building societies etc less his liabilities – mortgage, HP commitment, unpaid gas bill etc) and thus find out how rich he is so a business prepares a balance sheet. It must be emphasised that the balance sheet shows only business assets and liabilities.

u) This figure is the balance sheet value of the assets less liabilities in total at the beginning of the year.

v) The net profit for the year adds to the net total of assets less liabilities.

w) This sum is always put in but does not have any real significance.

x) The proprietor usually withdraws cash and goods from the business at various times during the year and the total is shown here.

y) If all accounting has been done accurately and correctly, this figure of the capital at the end of the year will be the same figure as the assets less liabilities.

What a balance sheet is and is not

7. A balance sheet is a classified summary of the assets and liabilities of a business valuing the assets at cost or at a figure derived from cost. I should point out that the use of cost derived figures can be modified in certain circumstances. Assets which had no cost are normally omitted. The most notable asset under this heading is *goodwill* which is only included if it had an actual cost ie it was bought.

8. A balance sheet does not show the value of the assets if they were sold. The reasons for this include:

a) The long established convention is to use cost based values.

b) The possible selling value of an asset is very subjective and accountants like to be objective.

c) The possible selling value of an asset cannot always be easily estimated. For example what is the second hand value of an oil refinery?

9. The balance sheet does not show what the business *as a whole is worth*. That could only be reliably determined by actually selling the business and any estimate is unlikely to be more than approximate.

Theory

10. Balance sheets have been produced for many years without recourse to any theory but in recent years a body of theory has been established. This body of theory has been established in the same way is theory in physics – observations are made of the real world, hypotheses are then made about possible theories that may explain the observations and the hypotheses are tested by making predictions which can be observed to be correct or incorrect.

    In accounting the theory about balance sheets is that there are a number of conventions which explain how balance sheets are actually constructed. These conventions include:

    a) *Business entity* – a business (or other non-profit making enterprise) has to be identified as the subject of the balance sheet and only its assets and liabilities are included.

    b) *Cost* – all assets are included at values which are at or are derived from historical input cost

    c) *Going concern* – it is assumed that the business will continue to function in the future and will not be liquidated in the near future. If the business is not a going concern then the cost based values would be replaced by realisation (what they can be sold for) values.

    d) *Accruals* – the unexpired portion of expenditure like insurance should be included. This convention can be controversial if, for example, a company makes aero engines and wishes to include expenditure on research and development as an asset.

    e) *Prudence* (or conservatism) – current assets such as stock and debtors should be valued at the lower of cost and net realisable value.

    ### Examples

    i) A widget is in stock. It cost £30 to buy and is usually sold for £50. It would be valued in the balance sheet at its cost £30. However if it was damaged and could only be sold for £10 then it would be valued at £10 as that is the net realisable value and is lower than cost.

    ii) A customer owes £100. This would normally be included in debtors at £100 but if the customer was in financial difficulties and it is estimated that he will pay only £50 then £50 only will be included in debtors.

Capital

11. Capital is simply defined as assets less liabilities. The Balance Sheet firstly lists and values the assets and then the liabilities. In a sole trader or partnership the final section of the Balance Sheet is as in paragraph 4 (t to y). In a company the corresponding section is called the Capital and Reserves and will be explained In Information Bank Topic 6. In the Balance Sheet of a club or society the corresponding section is usually called the Unappropriated Surplus or the General Fund.

 **Key principle summary**

○ Businesses produce balance sheets at intervals of not more than one year.

○ A balance sheet is a classified summary of the assets and liabilities of the business at the balance sheet date.

○ The balance sheet is a formal financial statement and should be in an appropriate neat and tidy format

○ The sections of a balance sheet include:

    fixed assets;

    current assets;

current liabilities (or creditors: amounts falling due within one year);

long term liabilities (or liabilities: amounts falling due after more than one year);

and capital.

○ Fixed assets are assets such as land and buildings, plant and machinery and vehicles.

○ Current assets include stocks, work in progress, debtors, prepayments and cash at bank and in hand.

○ Current liabilities include creditors and bank overdrafts.

○ Long term liabilities include loans and mortgages.

○ The capital is the assets less liabilities expressed as a single sum. It is usual to show

the capital at the date of the previous balance sheet + the profit in the period − the drawings = the capital at the date of the balance sheet date*

* which should also equal the assets less liabilities.

○ The balance sheet shows the assets at cost derived figures. It does not pretend or purport to give the saleable values of the assets or of the business as a whole.

○ The rules or conventions which accountants use in drawing up a balance sheet have been identified in a body of theory. The conventions used include the cost convention, the accruals convention, the going concern convention, the business entity convention, and the prudence convention.

---

3 | Depreciation

1. A business can have at least two types of expenditure:

   Revenue expenditure

   Capital expenditure

   Revenue expenditure is on goods and services that are consumed in the short term. It includes the input cost of the business's products. These costs can be simply the cost of goods purchased for resale or the costs (materials, labour etc) of goods manufactured for sale. Revenue expenditure also includes overhead costs such as rent, rates, insurance, salaries, electricity, repairs, motor running expenses and many others.

   Capital expenditure is the cost of acquiring fixed assets.

2. Assets are things possessed by a person or business and include real things like stocks, motor cars, cash in the bank and also debts due from other people or firms.

   Fixed assets are assets which cost a significant amount and give economic benefits for more than one accounting year. Examples are land and buildings, plant and machinery, motor vehicles and office equipment. Items of very small value (for example a ruler or stapler in the office) may well last for several years but are not regarded as fixed assets.

Depreciation

3. If a fixed asset is acquired in a particular accounting year then it will give economic benefit to the enterprise not just in that year but for one or more years after that.

   For example Martin's business might buy a new machine in 1994 for £2,000. This machine may well last for say five years and cease to be effective only in 1998.

4. In measuring the profit for 1994 it would be unfair to include the whole £2,000 as an expense reducing the profit for that year. This is because the machine will give economic benefit for each of

the years 1994 to 1998. It is necessary to spread the £2,000 over these years on some rational basis.

Allocating an appropriate share of the £2,000 over these years is called the depreciation process.

5. Before considering how this is done, it is necessary to gather together some data: the cost (which we know to be £2,000) and some estimates. We need to estimate the useful economic life of the machine. We will suppose this to be 5 years. We also need to estimate the salvage value at the end of the asset's life. This is clearly more difficult but we will suppose this to be £200.

Using this data and these estimates we can quickly see that the ultimate cost of the machine will be £2,000 less £200 = £1,800. As the machine will give benefit over 5 years, the most logical way of spreading the cost will be $\frac{£1,800}{5}$ = £360 a year.

This approach is called the straight line method and is the most frequently found in practice.

The consequences for profit measurement are that the profits of each of the years 1994 to 1998 are reduced by £360 each year. Note that cost in 1994 does not reduce the profit of 1994 by £2,000 but by £360.

6. Many accountants consider that the *straight line* method does not reflect reality in that the machine gives up its value more quickly in its early years than it does in its later years. They consider that the £1,800 should be allocated between the years 1994 to 1998 so that there is more depreciation in the earlier years. A way of doing this is to use the *reducing instalment* method of depreciation.

This is best explained by an example.

Example

	£
1994 Cost of machine	2,000
1994 Depreciation 37% of £2,000	740
	1,260
1995 Depreciation 37% of £1,260	466
	794
1996 Depreciation 37% of £794	294
	500
1997 Depreciation 37% of £500	185
	315
1998 Depreciation 37% of £315	116
	199

You will notice:

a) The depreciation and, hence the profit measurement, is unevenly distributed over the years. The reduction of profit in 1994 is £740 and in 1998 only £116.

b) The adoption of 37% as the rate does not exactly reduce the final value to the estimated salvage value of £200. This is because the rate chosen should be 36.9% and you may be wondering where the 37% came from. It comes from a formula linking cost, salvage value and expected life. Most accountants do not know this formula and fewer still actually use it. So I will not give it.

In practice the reducing instalment method is much used but accountants tend to ignore the salvage value and the expected life and simply take a fixed percentage. A very common percentage is 25%.

Note that the total depreciation over the 5 years is the same for both methods. Only the distribution over the years is different.

7. Depreciation will normally appear in the profit and loss account as:

Depreciation £x

This will be the whole depreciation for the year for all fixed assets.

Balance sheet values

8. So far we have considered the effect on profit measurement of the depreciation **process**. The depreciation process also affects the valuation put on assets in the balance sheet.

    Using our example we can draw up a table showing the valuations which would **appear** in the balance sheet at the end of each year:

	1994	1995	1996	1997	1998
	£	£	£	£	£
Straight line	1,640	1,280	920	560	200
Reducing instalment	1,260	794	500	315	199

You will notice that the valuations are different for the two methods.

It is necessary to appreciate what is meant by value. If a person is asked "What is the value of your car?". She will assume the value requested is the estimated price for which the car can be sold based on advertised prices, guides to car prices etc. Balance sheet values are *not* intended to indicate the prices for which assets can be sold. Consider a machine which is purchased for a special use unique to the buying company. It may have five years of economic use but at no time will it have any saleable value except as scrap.

A way of considering balance sheet values of fixed assets is to assume that when purchased the cost price represents the *utility* of the asset to the firm. As time progresses and the machine becomes worn out it gradually gives up its utility. The amount of utility given up in the year is the depreciation and the balance sheet value is the utility remaining.

9. The balance sheet value is called the *net book value* or the *written down value* or sometimes as the *carrying value*. You will now appreciate that this value may be below or above the second hand or resale value of the asset. Bear in mind that some assets have little or no second hand value – an example is special purpose machinery.

10. Fixed assets are usually shown in balance sheets like this:

	£ Cost	Depreciation	Net book value
Land	10,000	–	10,000
Buildings	80,000	12,000	68,000
Plant	32,000	11,306	20,694
	122,000	23,306	98,694

Note that the *original cost* of the fixed assets (which were bought at various times in the past) is always shown. This information is not of great value but it always given. The depreciation is all the depreciation on the fixed assets for *all years* up to the present. It is *not* just the depreciation for the year.

Types of fixed asset

11. There are several categories of fixed asset:

    land, buildings, plant, vehicles, office equipment etc.

    The theory is that they all have limited lives except land. Consequently they all need to be depreciated except for land. The causes of having limited lives include wear and tear, effluxion of time (this strange phrase is always used and it means assets depreciate because of the passage of time) and obsolescence.

    Land does not depreciate.

    Buildings have limited useful lives and therefore are depreciated. Commonly the useful life is estimated at 40 or 50 years and the straight line method is normally used.

    Plant and vehicles have shorter lives (5 to 10 years?) and may be depreciated by either method.

Depreciation policies

12. Estimates are required of useful lives and salvage values and as these are subjective the depreciation and hence the measurement of profit will depend on who makes the estimates. In addition the firm has to have a policy on which depreciation method to use. But note that the method once chosen should be applied consistently.

13. Published accounts should give the useful lives and the depreciation policies in a statement included with the accounts called the statement of accounting policies.

Disposals

14. Anton's business started on 1 January 19x2 and he bought on that date a Rover car for £12,500. He depreciated on the basis of a life of 5 years with a salvage value of £2,000. Thus the depreciation was £2,100 a year.

In his balance sheet at 31 December 19x4 the car stood at:

	£
Cost	12,500
Accumulated depreciation	6,300
Written down value	6,200

On March 19x5, he sold the car for £4,500 and bought another. What should be the depreciation charge for the car in the profit and loss account of 19x5?

The answer is simply £6,200 – £4,500 = £1,700. This will appear in the profit and loss account simply as depreciation £1,700 (it will probably be included in a global figure of depreciation and not be shown separately) or possibly as *'Loss on sale of vehicle £1,700'.*

 **Key principle summary**

○ Capital expenditure is expenditure on fixed assets.

○ Fixed assets are not an expenses in the profit and loss account of the year in which they are purchased but are subject to the depreciation process.

○ The depreciation is calculated by reference to the cost, the expected economic life and the salvage value.

○ Two common depreciation policies are straight line and reducing instalment (also called reducing balance).

○ The value of a fixed asset on the balance sheet is its cost less accumulated depreciation.

○ Land is not depreciated but buildings are.

○ Depreciation policies should be disclosed in the statement of accounting policies.

○ On disposal the profit and loss account is charged or credited with the difference between the book value and the proceeds of disposal.

 Stocks

Stocks

1. Most businesses have stocks. There are several possible kinds:

   ❑ stocks of raw materials in a manufacturing business

   ❑ stocks of goods for sale to customers. These may have been manufactured by the business (as in the stocks of new cars held by a motor car manufacturer) or purchased (as in stocks of new cars held by a car dealer)

   ❑ stocks of consumable items. These may include spare parts for machines, small tools, heating oil, stationery.

   ❑ manufacturers and construction companies also have work in progress which is the stock of products for sale which are still in the course of manufacture.

2. At a balance sheet date all stocks held have to be identified and counted. This is often a major undertaking and unless it is very carefully planned and executed errors will occur. After booking the items in stock on a listing which is called an inventory, the stocks have to be valued at cost. Some of them may be valued at lower than cost but we will deal with this point later.

Valuation at cost

3. Valuation at input cost may seem easy but in practice major conceptual problems occur with the definition of cost.

4. The basic principle is that stock should be valued at:

   'The expenditure that has been incurred in bringing each item to its present location and condition.'

   This is further defined as the cost of purchase + the cost of conversion.

5. Cost of purchase includes the purchase price including import duties, transport and handling costs and any other directly attributable costs, less trade discounts, rebates and subsidies. Most of these costs and deductions are easily identifiable. For examples:

   i) 25,000 widgets are imported at £10 each from Hong Kong. Carriage to our works cost £4,000 for the consignment. Cost each is clearly £10 + $\frac{£4,000}{25,000}$ = £10.16.

   ii) A farmer bought 10 tons of fertiliser at £20 a ton. The government paid him a subsidy of £6 a ton. The cost is thus £14 a ton.

   iii) Hugh purchased a widget at £20 less 25% trade discount. He was allowed a 5% cash or settlement discount when he paid for them 3 days after the invoice date.

   Cost here is considered to be £20 − £5 = £15. The cash or settlement discount is ignored in computing cost. The theory is that the cost is £15. The cash discount is a financial benefit obtained by financial means (having the cash to pay quickly) and is nothing to do with the goods.

6. Cost of conversion is more difficult. In general there are two types of cost to be added to purchase price:

   i) Costs which are specifically attributable to units of production eg direct labour, direct expenses, and sub-contracted work.

   Example

   Guy imported 10,000 door handles from Taiwan. These cost £1 delivered to his warehouse. They were then lacquered by a subcontractor who charged 5p each. They were then reboxed and labelled by Guy's staff at a cost of 7p a box for the boxes and 20 hours labour at £3 an hour. Total cost is then £1 + 5p + 7p + $\frac{£60}{10,000}$ = 1.18.

ii) *Production overheads*. This is more difficult and is treated in more detail In Information Bank Topic 10.

Example

Julie makes a single product – plastic cartons of mushy peas. Costs of producing 500,000 in a year of these are:

	£
500,000 plastic cartons	5,000
Peas	4,000
Direct labour	12,000
Production overheads (rent, rates, power supervision etc)	16,000
	37,000

Total cost per carton is thus $\frac{£37,000}{500,000}$ = 7.4p

In practice, no businesses produce just one product and the production overheads have to be shared between the different products. This is a conceptual problem which is dealt with In Information Bank Topic 10. However you should now realise that the cost of manufacturing a product must include an appropriate proportion of the manufacturing overhead.

Companies also have non-manufacturing overhead (administration, selling, distribution, finance) but these are not normally regarded as part of the cost of a product.

Valuation at net realisable value

7. Some items in stock may be damaged, old, obsolete or otherwise difficult to sell. It may be that the possible selling price of these is actually lower than cost. In such cases the net realisable value has to be estimated and this value is then used for stock valuation purposes instead of cost.

Examples

20 old model widgets are in Ted's stock. These cost £30 each to buy. They can now only be sold for £15 and Ted will have to pay £1 each carriage and 10% commission on the sale.

The cost is £30 each.

The realisable value is £15 each.

The net realisable value is £15 – £1 – £1.50 = £12.50.

Since £12.50 is below £30, the value for inclusion in the balance sheet is £12.50.

Like items

8. Some items in stock are indistinguishable from similar items. For example a dealer has a stock of identical exhausts for 1968 Morris Minors. Each of these is equally good at its function as the others. This means the items are *fungible*. However not all the items had the same cost because they were bought at different times and at different prices.

Example

Wilf bought 5 exhausts in October 19x2 for £30 each

and 7 exhausts in November 19x2 for £40 each.

In December he sold 8 of them.

At 31 December 19x2 he took stock and found he had 4 left and wondered what he should consider the cost of these to be. Remember that they are identical and he does not know from which consignment they came.

Accountants have developed three possible solutions for this problem:

First in first out	– FIFO
Last in last out	– LIFO
Average cost	– AVCO

We will consider each:

FIFO

		In	Out	Balance
	October	$5 \times 30 = 150$		$5 \times 30 = 150$
	November	$7 \times 40 = 280$		$\left\{ \begin{array}{l} 5 \times 30 = 150 \\ 7 \times 40 = 280 \end{array} \right.$
	December		$\left\{ \begin{array}{l} 5 \times 30 = 150 \\ 3 \times 40 = 120 \end{array} \right.$	$4 \times 40 = 160$

In FIFO we consider or assume that the oldest go out first so that what remain in stock are the later deliveries.

LIFO

		In	Out	Balance
	October	$5 \times 30 = 150$		$5 \times 30 = 150$
	November	$7 \times 40 = 280$		$\left\{ \begin{array}{l} 5 \times 30 = 150 \\ 7 \times 40 = 280 \end{array} \right.$
	December		$\left\{ \begin{array}{l} 7 \times 40 = 280 \\ 1 \times 30 = 30 \end{array} \right.$	$4 \times 30 = 120$

In LIFO we consider or assume that the newest go out first so that what remain in stock are the earlier delivered items.

AVCO

		In	Out	Balance
	October	$5 \times 30 = 150$		$5 \times 30 = 150$
	November	$7 \times 40 = 280$		$12 \times 35.8* = 430$
	December		$8 \times 35.8 = 287$	$4 \times 35.8 = 143$

* This is calculated by $\dfrac{150 + 280}{5 + 7}$

In average cost we assume or consider that a mixture of old and new go out each time there is a sale or a use of the items.

9. In practice LIFO is rarely used in the UK because it is not an acceptable valuation method for tax purposes and because it is frowned upon in the accountancy profession's statement of standard accounting practice No 9 on stocks and work in progress. It is however used in the USA and other parts of the world.

   FIFO and AVCO are both found extensively in the UK. Note that the assumptions for valuation purposes may not correspond with reality. In some real situations FIFO is always the reality. An obvious example is with perishable foodstuffs.

Stock costs and standard prices

10. A fourth common valuation method for stocks is to use a standard price. This is only used where a system of standard costing is in use and this is described In Information Bank Topic 14. Standard cost cannot be used for financial statement purposes unless it approximates reasonably to actual cost.

 **Key principle summary**

○ Stocks are of various kinds: raw materials, work in progress, finished goods awaiting sale, purchased goods awaiting sale, consumable stores.

○ For financial statement purposes stocks are valued at the lower of cost and net realisable value.

○ Cost is the expenditure incurred on bringing the good or service to its present location and condition.

○ Cost is the cost of purchase + the cost of conversion.

○ Cost of purchase includes import duties, transport and handling costs less trade discounts rebates and subsidies.

○ Cost of conversion includes specifically attributable direct costs + an appropriate proportion of production overheads.

○ Net realisable value is the expected selling price less all further costs to completion and all costs in marketing, selling and distribution of the product or service.

○ Fungible items can be valued on the basis of FIFO, LIFO, AVCO or standard cost.

5 | Manufacturing accounts

1. The measurement of profit in a manufacturing business requires a long financial statement called a 'manufacturing, trading and profit and loss account'. Though long its layout is very logical and the train of thinking usually very clear.

2. A common format is:

a)
b)
c)

Widget Manufacturing Company
Manufacturing, Trading and Profit and Loss account
for the year ending 31 December 19x2

(£'000)

d)	Raw materials		
e)	Opening stock	67	
f)	Purchases	534	
		601	
g)	Less closing stock	74	
h)	Consumed		527
i)	Direct labour		445
j)	Other direct costs		62
k)	Prime costs		1,034
l)	Production overheads		690
m)	Factory inputs in the year		1,724
n)	Opening work in progress		180
			1,904
o)	Less closing work in progress		201
p)	Works cost of finished goods output		1,703
q)	Opening stock of finished goods		299
			2,002
r)	Less closing stock of finished goods		350
s)	Cost of finished goods sold		1,652
t)	Sales		2,311
u)	Gross profit		659
v)	Administration costs	128	
w)	Selling and distribution costs	243	
x)	Financial charges	102	473
y)	Net profit		186

3. Considering this financial statement line by line:

   a) It is customary to identify the enterprise.

   b) It is also customary to identify the financial statement.

   c) And the period covered.

   d) Manufacturing starts with raw materials and so do we.

   e) There was a stock of raw materials (valued at cost of course) at the beginning and

   f) We must add the deliveries of raw materials that arrived during the year.

   g) However not all were used so we take away that part of (f) and perhaps (e) that were still there at the year end. This gives us –

   h) – the raw materials consumed in the year.

   i) Raw materials have to be worked on and so we add the costs of working on them which will include the wages of the workers who work on the raw materials and

   j) Any other costs directly associated with particular products. These may include royalties payable on production, work done on the products by sub-contractors and other outside firms.

   k) This gives us a total of direct costs and is usually termed the prime cost.

   l) Product cost is not just the direct costs but must also include the production overheads. So we add these. They would include rent, rates, insurance, supervisory and management salaries, telephone, repairs, machinery depreciation and numerous other headings of cost.

   m) Total inputs to the cost of products in the factory in the year.

   n) (m) gives us the total cost of inputs in the year but there was also some part-finished products at the beginning of the year which presumably were finished during the year by some of the inputs (d) to (l).

   o) Some of the inputs did not result in finished goods in the year but part finished goods which will be completed in 19x3. The costs included in (d) to (l) attributable to work in progress must be identified. This is actually a considerable task.

   p) Finally we arrive at the total cost of the products completed in the year and actually or metaphorically transferred into the warehouse and ready for sale.

   q) The products made in the year are not the only ones which could be sold. There were also some left over from the year before.

   r) Some of (p) and perhaps (o) were not sold in 19x2 and we take off the costs included in (p) and (o) for them as closing stock. This also is a formidable task in practice.

   s) We finally arrive at the cost of the finished goods which actually left the warehouse. These will have been sold but some may not have been sold but have been scrapped or stolen.

   t) The amount we sold them for.

   u) Gross profit is then the selling price of the goods sold in the year less the production cost of those goods.

   v) There are some non-manufacturing overhead costs and we summarise these over three headings (v), (w) and (x).

   w) These like the administration costs and financial charges could be itemised under sub-headings eg reps' salaries, reps' expenses, advertising, sales office costs etc.

   x) Financial charges could include interest and settlement discounts.

   y) Finally the bottom line which is the net profit.

4. A manufacturing, trading and profit and loss account has three sections which are not usually so labelled. These are:

    ❏ The manufacturing account (d) to (p).

    ❏ The trading account (p) to (u).

    ❏ The profit and loss account (u) to (y).

Conventions

5. The conventions used in preparing manufacturing etc accounts are the same as those used in preparing trading and profit and loss accounts. See Information Bank Topic 1.

    These conventions include:

    i)   The realisation convention. All sales made in the year are included irrespective of the date of payment. This applies also to the purchases of materials.

    ii) The accruals convention. All costs and expenses are included in the period to which they relate irrespective of the date of payment.

    iii) Prudence/conservatism. Stocks are valued at the lower of cost and net realisable value. Suppose the total cost of product X was £100 and was included in line (p).

    It is in stock at the year end and has to be valued. It is damaged and can only be sold for £80 and as this is less than the cost of £100, £80 is included in line (r).

    This means that £20 is included in line (s) but nothing in line (t) (it will be in sales in 19x3 hopefully). Consequently (u) and (y) are £20 less than they would have been. This means that the expected loss is taken this year and not in the year of sale.

    Next year £80 will be in lines (q) and (s) and £80 in line (t) so there is nil in lines (u) and (y).

Stocks and work in progress

6. The value of stocks and work in progress is often very large. As an example consider the 1991 accounts of Triplex Lloyd plc. Stocks and work in progress are valued at £18 million and the profit after tax is only £5.6 million. The effect of differing methods of valuing stocks, or indeed of errors, on profit can easily be seen.

7. The actual method of valuing stocks and work in progress follows the methods outlined in Information Bank Topic 4 and the inclusion of production overheads is in Information Bank Topic 10. The important principle to grasp is that the valuation of stock and work in progress takes out expenditure (eg from lines (h) to (l)) from 19x2 and puts it into lines (e), (n) and (r) of 19x3.

🔑 Key principle summary

○ The profits of a manufacturing enterprise are measured and demonstrated in a financial statement called the manufacturing, trading and profit and loss account.

○ This document is in a logical order:

materials + labour +	production overhead (adjusted for stocks) =	cost of production of finished goods
sales –	cost of finished goods =	gross profit
gross profit –	non-manufacturing overhead =	net profit

○ Stocks and work in progress are valued at total absorption cost which extracts expenditure on identified stocks from year x and charges it to year x +1. Often stock values are many times the annual profit and the inaccuracies of counting and measurement and the variability of costing methods make profit measurement a very inexact art.

6 | Company accounts

1. Accounting for company results is governed by the Companies Act 1985 (as amended in the Companies Act 1989). The Act specifies:
   - The financial statements to be produced
   - The format of the financial statements
   - The minimum information which must be given
   - The accounting principles to be followed
   - The dates by which the financial statements must be laid before the members(= shareholders) of the company in general meeting (at the AGM) and delivered to the Registrar of Companies (where they are filed and can be seen by members of the public)

2. The financial statements which must be produced are:
   - a profit and loss account
   - a balance sheet

   In addition, there must be notes which are attached to, and form part of, the profit and loss account and balance sheet.

   There must also be a directors' report with minimum content and an auditors' report.

   In addition a cash flow statement must be given. This is not a statutory requirement but is required by the quasi statutory Accounting Standards Board.

3. In this book, I shall cover the formats of the required financial statements. But I will not consider the information requirements, the directors report, the auditors' report or the laying and delivering requirements in detail. All these matters could take up an immense volume and the general student does not need to know them.

4. All companies produce an 'annual report and accounts' which is often a glossy product. You are strongly advised to obtain some of these. They are sent to all shareholders and you should have relatives or friends who are shareholders in at least the privatised utilities. They can also be obtained directly from the Secretary of any public company.

The profit and loss account

5. A common format which complies with the Companies Act is:

Stubby Widgets plc
Profit and Loss Account
for the year ending 31 December 19x2

			£'000
d)	Turnover		4,200
e)	Cost of sales		2,300
f)	Gross profit		1,900
g)	Distribution costs	945	
h)	Administration expenses	563	1,508
i)	Operating profit		392
j)	Interest payable		50
k)	Profit on ordinary activities before taxation		342
l)	Taxation		102
m)	Profit on ordinary activities after taxation		240
n)	Extraordinary items		50
o)	Profit of the year		190
p)	Dividends		60
q)	Retained profit for the year		130
r)	Earnings per share	6p	

a) The name of the company must be given (i.e in this case Stubby Widgets plc).

b) The title of the financial statement should be indicated.

c) The period which is normally one year should be stated

d) *Turnover* is the word used in the Act. *Sales* is the same thing but turnover can also be used for total fares in a transport company where 'sales' would be inappropriate. Do not forget that all sales made in the year must be included whether the customer paid in the year or not – the realisation convention.

e) Cost of sales. This idea has been met in Information Bank Topics 1 and 5. However it is usually wider here and will include all costs except those in lines (g), (h) and (j).

f) *Gross profit* is simply the difference between turnover and cost of sales.

g) *Distribution costs* are undefined in the Act but usually include sales salaries and commissions, advertising, warehousing costs of finished goods, travelling and entertaining of reps and customers, carriage of goods to customers including depreciation of vehicles, overhead costs of sales outlets and settlement discount allowed to customers.

h) *Administration costs* are also undefined in the Act but usually include salary costs of administrative personnel (eg in accounting function, directors and general management), overhead costs of administration buildings, professional fees and bad debts.

i) The *operating* profit. You will have realised that the word profit occurs in lines (f), (i), (k), (m), (o) and (q) So that a question such as 'What was the profit?' can only be answered if the question is specified more precisely. Each 'profit' is significant. The operating profit is significant in that the business can be seen as a set of resources (assets) provided by suppliers of capital (both shareholders and lenders) which the directors have to use to make a profit. The operating profit measures the profit they managed to make in the year from using the resources in their charge.

j) Resources are supplied to a company both by the shareholders and by long term lenders. The reward to lenders is *interest* and this line measures the amount payable to lenders for the use of capital in the year.

k) What is left is the profit on *ordinary activities* before taxation. This is the reward to shareholders for the use of their capital but is subject to corporation tax.

l) *Corporation tax* is payable on profit at rates decreed by parliament in the annual Finance Act. The calculation of corporation tax can be very complicated and it is enough to know how much will be payable on the profits shown in line (k).

m) This is the reward for shareholders after tax.

n) Company accounting makes a distinction between profits or losses on ordinary activities and those which are extraordinary. *Extraordinary items* are those which derive from events or transactions that fall outside the ordinary activities of the company and which are therefore expected not to recur frequently or regularly. The idea is to show the profit which can be *compared* reasonably with previous years without having it enhanced or reduced by the one off or the unusual.

Examples of extraordinary items are profits or losses on discontinuance of a business segment, profits or losses on the disposal of fixed assets or the sale of an investment.

Companies have tended to try to include windfall gains in ordinary profits and to treat windfall losses as extraordinary. The whole matter is regulated by the accountancy profession's statement of standard accounting practice number 6 and by the pronouncements of the Accounting Standards Board.

o) This brings together all the profit which is available for shareholders.

p) The shareholders are entitled to all the profits of the company but the custom is to make payments to them which are less than the total profit. The amount paid or payable is called the *dividend*. Directors dislike paying dividends as a dividend means that resources leave the company Dividends are expressed as so many pence per share.

q) The amount of the profit which has been made but not paid out to the shareholders is called the *retained profit* of the year.

r) This statistic is required for all companies which are quoted on the stock exchange. It is obtained by dividing line (m) by the number of shares which have been issued. There can be, as always, complications but we need not consider them.

6. Students often think of the annual profit as a sum of money. It is not. To make this clear, consider:

☐ sales are the sales made in the year irrespective of the date of settlement by the customer

☐ capital expenditure costs money in the year but only the depreciation appears in the Profit and loss Account.

☐ expenses follow the accruals convention so that the correct expense of the year is shown irrespective of the payments made.

The balance sheet

7. Companies can be listed on the stock exchange but most are not. The larger ones are usually listed and their shares are bought and sold by investors. Another feature of the larger companies is that they are usually holding companies with subsidiaries. They are groups like this

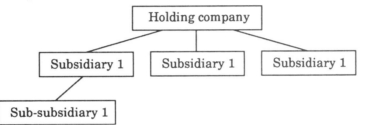

The public hold shares in the holding company and in turn the holding company holds shares in each subsidiary. Sometimes the subsidiary companies own the share in sub-subsidiaries.

Often the holding company holds all (100%) of the shares in its subsidiaries but sometimes it does not own all of the shares and there are outside shareholders called *minorities*.

You are most likely to have access to the published annual reports and accounts of listed companies and most listed companies are groups so that I shall illustrate the balance sheet of a group. In the annual reports you will find four balance sheets. These are:

☐ The current balance sheet of the group

☐ The current balance sheet of the holding company

☐ The previous year end balance sheet of the group

☐ The previous year end balance sheet of the company

The company balance sheets have to be given but are usually of no interest. The important balance sheets are the group ones.

Group balance sheets are drawn up on the assumptions that:

☐ the group is not a set of separate companies

☐ the group is one single company

☐ the group is owned by the shareholders of the holding company

The effect is:

☐ that a group balance sheet shows the assets and liabilities of all the companies as if they were one company.

☐ the capital and reserves sections relates to the holding company as the holding company shareholders in fact own all the group.

8. A typical group balance sheet:

Stubby Widgets plc
Group Balance Sheet as at 31 December 19x2

		£'000
a)	Fixed assets	
b)	Intangible assets	87
c)	Tangible assets	1,648
d)	Investments	44
		1,779
e)	Current assets	
	Stocks	431
	Debtors	590
	Cash at bank and in hand	32
		1,053
f)	Creditors: amounts falling due within one year	
	Creditors	400
g)	Bank overdrafts	228
h)	Taxation and social security	87
i)	Corporation tax	102
j)	Dividends	40
		857
	Net current assets	196
	Total assets less current liabilities	1,975
k)	Creditors: amounts falling due after more than one year	
l)	Bank and other loans	220
m)		1,755
n)	Capital and reserves	
o)	Issued share capital	800
p)	Share premium	100
q)	Revaluation reserve	200
r)	Profit and loss account	652
s)	Shareholders funds	1,752
t)	Minority interests	3
u)	Total capital employed	1,755

9. The balance sheet is similar to the one you have already met in Information Bank Topic 2 but there are some special company things:

    a) Fixed assets are usually divided into the three categories b. to d.

    b) *Intangible assets* are those like goodwill, patents and trade marks which have value but no physical substance. They appear in balance sheets at cost or less so they only appear if the goodwill etc was *purchased*. Non-appearance of intangible assets does not mean the company has none but that none has been purchased or any purchased goodwill etc has been written off.

    c) *Tangible* fixed assets are the physical ones like buildings, plant and machinery and vehicles. The detail is always given in notes to the accounts.

    d) Groups may also own shares in other companies where the holding is less than 50% and these are included using somewhat complex valuations.

    e) These are as explained in Information Bank Topic 2. There may be other headings and prepayments are normally included with debtors.

f) There are more sub-headings for this line than in Information Bank Topic 2. I have shown 5. You may meet others.

g) Many groups have both overdrafts and cash at bank. This may seem strange but each separate company may have either and in the group balance sheet they are not normally netted off.

h) This is required to be shown separately and shows the amount due but unpaid at the balance sheet date of VAT, PAYE Income Tax and National Insurance.

i) This is usually the corporation tax payable on the profits of the year and you will see that it is the same amount as in the profit and loss account. It is payable on 1 October 19x3.

j) The dividends in the profit and loss account are £60,000 divided into:

- an *interim* dividend paid on 30 September 19x2   £20,000
- a *final* dividend to be paid in May 19x3   £40,000

Companies usually make two dividend payments. One is after publication of the abbreviated unaudited results of the first half year and a final one when the full year results are published and the AGM has been held.

k) Most groups have long term liabilities. They are often called 'borrowings' or sometimes simply 'debt'.

l) Details are given in notes. Loans can be termed simply loans but may also be termed stock, notes, debentures, lease obligations, etc. The interest rates payable and the dates for repayment (repayment may be called *redemption*) are given for each loan. The total amounts owing may be surprisingly large.

m) This line concludes the list of assets and liabilities. Most students find the balance sheet up to now reasonably understandable although the valuation methods (based on cost) may be unexpected. The difficulty lies in lines (n) to (u).

n) The next section explains where the resources came from to enable the Group to buy the assets less liabilities. If X is a rich man, it may be reasonable to say how did he get to be rich. The answer may be:

- he was left a fortune by his aunt
- he has, over his life, spent less than his income
- his investments have increased in value since he bought them.

The company 'Capital and Reserves' section explains a Group's wealth in a similar way. It is very important to realise that the word '*Reserves*' is a technical one and its meaning bears no resemblance at all to the normal meanings given to it.

o) Companies obtain their initial resources from the people and institutions who become the shareholders. Each shareholder *subscribes* for so many shares. Each share is given a *nominal* or *par* value which has no real meaning at all. In the case of Stubby Widgets plc each share has a par value of 20p so that the total number of shares is 20p × £800,000 = 4,000,000. You may now work out that the earnings per share given in the profit and loss account are $\frac{£240,000}{4,000,000}$ = 6p. You could also work out that the dividends per share are:

$$\text{interim} \quad \frac{£20,000}{4,000,000} = \quad 0.5p$$

$$\text{final} \quad \frac{£40,000}{4,000,000} = \quad 1p$$

p) All the share capital may not have been subscribed at the formation of the company. The shareholders may have subscribed for shares later in the life of the company when they may have paid more than the par value for each share. The excess of amount paid over the par value is called the *share premium*. So the total amount of resources provided to the company by the shareholders is the share capital + the share premium.

q) The fixed assets may include land and buildings. These usually increase in value due to inflation and other causes. However accounting practice requires the land to be valued at original cost and the buildings at cost less depreciation. The effect of this is that a major asset of the company is valued at what may be a small fraction of its 'real' value. It is felt that this may mislead readers of the accounts even if an up to date valuation is included in the notes to the accounts. A way out of the problem is to commission a professional *revaluation* of the land and buildings and substitute this for the historical cost less depreciation. Note that in later years depreciation will continue to be applied to the buildings but at a higher rate as it will be based on the new valuation.

The balance sheet is based on an equation:

Assets less liabilities = capital and reserves.

In effect this means that the assets and liabilities are stated and the capital and reserves explains the sources of finance for their acquisition.

By unilaterally increasing the carrying value of land and buildings the equation is unbalanced. To restore the balance and to show the source of the increase in assets less liabilities, a line is included described as *revaluation reserve*.

r) Profit and loss account is the amount of profit after tax made since the company started less all dividends. Profit is a measure of the increase in assets less liabilities as a result of trading. Every year in which a profit is made there is an increase in the assets less liabilities. The profit and loss account figure on the balance sheet measures the total effect of such profits since the company began. It is sometimes called the *accumulated profit*.

Just as profit increases assets less liabilities so dividends decrease them and the accumulated figure shows the effect of profits less dividends.

s) Shareholders put funds into the company (the share capital and share premium) and the funds then grow and profit is the measure of growth. All growth represented by retained profits and revaluations belongs to the shareholders. So this figure represents the shareholders stake in the net assets of the company.

t) If one or more of the subsidiaries companies have minority shareholders then there will be *minority interests* shown here. The assets less liabilities of these subsidiaries are included in the group balance sheet in full so it is necessary to show the portion of them which in effect belongs to the minorities.

u) This concludes the explanation of the sources of finance for the assets and liabilities of the group. It can also be seen as an explanation of who owns the assets less liabilities of the group.

Shares – par and other values

10. The capital and reserves section of a balance sheet seems to have been designed to mislead and mystify everybody except accountants. We will try to unravel its meanings by considering a series of values – par or nominal values, net asset values and quoted values.

Firstly remember that the balance sheet must balance and so the total of capital and reserves must equal the total of assets less liabilities. Thus any change in assets and liabilities must lead to a change in capital and reserves.

When a company is formed it has no assets or liabilities, capital or reserves.

To acquire assets, the company issue shares to persons who become its shareholders. Supposing the first sale of shares is of 10,000 shares of £1 each then the first balance sheet will show:

Assets:	£
Cash	10,000
Capital and reserves:	
Share capital	10,000

ısh will be spent on fixed assets etc and rapidly will be replaced by a complex mixture of
and liabilities.

ach share is a £1 share and £1 is known as the par or nominal value. The shares could have been
issued at any par price. If par had been 50p then, to raise £10,000, 20,000 shares would have been
issued.

After a period of trading at a profit, a Balance Sheet can be drawn up as:

	£
Net assets:	24,300
Capital and reserves:	
Share capital	10,000
Profit and loss account	14,300
	24,300

To explain this:

a)   The original £10,000 cash has become a complex mixture of assets and liabilities valued at
£24,300.

b)   The capital and reserves explain where the resources to acquire the net assets came from.

c)   £10,000 came from the shareholders originally

d)   The remainder (£14,300) came from profitable trading.

The nominal or par value of each share is still £1. However as the company now has net assets of
£24,300 and is divided into 10,000 shares, each share is represented by net assets of £2.43. We can
say the net asset value of each share is £2.43.

If a shareholder wished to sell one of his shares to another person, the price would be decided by
negotiation between the parties. Suppose this was £3.60 then the value of the share is clearly
£3.60. If the company is quoted (another word is listed) on the Stock Exchange then this price
varies continuously and potential buyers and sellers can know the current price by consulting a
broker or the newspapers.

Thus the par value means very little in reality. The net asset value is useful knowledge (although
assets like goodwill may be omitted and accounting values are strange). The really useful value is
not given by the financial statements and that is the real value of the share.

Later in its life the company may issue more shares. Probably this will not be at the par value.
Suppose our company sold a further 5,000 £1 shares at £3 each. The par value remains at £1 but
the market allows the company to sell them for £3 and will receive £15,000 from the new
shareholders.

The balance sheet will show (presume the new shares were sold immediately after the last balance
sheet):

	£
Net assets:	39,300
Capital and reserves:	
Share capital	15,000
Share premium	10,000
Profit and loss account	14,300
	39,300

To explain this:

a)   The net assets have gone up by the extra money (£15,000) subscribed by the new
shareholders.

b)   The share capital has gone up by the 5,000 shares at par value.

c) The Share Premium is the difference between the cash obtained from the issue and the par value.

When you see a Capital and Reserves section of a Balance Sheet with Share Premium you know that at some time in its history, the company sold shares at a price above par.

Remember that the Capital and Reserves section shows where the resources came from to provide the net assets.

Bonus, rights and other issues

11. Many companies make bonus issues. These can be called scrip issues, capitalisation issues and in jest, bogus issues.

Suppose Q PLC has a balance sheet as:

	£
Net assets:	1,650,000
Capital and reserves:	
Share capital in 20p shares	500,000
Profit and loss account	1,150,000
	1,650,000

The directors wish to please the shareholders but do not wish actually pay money to them in the form of dividends. They can make a bonus issue of new free shares to the shareholders. This might be say a one for two issue, in which case Martin who has 100 shares will receive 50 new shares. The effect on the Balance Sheet will be:

	£
Net assets:	1,650,000
Capital and reserves:	
Share capital	750,000
Profit and loss account	900,000
	1,650,000

Note:

a) The net assets remain the same.

b) An issue of one new share for each two held will increase the share capital by 50%.

c) As net assets remain the same, so must capital and reserves and to keep capital and reserves in balance, profit and loss account must be reduced by £250,000.

d) Before the issue each share was quoted at 90p and as the company was divided into 2,500,000 $\left(\frac{500,000}{20p}\right)$ shares the company was worth £2,250,000. After the issue the company is still worth £2,250,000 but is now divided into 3,750,000 shares. Thus the quotation will go down to approximately 60p.

e) This seems a pointless exercise but shareholders will be pleased at receiving (apparently) something for nothing and the Market sees a bonus issue as a signal of confidence from the directors.

The company may also make a rights issue. This is a real issue of shares for cash. New shares are offered to existing shareholders in proportion to their holdings. They are not obliged to take up the offer and instead may sell their rights to other investors.

Suppose Q PLC make a rights issue of one new share for every three held at 50p each then 1,250,000 new shares will be sold and net the company £625,000.

The new Balance Sheet will look like this:

	£
Net assets:	2,275,000
Capital and reserves:	
Share capital	1,000,000
Share premium	375,000
Profit and loss account	900,000
	2,275,000

Note:

a) The net assets will rise because money has flowed into the company.

b) The share capital has risen as more shares have been issued

c) The new shares have a par value of 20p and were issued at 50p so the share premium is 1,250,000 × 30p = £375,000.

d) The company was worth £2,250,000 before the issue. In theory it will be worth £2,250,000 + £625,000 = £2,875,000 after the issue. It is now divided into 5,000,000 shares so each share may be quoted at £57.50p.

A form of bonus issue is the common practice of offering shareholders new shares instead of dividends. This saves the company paying out cash and is therefore popular with directors.

Q PLC determine to pay a dividend of 2p a share but offer instead one new share for every 30 held. Holders of 1,200,000 shares accept the shares and the remainder opt for the dividend. The Balance Sheet will now look like this:

Net assets:	2,199,000
Capital and reserves:	
Share capital	1,008,000
Share premium	391,000
Profit and loss account	800,000
	2,199,000

Note:

a) Net assets have gone down by £76,000. This is the payment of the dividend – (5,000,000 – 1,200,000) × 2p = £76,000

b) The share capital has risen by the issue of new shares – $\frac{1,200,000}{30} \times 20p = £8,000$

c) The share premium on the issue of 40,000 new shares, issued effectively at 60p, is 40,000 × (60p – 20p) = £16,000. The issue price is effectively 60p because the dividend foregone by the holder of 30 shares is 30 × 2p = 60p.

d) The dividend, whether in cash or shares reduces the Profit and Loss Account by 5,000,000 × 2p = £100,000.

Auditing

12. The annual report and accounts of a company is an important document and it is important that it should at the very least:

☐ give a true representation of facts

☐ fairly present information where judgement is required or choices are possible (eg on the lives of fixed assets and the depreciation policy)

☐ disclose all facts relevant to a shareholder

☐ comply with the Companies Act 1985 requirements.

Directors may have a vested interest in producing misleading or incorrect information or in suppressing information. They may perhaps wish to show a small profit when a small loss has been incurred!

To ensure that accounts can be relied upon, the Act requires that every company shall have an auditor who must give an opinion on the accounts. Auditors are qualified accountants who have been trained and licensed by their professional body to do this kind of work. Auditing is a very complex business and the relationship between the company, the shareholders and the auditors is a delicate one. Suffice it to say that you can rely on annual accounts in general despite some well publicised cases where the accounts proved unreliable after a scandal was revealed.

 **Key principle summary**

O   Registered companies are required to produce an annual report and accounts. This contains:

a profit and loss account;

a balance sheet;

a cash flow statement;

a directors' report;

an auditors' report;

notes giving details expanding the accounts;

a chairman's statement;

notice of the AGM;

other statements and information.

O   The Companies Act 1985 (amended 1989) specifies much of the detail required and also the format and accounting principles to use.

O   The profit and loss account is of the group if the company has subsidiaries.

O   The balance sheet is of the company also a balance sheet of the group is included.

O   The balance sheet lists the assets and liabilities with values. It also shows the sources of finance of the assets less liabilities in the capital and reserves section. This section can also be interpreted as showing the ownership of the assets less liabilities. Remember that reserves is a technical term which does not have its common meaning in this context.

O   Companies may issue new shares free to shareholders by a bonus issue.

O   Companies may raise cash by a rights issue to existing shareholders.

O   Companies may offer new shares in lieu of dividends.

O   Company accounts can usually be relied on as they are audited.

7 | Accounting conventions

1. The measurement of profit in the profit and loss account and the measurement of capital employed in the balance sheet has developed over the last century and a half in a largely pragmatic way. Only in the last few decades has development been regulated or planned.

2. Accounting was taught until at least the 1960s in a totally prescriptive way. Students were told that this or that was the way to do it. This approach meant that when new business developments required new developments in accounting no body of theory was available to assist accountants.

3. The body of theory was developed by academic accountants observing the way profit and capital measurement was carried out in practice and trying to deduce any common rules which were normally followed. This led to the discovery that there were a number of conventions that were normally adhered to.

4. In the 1970s in the UK (and much earlier in the USA) accounting development became more regulated by the formation by the professional accounting bodies of the accounting standards committee which produced a series of Statements of Standard Accounting Practice (SSAPs). This committee was replaced in 1990 by an independent body with statutory backing – the Accounting Standards Board. This Board has accepted the existing SSAPs and at the time of writing had issued the first of its pronouncements – Financial Reporting Standard(FRS) 1 on Cash Flow Statements.

5. In addition statutory recognition was given to accounting conventions in the Companies Act 1981 and to SSAPs in the Companies Act 1989. Also the Companies Act 1981 introduced mandatory formats for company financial statements which implicitly recognised the conventions and contemporary practice in accounting measurement.

6. An actual list of accounting conventions with definitions has not yet emerged and writers tend to disagree on the detail. You may read a slightly different list in other texts but the fundamentals do now seem to have achieved general acceptance.

7. Some of the conventions may seem strange and perhaps would not be adopted if accounting had to start again on a green field site. Many can be explained by historical circumstances. The driving force was often the conventions of double entry bookkeeping which was developed in renaissance Italy.

8. I have listed each convention together with a justification and a note of the consequences of adopting it.

The accounting conventions

Business entity

The business is seen as an entity separate from its owner(s) or proprietor(s).

The justification for this convention is that the proprietor and other interested parties (eg lenders, taxman etc) are concerned to know the profit earned by and the capital employed in the business or each business if the proprietor has more than one. Essentially the focus is on the business and not on the owner.

The drawbacks of this convention are:

☐ It is artificial – the assets and liabilities of the business are in law those of the proprietor not of some artificial entity 'the business'.

☐ The accounts of sole traders and partnerships do not make clear to creditors what actual assets are available to meet their claims or what other liabilities may have to be met from the assets. This is because in law it is the proprietor who owns the assets and owes the liabilities.

The consequences of the convention are:

☐ assets and liabilities are arbitrarily included in the balance sheet on a subjective view of what is the business. Some assets (eg motor cars) are both business and private.

❏ the capital of the business is seen as a liability of the business to the owner and drawings are seen as a reduction of this liability and profit as an increase in it.

Companies are actual legal entities and accounting is done for each company as a unit. However two problems have emerged.

❏ a company may really be several separate businesses or 'business segments' and investors and others really want to know the performance of each segment as well as the company as a whole.

❏ large companies are usually composed of a holding company with subsidiary and associated companies collectively known as the 'Group'. Each company is a separate legal entity but reporting is normally done for the group as a whole.

Money measurement

Transactions are recorded in money terms and financial statements are drawn up with assets, liabilities, revenues and expenses expressed in money terms.

The justification for this may seem obvious and in fact the objective is to report results using a common unit of measurement – money.

The drawbacks of this convention are:

❏ transactions and events that are not expressed in money terms tend to be ignored. For example relevant facts about a business such as the quantity of orders on hand, the quality of management, the existence of satisfied customers or even the existence of profitable contracts such as franchises are not included in financial statements. However the consequences of having these non-monetary assets will be result in higher profits.

❏ accounts are drawn up with the assumption that there is no inflation (or deflation). This clearly distorts results and attempts have been made to develop alternative accounting measurements which reflect the changing value of money but they have not really met general acceptance.

Historical cost convention

Assets and expenses are included at their actual cost to the business.

The justification for this critical convention is that historical cost is objective and verifiable. Any alternative convention (eg showing assets at realisable value) would be highly subjective and lead to a wide variation in measurement.

The consequences of the convention include:

❏ assets are valued at cost or cost derived figures (eg fixed assets are shown at cost less depreciation)

❏ items which had no cost are ignored

❏ unrealised gains are ignored.

The drawbacks of the convention are:

❏ the actual information required by managers, investors and others may be the current values of assets and values based on historical costs may be irrelevant for their purposes.

❏ in inflationary times profit is measured as sales at current prices matched against expenses which will include depreciation based on the original costs of the fixed assets.

Some fixed assets, particularly land and buildings, are sometimes revalued to market or resale values. So the fixed assets of a company may include some assets valued at recent prices and some by reference to historical cost. If buildings are valued upwards, depreciation continues to be applied but based on the revalued figures.

Realisation convention

The profit on any given transaction is included in the accounts of a period when the profit is realised. Realisation means when a transaction has occurred which gives legal rights to the receipt of money. What this means is that profit is counted on the sale of a good and not on payment. So if goods are sold on 12 December 19x2 the profit is earned in the year to 31 December 19x2 even though the goods were not paid for until 19 January 19x3.

The justification for this convention include:

❏ the critical event principle. The hard part of business is to make a sale and collecting the cash afterwards is relatively easy (credit controllers might disagree!). Thus the profit should be considered to be earned when the hard bit has been concluded.

❏ the certainty principle. At the point of a sale it is known that a profit has been made and precisely how much it is.

❏ the asset transfer principle. On the sale the goods cease to be the property of the trader and become the property of his customer. The trader ceases to own the goods and instead has a debt due to him.

Among the consequences of this convention is that unrealised holding gains are ignored. A profit is not recognised until a sale is made.

Two problems occur with this convention:

i) Goods are often sold subject to reservation of title which means that ownership of the goods does not in law pass until payment has been made. A reservation of title clause in a contract is often known as a Romalpa clause after the case which established its legal validity. In profit measurement the reservation of title is ignored and the realisation convention is followed.

ii) In civil engineering, shipbuilding and other long term contracting the precise point of a sale of a product is not really determinable and usually profit is deemed to be earned over the course of the contract. The realisation convention is thus ignored in such cases.

Accruals

This is somewhat similar to the realisation convention. Revenues and costs are recognised and included in the profit and loss account as they are accrued (= earned or incurred) not as they are paid or received.

The justification of this convention is that receipts and payments are to a degree random as to timing, whereas the earning of a revenue (eg a rent) or the consumption of a resource (eg electricity) can be accurately related to specific time periods.

The drawbacks to this convention include:

❏ the work required to apportion expenses to time periods.

❏ financial statements become more complex (than say cash flow accounting) with a consequent loss of intelligibility to the layman.

❏ balance sheets have to include prepayments and accruals. These are words that are not readily understood by the untutored in accounting.

Conservatism or prudence

This can be seen as having two aspects – income and costs:

i) revenue and profits are not anticipated but are recognised in the profit and loss when realised in the form of cash or other assets (eg a debt).

ii) Provision is made for all known liabilities (expenses and losses) whether an amount is known with certainty or is a best estimate in the light of information available. Provision means including in the profit and loss account.

Two examples

a) Gribble who tarmacs drives is preparing his accounts for the year ending 31 December 19x2. He is reviewing two contracts for resurfacing of drives for which he has signed contracts and which he will carry out in January 19x3. Contract A is expected to make a profit and in consequence of (i) above he ignores it for the purposes of 31 December 19x2 profits. The profit will fall in to the 19x3 accounts. Contract B was a mistake and he expects to lose approximately £500 on it. In consequence of (ii) above he will provide for the £500 in the 19x2 accounts. This means that there will be an expense in the 19x2 profit and loss account – *provision* for loss on Contract B.

b) Howe has two widgets in his stock at 31 December 19x2, his year end. Widget A cost him £100 and it is expected to sell in 19x3 for £150. In consequence of (i) above it will be valued in his accounts at cost £100 and any profit on its sale will fall in the year of sale – 19x3. Widget B cost him £100 also but it is obsolete and will probably be sold in 19x3 for £80 less 10% sales commission. As a consequence of (ii) widget B will be valued at its net realisable value of £72 and the expected loss of £28 will fall into the 19x2 accounts.

This convention is often seen as unnecessarily cautious.

Going concern

The going concern convention assumes that the enterprise will continue in operational existence for the foreseeable future. The balance sheet and profit and loss account are drawn up on the assumption that there is no intention or necessity to liquidate or curtail significantly the scale of operations.

The justification for this convention is that it is usually simply true. Most enterprises will continue to exist in the future.

The consequences of the convention can be seen with two examples.

Two examples

a) Magnolia Ltd has specialised plant and machinery in its balance sheet valued at Cost £25,000 less depreciation £8,500 net book value £16,500. The company is a going concern and is expected to trade for many years and use its plant well in to the future. The future plant depreciation will be included in future profit and loss accounts. If however the company were not a going concern and liquidation were expected shortly then the plant would need to be valued at its realisation value, that is what it can be sold for viz about £1,000 only.

b) Geranium Ltd have a branch in Bilston with 6 long serving employees. They are considering closing the branch down and making the employees redundant. If the branch is to be closed down it cannot be regarded as a going concern and redundancy pay will have to be included in liabilities. If it is not to be closed down it is a going concern and potential redundancy pay can be ignored.

Matching convention

The matching convention requires that in an accounting period, costs are matched with related income. Where costs have been incurred and there is no related income in the period or in future periods, with which the costs can be matched, they are treated as an expense of the accounting period.

Two examples

a) Penn writes a book in 19x2 and incurred research costs of £5,000 related to the book and £2,200 related to a book he decided not to write. He has the book typeset in 19x2 at a cost of £3,000 and has 5,000 copies printed at a cost of £5 each. He sells 1,000 copies in 19x2 at £11 each. What is his profit in 19x2?

Revenue is clearly 1,000 × £11 = 11,000.

Costs to be matched against it are:

- printing costs 1,000 × £5 = £5,000

- research costs: $\frac{1,000}{5,000}$ × £5,000 = £1,000.

- typesetting costs $\frac{1,000}{5,000}$ × £3,000 = £600

Some of the remaining costs can be matched against future revenue in future years. These are the remainder of the associated research costs (£5,000 – £1,000) and typesetting costs (£3,000 – £600). In the meantime they will be included on the balance sheet as an asset together with the stock of books (valued at cost £5 each). This assumes that the remaining stock will all be sold.

The unrelated research costs cannot be matched against revenues in this or any future year so they are treated as an expense of 19x2.

The profit will thus be:

$$£11,000 - (£5,000 + £1,000 + £600 + £2,200) = £2,200.$$

b) Strikneen Ltd are manufacturers of pharmaceuticals. In 19x2 they spent £1 million on research and development of Koorall which is a cure for the common cold. Testing and licensing will take until 19x6 when the drug will be begin to be sold with enormous profits. Is the £1 million an expense of 19x2 or should it be regarded as an asset and carried forward on successive balance sheets until 19x6 when it can be matched against the revenues earned in that and subsequent years? The answer accountants would give is that the answer depends on a reading of SSAP 13 (Research and development) and the certainty or otherwise of successful sales of Koorall.

Consistency

This convention requires that there is consistency of accounting treatment of like items within each accounting period and from one accounting period to the next.

For example if the straight line method of depreciation is used for vehicles by XY plc it must be used for all the company's vehicles and for all periods. It is possible to change but the fact of the change and its financial effect must be made clear.

Materiality

Accounting is concerned with the measurement of profit and capital and the presentation of the results to interested parties. In essence it is a summarising process. Too much detail in the annual accounts and the view is obscured. Insignificant items are merged with others and are not shown separately. An item is considered material if its non disclosure as a separate item would give a different view of the accounts as a whole than if it were disclosed.

Example

Marigold Ltd always incur bad debts but these are usually relatively small and the total amount is not shown separately but is included in the total of administrative costs. In 19x2 the company incurred a very large bad debt with the collapse of a customer Aster Ltd. Accounts were prepared with the bad debt included in administrative costs which were consequently much larger than in previous years and the profit was consequently much lower. Unless the bad debt is shown separately readers of the accounts may assume that the company has allowed administrative costs to get out of hand. In this year bad debts are considered material to the view given by the accounts and must be shown as a separate item.

Periodicity convention

This is simply the convention which says that profits and capital should be measured regularly for distinct periods of time. The usual time interval is one year but many companies produce accounts on a monthly, quarterly or half yearly basis.

Substance over form

Some transactions have a legal form which is different from their underlying commercial reality or substance.

The convention is to account for the substance rather than the legal form.

Two examples

a) Hire purchase transactions. The legal form is that the subject matter (eg a car) is on hire from the finance company and ownership only passes on the final instalment being paid. The substance is that the buyer acquires the car with the aid of a loan and this is how it is accounted for.

b) Some equipment or vehicles are leased from finance companies. Some leases are genuine rentals but some leases are arranged so that in effect the lessee buys the property with the aid of a 100% loan and the lease payments are in the nature of repayments with interest of that loan. Such leases are termed finance leases and are accounted for as purchase with loan.

⊙⟞═⟩ Key principle summary

○ The accounting conventions were deduced by academic accountants from observations of what accountants actually do.

○ They now have recognition from the Accounting Standards Board and from the Companies Act.

○ The conventions are:

Business entity –	the business is seen as separate from its owner;
Money measurement –	transactions and financial statements are drawn up in money terms;
Historical cost –	assets and expenses are entered into the records at their cost to the business;
Realisation –	profit is deemed to be earned at the point of sale not the point of payment;
Accruals –	revenues and costs are recognised and included in financial statements as they are earned or incurred not as they are received or paid;
Conservatism or prudence –	provision is made in current financial statements for all known liabilities or losses (present or future) but gains and profits are included only when they have been realised;
Going concern –	it is assumed that the enterprise will continue in operational existence into the foreseeable future;
Matching –	costs are matched with related income in each successive accounting period. But costs which cannot be related to income are included in the accounting period in which they are incurred;
Consistency –	consistency of accounting treatment between like items within accounting periods and from period to period;
Materiality –	financial statements should disclose separately items which are significant enough to affect evaluation or decisions;
Periodicity –	accounts are prepared at regular intervals;
Substance over form –	the commercial substance of a transaction is preferred to its legal form.

Accounting conventions and financial statements

Entity ———————→ **Nasturtium Ltd**

Periodicity ———————→ **Trading and Profit and Loss Account**
for the year ending 31 December 19x2

		£ ← Money
Realisation → Sales		400,000
Matching → Less: Cost of goods sold		250,000
Gross profit		150,000
Wages	61,000	
Accruals → Rent and rates	13,500	
Sundry overheads	31,900	
Provision for loss on future contracts	4,700	← Prudence
Materiality → Uninsured loss of stock by fire	6,800	
Cost → Depreciation	6,910	124,810
Net profit		25,190

Balance sheet as at 31 December 19x2

Cost → Fixed assets at cost		52,500
less Depreciation		21,000
		31,500 ←
Current assets		
Prudence → Stock	28,000	
Accruals → Debtors	61,000	Going concern
Prepayments	1,900	
	90,900	
Creditors: amount falling due		
within one year		
Creditors	38,000	←
Overdraft	26,480	
	64,480	
Net current assets		26,420
Total assets less current liabilities		57,920
Creditors: amounts falling due		10,000
after more than one year		
		47,920
Capital and reserves		
Called up share capital		2,000
Share premium account		6,000
Profit and Loss Account		39,920
		47,920

8 | Ratio analysis

1. Financial statements – profit and loss accounts and balance sheets- are designed to present *historical information* in a stylised form to *owners* primarily but to other interested parties secondarily. They are not designed to enable detailed analysis of the performance of the business or for a ratio analysis to be carried out on them.

2. In the light of the warning in paragraph 1, extreme care must be applied in using financial statements for analysing company performance and in doing ratio analysis. The probability of coming to the wrong conclusion is very high. At best, ratio analysis enables the analyst to determine areas where awkward questions can be asked or further information sought.

3. Ratio analysis has the following components:

   a) *Trends* – a gross profit ratio that is below industry average but is getting better may be more hopeful than a ratio that is above average but getting worse.

   b) *Similar companies* – clearly it is helpful to compare a company with other similar companies. However caution has to be taken as no two companies are exactly alike or use the same accounting policies.

   c) *Industry averages* – if these are available from inter firm comparisons or other sources

   d) Comparisons with *budgets* – a company may have intended ratios and a comparison with actual gives the actual outturn some objective standard for comparison.

4. Ratios are usually extracted for two purposes:

   a) To assess the *performance* of the management

   b) To assess *liquidity*. This has three sub-purposes:

      i) to determine how long a company will take to pay a supplier who is considering selling goods or services to the company on credit

      ii) to determine if the company will remain as a *going concern* or go into receivership or liquidation.

      iii) to assess the ability of the company to repay a loan

5. The persons or institutions who might apply ratio analysis to a company may include *actual* or *potential*:

   ❐ management

   ❐ owners / shareholders

   ❐ lenders

   ❐ customers

   ❐ suppliers

   ❐ employees

   ❐ competitors

   and also

   ❐ companies contemplating takeovers

   ❐ government agencies including the taxman and those concerning the control and regulation of business

   ❐ the public especially those who belong to pressure groups.

   Their purposes in doing an analysis will of course differ and the particular ratios they use will also differ.

6. Despite my opening paragraphs we will attempt to analyse the performance of Stubby Computers Ltd. The company operate a shop, retailing computer hardware and software from a high street

site. They belong to an interfirm comparison scheme whereby many firms in the same industry send in their accounts and mean ratios are extracted which enables all participants in the scheme to compare their performance with the average for the industry.

Stubby Computers Ltd
Trading and profit and loss account
For the years ending 31 December:

	19x2	19x3
	£'000	£'000
Sales	980	1,170
Cost of goods sold	600	750
Gross profit	380	420
Occupancy costs	25	34
Employee costs	110	111
Advertising	30	40
Administrative costs	31	34
Directors salaries	40	45
Depreciation	30	30
	266	294
Net profit before interest	114	126
	30	35
Net profit after interest	84	91
Corporation tax	23	28
Net profit after tax	61	63
Dividends	30	35
Retained profit for the year	31	28

Balance sheet as at 31 December

	19x2	19x3
Premises	200	188
Equipment and shop fittings	80	92
Vehicles	50	40
	330	320
Current assets		
Stocks	85	120
Debtors	90	87
	175	207
Creditors: amounts falling due within one year		
Creditors	70	90
Overdraft	20	32
Corporation tax	23	28
VAT and PAYE	18	20
Dividend	30	35
	161	205
Net current assets	14	2
Total assets less current liabilities	344	322
Creditors: amounts falling due after more than one year		
15% Bank loan	150	100
	194	222

Capital and reserves		
Called up share capital (20p shares)	100	100
Profit and loss account	94	122
	194	222

The mean ratios supplied by the interfirm comparison are:

Gross profit ratio	35%
Net profit to sales	10%
Overheads to sales	25%
Asset utilisation ratio	2.8 times
Annual sales growth	11%
Occupancy costs to sales	6%
Employee costs to sales	8%
Advertising costs to sales	3%
Return on capital employed	25%
Return on shareholders funds	32%
Dividend cover	1.9
Gearing ratio	40%
Stock turnover	65 days
Debtors average payment time	70 days
Creditors average payment time	60 days
Current ratio	1.6
Acid test ratio	1.1
Operating cycle	75 days

7. Before calculating any ratios we should extract as much *information* from the accounts as we can *without* ratios. The following points may be made:

   a) The company own its own premises and therefore, presumably, no rent is payable.

   b) The property is being depreciated and has not been revalued. Therefore the market value is not known.

   c) Equipment increased during the year despite depreciation. The company is investing in improved facilities.

   d) Vehicles declined in the year presumably as a result of depreciation. There was no investment in new vehicles including presumably directors' cars.

   e) The company have borrowed at some time in the past from the bank on a fixed interest loan. This was probably in order to buy the premises. £50,000 has been repaid in the year. The remaining £100,000 is in creditors falling due after more than one year so is not payable until at least 19x4.

Ratio analysis

8. **Gross profit ratio**

   This is $\frac{\text{gross profit}}{\text{sales}} \times 100$, so for 19x2 the ratio is

   $$\frac{380}{980} \times 100 = 39\% \text{ and for 19x3 36\%.}$$

   This is a key ratio and shows the relationship between the input prices paid by the company and prices obtained from customers. 39% means that on average every £1 of sales, the product sold cost 61p giving 39p to pay overheads and give a profit. The reduction from 19x2 to 19x3 may be due to:

   ❑ failure to pass on higher prices from suppliers

   ❑ a change in sales mix to lower margin products

   ❑ competitive pricing to combat competition or to get sales

☐   a change in the type of customer

The ratio achieved by the company is better than the industry average.

Net profit to sales

This ratio shows the extent to which sales have resulted in a profit.

In this case the ratio for 19x2 is $\frac{114}{980} \times 100 = 11.6\%$

and for 19x3 10.8%. A drop of 3% in the gross profit ratio would usually lead to a drop of 3% in the net profit ratio. In this case the drop is only 0.8% so the company have actually done well despite the 0.8% drop. They also have a better return than the industry average.

Overheads to sales ratio

The ratio for 19x2 is $\frac{266}{980} \times 100 = 27\%$ and for 19x3 25%. The improvement in this ratio has enabled the net profit to sales ratio to fall only 0.8 % despite the fall of 3% in gross profit ratio. Probably the overheads were too high in 19x2 as the ratio has now come down to the industry average.

Asset utilisation ratio

This shows to what extent the assets used in the business have generated sales.

It is calculated as:

$$\frac{\text{sales}}{\text{operating assets}}$$

Operating assets are usually defined as total assets less current liabilities. We will take the figures at the year ends.

So for 19x2 the ratio is:

$$\frac{980}{344} = 2.8 \text{ and for 19x3 3.6.}$$

This is a big improvement. We could say that the business managed to generate a substantial sales increase with an actual reduction in net operating assets. It is also better than the industry average

Annual sales growth

Sales growth for 19x3 is 1,170 − 980 = 190 (in £'000) so sales growth as a percentage is $\frac{190}{980} \times 100 = 19\%$.

Sales growth has to be compared with inflation which was running at 8% in 19x3 so that there has been an increase of 11% in real terms compared with an industry growth of 11% in money terms and 3% in real terms. Prices of computer products actually fell in 19x3 so that the growth in volume is actually greater than 11%.

However the sales growth was accompanied by a reduction of gross profit ratio, so a possible hypothesis is that sales were obtained by price reductions.

Occupancy costs to sales.

Occupancy costs include rent, rates, heat and light, repairs to premises, fire insurance etc.

The ratio for 19x2 is $\frac{25}{980} \times 100 = 2.5\%$ and for 19x3 2.9%. The ratio has worsened but cannot be compared with the industry average as the industry average probably includes rent and our company owns its own property. Be warned against comparing unlike figures.

An alternative ratio for this industry might be sales per square foot but we have no data on this.

Employee costs to sales

This ratio tells us how effective the staff are.

In this case the ratio for 19x2 is $\frac{110}{980} \times 100 = 11\%$ and for 19x3 9.5%.

despite inflation of 8% and presumably corresponding pay increases the company have held their wage bill constant so that we can presume staffing levels have actually reduced. Hence the reduction in this ratio. It is however still well above the industry average and further action to reduce staff seems possible.

An alternative ratio might be sales per employee but we have no data on the number of employees.

Advertising costs to sales

This ratio for 19x2 is $\frac{30}{980} \times 100 = 3\%$ and 3.4%. The appropriate amount of advertising is clearly difficult to determine but in this case is about the industry average. It has increased in 19x3 and sales have increase but any connection must be speculative.

Return on capital employed

This is often seen as the key success indicator. The theory is that management have been entrusted with the net assets of the enterprise with a duty to make a profit from them.

There are problems of definition. We shall take the return as being the net profit before interest and the capital employed as total assets less current liabilities.

In our case the ROCE for 19x2 is $\frac{114}{344} \times 100 = 33\%$

and for 19x3 39%. This seems very good in comparison with the industry average of 25% and the gross return available from for example building society investments. However there are many difficulties in making comparisons here including:

❑ Profit does not include any increase in value of the property over the year.

❑ Assets include the property at cost less depreciation when its market value may be higher or, of course, lower.

Return on shareholders funds

This ratio measures how well the management have turned the return on capital employed into a return on the funds invested by the shareholders.

The return is the net profit after tax and the shareholders funds are the total capital and reserves.

The ratio for 19x2 is $\frac{61}{194} \times 100 = 31\%$ and for 19x3 28%. The ratio has declined and in both years was less than the industry average. However note that it is an after tax ratio whereas the return on capital employed was a before tax ratio. The remarks about valuation difficulties apply to this ratio also.

Dividend cover

This ratio measures the extent to which profits are distributed to shareholders in the form of dividends.

The calculation is simply:

$$\frac{\text{net profit after tax}}{\text{dividends}}$$

In our case the ratio for 19x2 is 2.03 and for 19x3 1.8.

You can interpret the ratio by saying the in 19x2 just under half the profits were distributed but in 19x3, just over half were distributed. The ratio is in line with the industry average.

Gearing ratio

Gearing is also called *leverage*. Gearing measures the extent to which the company is financed by borrowings as against *equity*. Equity is the investment by shareholders.

The calculation is:

$$\frac{\text{Long term loans}}{\text{total capital employed}} \times 100$$

In this case the ratio for 19x2 is $\frac{150}{344} \times 100 = 44\%$ and for 19x3 31%. The theory is that some borrowings (usually called debt) are a good thing as the company can earn a rate of return on capital employed (in our case 39% in 19x3) above the cost of borrowing (15% in this case). However excessive debt can dangerously increase risk as interest and debt repayment have to be made even in times of recession. The company decreased its gearing in 19x3 by repaying part of its long term loan and the gearing ratio is now below the industry average.

Stock turnover

Stock is necessary in this as in all retailing companies. Too much stock carries risk of deterioration and obsolescence and also has costs of storage and financing. Too little stock may cause loss of sales. The stock turnover ratio measures the amount of stock in relation to its throughput.

Its measurement is $\dfrac{\text{stock}}{\text{cost of goods sold}} \times 365$

In our case the ratio is $\frac{85}{600} \times 365 = 52$ days and 42 days in 19x3 as against an industry average of 65 days. The ratio indicates that the average item was in stock for 52 days in 19x2 and 42 days in 19x3. It seems that the company either have excellent stock control or frequently lose sales by not having stock. The ratio is often difficult to interpret as year ends are chosen when stock is low to facilitate counting and some companies postpone purchases for the few days around stocktaking so a true average stock is not determined. Also a large stock may seem to be a good service to customers but may hide shortages of frequently wanted items together with surpluses of obsolete and slow moving items.

Debtors average payment time

This ratio measures the ability of the company to collect debts from its customers. In practice debt collection is a major problem with many large companies being very slow payers.

The ratio is measured by:

$$\frac{\text{debtors}}{\text{credit sales}} \times 365$$

We are not given the credit sales but we shall assume that 50% of the sales in both years are on credit and 50% for cash.

With our company the ratio is:

$\frac{90}{490} \times 365 = 67$ days in 19x2 and 54 days in 19x3 against an industry average of 70 days.

Our company seem to be very good at credit control and collecting debts.

Creditors average payment time

This is the critical liquidity ratio. It measures the average time taken to pay suppliers. Firms normally take more time to pay than strictly allowed by their suppliers but taking excessive time (say three months or more) usually indicates inability to pay more quickly and may sooner or later cause the company to fail.

It is calculated by:

$$\frac{\text{creditors}}{\text{purchases}} \times 365$$

In this case purchases are not given but can be deduced as opening stock + purchases − closing stock = cost of goods sold. Three of these variables are known for 19x3 but only two for 19x2. If stocks are not radically different at each year end then an approximation is to use cost of goods sold which is usually available knowledge.

Thus for 19x2 the time is $\frac{70}{600} \times 100$ is 42 days and for 19x3 44 days. This is relatively quick and the company might well take longer to pay and reduce their overdraft accordingly. The industry average is 60 days.

Current ratio

This is simply current assets over current liabilities and for our company it is for 19x2 $\frac{175}{161} = 1.1$ and for 19x3 1.0. With industry average at 1.6, our company's ratio is significantly different.

Some writers suggest that any variation from industry average should be subject to enquiry but general feeling now is that this ratio has no value whatever.

Acid test or liquidity ratio

This ratio is defined as (current assets less stock) over current liabilities. In 19x2 it was:

$\frac{90}{161} = 0.6$ and in 19x3 0.4.

As with the current ratio, I can attach no significance to it.

Operating cycle

This is defined as stock turnover + debtors average payment time − creditors average payment time. The idea is that it measures the time taken between cash being paid for goods and the receipt of the proceeds of sale of those goods.

In our case the time is 52 + 67 − 42 = 77 days for 19x2 and 52 days in 19x3 as against an industry average of 75 days. We seem to be doing well.

Investment ratios

9. Analysts apply some additional statistics and ratios to companies whose shares are listed or quoted on the stock exchange. These include:

    ❐   dividends per share

    ❐   dividend yield

    ❐   earnings per share

    ❐   price earnings ratio

To consider these items we will select Stubby Group plc and its abbreviated accounts:

Profit and loss account

	£'000
Net profit after tax	1,420
Dividends	700
Retained profits	720
Earnings per share	4.06p

Balance sheet

	£'000
Net assets	12,700
Share capital (20p shares)	7,000
Share premium	1,000
Reserves	4,700
	12,700

Remember that reserves are not assets but an *explanation* of how the company acquired its net assets of £12,700,000, for example by retaining profits or by revaluing its property.

Dividend per share

This is calculated by:

$$\frac{\text{Total dividend}}{\text{Number of shares}}$$

In this case each share has a nominal value of 20p and the share capital is given in £s. So the number of shares is $5 \times 7,000,000 = 35,000,000$ and the dividend per share is $\frac{700,000}{35,000,000} = 2p$. This statistic cannot be compared with other companies as the number of shares into which a given company is divided is arbitrary but year on year comparisons can be made.

Serious newspapers give the dividend per share daily for each quoted company. They do however give it gross which is the net dividend (which we have calculated) $\times \frac{100}{75}$ to reflect a 25% income tax rate. In our case the gross rate is 2.67p,

Dividend yield

The dividend per share cannot be compared with other companies but the dividend yield can be. The dividend yield is calculated by:

$$\frac{\text{Dividend per share}}{\text{Quoted price per share}} \times 100$$

The quoted share price varies all the time but we will assume it to be 68p.

The yield is thus $\frac{2.67}{68} \times 100 = 3.9\%$.

This is much below the gross rate obtainable on building society deposits but remember that the dividend per share in Stubby plc is expected to grow.

Earnings per share

This statistic is calculated as:

$$\frac{\text{Net Profit after tax}}{\text{Number of issued shares}}$$

In our case it is $\frac{£1,420,000}{35,000,000} = 4.06p$. In practice the calculation is not always this easy and the last line of the profit and loss account of quoted companies gives it. It cannot be compared with other companies but a year on year comparison is very useful.

Price earnings ratio

This is calculated as:

$$\frac{\text{Quoted price per share}}{\text{Earnings per share}}$$

In Stubby's case it is $\frac{68p}{4.06p} = 16.7$

The serious papers give the PE ratio for all quoted companies daily. Its meaning is difficult to assess but in general higher PE ratios imply expected growth and a low PE implies a stagnant company. However a company that has a particularly poor profit in a year will show a high PE.

Key principle summary

○ Financial statements are historical and produced as a report to shareholders. They are not designed for ratio analysis to be applied but ratio analysis is applied nonetheless.

○ Accounts can be compared with previous years, similar companies, industry averages, and budgets.

○ Ratios are used to assess performance and liquidity.

○ Parties connected with a company who might be interested are actual and potential managers, owners, shareholders, lenders, customers, suppliers, employees, competitors, predators, government agencies and pressure groups.

○ Ratios of interest include gross profit to sales, net profit to sales, overheads to sales, asset utilisation, sales growth, return on capital employed, return on shareholders funds, dividend cover, gearing, stock turnover, debtors average payment time, creditors average payment time, operating cycle, price earnings ratio, dividend yield etc.

○ Individual companies may have ratios of especial interest such as sales per square foot, sales per employee, hotel occupancy rate etc.

---

9 | The cash flow statement

1. Every company needs to make a *profit* and shareholders look to the profit and loss account to determine if a profit has been made. It is however not necessary for a profit to be made every year but in the long term the company must have a *surplus of profits over losses* or it will be in danger of receivership or liquidation.

2. Companies also pay dividends and a company can pay a dividend in a year in which it makes a loss and many do. However in the long term the company can only pay *dividends* up to the amount of any profit.

3. Thus companies must make profits and these profits must exceed any dividends declared. Profit is not the only requisite of long term survival. In addition the company must not run out of cash or must have the ability to obtain money (eg by borrowing) to enable it to settle its obligations as they fall due. Failure to *manage cash resources* can lead to receivership or liquidation even in profitable companies.

4. Consequently directors of companies are *accountable* to shareholders not only for the extent of their *profit* making capabilities but also for their *cash management* proficiency. This proficiency or lack of it is evidenced by a financial statement called the *cash flow statement*. This is a fairly sophisticated statement and is not very easy to understand although it is easier than its predecessor the statement of source and application of funds. The requirement for a cash flow statement was the first pronouncement of the new Accounting Standards Board and it is embodied in Financial Reporting Standard 1 'Cash Flow Statements'. All companies (except small ones and subsidiaries of Groups) are required to produce one each year starting with accounting periods ending on or after 23 March 1992.

5. The easiest way of understanding these statements is to follow the production of one from the data in a profit and loss account and balance sheet and this we will do.

6. Here are the balance sheets of Cashflow Ltd as at two dates a year apart and also the **summary** profit and loss account for the year ending 31 December 19x2:

**Cashflow Ltd
Balance sheet as at 31 December**

	19x1	19x2
(all figures in £'000)		
Fixed assets		
Cost	2,560	2,720
Less depreciation	1,435	1,710
	1,125	1,010
Current assets		
Stocks	976	1,378
Debtors	1,450	1,769
	2,426	3,147
Creditors – amounts falling due within one year		
Creditors	830	860
Overdraft	234	117
Taxation	88	123
Dividends	40	47
	1,192	1,147
Net current assets	1,234	2,000
Total assets less current liabilities	2,359	3,010
Creditors: amounts falling due after more than one year		
16% Debentures	400	600
Net assets	1,959	2,410
Capital and reserves		
Share capital (£1 shares)	600	700
Share premium	350	500
Profit and loss account	1,009	1,210
	1,959	2,410

Profit and loss account for the year ending 31 December 19x2

Turnover		6,462
Cost of sales		4,040
Gross profit		2,422
Overheads (including depreciation)		1,920
Operating profit		502
Interest		101
Net profit before taxation		401
Taxation		123
Profit after tax		278
Dividends		
Interim	30	
Final	47	77
Retained profit		201

The cash flow statement is now given with supporting notes which are a part of the **statement:**

Cashflow Ltd
Cash flow statement for the year ended 31 December 19x2

a)	Net cash inflow from operating activities		243
b)	Returns on investments and servicing of finance		
c)	Interest paid	(101)	
d)	Dividends paid	(70)	
	Net cash outflow from returns on investments and servicing of finance		(171)
e)	Tax paid		(88)
f)	Investing activities		
g)	Payments to acquire tangible fixed assets	(360)	
h)	Receipts from sales of tangible fixed assets	43	
	Net cash outflow from investing activities		(317)
	Net cash outflow before financing		(333)
	Financing		
i)	Issue of ordinary share capital	250	
j)	Issue of debenture loan	200	
	Net cash inflow from financing		450
k)	Increase in cash and cash equivalents		117

Notes to cash flow statements

1. Reconciliation of operating profit to net cash inflow from operating activities

Operating profit	502
Depreciation charges	415
Loss on sale of tangible fixed assets	17
Increase in stocks	(402)
Increase in debtors	(319)
Increase in creditors	30
Net cash inflow from operating activities	243

2. Analysis of changes in cash and cash equivalents during the year

Balance at 1 January 19x1	(234)
Net cash inflow	117
Balance at 31 December 19x2	(117)

Not included as a note to the cash flow statement but necessary for you to see what has happened is a reconciliation of fixed assets:

		Cost	Depreciation	Book value
r)	at 1 January 19x2	2,560	1,435	1,125
s)	Sold in year	200	140	60
		2,360	1,295	1,065
t)	Addition in year	360		360
u)	Depreciation in year		415	(415)
v)	at 31 December 19x2	2,720	1,710	1,010

The items sold fetched £43,000 so the loss on sale was £60,000 less £43,000 = £17,000.

Line (r) shows the position at the beginning of the year. The company had fixed assets which had originally cost £2,560,000 and which had been depreciated by £1,435,000.

Line (s) removes from line (r) the fixed assets which were sold in the year.

Line (t) adds the fixed assets which were bought in the year.

Line (u) adds the depreciation for the year (which appears as an expense in the profit and loss account). Note that this is depreciation on both the old and the newly acquired fixed assets.

Line (v) shows the fixed assets held at the end of the year and the total or accumulated depreciation on them.

Firstly we will explore how the statement is constructed and then we will consider the story that it tells.

a) Operating profitably usually produces a positive cash flow measured here at £243,000. This is obtained from the profit and loss account but first some adjustments have to be made as the profit and loss account measures value flows not cash flows. The adjustments required are in note 1. Depreciation is not a cash flow but is in the profit and loss account so it has to be added back. Similarly with the loss on sale where the actual cash flow is shown separately in line (h). Intuitively you will realise that cash flow from sales is less than sales if debtors have increased as they have. Similarly increase in stocks must involve a reduction in cash resources and an increase in creditors means an increase in cash resources.

b) This company has no income from investments as it has no investments but these will appear in many statements.

c) Interest paid is on the debentures and the bank overdraft.

d) Dividends paid are the final dividend from last year (£40,000) + the interim of this year (£30,000). This year's final dividend will be paid in the year ending 31 December 19x3.

e) The tax paid in the year is the tax on the previous year's profits as corporation tax is paid nine months after the year end.

f) These are the acquisition of fixed assets but can also be the acquisition of subsidiary companies in groups.

g) During the year £360,000 was spent on fixed assets.

h) Some assets were sold and fetched £43,000

i) 100,000 new ordinary shares of £1 each nominal were sold for £2.50 each and as a result the company raised £250,000 and share capital increased by £100,000 and share premium by £150,000. New issues of ordinary shares for cash are normally issued to existing shareholders in proportion to their holdings and are called *rights issues*.

j) A further issue of debentures raised £200,000

k) Cash and cash equivalents includes cash, bank balances, overdrafts and any short term deposits like those in building societies. In this case the only relevant item is the bank overdraft.

So what does this cash flow statement tell us:

i) The company made a profit of £502,000 but after adjusting for depreciation and loss on sale of fixed assets the positive cash flow from trading was (£502,000 + £415,000 + £17,000) no less than £934,000.

ii) An increase in stocks of £402,000 and of debtors £319,000 was partly financed by an increase in creditors of £ 30,000. The net effect of these three things was an absorption of cash of £691,000 and so the net contribution of operations to cash was only £243,000.

iii) Finance was also obtained from shareholders £250,000 and by long term borrowings at £200,000.

iv) Total cash inflows are thus £243,000 + £250,000 + £200,000 = £693,000.

v) Outgoings of cash were:

	£
on interest	101,000
on dividends	70,000
on tax	88,000

and on fixed assets £360,000, partly financed by sales of old fixed assets £43,000.

vi) Total outgoings are therefore £576,000

vii) Income less outgoings is £693,000 less £573,000 = £117,000. As a result the bank overdraft has come down by this amount.

Cash flow statements in practice

7. The compilation of cash flow statements is difficult and is best left to accountants. However the statements are intended to be used by investors, managers and other people who may not be accountants.

8. The example I have given is relatively simple and the actual statements of public companies tend to be more complex. The complications do not necessarily obscure the basic message and with some practice it is possible for a non-accountant to obtain much information about a company from its cash flow statement.

9. The things to watch for are:

i) The major financing experience of companies is that most cash comes in from operations and most goes out on new fixed assets. Observe the extent that this is so.

ii) Frequently the positive cash flow from operations is diminished by absorptions from increases in stock and debtors only partly financed by increases in creditors.

iii) Interest is a large absorber of cash and the effect of high interest rates has become a cliché in analysing the ills of business.

iv) Dividends do not usually absorb major amounts of cash.

v) Tax payments are also not usually great absorbers.

vi) New financing in the form of rights issues or borrowings are sometimes found. If the borrowings are relatively large then see if the company has reached dangerous levels of gearing.

vii) The net effect on cash and cash equivalent can be seen.

viii) Many groups buy or sell subsidiaries and the effect of this on cash flow can be traced. Sometimes the effect is large borrowings or rights issues and sometimes there is no effect on cash as the consideration is new shares or loan stock.

ix) Some companies show net cash flow from operations as I have in line (a) but some companies will give more detail as:

Cash received from customers

Cash payments to suppliers

Cash paid to or on behalf employees

Other cash payments.

 **Key principle summary**

○ Companies in the long term have to make profits. The law will not allow dividends in the long term to be paid except from profits. These two points are germane to a company's survival. In addition cash flow is very important as failure to manage cash resources adequately can lead to insolvency (the inability to pay debts as they fall due) and receivership or liquidation.

○ Companies are required by FRS 1 to produce an annual Cash flow statement.

○ There are some exemptions including small companies as defined in the Companies Act 1985 and subsidiary companies.

○ The format required is that the following inflows and outflows of cash should be shown in this order:

    operating activities;

    returns on investments and servicing of finance;

    taxation;

    investing activities;

    financing.

○ Notes expanding the detail in the statement accompany the statement.

○ The preparation of a statement can be difficult but understanding it should be available to all interested parties with a little practice.

○ The essentials of a cash flow statement are:

    operating profit adjusted for depreciation;

    changes in debtors, stocks and creditors;

    investment income;

    interest;

    dividends;

    tax;

    acquisition and sale of fixed assets;

    acquisition and sale of subsidiaries;

    financing from rights issues and borrowings and also repayments of loans;

    net effect on cash and cash equivalents.

10 Total absorption costing

1. *Total absorption costing* involves the terms *direct cost* and *indirect cost*. A direct cost may be *materials* (eg wood in a piece of furniture), *labour* (eg the wages of a lathe operator turning a table leg) or *expenses* (eg a royalty payable on the production of a specific product. The characteristic of a direct cost is that it can be *traced* to or associated with a particular product. Note that a product can be a good (eg a table) or a job (eg a particular estate of a housing developer) or a service (eg an operation on Fred Smith in a private hospital or the 9.25 train service from Wolverhampton to London).

2. Traceability is the key. Some costs are actually direct but are treated as indirect as they cannot be traced without excessive expense. An example might be power. The specific electricity used in powering the lathe that is turning the legs of a particular table can in theory be measured but in practice such electricity is treated as an indirect cost.

3. Indirect costs are all costs including materials (eg lubricating oil), labour (eg the managing director's salary) and expenses (eg rent or rates) that cannot be traced to specific products. Indirect costs are often called *overheads*. They are *shared* by all of the products.

4. Indirect costs can be further categorised into:

   Production costs

   Administrative costs

   Selling and Distribution costs.

5. The total absorption cost of a product (which may be a job, a product or a service depending on the nature of the business) is the total of:

   Direct costs + an appropriate share of the indirect costs.

   In theory all indirect costs can be included in a total absorption cost but usually only *production* costs are so included.

6. The total direct costs of a product are termed the *prime cost*. They are conceptually not difficult to determine but complex systems are required in practice to collect and allocate costs. For example the operator of lathe may make many different items in the course of a day and the time spent on each has to be recorded accurately.

7. The appropriate portion of indirect costs is usually not clear cut and complex methods have been developed to establish these in *multiproduct* firms. We shall explore these later.

8. In single product firms the appropriate share of production overheads per product is more easily conceived.

   Suppose a firm make a single identical product – a widget and that they make 20,000 of these a year. The total indirect costs add up to £126,000 a year. Then the appropriate share of the £126,000 to be allocated to each widget is £126,000/20,000 = £6.30.

9. If the company is operating in a recession then output may be restricted because sales are reduced. Suppose that the output was only 18,000 but that overheads remained at £126,000 then the appropriate indirect cost of each product is £126,000/18,000 = £7. In practice, firms attempt to maintain unit cost by reducing overheads by for example making staff redundant or cutting back on training.

10. In practice the cost of a single product is not always measured but instead the cost of a set of products is found. The set of products is called the *batch*. For example in baking, individual loaves are produced in sets or batches and the unit cost measured is the cost of each batch.

11. Accountants tend to formalise their procedures by producing *formal statements* as for example the profit and loss account or balance sheet. In costing procedures formal statements are also produced. An example is the *job cost statement*.

Suppose that the cost of a widget is:

			£
Direct costs	– materials		3.89
	– direct labour 2 hours at £4 an hour		8.00
	– painting done by outworkers		2.10
Indirect costs	– as paragraph 8 above.		

then the accountant could produce a statement as:

Widget – Job Cost statement

	£
Direct costs:	
Materials	3.89
Labour	8.00
Outwork costs	2.10
Prime cost	13.99
Indirect production cost	6.30
Total production cost	20.29

The total production cost can also be called the *total absorption cost* as all production costs (both direct and indirect) have been or can be assigned to products. As a cost is assigned to a product it is said to be *absorbed* by that product.

12. The production cost of a product, job or service can be used in several ways:

   a) In measuring profit, it is necessary to establish the cost of stocks of finished and part-finished items at the period end. The total absorption cost is taken as the cost for this purpose.

   b) The TAC can be used in *pricing*. An enquiry may be received for the production of a made to measure widget from a prospective customer. The estimating department calculate the expected production cost and then add a percentage (say 20%) to it to produce a possible selling price to quote to the customer. The percentage added should be enough to cover non-production overheads and to give a profit. In the above case the selling price arrived at will be:

Estimate of selling price re enquiry No 299

	£
Total production cost	20.29
Margin added	4.06
Selling price	24.35

In practice the cost plus approach to selling prices has to be modified to reflect market conditions. But knowing this figure is very useful in pricing decisions

Multiproduct overhead costing

13. No firm produces just one product. Students often suggest water supply as a single product company but pricing by water rates or by differential tariffs effectively are the supply of separate products.

   It is relatively simple, at least in principle, to determine the *prime cost* of each product produced but *apportioning the overheads* is more difficult.

14. The method normally adopted is to divide the firm into separate *cost centres*. A cost centre is any location, function or items of equipment in respect of which costs may be ascertained and related to cost units for control purposes. Examples of the division of a firm into cost centres may include a factory which is divisible into shops or departments eg welding shop, plating shop, assembly shop etc. or each route covered in an airline, each department in a department store.

The procedure is then to list the overheads. As an example we will take a widget factory and the overheads are:

	£
Rates	200,000
Electricity	180,000
Management salaries	300,000
Canteen subsidy	60,000

There are three departments – welding, assembly and packing which have statistics as:

	Welding	Assembly	Packing
Floor area (m^2)	900	600	500
No of workers	40	80	30
Total HP of machinery	600	100	200

The second procedure is to apportion the overheads to the cost centres in accordance with some appropriate criteria. In this case these might be:

Overhead apportionment schedule

Cost	Method	Total	Welding	Assembly	Packing
Rates	Floor area	200,000	90,000	60,000	50,000
Electricity	HP of machines	180,000	120,000	20,000	40,000
Management	No of workers	300,000	80,000	160,000	60,000
Canteen	No of workers	60,000	16,000	32,000	12,000
		740,000	306,000	272,000	162,000

Note: The methods chosen here are common but would depend on the circumstances. For example electricity could be split and part apportioned by floor area representing heating and lighting and that part that is power divided up in accordance with machine HP or hours used or hours used × HP.

Some overheads are known to be for specific cost centres. Examples are the salaries of supervisors who work exclusively in specific cost centres. Such costs are not apportioned but are simply *allocated* to the appropriate cost centre to be added to the *apportioned* amounts to find the total overheads of each centre.

15. The next procedure is to find a method of dividing each cost centre overhead over the products which use it. There are several methods including the *machine hour rate*, the *labour hour rate*, *percentage on direct wages*. To illustrate, suppose the welding department was primarily a machine using department and total machine hours available in a period were 5,100. Then the machine hour rate would be $\frac{£306,000}{5,100}$ = £60. If job No 341 required 4 hours of machining in the welding shop then the overhead cost of the that machining would be 4 × £60 = £240. Job 341 is said to absorb £240 of the overheads. If enough jobs were available in the department to use all the 5,100 hours then all the overheads would be absorbed.

Note that the overhead total apportioned is a function of the apportioning method which may vary with different accountants and the extent of factual information (eg how much electricity used for heat and how much for power) and as such is imprecise. The total hours actually supplied may be less in a recession and more in a boom or may vary for other reasons. Thus a machine hour rate is not an exact scientific figure and so also a product cost is not either.

Overhead recovery

16. An objective of a firm may be to make full recovery of all its costs, including its overheads, in its selling prices. If the total costs of the assembly department are £272,000 and the total direct labour hours available in the department in a period are 12,000 then a labour hour rate for absorption of overheads will be $\frac{£272,000}{12,000}$ = £22.67 an hour. Full overhead recovery will depend on:

❏ All the 12,000 hours actually being available in the period.

❏ Enough work being available in the period to absorb all these hours.

Each job done is priced out at prime cost + absorbed overheads + profit. Thus each sale can be seen as recovering part of the overheads. Clearly in practice either under or over recovery of overheads always occurs.

 **Key principle summary**

○ A product cost under Total Absorption Costing principles is the sum of direct costs and an appropriate proportion of indirect costs.

○ Direct costs form the prime cost of a product.

○ The overheads to be included will be production costs only if a cost is to found for stock valuation purposes.

○ For other purposes, including selling price determination, administrative and selling and distribution costs may be added.

○ In multiproduct firms ascribing overheads to individual or batches of products involves:

    i)   Listing overheads;

    ii) Allocating and apportioning the overheads to cost centres;

    iii) Developing an absorption method such as a machine rate, a labour hour rate or a percentage on materials, labour, or prime cost.

○ If activity is less than budgeted underabsorption of overheads takes place.

---

11 Cost behaviour, marginal costing and breakeven charts

1. Costs can be categorised in many ways. One method is to divide all costs into either *fixed costs* or *variable costs*.

    Fixed costs are those costs which remain constant over wide ranges of *activity* for a specified time period.

    Variable costs are those which vary in direct proportion to the *level of activity*.

2. Examples of fixed costs include rent, rates, many salaries, leasing charges for cars etc. The rent of a factory is constant for at least the near future. It will be unaffected by the level of output. However if the output was to rise very significantly, it may be necessary to rent further space and then the rent would of course be greater.

3. Examples of *variable* costs include direct materials, direct labour (especially if paid on piecework) and probably power. Most variable costs are assumed to change in direct proportion (*linearly*) to output but variations may occur. For example doubling output may double the purchase of materials but quantity discounts may then be available so that the cost increase is slightly less than the increase in output.

4. Several other terms are also used. These include:

    ❐ *semi-variable costs*. These are costs which have both a fixed and variable component. Examples are telephone charges where there is a rental charge which is fixed and a charge for calls which is variable. Motor car costs include tax and insurance which are fixed and petrol which is variable with usage.

    ❐ *stepped fixed costs*. These are fixed costs which are constant over specific levels of output but which may jump when output rises to a critical level. The example of rent has already been mentioned. A further example might be supervision. One supervisor is required for all output up to say 10,000 units. At higher levels she cannot handle the production and an additional supervisor has to be engaged.

5. You should note the effect of fixed and variable costs on the costs of each unit of output at different levels of output. The following example illustrates this:

    Dave is a manufacturer of gold rings. If he doubles his output he will have to buy twice as much gold but each ring will still use 1.5 grams of gold and the cost of gold per ring will be the same. Gold is a variable cost. He can double his output from 5,000 rings a month to 10,000 rings a month without changing his rent of £300 a month. The rent is fixed and unaffected by levels of output but the cost per unit of output changes. The cost per unit will be $\frac{£300}{5,000}$ = 6p at 5,000 units a month but will be only 3p at an output of 10,000 a month.

Behaviour of costs

6. In theory it is easy to divide all costs into fixed and variable but in practice it turns out to be considerably harder. Some difficult items include:

    ❐   Direct labour. Piecework remuneration is clearly variable but labour paid per hour is less certain. Consider a small factory manufacturing aluminium castings. There are three direct labour employees who are paid a standard sum each for a 38 hour week. Observation shows that at an output of 20,000 castings a week they appear to be fully employed. However in a period of extra demand they succeed in pushing output to 25,000 units a week. They were unable to increase output beyond this level in a standard week and when demand increased to 30,000 units overtime had to be worked. Overtime is paid at time and one half. This means that if standard time is paid at £4 an hour, overtime is paid at £6 an hour.

    ❐   Telephone. Rentals are clearly a fixed cost. But it is questionable if call costs are related at all to output. If output is doubled do telephone calls double? The only way to discover the relationship between output and telephone call costs for a particular firm is to measure costs against output for several successive periods.

Contribution

7. Cost accountants have coined the word '*contribution*' for an important concept in decision making. The contribution made by a product is its sales price less the variable costs associated with it.

    An example

    ❐   in the gold ring factory. Sales price of each ring is £25 and the variable costs of production are £17 for the gold and £2 piecework labour in pressing, making and polishing. The contribution is thus £25 – £19 = £6. Two things can be said about this. Firstly every time one more ring is made extra income is £25 and extra outgoings are £19. For 'extra' accountants tend to use the word '*marginal*'. Approximately all other costs in the factory stay the same whatever the level of output. Secondly the total of all the individual contributions from each ring made and sold has to be sufficient to cover all the fixed costs and make a profit.

8. The concept of the extra cost of one more unit of output beyond the edge or margin of production has led to the whole concept of dividing costs into fixed and variable being called *marginal costing*.

    It is possible to value stocks at marginal cost instead of total absorption cost. Valuation at total absorption cost is now mandatory for legal reasons for published accounts and consequently marginal costing is not normally used for stock valuation.

    Marginal costing is however much preferred for *decision making*.

Breakeven

9. Suppose I am organising a barn dance. I have booked the hall and the band at a total cost of £162. These are the fixed costs. Each ticket sold will bring in £3 and will involve the purchase of a fish and chip supper for delivery from the local shop at £1.20. The variable costs are thus £1.20 a ticket and the contribution from each ticket is £3 – £1.20 = £1.80. How many tickets do I need to sell to break even, that is to make no profit or loss?

The answer is that I need to sell 90 tickets. This is calculated by dividing the amount required (the fixed costs) by the contribution from each ticket £1.80. If I sell 90 tickets I have 90 × £1.80 =£162 which is just sufficient to cover costs. If I sell 91 tickets I shall make a profit of £1.80 but if I sell 89 tickets I shall make a loss of £1.80.

10. It is possible to represent this break even concept in a *break even chart*. This is constructed on graph paper (or these days on a computer screen) as follows:

Vertical (y) axis   – £ sterling
Horizontal (x) axis   – output in units

Example

A garden fork factory

Fixed costs   £50,000 a month
Selling Price   £6 each
Variable costs   £2 each

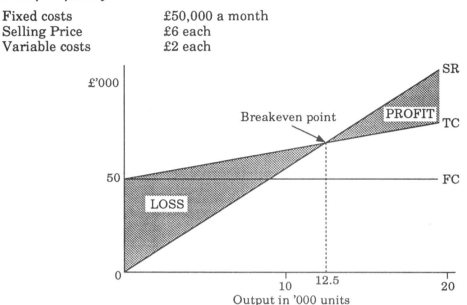

Note that the fixed cost (FC) line is usually drawn first. The total cost (TC) (fixed + variable costs) line is then drawn from the fixed cost level at the junction with the y axis.

The total sales revenue (SR) is then drawn from the origin.

The point were the total sales revenue crosses the total cost line is the *breakeven point*. Left of this point total costs are greater than sales revenue and the business is in loss. Right of the line the business is in profit.

Break even can be calculated from the contribution approach.

11. Special points about breakeven charts include:

❏ *relevant range*. There is little point in drawing the output from 0 to infinity. Output is likely to fall between certain levels. For example Jan has a boutique. Sales may in theory be anything but in practice they are exceedingly unlikely to fall below say £300 a week and equally unlikely to rise above £600 a week. The relevant range is thus between £300 to £600.

❏ *margin of safety*. Suppose that Fred's business makes gateaux for restaurants. He finds that his breakeven point is 2,000 gateaux a week. However he finds that his sales in a normal week average 2,500. He sees that his current sales give him a margin of safety of 500 gateaux a week before he would start to make a loss. The margin of safety can also be expressed as a percentage:

$$\text{Margin of safety} = \frac{\text{Margin of safety in unit sales}}{\text{Expected sales in units}} \times 100$$

❏ *output* (the x axis dimension) can be expressed in units as used in the barn dance example where the unit is one ticket sold. Output can also be expressed in sales in £s. In a shop many different articles are sold so unit sales are not usable but if the profit margin is fairly **constant** when averaged then a chart like this can be constructed.

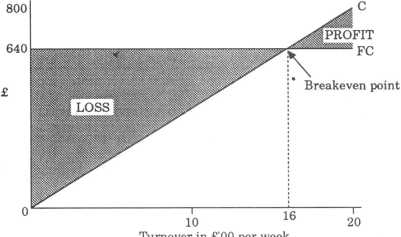

As before the y axis is in £ but this time the x axis is turnover per week. The fixed cost (rent, rates, wages etc) is labelled FC. The contribution line is labelled C. The contribution is calculated as 40% of turnover on the assumption that on each £1 of sales, a contribution of 40p is made as the average input cost per article sold is equal to 60p per £1 of sale price.

The break even sales can be seen as £1,600 a week. This is very useful for a shop owner for whom bookkeeping is a chore. He must keep a record of his daily sales and he knows that if his weekly sales exceed £1,600 he is at least not making a loss.

Key principle summary

- ○ Fixed costs remain the same (within certain limits of output and time) whatever the output.
- ○ Variable costs tend to vary with the level of activity.
- ○ Fixed costs per unit vary with output.
- ○ Variable costs per unit tend to stay the same at all levels of output.
- ○ Semi-variable costs contain both fixed and variable elements.
- ○ Stepped fixed costs increase/decrease by discrete amounts at critical levels of output.
- ○ The behaviour of costs in relation to changes in output is not easy to predict.
- ○ Contribution is the sales price less the variable costs. It can be expressed as a total, per unit or as a percentage of sales.
- ○ Marginal costing is that system of costing where only variable costs are related to products.
- ○ Marginal costing can be used to value stocks but total absorption costs are preferred for this purpose.
- ○ Marginal costing is preferred for decision making purposes.
- ○ The breakeven point is the level of activity where there is no profit or loss.
- ○ A breakeven chart is a chart which indicates approximate profit or loss at different levels of sales volume or output within a relevant range.
- ○ The margin of safety indicates the extent to which the forecast turnover exceeds or falls short of breakeven.
- ○ Relating breakeven point to some easily measurable statistic like weekly sales is of great use to management.

12 Uses of marginal costing

Marginal costing is not normally used in profit measurement but is extensively used in *decision making*. We will review a number of decisions which can be made with the assistance of *marginal costing*.

Note that accountants produce costs which are produced for management use. Many costs so produced are estimates and may turn out differently from the forecast. Accountants produce figures in terms of money and can also supply management with techniques to employ in using the figures in making decisions. Decision making is a *management* task and managers have other criteria to take into account in making decisions. The financial effect of a decision is always very important and financial survival is a necessity for most organisations. However other factors may be relevant:

a) Decisions may have effects not perceived by the management accountant in supplying his figures. For example, the dropping of a product on financial grounds may have effects on the sales of other products or on personnel morale.

b) Aspects of business such as quality control, health and safety, energy conservation and pollution control must be taken into account and altruism is not entirely lacking in business. The effect of a decision which involves redundancy or relocation should be taken only after due consideration of these consequences.

c) Management often have priorities and goals not known to the management accountant. Examples may be a desire to take a larger market share whatever the cost or to expand to feed a manager's ego.

Breakeven

The simple technique of determining the *breakeven point* can be useful in decision making. Here are two examples:

1. Danielle is considering using her redundancy money in starting a new boutique in a suburban precinct. She estimates that she should be able to sell about £1,000 worth of clothes a week. She has worked out all the overheads including rent, rates, depreciation, interest, and wages. These will total £21,000 a year. She estimates that on average her clothes will be sold at cost + 60%.

    Calculate her breakeven sales. Fixed costs are £21,000 so she must have a *contribution* or gross profit which at breakeven is £21,000. To calculate breakeven sales:

Sales	?		160
Cost of sales		?	100
Gross profit	£21,000		60

    Note that if cost of sales is seen as 100, then gross profit will be 60 and sales 160.

    Breakeven sales are 160/60 × £21,000 = £56,000 a year or £1,077 a week. This is slightly more than her estimated sales so the project may not quite be viable.

2. Daniel intends to start a part time business as a photocopying shop. He can either hire his equipment or buy it outright. Costs are likely to be:

	Hire	Buy
Variable costs	3p a copy	1.5p a copy
Fixed machine costs		£2,000
General fixed costs	£2,000	£2,000

    He estimates that he will sell 150,000 copies at an average of 7p a copy.

The profits at 150,000 copies would be:

	Hire	Buy
Sales (at 7p)	10,500	10,500
Variable costs	4,500	2,250
Contribution	6,000	8,250
Fixed costs	2,000	4,000
Net profit	4,000	4,250

He concludes that at his expected sales, he will make more profit by buying. He also calculates that every copy sold over 150,000 will bring him extra profit of 4p if he hires and 5.5p if he buys.

However his accountant, who is ever cautious, advises him to calculate his breakeven point on each mode of operation:

	Hire		Buy	
Fixed costs	£2,000		£4,000	
Contribution per copy	4p		5.5p	
Breakeven	$\frac{£2,000}{4p}$	= 50,000	$\frac{£4,000}{5.5p}$	72,727

Daniel is worried that he will not achieve the expected sales and can gain comfort from hiring his machines and having a lower breakeven point. He takes a smaller risk by hiring.

Make or buy

A common problem in industry is whether to make a product in house or to buy it in from a supplier.

Sheinton Ltd make cast iron door furniture. A new product has been developed and the management are considering whether to make it in the factory or to have it made in Hungary. Cost data for a year are:

	Make	Buy
Fixed costs	£70,000	£2,000
Variable costs (per 100 items)	£10	£50

Sales price is 70p and expected sales are 200,000 items.

Profits expected are

	Make	Buy
Sales	140,000	140,000
Variable costs	20,000	100,000
Fixed costs	70,000	2,000
Net profit	50,000	38,000

At the turnover predicted, it would be cheaper to make the product. However various other scenarios are possible:

❐ turnover may be less and below 170,000 items it is more profitable to buy in.

❐ once the figures are known it may be possible to obtain an even lower price from the Hungarians.

❐ other matters may be important – continuity of supply, control over quality, staff morale etc.

Special order pricing

Burn Ltd manufacture cookers for the home camping market. These sell at £65 each and the costs of manufacture are:

Variable manufacturing costs	20
Fixed manufacturing costs	18 *
Administration costs (all fixed)	8
Fixed selling/distribution costs	6 †
Variable selling /distribution cost	3
	55

* based on total costs of £180,000 and output of 10,000 units.
† based on total costs of £60,000

The company have received an enquiry from a Dutch company for the supply of 3,000 cookers. The price they are prepared to pay is £40 a unit.

Burn Ltd reckon that the additional output is possible with the use of overtime such that the variable manufacturing cost will be £22 a unit. There will be an increase of £6,000 in fixed manufacturing costs and £9,000 in administration costs. The variable selling/distribution costs will not apply but a carriage cost of £4 a cooker will have to be paid.

Should the order be accepted?

The marginal costs of making and supplying the 3,000 cookers will be:

	£
Variable manufacturing costs	66,000
Fixed manufacturing cost	6,000
Fixed Administration costs	9,000
Carriage	12,000
	93,000

or £31 a unit

Thus the marginal revenue £40 is greater than the marginal cost so the order should be accepted.

Note that:

❑ original fixed costs remain the same whether or not the order is accepted and therefore they can be disregarded in the decision.

❑ Additional fixed costs will be incurred and they must be part of the decision.

❑ all the relevant variable costs must be taken into account

❑ the order is at a price much below the UK selling price. If this price becomes known then UK customers may demand a price reduction. Also the items sold to the Dutch may find their way back to the UK and undercut normal UK sales.

❑ It is clearly of advantage to sell goods at above marginal cost in new markets as long as current markets are not disturbed. This is a matter of management judgement.

Scarce resources

In some situations there is a shortage of a some resource and output has to be restricted. The shortage may be of a material, of skilled labour, of machine time or even of money to fund output. The resource in short supply may be called the *limiting factor* or the *key factor*.

An example

Penny Widgets Ltd manufacture three products whose per unit sale prices, variable costs and potential sales are:

	Alpha	Beta	Gamma
Sale price	£28	£44	£56
Variable costs	£16	£24	£38
Potential sales	6,000	8,100	4,500

The limiting factor is the supply of skilled labour. The quantity of skilled labour to make each product is 30 minutes for an Alpha, 20 minutes for a Beta and 12 minutes for a Gamma. The total supply of skilled labour is limited to 4,600 hours in period X. The problem is to decide which items to manufacture to maximise profit.

The answer can be found by a table as:

	Alpha	**Beta**	**Gamma**
Sales price (£)	28	44	56
Variable costs	16	24	38
Contribution	12	20	18
Skilled labour(minutes)	30	20	12
Contribution per minute of skilled labour	*40p*	*100p*	*150p*
Ranking	3	2	1
Manufacture Gamma			4,500
Skilled labour used(hrs)			900
Manufacture Beta		8,100	
Skilled labour used(hrs)		2,700	
Total skilled labour(hrs)		3,600	
Manufacture Alpha	2,000 (b)		
Skilled labour use(hrs)	1,000 (a)		
Total skilled labour used (hrs)			
	4,600		

a) Only 1,000 hours remain and all of these can be used in making Alphas.

b) The 1,000 hours will enable 2,000 Alphas to be made.

The secret of this type of exercise is in the line in italics. The greatest profit comes from using the scarce resource to the greatest advantage and the products which give the *greatest contribution per unit of scarce resource* are to be preferred. Beta may give the highest contribution per unit but only 3 of these an hour can be made. Whereas 5 gammas can be made in an hour of scarce labour.

Deletion of a segment

Management expect all segments of a business to make a profit. Any segment which fails to make a profit is normally discontinued. Here is an example.

Poshshop plc is a department store in Walsall. The Pottery department is on the second floor and the latest profit statement for the department shows:

	£
Sales	80,000
Cost of goods sold	50,000
Wages	16,000
Share of fixed overheads	18,000
Net loss	(4,000)

Note:

❏ the cost of goods sold and wages are variable costs, changing more or less in line with sales.

❏ the fixed costs (rent, rates, insurance, heat and light, administration etc) would remain unchanged if the department were closed.

Should the department be closed?

We can answer this question by considering what would *change* if it was closed. The contribution made by the department is (£80,000 − £50,000 − £16,000) £14,000 and this would be lost if the department closed but fixed overheads would remain the same. Consequently the company would be £14,000 worse off if the department closed.

Another point to consider is that the space occupied by the department might be more profitably used. Suppose that the space could be let on concession to Fred's China Figures at a rent of £17,000. Then the rent would be greater than the contribution from the department and the letting would be more profitable. It is possible to say that the *opportunity cost* (the value of a benefit sacrificed in favour of an alternative course of action) of continuing the department would be the rent foregone

 **Key principle summary**

○ Marginal costing is not usually employed in profit measurement but is an excellent tool for decision making.

○ Accountants provide figures to management and also techniques for using them (eg Scarce Resource analysis) but decisions are made by management.

○ Management often make decisions by considering non-financial as well as financial data.

○ Breakeven analysis can be used as a measure of risk and in choosing between alternatives including whether or not to start a new business or business segment.

○ Make or buy decisions are assisted by marginal costing.

○ Special order pricing at any price above marginal costs may be beneficial but may have unfortunate consequences.

○ In the presence of a scarce resource the most profitable course of action is to maximise contribution per unit of scarce resource.

○ The deletion of a segment can be assessed by measuring the contribution foregone and the measurement of opportunity cost as contribution foregone has many applications.

---

13 Budgeting

1. It is possible to manage a business by continuing as before and responding to events as they occur. Many small and some large businesses behave in this way and survive. However even in these businesses the management have some implicit plans which might be simple such as 'to increase sales' or 'reduce costs' or to explore the possibilities of additional products.

2. Most businesses prefer to make their plans explicit and may do so in qualitative or in quantitative terms. One of the best ways of approaching the *future* is by *budgeting*. Budgeting is making a *plan* expressed in *money* terms.

3. The objectives of budgeting are multifold and seven are usually identified specifically. These are:

   a) *Planning*. A budget is a plan expressed in money terms. The budget is normally for one year ahead and should take into account:

      ❑ any longer term planning processes

      ❑ expectations of economic conditions and events in the ensuing year

      ❑ anticipate problems and difficulties as they may arise

   b) *Coordination*. A budget in a firm is made up of *subsidiary* or *sectional* budgets. It is important that each budget coordinates with all the others. For example the sales budget may be for a specific quantity of specified products. Production must be budgeted to meet the needs of sales. Similarly, capital expenditure may need to be planned to enable the planned output to be achieved and new labour may need to be hired and trained (or labour may need to be shed). All this has implications for cash levels and borrowing may need to be planned. Overall the budget must indicate a satisfactory level of profit or must be reprogrammed until it does. All this coordination is not usually achieved at the first draft and much negotiation amongst managers is often required before the budget can be adopted. A side effect of all this is that a manager becomes more aware of the activities of other departments and how his/her department fits into the whole.

c) *Communication*. Once the master and subsidiary budgets have been adopted they need to be communicated to all appropriate personnel in the company. The management have expectations in the budget and the budget also implies the means to fulfil them. By communicating the budget to relevant personnel the management are able to inform staff of the management's hopes and aspirations. In addition the formation of the budget requires that much learning of company objectives and inter-relationships is acquired by staff.

d) *Motivation*. The budget can be seen as a device for motivating staff to fulfil the plans of the management expressed in the budget. There is a large literature on the *behavioural* effects of budgeting and especially on its dysfunctional effects.

e) *Control*. Control means finding means of ensuring that the plans are *achieved*. Essentially this means that where the outcome of activities varies from the budget these variations can be identified and management can correct them. A technique which has grown up with budgeting is *management by exception*. The great mass of activities that go according to plan require little management attention and all their concern can be put into matters that diverge from the budget.

f) *Evaluation*. Budgets form an objective standard of attainment that actual performance can be measured against and managers are motivated to achieve budgets. Senior management can evaluate the performance of line managers and other staff by reference to the budgets.

g) *Delegation*. Budgets can be broken down into sub-budgets by function (eg capital expenditure, personnel, purchasing, sales, manufacturing, marketing, accounting etc) and each of these can be further subdivided if required (eg sales into regions, manufacturing into departments or sections). Each sub-budget can be given to a specific person who is then *responsible* for that budget. Once the budget has been agreed and approved then each budget holder has a plan to work with and higher management can leave her to it. Adherence to the budget will be monitored and only *variances* need to take up management time. The alternative is either for higher management to supervise the line management continuously or to allow the line managers to act independently with the risk of uncoordinated activity and actions which run counter to management policy.

The above are usually seen as the functions of budgeting. Successful budgeting is realised when the budget is the result of a process of *consultation* and *negotiation* when all relevant personnel are involved and can bring their special knowledge to the issue. Budgets imposed from above are rarely effective as dysfunctional behaviour often follows.

Budgeting can be effective in all types of enterprise including non-profit ones. It is important to realise all the objectives and not the simple approach of many line managers who may see the budget simply in terms of *authorisation*. Ellen, the head of department X, has a budget of £y which is agreed under a series of expenditure headings. Her attitude might be that she has to spend all the amount allowed by the budget or she will lose the benefit of any unspent sums both this year and probably next year as well as next years budget will be less to follow reduced actual expenditure this year. This is clearly against the best interests of the organisation as a whole which could benefit from more economical spending. Many organisations now apply *virement* which means that sums unspent under one heading can be transferred to overspent headings.

Preparation of a budget

This is normally a process requiring much expenditure of time on the spreadsheet and acres of printout but we will try to simplify the process to give you the bones of the process.

Gubbins Marketing Ltd have a balance sheet at 31 December 19x2 as

Balance Sheet as 31 December 19x2
(all figures in £'000)

Fixed assets			
Cost			340
Less Depreciation			162
			178
Current assets			
Stocks		90	
Debtors		87	
		177	
Creditors – amounts falling due within one year			
Creditors		67	
Overdraft		44	
		111	
Net current assets			66
Total assets less current liabilities			244
Capital and reserves			
Share capital (£1 shares)			100
Share premium			50
Profit and loss account			94
			244

The first action is to determine the *principal budget factor* which is the item which restricts activity. We shall assume that it is sales (it usually is).

The second action is to determine the sales budget – itemised by product with quantity and price. We will make this £600,000 in total.

The third phase is to identify any management policies which need to be incorporated in the budgets. These are:

❐ stock must be held down to no more than £95,000

❐ creditors must be paid on average no more than two months after the goods are invoiced.

The fourth phase is to construct the subsidiary budgets:

a) The purchases budget. On average the mark up on cost is 50%. Therefore given the sales, cost of goods sold will be £400,000. As opening stock is £90,000 and closing stock can be no more than £95,000, purchases will be £405,000. I assume that stocks in the past have been a lower portion of cost of sales than that planned in 19x2.

b) The labour budget. The expected throughput requires a staff of 8 and at an average cost of £8,500 each, labour will cost £68,000. Currently only 6 are employed so two more will have to be recruited.

c) The Overheads budget. Knowing the expected levels of rent, rates etc a total budget of £58,000 is envisaged.

d) The capital expenditure budget. The expected level of sales implies additional handling equipment and an additional van so that £40,000 needs to be spent.

The fifth phase is the construction of the master budget. This will be in the form of a trading and profit and loss account:

Budgeted trading and profit and loss account for 19x2

Sales		600
Cost of sales		400
Gross profit		200
Labour	68	
Overheads	58	
Depreciation	38	164
Net profit		36

I have assumed a depreciation rate of 10% straight line.
and a balance sheet:

Budgeted balance sheet as 31 December 19x3
(all figures in £'000)

Fixed assets			
Cost			380
Less depreciation			200
			180
Current assets			
Stocks		95	
Debtors		150	
		245	
Creditors – amounts falling due within one year			
Creditors		67	
Overdraft		78	
		145	
Net current assets			100
Total assets less current liabilities			280
Capital and reserves			
Share capital (£1 shares)			100
Share premium			50
Profit and loss account			130
			280

I have assumed that debtors will be equal to three months sales. All the other figures but one can be calculated from the figures so that the only figure to put in is the overdraft. In practice this would be calculated on a month by month basis. However it can be seen that an increase has to be negotiated with the bank manager.

Budget Review

The above budget setting exercise is simple and is for a trading company of a small size. Larger companies who manufacture and have large numbers of products, complex production systems and numerous departments find the budgeting process very expensive. However the principles are the same in all budget setting routines. At the end of the process, a review can be made and questions asked such as:

Is the profit satisfactory?

Is return on capital employed sufficient?

Is cash flow acceptable?

If the answer to any of these questions is no, then it is possible to review the budget in detail and make changes as desired. In effect the budget is a proposed plan. Alternative plans are possible. However the proposed budget is coordinated and any alternative would require the detailed working that would make it also a coordinated plan.

⌀══ Key principle summary

○ Enterprises can operate without budgeting and many do.

○ Most enterprises now do budget.

○ A budget is a plan expressed in money terms.

○ The objectives of budgeting are:

    a) planning;

    b) coordination;

    c communication;

    d) motivation;

    e) control;

    f) performance evaluation;

    g) delegation.

○ The processes of budget forming may be:

    a) determine responsibilities including the composition of a budget committee;

    b) derive key forecasts (usually sales);

    c) establish company policies;

    d) prepare quantity budgets with appropriate managers;

    e) coordinate quantity budgets;

    f) prepare financial budgets;

    g) coordinate financial budgets;

    h) produce master budget;

    i) review;

    j) approve;

    k) disseminate to relevant parties.

14 Standard costing

1. Standard costing is an extension of budgetary control. It began in manufacturing but it can be applied in all industries. The objective is to set up *predetermined* standards of cost and other aspects of performance such as sales. The actual outcome can then be compared and *variances* between *standard* and *actual* can be computed. If a variance is significant then it can be investigated and if necessary corrective action taken. The setting up of standards is the essential since they supply objective criteria against which performance can be measured.

2. Standards must be set up realistically using all available technical knowledge. For example if the standard cost of making a widget is to be established then the material quantities must be evaluated by production personnel and prices established by purchasing personnel. Labour time must be evaluated by work study engineers and cost by wages staff. The standards to be adopted should be *attainable* standards that is those standards of performance that are achievable if machinery is operated efficiently, material properly used and appropriate allowances are made for normal losses, waste and machine downtime. *Ideal* standards which can only be achieved in exceptional circumstances are not normally adopted.

3. Once set up, standard costs have several uses. Measuring *profit* for regular internal performance reports is much easier if standard costs are used for valuing stocks of raw materials, work in progress and finished goods rather than determining the actual costs. Note that actual costs have to be used for external profit reporting. Standard costs are also used for cost measurement when determining the *price* to be quoted to potential customers. However the principal use of standard costs is in *variance analysis*.

Variance analysis

4. *Material variances*

    The standard material cost of one mark IV widget is 24 kg of Hedonite at £2.40 a kg.

    In period 12,420 widgets were made. The actual material cost of these was 10,710 kg at £2.30 a kg.

    The standard material cost of making 420 widgets is:

    $$420 \times 24 \times £2.40 = £24,192$$

    The actual cost turned out to be:

    $$10,710 \times £2.30 = £24,633$$

    The difference at £441 is an adverse variance as the actual cost was more than the standard cost.

    Now we can break this variance down into two sub-variances:

    a) Material price variance:

        $$10,710 \times 10p = £1,071 \text{ FAV}$$

        Obviously the Hedonite was bought at a slightly cheaper price than the standard and we have a favourable variance. How can we interpret this? Possibly the price of the material has simply changed and the firm have to accept the price given by the market. This might be called a *planning* variance since effectively the standard is now wrong as the market price has changed. An alternative possibility is that the buying department were successful in securing the material at a lower price or perhaps deliberately bought an inferior grade of material. These interpretations would imply that the variance was a *performance* variance.

        Generally the objective of calculating of variances is not to explain but to alert management to the existence of non-standard costs so that they can enquire the reasons from the persons responsible.

        Now that we have extracted the price variance we can calculate any further variances at standard cost.

b) Material usage variance.

$$((420 \times 24) - 10{,}710) \times £2.40 = £1{,}512 \text{ ADV}$$

$$\uparrow \qquad\qquad \uparrow$$

Std Usage   Actual

Clearly more material was used than standard and the explanation is likely to be caused by *adverse* performance. Perhaps supervision was lax or perhaps the process results vary naturally and this was one of the bad periods. It may be that the adverse usage variance was connected with the price variance as poorer quality material (favourable price variance) caused excessive usage. Different variances are often *connected*. Management are now alerted to determine the cause and if necessary take some action to prevent recurrence.

The two variances are now

$$£1{,}071 \text{ FAV} + £1{,}512 \text{ ADV} = £441 \text{ ADV}$$

so we can check our calculations.

5. *Labour variances*

The standard labour cost of making one Mark IV widget is 9 hours at £3.50 an hour = £31.50.

Therefore the standard labour cost of making the 420 widgets was:

$$420 \times 9 \times £3.5 = £13{,}230$$

The actual cost of making the 420 widgets was 3,600 hours at £3.72 an hour = £13,392.

The variance is thus £162 ADV

This variance can broken down into sub-variances:

a) Labour rate variance.

$$3{,}600 \times 22\text{p} = £792 \text{ ADV}$$

The cause of this may be planning in that the standard is now out of date following an agreed wage increase. Or it may be a performance variance as the mix of labour (skilled, semi-skilled or unskilled) was slightly more skewed than standard toward the skilled. Another alternative may be some overtime working.

Having extracted the rate (equivalent to price) variance, all further variances will be at the standard rate of £3.50 an hour.

b) Efficiency variance

$$((420 \times 9) - 3{,}600) \times £3.50 = £630 \text{ FAV}$$

$$\uparrow \qquad\qquad \uparrow$$

Std Usage   Actual

The explanation for this may be that conditions were just right or that fewer breakdowns or hold-ups occurred than the standard foresaw. There may be a connection with the rate variance if that was caused by a higher than standard proportion of more skilled labour.

The two sub-variances are £792 ADV and £630 FAV = £162 ADV

6. *Variable overheads*

The variable overheads are costs such as power and consumable stores which vary linearly with output. Suppose that the standard variable cost for the production of one widget was £27 then the standard variable overhead cost for 420 widgets is £11,340. In period 12 the actual variable overheads were £12,743. The total overhead variance is thus:

$$£11{,}340 - £12{,}743 = £1{,}403 \text{ ADV}$$

The total variance can be broken down:

a) Efficiency variance. The variable overheads are associated with labour hours. Cost accountants say the variable overheads are *driven* by the labour hours. In fact the standard labour hours required for 420 items of output are $420 \times 9 = 3{,}780$. We have seen that the standard variable overheads per widget are £27 or £3 a labour hour. Therefore we might expect the variable overhead cost to be $3{,}780 \times £3 = £11{,}340$. However the actual labour hours were 3,600 and if variable overheads are driven by labour hours then the variable overheads should be $3{,}600 \times £3 = £10{,}800$. By using less labour hours than standard on our output, we would expect a saving on variable overheads of:

$$£11{,}340 - £10{,}800 = £540 \text{ FAV}$$

This is called the efficiency variance.

b) Expenditure variance.

The standard variable overhead cost driven by labour hours is:

$$3{,}600 \times £3 = £10{,}800$$

The actual expenditure was £12,743 and so the expenditure variance is:

$$£10{,}800 - £12{,}743 = £1{,}943 \text{ ADV}$$

The total variance is:

$$£540 \text{ FAV} + £1{,}943 \text{ ADV} = £1{,}403 \text{ ADV}$$

The cause of the efficiency variance is simply the efficiency of labour and the cause of the expenditure variance is probably that prices of the variable overhead constituents have risen or that the outlays were excessive in relation to standard. Perhaps excessive lubricating oil was used.

In practice the variable overheads are not simply driven by labour hours and meaningful variances are best obtained by looking at each variable overhead expenditure heading in turn.

7. *Fixed overheads*

Fixed overheads are those that do not vary with output and the standard will be a lump sum not an amount per unit of output. We will suppose the lump sum is £16,000. A standard cost per widget is calculated and must include an amount for fixed overheads. This can only be done by having a budgeted output. Suppose this was 400 widgets. Then the fixed overhead cost per widget is:

$$\frac{£16{,}000}{400} = £40$$

In period 12 the actual fixed overhead expenditure was £15,700.

The total fixed overhead variance is:

$$(420 \times £40) - £15{,}700 = £1{,}100 \text{ FAV}$$

The idea is that by including £40 a widget in the standard cost every unit produced (and sold) recovers £40 from the customer. As 420 units were produced then recovery is $420 \times £40 = £16{,}800$. Since actual expenditure was only £15,700, £1,100 more was recovered than was expended.

The total variance is broken down into:

a) Expenditure variance. This is:

$$£16{,}000 - £15{,}700 = £300 \text{ FAV}$$

Fixed overheads should be the same regardless of output and at standard are £16,000. In fact they were £15,700 so some savings were made. Perhaps less than standard was spent on maintenance or a supervisor left and was not replaced.

b) Volume variance. This is:

$$(420 - 400) \times £40 = £800 \text{ FAV}$$

The calculation is the extra output over budget viz 20 widgets at standard cost.

This is a very useful measure because the effect of output over budget is to increase profit not only by the profit margin on the extra output but also by the recovery of fixed overheads that have already been recovered by the budgeted output.

8. *Sales margin variances*

The variances so far have been concerned with costs. Clearly these variances affect profit. So also do sales volume and prices.

We will first summarise the position with the standard cost per widget which is:

		£
Materials	24 Kg at £2.40	57.60
Labour	9 Hours at £3.50	31.50
Variable overheads		27.00
Fixed overheads		40.00
		156.10

Suppose the selling price is £180 then the standard *margin* of profit per widget is:

$$£180 - £156.10 = £23.90$$

In period 12 actual sales were 420 units at £175 = £73,500

The total sales margin variance is:

$$(400 \times £23.90) - (420 \times £18.90) \quad = £1,622 \text{ ADV}$$

$$\uparrow \qquad\qquad \uparrow$$

$$\text{Std} \qquad\qquad \text{Actual}$$

This is the budgeted profit less the actual sales at actual sales margin assuming standard costs. Clearly the actual costs were not standard but the variances from standard are dealt with as cost variances and we have already done this. Since the selling price is £5 less than the standard the actual margin is £18.90.

This total variance can be broken down as:

a) Sales margin price variance.

This is:

$$420 \times £5 = £2,100 \text{ ADV}$$

The sales margin achieved was 420 (the actual output) at £5 which is the reduction in price.

The reduction in price of £5 caused a reduction in profit of £2,100.

b) Sales margin volume variance. This is:

$$(400 - 420) \times £23.90 = £478 \text{ FAV}$$

This isolates the effect on profit of the extra 20 units sold over budget.

Notice that this is a sales margin variance not a sales variance.

The total variance is thus confirmed as:

$$£2,100 \text{ ADV} + £478 \text{ FAV} = £1,622 \text{ ADV}$$

9. *Reconciliation of actual and budgeted profit*

In period 12 the budgeted output is 400 units and so the budgeted profit is:

$$400 \times £23.90 = £9,560$$

The actual costs were:

		£
Materials 10,710 Kg at £2.30		24,633
Labour 3,600 hours £3.72		13,392
Variable overheads		12,743
Fixed overheads		15,700
		66,468

As sales were 420 units at £175 = £73,500 then the profit was:

£73,500 − £66,468 = £7,032

This is different from the budgeted profit of £9,560 and we can now produce a statement reconciling the standard with the actual profit as:

			£
Budgeted net profit			9,560
Sales variances			
Sales margin price	2,100 A		
Sales margin volume	478 F	1,622 A	
Material variances			
Price	1,071 F		
Usage	1,512 A	441 A	
Labour variances			
Rate	792 A		
Efficiency	630 F	162 A	
Variable overhead variances			
Expenditure	1,943 A		
Efficiency	540 F	1,403 A	
Fixed overhead variances			
Expenditure	300 F		
Volume	899 F	1,100 F	2,528 A
Actual profit			7,032

Key principle summary

○ Standard costs are established as the costs of production of products. They are usually attainable but should also be challenging and stimulating.

○ Standard costs can be compared with actual costs and variances extracted.

○ Significant variances can be investigated to determine the causes and take corrective action.

○ Causes can be planning which indicates that the standard is now unrealistic or out of date or performance which means that they are caused by operations which were different from standard.

○ Variances are usually analysed as:

material	price:	actual usage × price difference
	usage:	(std − actual usage) × std price
labour	rate:	actual usage × rate difference
	efficiency:	(std − actual usage) × std rate
variable overheads	efficiency:	(std − actual labour hours for output) × std rate
	expenditure:	((std labour hours for output × std rate) − actual expenditure

Fixed overheads	expenditure:	Std – actual expenditure
	volume:	(Std – actual output) × std rate
Sales margin	price:	Sales volume × price difference
	volume:	(budget – actual volume) × std margin

○ Once the variances have been extracted, it is possible to draw up, a reconciliation between budgeted profit and actual profit.

○ Price variances are usually extracted first and subsequent variances are calculated at standard prices.

○ Sales margin variances are extracted not sales variances. Sales margins are calculated assuming standard costs.

---

15 | Cash flow forecasting

1. Every business needs to make a *profit*. In the short term (for example for one year) a business can make a loss but in the long run a business must be profitable to *survive*.

   Further, *withdrawals* from a business by its owner must be less than profits. Again, in the *short term*, a proprietor of a business can continue to draw from the business which is making losses or profits less than the drawings. But in the *long term* profits must exceed drawings. In companies, withdrawals by the proprietors are called *dividends* and these can also in the short term be paid even when the company has made a loss or has made a profit which is less than the dividend. However in the long term, companies must make profits which exceed dividends to survive. In fact company law prohibits a company from paying dividends except out of profits. This restriction does not apply for any one year but means that a dividend in a year can only be paid to the amount that total profits since the formation of the company exceed total dividends already paid.

   However even profitable companies can fail if they do not manage their *cash flow* satisfactorily. A simple example:

   Simon starts a business with £100. He buys stock, paying the supplier £100. He sells the stock for £200 and the customer will pay him in three months. He borrows £100 from the bank and buys £200 more stock from a supplier agreeing to pay £100 now and £100 one month later.

   He is now in a position where he has:

Assets:		Liabilities:	
£200	stock	Bank	£100
£200	debt	Creditor	£100
£400			£200

   His business now has net assets of £400 – £200 = £200.

   This came from £100 original investment and £100 profit.

   However he has no *cash* and if his debtor delayed payment he would be unable to repay the bank and pay his creditor.

   This scenario happens continually with numerous businesses which are profitable but which run out of cash. The effect is often *bankruptcy*, *receivership* or *liquidation*.

2. The need is for a business to manage its cash flows. It can only easily do this by:

   ❏ *forecasting* cash flows

   ❏ identifying likely shortages

   ❏ *arranging finance* to eliminate the revealed shortages

❐ continually reviewing the current and future cash position

Indeed before lending to a business, the bank always requires a cash flow forecast. There are many advantages to this:

❐ the bank can see that the business will be able to survive

❐ the bank can see that the business can pay interest and repay the loan as agreed

❐ the business owners have the importance of cash flow management impressed upon them.

Cash flow forecasts

The easiest way to construct a cash flow forecast is to use one of the forms supplied by the bank. The following is a slightly abbreviated example:

Month	Jan		Feb		...
	Budget	Actual	Budget	Actual	

Receipts
1. Sales – cash
2.   – debtors
3. Loans received
4. Capital introduced
5. Disposal of assets
A. Total receipts

Payments
6. Cash purchases
7. Payments to creditors
8. Principals remuneration
9. Wages/salaries
10. PAYE/NHI
11. Capital items
12. Transport/packaging
13. Rent/rates
14. Services
15. Loan repayments
    HP/Leasing payments
16. Interest
17. Bank/finance charges
    Professional fees
    Advertising
18. VAT
19. Corporation/income tax
20. Dividends
B. Total payments
C. Opening bank balance
D. Closing bank balance

All that is necessary is to fill in the form with appropriate figures. In practice this is difficult because:

❐ business people do not understand all the terms and concepts used

❐ forecasting is virtually impossible especially with a new business.

However forcing a new businessperson to think and plan and forecast is highly desirable.

An explanation of some of the terms is:

Line:

1. Sales – Cash. Some businesses sell *on credit* where the sale and invoice take place and then payment is received at a later date. The later date can be anything from a few days to many months. It is often very difficult to forecast. Some businesses sell for cash at point of sale. Examples are retail shops, bus companies and cinemas. Some businesses are fortunate enough to

receive money in advance of providing the service. An example is a travel agency. Line 1 requires a forecast of all cash to be received in each month.

2. Where sales are made on credit, it is necessary to forecast:

   ❏ how much will be sold on credit in each month

   ❏ when the customers will pay

   In practice people who set up businesses are often surprised to find how long customers wait before paying. The worst offenders are large firms.

3. Loans received. This row will only be filled in if loans have been negotiated. At least there is a reasonable degree of certainty over this row.

4. Capital introduced. The proprietor(s) of the business will normally introduce actual money into the business at its beginning. Banks normally expect proprietors to introduce money and not rely solely on bank finance. In the case of companies, capital introduced is usually to pay for shares in the company. However many company founders also make loans to the company in addition to buying shares. Note that only money is included in a cash flow forecast. Many new business founders introduce other assets (goodwill, motor vehicles, tools, initial stock etc) but these do not go on a cash flow forecast or statement.

5. Disposal of assets. This is unlikely in a new business. If it does occur include only the actual *proceeds* of sale.

6. and 7. Purchases. Just as sales can be made for cash or on credit so purchases can be made for cash or on credit.

   These can more easily be forecast since they are under the control of the business. However payments later than desired often occur if the business finds itself short of cash.

8. Principal(s) remuneration. A person who starts a new business usually has to rely on the business for his living expenses. He thus has to make cash *drawings* from the business. In a company these drawings are usually called *directors' salaries* or directors' *emoluments* as technically a director is an employee of the company.

9. and 10. Wages/salaries. Most employees are paid weekly or monthly and are paid net of PAYE and National Insurance. Technically the sums deducted together with employer's national insurance are payable in the month following the pay to which they relate. It is highly desirable to keep to this requirement.

11. *Capital* items. These are items such as purchase of buildings, plant, machinery and vehicles. They are especially likely in a new business. Enter only the cash payable for them. Note that if the capital items are acquired by leasing or on HP they go in row 16.

12. Transport/packing. Note that a new vehicle will go into row 11. This is for running expenses. Remember that some items are purchased on credit (eg a garage bill paid the month following the repair) and the payment in its appropriate month is what goes in the forecast.

13. Rent/rates. These are obvious. However new businesses in new premises often find that there is a long delay before rates bills are assessed and agreed.

14. Services. These may include telephone, gas, electricity and water. Remember that they are payable usually after consumption.

15. Loan repayments. Profits have to be large enough to allow for drawings and dividends and loan repayments.

16. Interest. Banks sometimes charge *interest* monthly and sometimes quarterly. Amounts are surprisingly large.

17. Bank/finance charges. Banking is not free to commercial customers and again bank charges are often considerable. They are however negotiable.

18. Value added tax. This is usually payable quarterly although there are other schemes. VAT is a subject of remarkable complexity and I shall not pursue it here.

19. Corporation/Income tax. Taxes are inevitable even with expert advice. Companies pay corporation tax on their profits about nine months after the conclusion of the year in which the profits were earned. The proprietors of unincorporated businesses pay income tax on the profits of the businesses. The timing and amount of corporation tax, advance corporation tax and income tax is a knotty subject and professional advice is essential. Sufficient to say that most new businesses will not pay any such taxes until eighteen months or so after the commencement of the business.

20. Dividends. Company can pay dividends to their shareholders. It is unlikely that a new company will declare and pay a dividend until at least the first year is over.

Having entered the forecast payments and receipts month by month, it is necessary to total the amounts in rows A and B. Then the opening balance at bank is entered in the first column in row C and the month end balance computed by adding row A and deducting row D to give the month end balance which goes in row D and then into the second month of row C.

An example

Federico intends to start in business on 1 January 19x2 as a wholesaler of decorative tiles. He will sell some tiles retail to local customers.

Details about his intentions are: (note that I have confined this example to three months. Most forecasts cover twelve months)

☐ He has acquired the lease of a small warehouse paying £5,000 at the beginning of January and an annual rent of £2,400 payable on the usual quarter days in arrears.

☐ Gas and electricity will cost £500 in January, £600 in February and £550 in March. These are payable in the month following consumption.

☐ He will buy £12,000 of tiles in January, £8,000 in February and £8,000 in March. His supplier expects payment in the month after supply.

☐ He will also buy about £400 a month of tiles locally for cash.

☐ He has arranged to borrow £5,000 in January from his mother repayable at £1,000 a year on December 31 each year. There is no interest on this loan.

☐ He will put in £4,000 from his own savings, his old van worth £1,500 and his collection of tiles valued at £2,500.

☐ He hopes to sell £800 a month for cash and credit sales of £4,000 in January, £14,000 in February and £16,000 in March. He estimates that payment will be 50% in the month following sale and 50% in the month after that.

☐ Federico intends to draw £400 a month for himself.

☐ He will employ Maria who will earn £300 a month less £60 tax and insurance. Employers national insurance will be £30 a month.

☐ He will need some shelving which will be delivered and paid for in January and cost £7,000. This should last 10 years

☐ He will lease a car for himself at a cost of £250 a month.

☐ He will have to pay professional fees re the warehouse lease purchase and the cash flow forecast of £600 in February.

☐ Advertising will be payable in advance at £180 a month. The first adverts will appear in February and be paid for in January.

☐ We will ignore VAT and any other payments.

Federico
Cash flow forecast for the first quarter of 19x2

	Jan	Feb	Mar	Total
Receipts:				
Loan – mother	5,000			5,000
Capital introduced	4,000			4,000
Cash sales	800	800	800	2,400
Credit sales		2,000	9,000	11,000
Total	9,800	2,800	9,800	22,400
Payments:				
Lease	5,000			5,000
Rent			600	600
Gas and electricity		500	600	1,100
Creditors		12,000	8,000	20,000
Cash purchases	400	400	400	1,200
Drawings	400	400	400	1,200
Wages	240	240	240	720
PAYE/NHI		90	90	180
Shelving	7,000			7,000
Lease of car	250	250	250	750
Professional fees		600		600
Advertising	180	180	180	540
Total	13,470	14,660	10,760	38,890
Opening balance	0	(3,670)	(15,530)	0
Closing balance	(3,670)	(15,530)	(16,490)	(16,490)

Federico takes this forecast to his bank and asks for an overdraft facility of £20,000 as he foresees that he will need £16,490 according to his forecast but would like more to cover things not going according to plan. The bank manager refuses to offer more than £10,000 and asks Federico to reconsider his proposals to keep the overdraft under £10,000.

Possible actions are:

❐ put in more capital himself, perhaps by second mortgaging his house.

❐ obtain a special loan secured on the lease

❐ reduce or delay some of his purchases

❐ negotiate more credit from his supplier

❐ attempt to buy the shelving on hire purchase or lease it

The advantage of a forecast is that it enables cash flow difficulties to be seen in advance and action taken to avoid disaster.

Problems in cash flow forecasting

Cash Flow forecasting is not intrinsically difficult but there are some pitfalls:

❐ include only cash flows. Remember that depreciation is not a cash flow.

❐ be careful about tax flows – VAT, PAYE and NHI. Professional advice is desirable.

❐ customers are likely to pay more slowly than expected.

❐ Allow for bad debts and disputes with customers that may slow payment.

❐ Allow for all expenses. It is easy to omit some. Provide a sum for contingencies like repairs.

❐ Do not forget that the proprietor must make drawings to live on.

❏ Loans and overdrafts require interest to be paid. With fixed term loans interest payments are usually determinable. However the amount of interest payable on an overdraft is difficult to forecast. Consult with the bank manager.

 **Key principle summary**

○ Businesses must, in the long term, earn profits which are greater than drawings and dividends.

○ Businesses must also manage their cash flows to ensure that payments can always be made when they fall due.

○ Cash flow forecasting is desirable at all times and is an essential requirement for businesses requesting loan or overdraft facilities.

○ Cash flow forecasts usually cover twelve months and each month has a column for the forecast and for the actual flows which are of course filled in after the event. A total column is useful to check accuracy.

○ If a cash flow forecast shows a cash flow problem is possible, action can be taken to avert the difficulty.

○ Professional advice on the forecast by an accountant is usually sought by people who intend to start a business.

○ The modern way of preparing a cash flow forecast is to use a computer spreadsheet package.

○ Do not include non-cash flows like depreciation. Do include all costs include taxes, drawings and interest.

---

16 | Investment appraisal

1. Capital expenditure is expenditure on fixed assets. Fixed assets are long lived items like land, buildings, plant and machinery and vehicles. These are called tangible assets. For the purposes of this chapter we will include also the acquisition of intangible assets such as goodwill, patents and trade marks.

   Fixed assets can be acquired singly as in the purchase of a replacement lorry or lathe or the construction of a factory extension. They can also be acquired as a set as in the setting up of a new branch, a new production line or a whole business.

2. The important thing is to distinguish between capital expenditure and revenue expenditure. Revenue expenditure is spending on the supply and manufacture of goods and the provision of services charged in the profit and loss account in the accounting period in which they are consumed.

3. In most companies, revenue expenditure is controlled by systems of budgetary control perhaps with standard costing and variance analysis. Capital expenditure often involves very large sums and is non-routine, so it is very important to have a system to deal with projected capital expenditure. Such systems are called *investment appraisal* or *capital budgeting*.

Payback

4. A simple way of appraising projected capital investment is to use payback. This is simply considering the length of time which is required for a stream of *cash receipts* flowing from the investment to recover the initial investment.

   Suppose a replacement machine was being considered. The cost (after deducting the proceeds of sale of the old machine) will be £5,000. The new machine will cost less to run and the annual savings are estimated at £1,500 a year. The payback period is $3\frac{1}{3}$ years ($3 \times £1,500 + \frac{1}{3} \times £1,500$).

For management, knowing the payback period is useful in deciding whether or not to go ahead with an investment and deciding between possible alternatives. Some managements have a *hurdle* such that investments are not accepted unless the payback period is say less than three or four years.

Points about payback include:

a) Cash flows are considered, not accounting flows

b) Future cash flows are not equivalent to current cash flows as current cash held can be invested to earn interest. £1,000 today can be invested at say 10% so that in one years time it is equivalent to £1,100. This important idea is not recognised by payback.

c) Payback prefers short term investments rather than investments which take a long time to pay off. *Short-termism* is a criticism often levelled at British management.

d) In a time of rapid technological change, payback has some obvious benefits.

e) Projects that pay back quickly may present less *risk* and payback is sometimes used as a proxy for the riskiness of the project.

Discounted cash flow

5. This is a more sophisticated approach to capital investment appraisal but is not so simple to understand.

The important concept is that money has a time value.

If you have £1,000 today (the *present* time) then it can be invested to earn say 10% interest. This means that its value grows as:

	£	
now	1,000	
Interest year 1	100	
value after one year	1,100	
Interest year 2	110	(10% of £1,100)
value after two years	1,210	

This is easy to understand. However we can see the process in a different way. We can say that the £1,210 after two years is equivalent in value to the £1,000 now. We can also say that the *present (= now) value* of £1,210 receivable in two years time is £1,000.

If the interest rate was say 15% the figures would be:

	£
now	1,000
Interest year 1	150
value after one year	1,150
Interest year 2	172.50
value after two years	1,322.50

So the present value of £1,322.5 two years in the future at 15% rate of interest is £1,000.

It is possible to calculate the present value of any future sum, given its date and a rate of interest. We can use a formula:

$$\text{Present value} = \frac{\text{future sum}}{(1 + r)^n}$$

where r = the rate of interest. This has to be expressed as a percentage divided by 100 ie if the rate is 16% then r = 0.16. and n = the number of years.

If we take the figures already calculated then £1,322.50 at 15% two years in the future:

$$\text{Present value} = \frac{1,322.5}{(1.15)^2} = £1,000$$

Alternatively, tables can be used. This is an extract from a table:

	Interest rate			
Year	10%	12%	14%	16%
1	.91	.89	.88	.86
2	.83	.80	.77	.74
3	.75	.71	.67	.64
4	.68	.64	.59	.55

You can read off that the discount factor for a sum three years away at 14% is .67. So if we need the present value of £4,800 three years away at 14% then the answer is

£4,800 × .67 = £3,216 or as .67 is a rounded figure we should perhaps specify it as £3,200.

The formula gives £3,239.86...

An example

Upandaway plc are considering an investment in a company aeroplane. Projected cash flows are:

Cost now £600,000.

Resale value after 4 years £100,000

Savings each year on other forms of transport £380,000

Running costs year 1 £150,000, year 2 £180,000, year 3 £200,000 year 4 £200,000.

We can set this up as a table:

	(all figures in £'000)				
Year	0	1	2	3	4
Outflow	− 600				
Savings		+ 380	+ 380	+ 380	+ 380
Costs		− 150	− 180	− 200	− 200
Resale					+ 100
Net cash flow	− 600	+ 230	+ 200	+ 180	+ 280
Discount factor		.89	.80	.71	.64
Present value	− 600	+ 200	+ 160	+ 130	+ 180

Note:

a) I have used a discount rate of 12%. The discount rate to be used is the '*cost of capital*' to the company. Its calculation is a very large subject and we will not attempt to calculate it in this manual.

b) The original outlay is described as year 0 and subsequent flows as being in year 1, 2 etc. Cash flows in a year are usually considered to be received or paid at the *year end*.

c) The estimates of future cash flows are very *uncertain* and the effect of multiplying an uncertain number say £380,000 by a discount factor which is a rounded fraction of an uncertain discount rate should not be a precise number. I have therefore given the discounted cash flows to two significant figures.

d) The net present value is:

$$-£600,000 + £200,000 + £160,000 + £130,000 + £180,000 = + £70,000$$

As this is positive, the project is a good one and should be undertaken. Essentially, we can say that it will earn income which represents a rate of interest greater than 12% which is the cost of capital.

e) It is possible to calculate a profitability index:

$$\frac{\text{Discounted inflow}}{\text{Initial outlays}} = \frac{£670,000}{£600,000} = 1.1$$

This can also be used as a measure of risk as the higher the projected discounted inflows in relation to the initial outflow, the less likely it is that the actual discounted future inflows will return a negative net present value.

f) In order to appraise a project using this method, it is necessary to specify all cash flows and an interest rate. In specifying future cash flows, a *time horizon* has to be specified. In the example I have suggested that the aeroplane will last four years. In practice the life of new projects is uncertain and stating a time horizon adds yet another layer of unreality to the process.

Internal rate of return

6. This is a similar but more difficult alternative to net present value. It actually presents a number of conceptual and practical problems which I will not address here. As a result it is not very commonly used in business.

The objective of this approach is to see what rate of interest a proposed project will *return*. Suppose that Upandaway plc are considering a joint venture project in Poland which will involve an outlay now (year 0) of £65,000 and the expected returns over the three year life of the project are:

Year 1 £20,000 Year 2 £30,000 year 3 £40,000

What rate of return is given by this project? An alternative statement of the problem is: what rate of discount will discount the cash flows in years 1,2 and 3 back to the outlay in year 0? This can only be found by *trial and error*. Let us start with 14%

Year	1	2	3
	£'000	£'000	£'000
Cash flows	20	30	40
Discount factor at 14%	.88	.77	.67
Present values	18	23	27

Net present values in total are £68,000.

This is more than the outlay, so we can say the project pays more than 14% and we should try 15%.

This gives figures of £17,000 + £23,000 + £26,000 = £66,000

This is approximately correct and we can say the project will pay about 15%. The company may have a rule that all projects which pay above the cost of capital of 12% are acceptable and then this project would be considered to be acceptable.

Some points about internal rate of return are:

a) Most text books calculate the rate exactly (eg 14.63%). However the forecast cash flows are estimates with a large margin for error and it is not really possible to specify the rate of return accurately. In fact it may give management a spurious confidence in the accuracy of the forecasts.

b) The calculations can be tedious and in practice are carried out on a computer.

c) The higher the internal rate of return in relation to the cost of capital, the less risky the project appears to be.

Accounting rate of return

7. The net present value and internal rate of return approaches use cash flows. A disadvantage of this approach is that measurements of cash flows are not made or are not reported so there is often no feedback on the success of the forecasts made. As measurement and reporting is done of accounting flows, some writers advocate appraising projects by using the accounting rate of return. Suppose Upandaway plc are proposing to open a branch in Tipton and expected initial outlays are £20,000. Expected returns are:

Year	1	2	3	4	5
(in £'000)	5	6	8	6	5

These returns are after depreciation.

Average return is $\dfrac{£30,000}{5}$ = £6,000

The accounting rate of return is $\dfrac{£6,000}{£30,000}$ × 100 = 20%

An alternative is to take the *average capital employed* which, assuming that the investment will be steadily depreciated to nil over the five years is $\dfrac{£30,000}{2}$ = £15,000. In this case the accounting rate of return will be $\dfrac{£6,000}{£15,000}$ × 100 = 40%.

Points about this method include:

a) It is in effect a rate of return on capital employed.

b) The accounting flows are subject to the vagaries of accounting measurement including different depreciation methods.

c) The method is not intellectually rigorous and there are no universally accepted methods of applying it.

d) I do not recommend it.

Practical investment appraisal

8. There is agreement that some approach to formal capital investment appraisal is desirable if only to clarify thinking. For example management may decide they fancy a company aeroplane but to do so without careful estimates of costs, revenues, savings, alternatives etc may well lead to a bad decision.

   However the intellectually rigorous methods of appraisal (net present value and internal rate of return) do have drawbacks including the fact that management do not always understand them.

   The simple methods (payback and accounting rate of return) are easier to understand but lack rigour. Many companies adopt a combination of methods. This may mean net present value as a first hurdle and payback as a second hurdle. Also in practice many proposals may pass the tests and be rejected by management and many fail the tests but are adopted anyway!

 **Key principle summary**

○ Capital expenditure is in some ways the most important activity of enterprises.

○ It is vital that projected capital investment should be subject to careful scrutiny and consideration including the use of capital investment appraisal techniques.

○ Capital investment appraisal can also be called capital budgeting.

○ The simplest technique is payback where the time taken by estimated future cash inflows to cover the initial outlay is calculated.

○ The best technique is the calculation of net present value. This is carried out by discounting all cash flows (except the initial outlay) by a rate of interest equal to the cost of capital.

○ A similar, but more difficult, technique is the internal rate of return. This method involves the calculation of the discount rate which will just discount the future cash flows back to the initial outlay.

○ The accounting rate of return involves the calculation of a return on capital employed using the average after depreciation returns and the actual or average capital employed.

○ In practice, enterprises may use none, any or a combination of these or make decisions on other grounds altogether.

17 Sources of finance

1. Companies have sources of finance under three general headings:

    Retained profits

    Equity

    Debt

    Each have different costs and we will consider these as we review each type.

Retained earnings

2. The principal source of finance for companies is retained profits. This can be illustrated by Stubby Ltd buying a widget for £50 and selling it for £75. There may be time delays involved as credit is given by the supplier and taken by the customer and there will be a delay between purchase and sale when the widget is in stock. However the effect of the transaction is that the company has £25 more cash. The total cash gains of this kind will be reduced by the payment of overheads and subsequently by tax and dividends. However if the company makes a profit there will be a net increase in financial resources.

    It appears that retained earnings have no cost to the company but in fact the expansion in the company, which retained earnings are, will give shareholders expectations of higher dividends. Dividends are the cost to the company of all forms of equity finance.

Equity

3. Equity is the investment in the company by persons and institutions who become shareholders. Such investment is normally for the long term and is risk bearing. If the company does well, the equity shareholders receive large dividends but if the company fails, the equity shareholders lose all their investment.

    In company law, the money invested by shareholders is not normally returnable. If a shareholder wants his money back he cannot look to the company but has to find a buyer for his shares. Shareholders in private companies often find themselves locked into their shares and can only find buyers amongst the other shareholders or when the company as a whole is sold. Shareholders in companies quoted on the stock exchange can always sell their shares as the stock exchange provides a market for them.

    Companies obtain finance by issuing shares:

    a) In exchange for a business usually because the company is formed to take over a business.

    b) By a general issue of shares to the public by a prospectus. This usually happens only when a private company becomes a public company and obtains a listing on the stock exchange.

    c) By a rights issue. This means that new shares are issued for cash to existing shareholders in proportion (the usual expression is *pro rata*) to their existing holdings.

    d) In a takeover of another company. Sometimes a takeover does not involve buying another company for cash but issuing new shares in the predator company to the shareholders of the victim company in exchange for their shares in the victim company. The predator company does not get cash for the new shares but does get a subsidiary company.

    The cost of equity is a difficult concept. Essentially, when a company obtains finance by issuing shares it incurs at least a moral obligation to pay dividends. The dividends are the cost to the company of obtaining equity finance. Investors have expectations of increasing dividends as the years go by.

Preference shares

Preference shares are shares which have many of the characteristics of loans. R plc issued 1,000,000 7% £1 preference shares in 1995. The shares are redeemable at par at the company's option at any time after 2006 and the dividends are cumulative.

The redeemable arrangement means that the company can repay the shares at any time after 2006. Par means that each £1 share will be repaid at £1. It is also possible to repay at a premium, for example repayment at £1.20 a share or at a discount, for example at 90p a share. The law requires that preference share can only be redeemed if profits are available greater than or equal to the redemption. Once used for redemption, the profits are not then available for dividend.

The company can pay dividends on the shares but the annual dividend will always be 7p a share (or less). Cumulative means that if the dividend is missed in a year it should be made good in subsequent years. Dividends on ordinary shares can only be paid if preference dividends are up to date. No dividends, ordinary or preference, can be paid unless the company has a credit balance on profit and loss account greater than the amount of the dividend. The company have no legal obligation to pay dividends.

In a winding up or liquidation, preference shareholders are paid out in full before any payment to ordinary shareholders. However, in most liquidations no funds are available to either type of shareholders!

Preference share were once common but are now relatively rare.

Debt

4. Debt means borrowing. Borrowing can be in the short term, in the medium term (2-5 years) and for the long term. Borrowing can be *unsecured*, *secured* by operation of law, secured by a *floating charge* or secured by a *fixed charge* on a specific asset (see later in this Topic). Costs are usually expressed as an interest rate.

Short term debt

5. Most companies obtain supplies on *credit*. This means they have the supplies and can use them before they pay. Payment can be anything from a few days to several months after receipt of the goods. The exact time depends on the policy of the payer and the tolerance of the supplier. Large companies are notoriously slow in paying small suppliers.

In effect trade credit is a form of finance which companies see as free. In fact it may not be free as:

a) better prices may be negotiated if long credit is not taken

b) settlement discounts are lost by taking credit. If the terms offered are nett, one month or 5% discount for immediate payment then the taking of credit implies a cost of the lost discount.

6. The other common form of short term finance is the *bank overdraft*. This is normally regarded as short term as technically the terms of the loan are that the loan is repayable on demand. In practice overdrafts are renegotiated at intervals and often go on for many years so that companies see them as medium term or even long term finance. The cost of an overdraft is the interest rate agreed with the bank and often appears extortionate to the business borrower.

There are other forms of short term finance available including *bills of exchange* which we will not pursue further and factoring.

7. *Factoring* involves the following procedures:

❏ Stubby Ltd (the borrower) sells goods on credit to A Ltd, a customer and invoices them at £1,000.

❏ Natmid Factors Ltd (a factoring finance company) advances 80% of the value, that is £800 to Stubby Ltd on the same or the next day.

❏ when A ltd pay three months later, £800 goes to Natmid in repayment for the advance and £200 to Stubby Ltd

❏ in due course, Natmid charge up Stubby with interest on the £800 loan which was lent for three months.

Factoring finance is only used on sales so that the borrowings only occur to the amount needed to finance debtors.

Factoring companies usually offer other optional services to the lenders including:

- customer accounting
- credit control (assessing whether or not to give credit to a potential customer)
- chasing slow payers

Medium term debt

8. We will consider two forms of medium term debt: hire purchase and leasing. Other forms exist including bank lending which we will consider under long term debt.

9. *Hire purchase* is much used by small companies who often acquire assets such as machines and vehicles on hire purchase. You may be familiar with the concept as it is very common domestically. The parties to the contract are:

   - the seller of the goods (say a car) who sells the goods to the company who want the car (known as the hirer) and get paid by the finance company. The seller is then no longer involved in the transaction;

   - the hirer company who has use of the car and is in effect (but not in law) the owner;

   - the finance company. In law they own the vehicle and receive payments (instalments) from the hirer over the term of the HP agreement. The agreement normally requires the hirer to pay monthly equal instalments over a period of one, two or three years. The instalments are partly repayment of the amount lent and partly interest.

   On payment of the last instalment ownership of the car passes to the hirer. The law gives the finance company some rights of repossession which we will not consider here.

   The rate of interest is usually high and is given as an annual percentage rate (APR) which is equivalent to the internal rate of return.

10. Leasing is a rapidly expanding form of finance. If Stubby Ltd need a new machine, they can seek the aid of a leasing finance company who will buy the machine and then lease it to Stubby Ltd. Stubby Ltd as lessees pay equal monthly sums as agreed to the finance company who are the lessors. Failure to pay instalments gives the finance company rights of repossession and the problem of disposing of the repossessed asset.

    The essence of the deal is that Stubby do not own the asset but lease it. However many such lease agreements are effectively finance leases and the reality of the matter is that the deal is the same as a hire purchase transaction.

Long term debt

11. Companies are able to borrow in the long term with repayment required only after a period which can be twenty years. Lenders can be banks, other institutions such as insurance companies and members of the public.

    Such borrowings can be termed loans, *unsecured loan stock*, notes, *bonds* or *debentures*. They always pay interest at a specified rate called the *coupon* rate.

    Some loans are simply by a single institution which receives interest every year and final repayment when specified. Some loans are made by numerous individuals and are quoted on the stock exchange. Suppose that in 1992 Giant plc raised £10,000,000 by a public issue of 15% loan stock repayable in 2012. Small was a member of the public who subscribed for £2,000 worth of the stock. In 1997 he wished to dispose of the stock. Giant plc will not repay until 2012 but he was able to sell his holding to another investor through the medium of his broker. He would not receive £2,000 but whatever the stock was quoted at on the date of sale which may be more or less than the £2,000. The actual quotation depends on the prevailing interest rates and if interest rates generally had fallen, he would actually sell his holding for more than £2,000.

12. Loans can be *secured* by a *fixed charge*. Supposing B Ltd wish to raise £50,000 by a loan from Unutterable Assurance plc. B Ltd own a property valued at £100,000 and offer this as a security. This means that the deeds of the security will be deposited with the lender. If B Ltd default on the loan then the lender can appoint a *receiver* to seize the property and sell it. The proceeds of sale will firstly be used to repay the loan and only any remainder will be available to other creditors.

The lender cannot lose providing the property is worth more than the loan. The property is said to be subject to a *mortgage* and my readers will be aware that this is exactly what happens when houses are bought through a building society or bank mortgage.

13. Loans can also be *secured* by a *floating charge* on all the assets. C Ltd borrow £20,000 from the Natmid Bank who take a floating charge. If C Ltd default on the loan then the bank can appoint a receiver who must be a qualified insolvency practitioner. The receiver's duties will involve trying to save the company but if this is not possible then the assets will be sold and the loan repaid from the proceeds. Only any remainder is available for other creditors.

Convertible loans

14. Lending long term is not very attractive as interest rates may change and inflation reduces the capital in real terms. In order to attract investors to subscribe for loans, it is common to offer loans with rights to convert the loan into ordinary shares at specified dates. For example D plc issued £1,000,000 of 10% convertible loan stock in 1990. In any August from 1995 to 1999 each £100 of loan stock can be converted into 50 ordinary shares of 20p each. In 1995 Mrs P who has some stock finds the share price is £1.30 so that the value of 50 shares is $50 \times £1.30 = £65$ so she does not convert. However in 1996, she finds the share price is £2.40 so that the value of 50 shares is £120 and she does convert. On conversion she finds she has 50 shares of 20p each instead of £100 of loan stock. Instead of receiving interest she will in future receive dividends. You will see that she has made a capital gain and it is the possibility of this which makes convertibles attractive. This is especially true as she avoids the possibility of loss as the loan will eventually be repaid if it is not converted.

Warrants

15. Another way of attracting investors to loans is to attach warrants, which are rights to subscribe for shares, to the loan. E plc issued £2,000,000 of 12% loan stock in 1994 with warrants giving lenders of £100 rights to subscribe for 5 new 50p ordinary shares at a price of £1.80 at any time after 1998. In 1999, Ella who has £100 of the stock finds that the shares are quoted at £1.60 and does not exercise her warrants. But in 2,000 she finds that the shares are quoted at £2.50 and so she exercises her warrants and subscribes for the 5 shares at £1.80 and thus acquires shares worth £2.50 each. She still has her loan stock but of course no longer has the warrants.

Gearing

16. Gearing is called *leverage* in the USA and the term is now common also in the UK. Gearing describes the relative amounts of investment in a company of *debt* and *equity*.

The theory is that companies should have at least some borrowings because they can borrow at one rate say 15% and invest the money in productive assets to yield a higher rate say 20%. Failure to have some borrowings is to deprive the equity shareholders of this opportunity.

However too large an amount of debt (= too high gearing) can be dangerous. Debt interest has to be paid and debt capital repaid. Too much debt can be an impossible burden in bad times and lead to company failure. The optimum gearing ratio is a matter of much controversy but clearly depends on the type of company. There is a theory associated with two American economists, *Modigliani* and *Miller*, that the cost of capital is independent of the gearing ratio. This implies that high gearing does not increase the risk attached to debt and equity. Their arguments are seductive but most observers take a view that high gearing does increase the risk accepted by both debt holders and equity holders.

What sources of finance to use?

17. There are no golden rules on this. Some debt is desirable as we saw in the last paragraph but too much debt puts the company into danger. There is a theory that *financing is a separate function* from investment in productive assets. Thus the directors of F plc should decide what investment in assets to make and then use a range of appropriate financing sources to finance the company. Clearly the two are connected but specific assets should not be associated with specific financing sources.

Clearly leasing, hire purchase and the factoring of debtors are sources of finance which are associated with specific assets but the decision on the amount of investment in the assets which are leased, hire purchased and the debtors should be taken independently of the finance available. Similarly these financing sources should be seen as just some of the range available in selecting the company's mix of financing sources.

Another theory is that short term assets should be financed with short term finance and long term assets with long term finance. I do not find this theory attractive as it contravenes the theory on the independence of financing and investment. However a mix of short term, medium term and long term finance is probably most appropriate.

Repayment and security

18. All borrowings have ultimately to be repaid. Most companies find that borrowings are repaid by further borrowings. Jason is considering supplying goods on credit to W Ltd. What should he look for in the balance sheet? He should look at the repayment dates for all borrowings as it may be that the company have to borrow soon to make a repayment and that replacement borrowing may be difficult. Cash flow difficulties may then follow making payment of creditors tricky. He should also look to see if any of the borrowings are secured. Hire purchase and leasing means that most or all of the value in the corresponding assets will go to these lenders. Some of the lenders, especially bankers, will have fixed or floating charges.

19. Many loan stocks have redemption dates as 2002-2004. This means hat the company must repay the loans at some time between these dates. G plc have £10,000,000 of 12% loan stock 2002 –2004 outstanding. If interest rates are less than this, say 9%, they will borrow at 9% and repay the loan early in 2002. But if interest rates are higher, say 14%, they will postpone borrowing until the end of 2004 and repay then.

 **Key principle summary**

○ Companies finance themselves by a mixture of retained earnings, equity and debt.

○ Retained earnings are the major source of company finance. Their cost is the higher dividends expected.

○ Equity comprises the interest in the company of its owners, the shareholders. Equity arises from retained earnings and from new issues.

○ Shares can be issued in exchange for businesses, companies or cash. New cash issues are nearly always rights issues.

○ Preference shares pay fixed rates of dividend and are usually redeemable and cumulative.

○ Debt can be short term, medium term and long term.

○ Trade credit, debt factoring and overdrafts are the principal forms of short term debt.

○ Hire purchase and leasing are common forms of medium term debt.

○ Long terms loans are often called debentures, bonds, notes or other terms.

○ They can be unsecured or secured by fixed or floating charges.

○ Loans can be quoted.

○ Loans can be convertible or have warrants attached.

○ Gearing is desirable but too high gearing can be very dangerous.

○ Financing and investment in productive assets can be seen as separate activities.

18 Working capital

1. Working capital can be defined simply as current assets less current liabilities or also as current assets less creditors and overdraft if any. Managers and accountants often speak of having a working capital problem. Essentially what they mean by this is an inability to pay creditors when they want to as the overdraft has a ceiling which cannot be exceeded. The reason why working capital comes into this problem can be explained by regarding working capital as a *single entity* which can be *subdivided*.

    Suppose Stubby traders ltd was formed to market pencils. Initially the company was formed with a share capital of £30,000. Of this £20,000 was required for fixed assets and the balance was available to be invested in working capital. After some 9 months trading, during which no profit was made, the working capital looked like this:

	£	£
Current assets		
Stock	28,000	
Debtors	43,000	
		68,000
Current liabilities		
Creditors	28,000	
Overdraft	30,000	58,000
Working capital		10,000

    The amount of working capital (£10,000) can only be changed by either raising *new finance* from shareholders or long term loans, and we will presume this is not possible, or by making *profits* and this has not occurred yet.

    Stock is the minimum necessary to continue trading. Anything less would lead to stock outs and loss of sales.

    Debtors cannot be reduced without turning away customers and collection is as fast as can be achieved without alienating good customers.

    The bank overdraft is as high as the bank will allow and any increase may lead to the bank dishonouring cheques.

    The only flexible item is creditors. This represents unpaid accounts and represents 3 months supplies on average. Some suppliers are very tolerant but others are restive. Some have refused further supplies and some have threatened court action if payment is not made in a few days. Stubby Traders' bookkeeper is reduced to such excuses for non-payment as: the cheque is in the post (it is not); I cannot send a cheque today as the director is out of town (he is sitting on the desk); we have used the last cheque in the book and the bank is closed (just untrue); we will not pay your £3,000 bill going back 4 months because we are waiting for a credit note to correct the price of the four sprockets invoiced at £2.50 each instead of the agreed £2.40; we will send you a cheque today (we will, but it will not be signed and you will have to send it back for signature thus giving us a week more time).

    The problem is that the company cannot pay its bills but the cause is that the total of working capital is too low. How can this be corrected? This chapter will pursue some solutions.

Increasing working capital

2. If working capital is too low then some way should be found to increase it by raising finance from other sources. These may include:

    a) An issue of shares to existing shareholders if they have any cash available.

    b) An issue of shares to an institution that will buy equity in small companies. There are now several *venture capital* suppliers in the market.

c) Raising a long term loan from the bank or other institution. Normally security in the form of a fixed or floating charge will be required and the overdraft may be restricted further if the bank's security is lessened by a prior charge.

d) Financing the fixed assets by leasing or hire purchase.

e) Factoring the debts.

Stocks

3. Return to the working capital calculation in paragraph 1. You will see that if stocks can be reduced, creditors can be reduced if all the other figures remain unchanged.

The amount of stocks carried is of great importance to the management of most enterprises. Large amounts of stock prevent stock outs and enable all the demands of customers to be met. However holding stock has costs including:

storage space costs

financing costs

risk of damage or spoilage

risk of obsolescence.

Deliberately carrying small stocks also means buying in small quantities which involves extra handling costs and loss of bulk discounts.

In practice stocks are of many different lines. Some of these sell well and sometimes stock outs occur. Some stocks sell very slowly if at all. The tendency is for stocks of slow selling lines to multiply so that stock becomes too large and consists of the wrong items. Effectively the firm suffers from the penalties of holding large stocks without the benefits of being able to supply popular items to customers. The remedy for this situation is vigilance. All purchasing should be carefully considered and stocks continually monitored. Any that do not move rapidly should be studied and movement hastened by a special promotion or price reductions.

There is a theory about the optimal amount of a particular line of stock. This concerns the economic order quantity (the optimal size of order) and is given in the formula:

$$EOQ = \sqrt{\frac{2BN}{C}}$$

where
B = the costs (clerical, transport etc) of making one order.
N = the number of units used in a year
C = costs associated with holding the stock in £ per year.

Suppose T Ltd use 5,000 mark 3 widgets a year, the holding cost is 30p a unit a year and the buying cost is £20 an order then:

$$EOQ \text{ is } \sqrt{\frac{2 \times 20 \times 5,000}{0.30}} = 816 \text{ units}$$

Once the economic order quantity has been calculated it is then desirable to calculate the re-order level. This is the level of stock at which an order should be placed.

It is given by:

$$\text{Re-order level} = \frac{DN}{W}$$

where
D = the delivery time taken by suppliers in weeks
W = the number of working weeks in the year.

T Ltd find that the supplier of mark 3 widgets takes 7 weeks from order to delivery and there are 50 working weeks in the year. Then:

$$\text{Re-order level} = \frac{7 \times 5,000}{50} = 700 \text{ units}$$

Thus the purchasing officer should be told to order 816 units every time the stock falls to 700 units. In practice 816 units may be an unacceptable order and an order of 1,000 may be necessary or perhaps 6 gross – 864 units.

This explanation works well in theory but in practice:

a) Estimation of purchasing costs and holding costs is difficult and subjective.

b) The numbers change constantly – demand increases or reduces and delivery times vary greatly.

c) Doing the calculations for perhaps thousands of lines is a formidable task.

but

d) Attempting the calculations keeps the stock constantly under review.

e) Stock records are ideal for computerisation and once EOQs and re-order levels have been input, the computer can re-order automatically.

Note that the most modern manufacturing systems use *'just in time'* stock deliveries so stock levels of raw materials and components are effectively nil.

Manufacturing companies also have work in progress and stocks of finished goods. To optimise holdings:

a) The work in progress at any one time depends on the cycle time in manufacture. This should be kept as short as possible and constantly monitored. Delays caused by machine breakdown should be minimised by planned maintenance and delays caused by material or component shortages should be minimised by stock controls like the use of EOQ and re-order levels.

b) Finished goods levels are a function of production and sales. Production should be planned in relation to sales forecasts and the up to date position constantly monitored.

Debtors

4. Some firms are fortunate in that they sell goods with cash paid at the time of sale or even earlier. Examples are supermarkets where cash is paid as sales are made and travel agents who collect the cash before the holidays are taken. Many firms however have to sell on credit. It is very easy to put 'nett cash 30 days' on the invoice but many customers ignore this and pay only after several reminders and threats, months after the invoice date. For many firms, collecting debts is a major headache. How can debtors as a total be kept as low as possible?

Possible procedures are:

a) Avoid selling to firms that are very slow in paying.

b) Raise selling prices to such customers to compensate for slow payment.

c) Invoice promptly and send monthly statements on time.

d) Chase slow payers by stickers on statements, letters, telephone calls, cutting off further supplies and finally legal action.

e) Offer discounts for prompt payment. This is a common device but often misfires and can be very costly. The cost can be expressed as a rate of interest using the formula:

$$\text{cost of discount} = \frac{12r}{m}$$

where r =   rate of discount as a percentage

          m =   the average credit, in months, taken by the customer.

Suppose C Ltd, a customer, takes 3 months on average and is offered 5% discount for immediate payment on receipt of the invoice then:

$$\text{Cost of discount} \frac{12 \times 5}{3} = 20\%$$

This is high and it would pay to borrow from the bank if the APR were lower than 20% rather than give the discount.

In practice the situation is usually *worse* as:

a) Slow paying customers do not take advantage of the discount.

b) Quick paying customers do take advantage, Suppose X ltd normally pay in the 30 days but, along with other customers, are offered 5% for immediate payment. If they accept (they are almost sure to do so) then the cost is:

$$\frac{12 \times 5}{1} = 60\%$$

c) Some customers will take the discount and still pay late. This leads to acrimonious relations with the customer and often the discount has to be conceded.

A point about slow payers is that they if they fail then the amount lost is say four months sales rather than the say one month of a quick payer. It is worth noting that the actual loss in a bad debt is the cost of the goods sold not the selling price and also that the VAT is now recoverable.

The protection of selling goods on reservation of title contracts (so-called Romalpa contracts where the title to the goods remains with the seller until payment is made) is largely illusory in practice.

Creditors

5. Prompt payment of suppliers is good practice and wins supplier goodwill which can result in good service and preference in time of shortage. However to minimise working capital requirements many firms take excessive credit. This may have a number of effects:

a) Supplier badwill

b) Some suppliers may increase prices to slow payers.

c) Some essential suppliers may refuse further credit and insist on cash with order.

d) A reputation for slow payment may lead to some desirable suppliers refusing credit.

e) A supplier may lose patience and issue a writ. This can have a snowball effect if other suppliers hear of it and do likewise. The effect may be receivership or liquidation.

f) Loss of potential settlement discounts. It is almost always advantageous to take settlement discounts.

Overtrading

6. Refer back to the working capital calculation in paragraph 1 and consider the effect of a 20% increase in sales.

If sales are increased by 20% then working capital will be:

Stock	33,600	
Debtors	51,600	
		85,200
Creditors	45,200	
Overdraft	30,000	
		75,200
		10,000

I have assumed that working capital remains at £10,000 and the overdraft at £30,000. The effect is that creditors have been increased by 61%. If we assume that creditors were at the limit of tolerance on an average of three months then an increase of 20% would keep the situation stable but an increase of 61% would push the creditors too far and lead to receivership.

The phenomenon of being unable to pay creditors because of an increase in business is called overtrading. It is quite common. The solution is to ensure that before increasing sales (which is obviously desirable) extra finance is available from long term or short term sources.

Taxes

7. At one time the response of many firms to difficulty in paying trade creditors was to delay payment of taxes including corporation tax, PAYE and National Insurance and VAT. The taxing authorities now have sanctions against late payment in the form of interest and penalties.

    Delay in payment of taxes is no longer recommended

Key principle summary

○ Working capital is defined as current assets less current liabilities or current assets less creditors and overdraft.

○ The working capital problem arises from the fixed sizes of working capital as a whole, stock, debtors and the overdraft. The result is difficulty in paying creditors.

○ Stocks should be the minimum required to satisfy production or sales needs.

○ An economic order quantity and a re- order level can be calculated for each stock line.

○ Debtors should be minimised by a range of policies.

○ Offering settlement (often called cash) discounts can reduce debtors but is very expensive.

○ Paying creditors slowly can be construed as giving free finance but can be bad practice both morally and commercially. Taking cash discounts is usually good.

○ Increasing sales without considering the effects on working capital components can lead to overtrading and disaster.

○ The payment of taxes should not be delayed.

---

19 | The stock exchange

1. The stock exchange is a market. A market is a place where things are bought, sold and exchanged. The things traded on the stock exchange are financial securities and we will review these later in this chapter. Originally the stock exchanges were places in London and other cities, containing a floor where the actual trading took place. This is still partly true and the magnificent stock exchange building in London can be visited and I commend it to you. There are also stock exchange buildings in other cities in Britain and Ireland. There are also stock exchanges in most countries in the world.

    Today trading is not done on the floor of the exchange but through the medium of electronic communications and especially the *computer screen*. The stock exchange is now a world wide market.

Investors

2. The most important people on the stock exchange are the investors. Investors are people and institutions who buy and sell financial securities. Several million people in the UK now invest through the stock exchange directly and nearly everybody invests through the stock exchange indirectly.

    Private investors now account for a diminishing proportion of stock exchange investors but private investment has received a boost through the eighties due to the privatisation issues. People who never considered stock exchange investment now have shares in British Gas, British Telecom and the others. There is however a tendency for buyers of privatisation issues to hold these without further dealing. If they do sell there is a tendency for the shares to be sold to *institutions* so that the long term trend is still away from private shareholders towards institutional investors.

3. The principal institutional investors are:

    Pension funds

    Insurance companies

    Unit trusts

    Investment trusts

4. Large numbers of people in the UK are in occupational pension schemes. Pension schemes often work as:

    Deductions are made from salaries and wages.

    Contributions are made by the employer.

    These two sums are handed by the company to pension fund trustees (who can be representatives of the company and unions).

    The trustees invest these sums in securities or other investments using professional advice.

    Pensions are paid as agreed.

    The essential points are that pension fund investment outside the sponsoring company ensures that pensions are safe even if the sponsoring company fails. In general pension fund investment is well done but occasional scandals occur such as the Maxwell and Daily Mirror pension fund disgrace. Pension fund investment is now megabillion.

5. Insurance companies receive premiums from their policyholders and invest them. At a later date claims will be met. This is true of accident insurance but the principal investment is from life assurance and pensions. Premiums on life assurance, endowment, personal pensions and other policies are collected by the assurance companies and invested. Payment on maturity, death or pensionable age may be decades later.

6. Unit trusts work like this:

    ❏ A management company forms a trust and appoints a trustee

    ❏ The trustee is usually an institution such as a bank or insurance company. It holds the securities in safe custody

    ❏ The management company advertise the units for sale and members of the public send in their money.

    ❏ The money is invested in securities and the whole portfolio is regarded as so many units

    ❏ The value of each unit varies according to the value of the underlying portfolio

    ❏ New units are sold to the public continuously and the money collected adds to the portfolio and the number of units it is divided into.

    ❏ Investors can sell their units back to the trust at the quoted rate. If more investors sell than buy then the trust will have to sell securities to fund the buying back from investors.

    ❏ Unit trust investment can be in shares generally or in specific sectors eg Fixed interest, high income shares, European shares, smaller companies etc

    ❏ Units are sold to investors at the offer price and bought back at the bid price which is less.

    ❏ The advantages of unit trust investment are that they are professionally managed and a diversity or spread of investment is obtained.

    ❏ The disadvantages are that the management of the trust has to be rewarded with fees.

    Unit trusts are very popular as a form of investment for the small investor. There are numerous management companies (including the high street banks) and thousands of unit trusts. Latest prices are given regularly in the newspapers.

7. Investment trusts are not trusts but limited companies whose business is investment in securities. The operation is:

- ❑ A company is formed (usually a plc);

- ❑ Shares in it are sold to the public in a public issue advertised in the press (only PLCs can do this);

- ❑ The sums collected from the shareholders are invested in securities or other investments (eg property);

- ❑ Investment trusts are permanent companies and invest for the long term although they do change their investments as they are professionally managed;

- ❑ Investment trust companies can borrow money (unlike unit trusts) and so can engage in gearing;

- ❑ Shareholders cannot recover their money from the company but can sell their shares to other investors as the shares are quoted on the stock exchange.

Investment trusts are a useful medium for investors as a shareholding in an investment trust is in effect an investment in a *diversified portfolio*.

Operators on the stock exchange

8. The principal operators on the stock exchange are the investors. Investors include private citizens like you and me and the institutions. Institutional investors are managed by *fund managers*.

When investors buy or sell securities on the stock exchange they actually buy or sell to *market makers*. A market maker is a firm that maintains a portfolio of specific securities and holds itself out as a dealer in those securities. Its profit comes from changes (which can be up or down) in the value of its portfolio and also from dealing as it buys from the investor at a lower price than it sells to the investor. The difference is known as the *turn*.

Investors do not deal direct with market makers but through stockbrokers who arrange the deals. Stockbroking firms are remunerated by *commissions*. Firms can offer various services as well as arranging deals for investors including advice and portfolio management. You can deal direct with a broker or deal with a firm through your bank. Firms can now be both market makers and brokers.

What is traded on the stock exchange?

9. The stock exchange provides a market for:

Government securities

Shares in companies

Debentures and other securities of companies

Overseas securities

etc.

10. Government securities are usually called gilt-edged securities. An example of a gilt-edged security is $3\frac{1}{2}\%$ War Loan. This was issued during the 1939-1945 war when £100 worth was sold to investors for £100. The holder of £100 worth will receive £3.50 a year in interest for ever. As this is an *undated* stock the *capital* is not likely to be repaid. £100 worth of the stock is being bought and sold at the date of writing at about £36. As a result an investor who has held the stock since the war has made a *money* loss and a much greater *real* loss on the stock. The reason why it sells at 36 is that at that price its *yield* is:

$$\frac{3.5}{36} \times 100 = 9.7\%$$

and that is the going rate of interest on this relatively *risk free* security.

Another gilt-edged security is Treasury $14\frac{1}{2}\%$ 1994. £100 worth of this stock pays £14.5 annual interest and will be redeemed at par in 1994. This is known as a short as it will be repaid in less than five years from 1992, the time of writing. The stock is quoted at about £108 so the yield on this stock appears to be:

$$\frac{14.5}{108} \times 100 = 13.4\%$$

However investment in 1992 is £108 and repayment in 1994 will be only £100. Taking this into account the *redemption yield* is actually 10.1% which is much the same as the war loan.

There are billions of pounds of gilt-edged securities and new ones are issued from time to time to fund the public sector borrowing requirement which is the difference between the amount spent by government and the amount raised in taxation.

11. Shares in companies offer investors an exciting medium of investment and many people enjoy much pleasure in receiving dividends and seeing how the quoted price of their investment has risen. Conversely, a company may pass (= omit) its dividend and the share value may go down and the company may go into liquidation.

12. Other company securities listed on the stock exchange include preference shares, loan stocks, convertible loan stocks and warrants.

13. Some overseas company shares are quoted and some foreign government stocks. Investors can buy these stocks directly or through the medium of unit or investment trusts. Direct investment through foreign stock exchanges is also possible.

Other forms of investment

14. There are an enormous range of investments available for investors including:

> Securities listed on the stock exchange
>
> Unit Trusts
>
> Life assurance
>
> Pension schemes
>
> National Savings
>
> Deposits in Building Societies and Banks
>
> Property (including the home)
>
> Chattels (including stamps, antiques etc)

The best form of investment for a particular person depends on many factors and professional advice should be sought if more than a simple bank or building society deposit is contemplated. The choices are usually between:

> Income and capital growth
>
> High risk and low risk

Shares in companies generally offer low income (gross yield on ICI is about 6%) and fixed interest securities like gilt-edged stocks yield higher income. However shares offer a chance of *capital gains* and fixed interest securities generally do not.

Investing in shares offers some risk of loss. This is less in *blue chip* shares. Blue chip shares are those in large reputable well established companies like ICI and Unilever. Investing in National Savings offers little risk of loss. In general the higher the risk, the higher the yield and vice versa.

Primary and secondary markets

15. The exchange also acts as a primary market. This refers to the sale of securities to the public by a company or other institution (including the government) raising new money from investors. New issues can be:

> new shares in companies
>
> new gilt edged or local authority stocks
>
> existing shares sold by a single or a few investors.

Many issues appear to be issues of new shares in a company but are in fact sales by one or more investors. As an example, the sale of the privatisation issues have been the sale by one investor (the government) of existing shares to the public.

New issues can be sold by:

a prospectus issue

an offer for sale

a placing.

A prospectus is an advertisement offering the shares for sale. A prospectus must be in the form required by the Companies Act and the Stock Exchange. It contains an amazing amount of detail.

An offer for sale is similar and also involves a prospectus. However an offer for sale comprises the sale of the shares firstly to an issuing house (a bank or a stock exchange firm) and it is the issuing house which offers the shares for sale to the public.

A placing is usually a relatively small issue and the securities are placed with (= sold to) the clients of a stock exchange firm. The firm also make some available to interested members of the public.

Benefits and drawbacks of flotation

16. Businesses are started by one or a few people with an idea and a little capital usually supplemented by family and bank loans. Initially the legal form of the enterprise is sole trading, a partnership, or like Martin Padlocks Ltd as a small private limited company. The main advantage of trading as a company is limited liability. If the company goes bust the owners do not go bust with it unless they have guaranteed the bank overdraft in which case their liability extends as far as having to repay the bank. The shareholders in a company do not usually have any liability to pay the company's creditors. Taxation advantages are minimal unless very large profits are earned and trading as a company has disadvantages in terms of taxation and strict regulation under the Companies Act.

Most businesses either fail or remain small. However some grow and become large enough to seek quoted status on the stock exchange. There are some advantages in this:

a) The shareholders can sell some or all of their shares to investors

b) The company has access to finance

c) The company can finance the takeover of other companies (see later).

d) The company will have a larger public profile

e) The company can reward and motivate its employees with share option schemes.

The main disadvantages are:

a) Requirements to keep investors and the Stock Exchange informed of all significant developments

b) The need to maintain performance and make dividend payments

c) Vulnerability to takeover

Nonetheless flotation offers a company substantial benefits and brings with it prestige both for the company and for its directors.

Procedures for flotation

17. Suppose Adam Ltd, a dealer in widgets has reached a size which is large enough to seek a listing on the Stock Exchange. The company has 12 shareholders, all members of the Eden family. The company is currently divided into 10,000 share of £1 each. Procedures might be:

a) Make a bonus issue of 39 new shares for each share held there will now be 400,000 shares.

b) Split each share into 10 shares of 10p each. There will now be 4 million shares.

c)   Create 3 million new shares.

d)   Sell shares to the public by an Offer for Sale at £1.30p each.

The shares to be sold will be:

all the new shares

30% of the existing shareholders' shares

You may be able to calculate that:

i)   The company will gain £3,900,000 from the sale of the new shares

ii)   Eve Eden who held 1,200 shares in the company will gain £187,200 and still hold 336,000 shares worth £436,800.

iii) The original shareholders still own 2,800,000 shares out of 7,000,000 – 40%.

Takeovers

18. A feature of the Stock Exchange is the extent of takeovers of companies by other companies. Suppose Adam PLC has now been trading as a listed company for two years and its shares are now quoted at £2.00. It would like to buy Abel Ltd from its existing shareholders. Adam has agreed to buy the 20,000 shares at £30 each – a total of £600,000. It can pay for the shares in several ways:

a)   Pay cash – this is possible only if Adam PLC have cash or can borrow it. Abel's shareholders may not like cash as they will have to pay capital gains tax.

b)   Create 300,000 new shares in Adam PLC and issue these to the shareholders of Abel. The balance sheet of Adam will change by:

adding an asset – investment in Abel Ltd £600,000 – to its net assets

adding: Share Capital 300,000 × 10p   = £30,000

Share Premium 300,000 × £1.90   = £570,000

to the Capital and Reserves.

c)   Creating and issuing loan stock or, more likely, convertible loan stock in Adam PLC to Abel's shareholders.

You will realise that it is possible to issue shares or loan stock as a consideration instead of cash.

It is possible for a large company (often a sluggish one) to be taken over by a small one (usually a thrusting one). This is achieved by the large company creating and issuing new shares to the shareholders in the small one (as with Adam and Abel) such that the old shareholders in the small company have a commanding holding in the large company. Commanding can be 10% or more if the shares in the large companies are diversely held. This is called a reverse takeover as the reality is the taking over of the large by the small whereas the appearance is the reverse.

Insider dealing

19. Much money can be made on the stock exchange by dealing in shares as the prices of shares go up or down as new information becomes available. For example Wulfrun Airlines PLC moved down from 340p a share to 315p a share on news that the price of aviation fuel had risen 20%. A person who has advance news of price-sensitive information can make money. For example Mary works for Stubby PLC and attends a Board Meeting at which the Board agree to make a bid for Adam PLC. Mary left the meeting and rang her Broker to buy some shares in Adam before the news was announced to the public and the price of Adam shares rose.

Mary is an insider in that she is privilege to price sensitive information about Adam PLC before it is known by the investing public at large. Insider dealing is illegal.

Bulls, bears and stags

20. The stock exchange contains many mythical animals including:

Bulls are optimistic investors who buy shares in the expectation of a rise in price. The stock exchange operates on a year of 24 accounts of usually 10 days each. If an investor buys early in an account and sells later in the same account, then he can make settlement on the same day, usually ten days after the account has ended. So he can make a gain without actually putting up any money.

Bears are pessimistic. A bear investor will sell shares he has not got early in the account in the expectation that the price will fall and she can buy in at a lower price before the account ends and she has to make delivery.

Stags are investors who deal in new issues. The idea is that new issues are often oversubscribed. For example 1,000,000 shares may be offered and ten times that number may be subscribed for by the public. If this happens the available shares are allocated by some fair process which discriminates in favour of the subscriber for small numbers. If a stag gets an allocation, he will rapidly sell them and make a profit as the price will go to a premium over the issue price as demand clearly exceeded supply.

Key principle summary

○ The stock exchange is a market for financial securities.

○ Investors can be individuals or institutions.

○ The principle investing institutions are pension funds, insurance companies, unit trusts and investment trust companies.

○ The principal players on the stock exchange are investors, market makers and brokers.

○ The stock exchange provides a market for the securities of the government, foreign governments, local authorities and public companies whose shares are quoted (= listed).

○ Securities can usually offer above average income or capital growth but not both.

○ Higher returns (income and capital gains) usually accompanies higher risk.

○ The stock exchange is primarily a secondary market but new issues are made. These can be of new securities or previously owned securities.

○ New issues can be sold by prospectus issue, offer for sale or a placing.

○ Bulls are optimistic, bears are pessimistic, and stags hope for a quick capital gain on new issues.

○ Takeovers and mergers are a feature of British financial life.

○ Insider dealing is profitable but illegal.

○ Flotation has advantages and disadvantages.

Section 3

Developing knowledge and skills

Introduction

Via Sections 1 and 2 you will have been introduced to all the key principles, techniques, knowledge and understanding of accounting that you will need as a non-accountant manager.

This section provides the following:

1. Graded exercises and Case studies – to help confirm your understanding and enhance your knowledge and skills. Those marked with an asterisk have outline answers in the Appendix – to give you confidence that you are on the right lines – whilst the others have answers only in the Lecturers Supplement (see Preface).

2. Further developments of particular aspects – You may pursue them if they are applicable to your own circumstances (i.e. they are not essential for *all* non-financial managers). These further developments are clearly headed as 'Further development'.

How to use this section

If you are studying at College your tutor will advise you on what exercises, case studies and assignments to attempt and what sequence best suits your course of study.

If you are studying on your own, the following study plan is recommended.

❐ On completing each Unit in Section 1, you will be able to tackle some of the exercises in this section. A reference box directs you to the relevant exercises.

 The sequence of Topics in this section is the same as in Section 2 to make it easier for you to revise topics if you need to.

❐ If you find that the Further Development Topics in this section are pertinent to your interests then study them and work through the exercises, cases and assignments which relate to them.

Contents

1 The profit and loss account

The trading account

Here are some exercises to familiarise yourself with the trading account of a wholesale or retail business.

*1. Given the following separate sets of data for 19x2, calculate the gross profit:

Business	A	B	C
Cash Sales in 19x2	540,000	6,000	3,000
Sales on credit in 19x2	1,200	543,000	231,000
Cash received from customers in 19x2	540,950	521,000	236,000
Purchases in 19x2	412,000	490,000	134,000
Cash paid to suppliers in 19x2	398,000	502,000	139,000
Stock at end of 19x1	32,000	160,000	3,700
Stock at end of 19x2	38,000	152,000	3,900

One of these businesses is a supermarket and two are wholesalers of which one is in fresh fish and the other in expensive imported furniture. Which is the retailer and which is the fresh fish wholesaler?

*2. Given the following separate sets of data for 19x2, calculate the missing item:

Business	D	E	F	G
Sales in 19x2	450,000	?	980,000	28,000
Stock at end of 19x1	?	36,000	120,000	6,000
Purchases in 19x2	390,000	98,000	650,000	?
Stock at end of 19x2	76,000	?	230,000	7,400
Cost of goods sold	?	93,700	?	15,890
Gross Profit	80,000	31,000	?	?

A major problem in practice is *cut-off*. This is ensuring that a proper match is made between sales and the cost of the actual goods sold.

3. June has a a business retailing giftware. At 31 December 19x2, her year end, she took stock and included everything on the premises. On 5 January she received a consignment of goods which had been despatched and invoiced at £300 on 29 December. The goods had been in transit by rail. What could go wrong with the calculation of gross profit for 19x2?

4. Claude gave his assistant Cecil the task of taking stock at his antique shop on 31 December. Each item has a coded ticket which can be used to calculate the input price. The stock was duly evaluated at cost and the gross profit calculated as £79,304. Claude later discovered that the following matters may have a bearing on the stock:

    i.   A settee sold to Cyril (cost £500) for £890 on 30 December was not collected by Cyril until 4 January.

    ii. A table (cost £200) sold to Daniel in November for £700 was in the shop for repair.

    iii. A clock purchased from Odile for £500 on 27 December was not paid for until 25 January.

    iv. A barometer which had cost £950 in November was at the home of Ben, a customer. Ben was trying it out but eventually decided not to buy it.

    What should have been the gross profit?

Expenses

The accruals convention is applied to all expenses and the following exercises should increase your familiarity with this idea.

5. Rent: Dew paid rent as follows:

12 November	19x1	£3,000 for the half year to 31.3.19x2
4 April	19x2	£3,500 for the half year to 30.9.19x2
3 January	19x3	£3,500 for the half year to 31.3.19x3

What is the correct charge for the profit and loss account for 19x2?

*6. Sven pays his manager Brenda a salary of £15,000 a year. Employer's national insurance is 10.4%. Payment is made monthly and the payment for December was £925 being £1,250 less tax and insurance. The PAYE and national insurance on the December salary was paid on 18 January 19x3. On 12 February, a bonus was paid to Brenda for her excellent work in 19x2. The gross amount of the bonus was £1,200.

What is the correct charge in the profit and loss account for 19x2 in respect of Manager's Remuneration?

Completing a Trading and Profit and loss account.

*7. Given a set of data, it is only a matter of slotting these into a pro forma profit and loss account. Below are two sets of data:

Year ending 31 December 19x2

	Alpha	Beta
Sales on Credit	800,000	1,490,000
Cash Sales	630,000	
Opening stock	61,000	231,000
Closing stock	49,000	245,000
Purchases	840,000	780,000
Carriage inwards	17,000	12,000
Carriage outwards	23,000	35,000
Wages	187,000	202,000
Rent	30,000	
Insurance	6,700	31,000
Rates	16,800	58,000
Depreciation	32,000	62,000
New Car	15,000	
Sundry expenses	17,200	19,540
Advertising	67,900	102,000
Motor running expenses	12,450	35,000
Accountant's fee	3,000	5,600
Security costs	4,100	6,900
Stationery	2,600	9,100
Drawings	30,000	46,000
Loan Repayment	25,000	50,000
Loan Interest	13,500	21,000
Bank Charges	2,600	7,200
Settlement discount	4,700	
Rent Received	6,000	

Notes:

For Alpha:

i. Carriage inwards is regarded as part of the cost of purchases

ii. Wages do not include a bonus to the staff of £20,000 paid after the year end

iii. Rates include £7,200 for the half year to 31 March 19x3.

iv. Settlement discount is the amount allowed to customers for quick payment. It goes in the profit and loss account section.

For Beta:

i.   Carriage inwards is regarded as part of the cost of the purchases

ii. Insurance includes the fire insurance premium £2,400 for the year ending 31 May 19x2

iii. Stationery includes a consignment of posters £1,200 which were received on the last day of the year and were not opened until 4 January 19x3.

iv. Rent received is for a part of the premises let to another firm.

Interpreting a Trading and Profit and Loss Account

8. Below are the Trading and Profit and Loss Accounts for the two years 19x1 and 19x2 of Grace, a sportswear retailer:

Trading and Profit and Loss Account

For the Year Ending		19x1		19x2
Sales		215,000		262,000
Less Cost of Goods Sold:				
Opening Stock	36,000		52,100	
Purchases	162,100		178,600	
	198,100		230,700	
Less Closing Stock	52,100		46,000	
		146,000		184,700
Gross Profit		69,000		77,300
Less Expenses:				
Rent	10,000		10,000	
Rates	11,300		13,400	
Insurances	2,600		3,700	
Wages and Salaries	14,000		14,800	
Advertising	4,400		8,600	
Sundry Expenses	5,200		6,000	
Depreciation	4,300		4,300	
		51,800		60,800
Net Profit		17,200		16,500

Appraise the performance of the business over the two years considering especially:

❏ Turnover
❏ Stock levels
❏ Gross Profit to Sales ratio
❏ Each expense item
❏ the relationship between 19x1 and 19x2
❏ the relationship between each item in the accounts and all the others
❏ how much cash may have been generated by the profits

Note that Grace works full time in the business and that inflation was about 4% between 19x1 and 19x2.

Further development

Service industries

The measurement of profit in a trading (= buying and selling goods) business is relatively straightforward but there can be more difficulty with service industries and also with industries like agriculture and extraction.

Here are some exercises which could be used for group discussion or as assignments:

9. Virtreal set up on 1 January 19x2 as an independent writer of software working from his home. He commissioned a series of programmes suitable for local authority use from a friend. In 19x2 he sold 5 copies of the programme for £3,000 each and four of these were paid for in 19x2 and one in 19x3. He has obtained orders for 6 copies for delivery in 19x3 and is hopeful of several more orders.

    Some other data about the business in 19x2 are:

    i.   He purchased computer equipment for £6,000 which he reckons will have a three year life.

    ii. He paid his friend £5,000 for writing the programs and his friend did some revision work in December 19x2 which Virtreal paid for in January 19x3 at £1,200

    iii. His other overheads cost him £1,400 in 19x2.

    Discussion:

    i.   How much profit did Virtreal make in 19x2?

    ii. Do you think Virtreal could regard some of his household expenses as an expense of the business?

10. Giles is a farmer who set up on 1 January 19x2. He wonders how he should treat some of his activities in measuring his profit for the first year. These include:

    i.   He expended significant sums on seed and fertilizer in the year to produce a crop of wheat and potatoes. He kept the harvested crop in store until March 19x3 when he sold them.

    ii. He bought some goats and expended material amounts of money on feeding and caring for them. By the year end the goats had produced many offspring. A few of these had been sold but most were still on the farm.

    Discuss these problems in terms of annual profit measurement.

11. Sheinton are a pop group. The five members normally play gigs locally and charge modest fees for their work. In 19x2 they spent £2,000 on recording fees for an album and had 3,000 copies made at a cost of £4 each. They sold 300 albums in 19x2 and are hopeful of selling the rest in the next few years.

    Discuss the annual profit measurement problems here.

12. Icicle started a business on 1 January 19x2, servicing some specialised equipment. He signed a number of contracts including:

    Contract A. He received a lump sum of £3,000 to service some equipment over the ensuing four years. He should make a profit on the contract.

    Contract B. Similar to contract A but he reckons that the contract was a mistake and that it will cost him £5,000 to execute the contract over the four years.

    Contract C. He will receive an annual sum of £1,200 for the next four years and will be able to do the work for only £300 a year.

    Discuss these from an annual profit measurement point of view.

Published profit and loss accounts

All organisations produce annual profit and loss accounts. In the case of non-profit organisations like clubs ands societies the profit and loss account is called the *Income and Expenditure Account.*

Students of accounting should try to see as many profit and loss accounts and income and expenditure accounts as possible. You can obtain them from friends and relatives who own shares in public companies, from building society offices and from the treasurers of clubs, societies and churches and charities.

Note that some treasurers do not understand accounting sufficiently well to apply accrual accounting and produce simply a summary of receipts and payments.

Try to make sense of any accounts that you find.

Most sets of accounts are *audited*. See if there is an *auditor's report* and determine the qualifications, if any, of the auditor.

2 Balance sheets

Formation of Balance Sheets

Firstly, an exercise to enable you to practise the formation of Balance Sheets.

1. The following data relate to three businesses at 31 December 19x2:

all in £'000	A	B	C
Stocks	28	102	74
Trade creditors	21	140	68
Plant and Machinery at cost	46		
Equipment at cost		62	42
Equipment depreciation to date		51	12
Premises at cost	100		280
Debtors	53	203	
Loan to Philip repayable on 29 June 19x3	10		
Capital at 31 December 19x1	132	?	108
Vehicles at cost	54	180	74
Prepayments	2	6	9
Vehicle Depreciation to date	18	43	39
Premises depreciation to date	20		14
Drawings in 19x2	38	30	51
Net Profit in 19x2	41	51	73
Cash at Bank	17		
Bank Overdraft		62	?
Loan from Immutable Assurance at 18% repayable 19x8	80		170
Accrued rent and rates	5	12	4
Plant and Machinery depreciation to date	31		
Hire purchase commitment		36	

Required:

a. prepare a balance sheet for each business.

b. The businesses are a retailer, a manufacturer and a wholesaler. Which is which?

Profit and Loss Accounts and Balance sheets

It is not to difficult to slot the necessary data into a pro forma Profit and Loss Account or Balance Sheet. It can be more difficult to sort out data which might go into either or both. Here is an exercise to give you more familiarity with these financial statements:

*2. The following data relate to the businesses of Alan, Brian and Kate for the year ending 31 December 19x2:

All in £'000	Alan	Brian	Kate
Sales	750	310	510
Creditors	35	31	80
Debtors	150	12	130
Stock at 31 December 19x1	52	18	71
Stock at 31 December 19x2	56	23	65
Premises at cost	200		130
Premises Depreciation to 31 December 19x1	20		52
Equipment at Cost	65	78	90
Equipment depreciation to 31 December 19x1	21	16	59
Purchases	520	153	340
Rent, Rates and Insurances	32	45	32
Wages	128	43	154
Other Overheads	21	24	46
Bank Interest and Charges	12	2	31
Cash at Bank	49	12	
Bank Overdraft			76
Capital at 31 December 19x1	438	48	241
Drawings	35	18	34
Loan from David at 10% repayable in 19x5			40

Note:

Alan:

❐ Depreciation for 19x2 will be: on the premises £5,000 and on the equipment £13,000
❐ Rent rates and insurances include a fire insurance premium of £6,000 for the year ending 31 August 19x3 but do not include the rates for the quarter ending 31 December 19x2 £7,000.

Brian:

❐ Depreciation for 19x2 should be £6,000
❐ Wages does not include a bonus to the staff of 10% of the profit after charging the bonus.
❐ Other overheads includes a payment for a maintenance agreement £3,000 for 19x3

Kate:

❐ Depreciation for 19x2 should be £4,000 on the premises and £9,000 on the equipment
❐ No interest was paid on the loan in 19x2 and the 19x2 interest was paid in January 19x3
❐ Wages includes an advance of £3,000 to an employee which will be repaid by deduction from her salary in 19x3

Required:

a. Prepare a Trading and Profit and loss Account for the year ending 31 December 19x2 and a Balance Sheet as at 31 December 19x2 for each business.

b. Write short notes on the situations shown by these accounts.

Transactions and the Balance Sheet

A Balance Sheet shows the assets and liabilities of a business at a particular moment in time. All enterprises continuously engage in transactions such as the sale and purchase of goods and services and the receipt and payment of cash. Each transaction changes the Balance Sheet. To give you a deeper understanding of the Balance Sheet and of the effect of transactions, here is an example followed by an exercise. It may also give you an insight into the relationship between profit and the balance sheet:

Example – question

Joanne is a wholesaler of dresses and this is her Balance Sheet at 31 January 19x2:

Joanne
Balance Sheet as at 31 January 19x2

Fixed Assets

	Cost	Depreciation	Net Book Value
Equipment	98,000	56,000	42,000
Vehicles	41,000	17,000	24,000
	139,000	73,000	66,000

Current Assets

Stock	63,900	
Debtors	164,200	
Prepayments	1,800	
	229,900	

Less Creditors: amounts falling
due within one year:

Creditors	95,400	
Bank Overdraft	102,700	
	198,100	

Net Current Assets	31,800
Net Assets	97,800
Capital	97,800

The following transactions occurred in the day after the Balance sheet date:

a. Purchased 500 dresses on credit for £11,000 from Elaine

b. Sold 50 dresses on credit to Leeanne for £2,200. They had cost £1,500.

c. Paid Leo who had supplied dresses in January £4,200 (note that Leo was therefore one of the creditors)

d. Received £700 from Helen, who had been supplied with dresses in December (so Helen was one of the debtors).

e. Purchased on credit a new car from Hawthorn for £18,000

f. Joanne drew £300 from the bank for private purposes.

g. Paid Fire Insurance premium for the year ending 31 January 19x3 £950.

Required:

    i. Draw up a table showing the effects of each transaction on items in the Balance Sheet.

    ii. Show the Balance Sheet after these transactions have been completed.

    iii. Draw up a Trading and Profit and Loss Account for the day.

    iv. Explain why items c to g do not appear in the Trading and Profit and loss Account.

Example – Answer

i. a. Add £11,000 to stocks and creditors

    b. Add £2,200 to debtors, deduct £1,500 from stock. We now have £700 more "Assets less Liabilities" so also add £700 to capital which must be equal to "Assets less Liabilities".

    c. Add £4,200 to the overdraft and deduct £4,200 from creditors.

    d. Deduct £700 from Debtors and from the overdraft.

    e. Add £18,000 to Vehicles and to creditors.

    f. Add £300 to the overdraft and as net assets (Assets less Liabilities) are now less deduct £300 from capital.

    g. Add £950 to the overdraft and to prepayments.

ii. Balance Sheet after completing these transactions:

Joanne

Balance Sheet as at 1 February 19x2

Fixed Assets

	Cost	Depreciation	Net Book Value
Equipment	98,000	56,000	42,000
Vehicles	59,000	17,000	42,000
	157,000	73,000	84,000

Current Assets

Stock	73,400	
Debtors	165,700	
Prepayments	2,750	
	241,850	

Less Creditors: amounts falling
due within one year:

Creditors	120,200	
Bank Overdraft	107,450	
	227,650	

Net Current Assets	14,200
Net Assets	98,200

Capital	at beginning	97,800
	net Profit	700
		98,500
	less Drawings	300
		98,200

iii. Trading and Profit and Loss Account

Sales		2,200
Less Cost of Goods Sold:		
Opening stock	63,900	
Purchases	11,000	
	74,900	
Closing stock	73,400	1,500
Gross Profit		700
Expenses		nil
Net Profit		700

Note that cost of goods sold was derived from opening and closing stocks and purchases. In this case it was possible to derive the gross profit directly as there was only one sale and it gave a gross profit of £700.

iv. c and d – It is the sale or purchase which affects profit and not the subsequent cash flows.

   e. The purchase of a fixed asset does not affect profit but subsequent depreciation does. As this is a one day profit measurement, depreciation is negligible.

   f. Drawings do not affect profit. Profit is made so that drawings can be made.

   g. The fire insurance does affect profit but as the period is one day only strictly only £950/365 would affect profit.

Exercise

3. Take the original balance sheet of Joanne and repeat the exercise above but with these transactions:

    a. Sold 400 dresses on credit to Jean for £700. They had cost £450.

    b. Purchased dresses for cash £2,000.

    c. Purchased dresses on credit from Howard £2,900.

    d. Paid Kaye, a creditor £820.

    e. Received from Louis, a debtor, £4,000.

    f. Purchased additional equipment on credit from Hugh £3,700.

    g. Borrowed £10,000 at 15% per annum interest from Tweed, repayable in 19x5.

    h. Joanne withdrew 2 dresses from stock as a present for her daughter. They had cost £300 each.

Further development

Finally two case studies for group use or as an assignment:

Case Study 1

Roy started in business on 1 January 19x2 as a dealer in widgets. (Note that all widgets are identical)

His transactions in the first month were:

January:

1. Opened a business bank account with £1,200, his personal savings.
2. Put his car valued at £2,400 into the business
3. Purchased 40 widgets on credit from Apple at £30 each.
14. Purchased 60 widgets from Bramble on credit for £36 each
16. Paid the insurance premium on his car for the year to 31 December 19x2 £720
18. Sold 10 widgets to Cherry for £60 each
20. Sold 20 widgets for cash to Greengage for £50 each.
21. Purchased 25 widgets on credit from Framboise at £40 each.
25. Sold 11 widgets on credit to Lemon for £70 each.
27. Received £2,000 from Bramble
29. Sold 50 widgets on credit to Logan at £70 each.
30. Paid Apple the amount due to him.
31. Discovered that Bramble had decamped and would be unable to pay him the balance due.
31. Took stock and found he had 31 widgets in stock.
31. Drew £50 from the bank for private purposes.

Note:

❑ the van depreciation is £600 a year.

❑ assume there are no other expenses.

Required:

a. Prepare a trading and Profit and Loss Account for the month of January 19x2 and a Balance Sheet as at 31 January 19x2.

b. Comment on the problems you have met in dealing with this problem and how you have solved them.

Case Study 2

Scoff rents a small unit on a trading estate and prepares dinners and buffets for commercial and other customers. His accounts for the two years 19x1 and 19x2 show:

Profit and Loss Account

		£ 19x1		£ 19x2
Sales		165,000		178,000
Cost of Materials	40,000		46,000	
Wages	52,000		56,000	
Rent, Rates and Insurance	18,200		19,900	
Electricity	6,900		7,800	
Van Expenses	13,700		15,400	
Sundry Expenses	5,600		6,200	
Depreciation:				
Vans	4,000		4,000	
Equipment	6,000	146,400	5,400	160,700
Net Profit		18,600		17,300

Balance Sheet

		19x1		19x2
Fixed Assets				
at cost less depreciation		37,000		35,000
Stocks of Materials	4,200		5,900	
Debtors	35,400		40,200	
	39,600		46,100	
Creditors	12,700		16,300	
Bank Overdraft	30,600		33,200	
	43,300		49,500	
		(3,700)		(3,400)
		33,300		31,600
Capital at beginning of year		33,900		33,300
Profit for year		18,600		17,300
		52,500		50,600
Drawings		19,200		19,000
at end of year		33,300		31,600

Note:

- Inflation was 4% between the two years

- The bank have written to Scoff requesting a reduction of the overdraft

- the vans desperately need replacing

- Scoff has a wife who helps in the business (her wages are in wages in the Profit and Loss Account), two children, a nice house with a large mortgage.

- Scoffs is very much in demand and at peak times, his services have to be booked a year in advance

Discuss the performance of the business over the two years and indicate his problems. Suggest some ways he might improve things.

3 Depreciation

Firstly some exercises in basic depreciation

*1. Judith started her computer programming business on 1st January 1992 and immediately bought some computer equipment at a cost of £6,000.

  a. What estimates will Judith need to make in order to decide on the depreciation of the equipment?

  b. What factors will cause the equipment to have limited life?

If she decided that the equipment would have a useful economic life of 3 years and have a salvage value at the end of 3 years of £2,500.

  c. Calculate:

    i. Depreciation for 1992, 1993 and 1994

    ii. The balance sheet values of the equipment at the end of each year.

    using (i) the straight line method and (ii) the reducing instalment method using a rate of 25%.

  d. Comment on the effect on profit and balance sheet values of the two methods.

In 1993, she realised that her equipment was becoming obsolete and she sold it for £1,500 and bought some replacement equipment for £9,000. The sale and purchase took place in August 1993.

  e. Assuming that she uses the straight line method, calculate:

    i. The depreciation for 1993 for the original equipment and the balance sheet value for it at the end of 1993.

    ii. The depreciation on the new equipment assuming that its estimated life is 4 years and its salvage value £1,000.

    iii. The balance sheet value at the end of 1993 for the new equipment.

In January 1994 she is in conversation with a computer equipment dealer who tells her that the second hand value of her new equipment is only £5,000.

  f. Comment on the dealer's remarks in the context of Judith's profit and Loss Account and Balance Sheet.

It turns out that the new equipment is excellent and at the end of 1996 she is still using it and expects to continue to do so for at least two more years.

  g. What will be the effect on profit and balance sheet values for the years after 1993.

2. Davinder has a parcels delivery service and has five vans. He bought these at various dates in the past and the position at the end of 1995 is:

	Ford	Rover	Renault	Seat
year of purchase	1991	1992	1993	1994
Estimated life (years)	5	5	6	4
Estimated Salvage value (£)	500	1,000	200	600
Cost (£)	8,500	7,000	7,400	3,800

Complete the entry in Davinder's Balance Sheet as at 31 December 1995:

Fixed Assets

	Cost	Accumulated Depreciation	Net Book Value
Vans			
Office Equipment	£3,500	£1,960	£1,540

Further development

Depreciation Policies

Mozart & Co are a string quartet.

In their first year they bought the following items:

2 modern instruments from Japan £7,000 each
A Guanieri violin, made in Cremona in 1720, £60,000
A Victorian double bass £7,500
A new Ford Minibus for transport £12,800
Sheet music £480
A computer to record their activities.
A former Church Hall as a practice room £45,000.

Discuss the depreciation policies which might be applied to these assets.

The answer to this, might be given by accountants as:

Modern Instruments – these have a limited life and may have a life of say 5 years but with a good resale value, perhaps £2,000.

The guanieri may be considered to have an infinite life and will be regarded as a fixed asset but not be depreciated.

Similarly the Victorian double bass will be regarded as a fixed asset but not be depreciated.

The Ford minibus clearly has a limited life. A possible life might be 5 years with a salvage value of say £2,000.

Sheet music may be said to have an economic life which will be as long as the paper is still legible and as long as the works are still played. In practice, however, the amount spent is relatively small and there will be money spent on music each year. Most accountants would see this expenditure as revenue and it would be written off (= put in the Profit and Loss Account as an expense) as it is incurred.

The computer clearly has a limited life caused less by use than by obsolescence and would probably be depreciated over a period of say three years with an estimated salvage value of nil.

The Church Hall is a really a mixture of land which has an infinite life and a building which has not. Land is not normally depreciated but buildings usually are. An estimate of useful life is clearly impossible to agree on but in this case perhaps 20 years is not unrealistic.

The lessons of this exercise are:

a.   Measurement of annual profit is a very inexact art.

b.   Estimates are required and may lead to disagreement amongst accountants and between management and auditor.

c.   Estimates required include useful economic life, salvage value, method of depreciation (straight line, reducing balance etc), division of expenditure between land and buildings and others.

d.   Fixed assets are usually depreciated but are not appreciated – increases in value (eg of the Guanieri or the land) are not recorded.

e.   Assets such as buildings which are often regarded as appreciating (eg buildings) but which do have a limited life are depreciated.

f.   Fixed assets of little cost are usually regarded as revenue expenditure and written off in the profit and loss of the year in which they are acquired.

Some more problems

*3. North started in business on 1 January 19x2.

He acquired the following fixed assets:

1 January 19x2   Lorry £35,000
5 March 19x2   Computer system £16,000
9 June 19x2   Delivery Van £10,200
19 November 19x2   Copier £4,000
13 December 19x2   Warehouse £105,000
8 March 19x3   Ford Car £16,000
24 July 19x3   Fax machine £800

Required

i.   Calculate the charge for depreciation in the accounts of North for the years ending 31 December 19x2, 19x3,19x4 and 19x5.

ii.   Show the Balance Sheet figures for each year end using the format:

	Cost	Accumulated Depreciation	Net Book Value
Land			
Buildings			
Vehicles			
Office Equipment			

You should use the following discrete set of assumptions and policies:

a.   ❐   Vehicles last 4 years and have a salvage value of 20% of original cost.

      ❐   Office Equipment has a life of three years with no salvage value

      ❐   Land is not depreciated

      ❐   Buildings are depreciated over 40 years

      ❐   the Warehouse includes land at £25,000

      ❐   straight line is used throughout

      ❐   items bought before 30 June in a year have a full year's depreciation but items bought later have only a half year's depreciation in the first year.

b.   ❐   Vehicles and office equipment are depreciated at 25% per annum on the reducing balance basis

      ❐   Land is not depreciated

      ❐   Buildings are depreciated over 25 years on the straight line basis

      ❐   the land part of the buildings is estimated at £35,000.

      ❐   all items bought in a year are given a full year's charge for depreciation in that year

4.   Dwight has a year end of 31 December and depreciates his vehicles on the basis of 25% per annum reducing balance. He sold a vehicle that he bought in 19x2 for £13,000, for £3,000 in 19x7.

    a.   Calculate the depreciation charge for the vehicle in 19x7.
    b.   Recalculate a. on the basis that the vehicle was sold for £5,000.

*5.   Durham Widgets Ltd operate from a warehouse they bought in 19x1 (land £10,000 + building £50,000). Depreciation of the buildings is over 40 years.

In 19x9 the warehouse was sold for £100,000 and another bought (land £30,000 + building £120,000).

Profit before including building depreciation in 19x9 was £34,000. Assuming the new building is depreciated over 40 years also calculate the depreciation on the warehouses for 19x9 and recommend a way of showing this in the profit and loss account of the company.

Further Development

Revaluation

Generally accounting recognizes depreciation and ignores appreciation. This has led to some distortion in the view given by financial statements. For example Stubby Breweries plc a small independent brewer bought its brewery premises in 1960 for £63,000 (land £7,000 + buildings £56,000). Depreciation policy was to write off the buildings over 50 years. Thus by 1990 the

brewery stood at $£63,000 - \left(31 \times \dfrac{£56,000}{50}\right) = £28,280$. In fact the buildings were well maintained

and an independent valuation gave the brewery a value of £480,000 (land £120,000 and building £360,000).

It is possible to take this valuation into the accounts. The effect would be:

- ❑ the land will be shown at valuation £120,000
- ❑ the buildings will be shown at valuation £360,000
- ❑ the buildings will be depreciated over the remaining useful economic life of the buildings. This was estimated at 30 years. Thus for 1990 and later years the depreciation will change from £1,120 a year to £12,000.
- ❑ the increase in value is £480,000 – £28,280 = £451,720. This is not regarded as an item in the profit and loss account of 1990 but is added directly to the figure of capital (capital and reserves in a company

Exercise

6. Whizzbang PLC is a manufacturing company with net assets of £6.4 million. Its profits before tax have hovered around £1 million which gives a return on capital employed of 15.6% which is considered good in the industry. A takeover is rumoured form Megabang PLC and as a part of its defence, Whizzbang PLC decide to have their property revalued. The property stands at:

    Land at cost £600,00

    Buildings at cost £4 million less 5 years of depreciation at £100,000 a year.

    The valuers give a value of Land £1.4 million

    Buildings £6.4 million

    Before incorporating the revaluation in the accounts the directors wish to see the effect it would have on profits and capital employed.

    Calculate:

    a. The surplus revealed by the revaluation. How would it be treated in the profit and loss account and the balance sheet?

    b. The annual profit if the estimated life of the building remained as before.

    c. The capital employed

    d. The return on capital employed

Other methods of depreciation

Several other methods of depreciation are found in practice as well as the straight line and reducing balance methods.

These include production unit and sum of digits.

Production unit method is illustrated by a Camrat Ltd which purchased a hedonite mine on 1 January 19x1 for £6 million.

The land itself has no real value (in fact it might cost money to restore it). The £6 million is really spent on the mineral Hedonite. Output is estimated at 4000 kilograms over its life. In 19x1 280 Kg were extracted. Depreciation is regarded in 19x1 as £6 million $\times \frac{280}{4,000}$ = £420,000.

Exercises

7. What will be the depreciation in 19x2 when 700 Kg were extracted? In 19x3, extraction was 800 Kg and at the year end a reappraisal of the mine indicated remaining reserves of 6,000 kg.

   Sum of digits:

   Suppose Dulcie starts a business on 1 January 19x2 with a machine which cost £10,000. She estimates its life at 4 years and its salvage value at £1,000. Total depreciation for the four years is thus £9,000. Under the sum of digits method, the depreciation is calculated by:

4	$\frac{4}{10} \times 9,000$	3,600
3	$\frac{3}{10} \times 9,000$	2,700
2	$\frac{2}{10} \times 9,000$	1,800
1	$\frac{1}{10} \times 9,000$	900
10		9,000

8. Contrast the depreciation of a machine costing £8,000 with a life of 4 years and a residual value of £2,500 on the straight line, the reducing balance and the sum of digits method.

The impact of depreciation on profit

The choice of depreciation policy (straight line, reducing balance etc) does not usually make a large difference to profit. Similarly varying estimates of salvage value and life do not often affect profit greatly. However in some industries, depreciation is of paramount importance.

9. Consider a company which operates in the shipping industry.

   It has one asset a ship which cost £6 million in year 1.

   Expected revenues and costs for the first three years are: (all figures in £'000)

year	1	2	3
Revenues	1,200	1,600	1,600
Expenses (excluding depreciation)	500	800	800

The ship will last at least 20 years but the directors note that comparable companies write off their ships in anything from 8 to 20 years.

Salvage value is likely to be about £0.5 million at any time except the first few years.

Discuss the attitudes of the directors in reporting profits to the suppliers of capital for the company. You may ignore taxation as tax calculations are unaffected by depreciation policy.

4 Stocks

Exercises

1. Cheepoh supermarkets plc categorise their stocks as goods for resale and miscellaneous (heating oil, stationery, spare parts for equipment and vehicles). How do you think the following might categorise their stocks?

   Giant Civil Engineering and construction plc

   Fork lift truck manufacturing company plc

   Shoo pharmaceuticals plc (research, design, manufacture, wholesale and retail)

   Mayne car dealers plc

*2. How would the following stocks be valued:

   a. 200 widgets purchased by A Ltd from B Ltd in Taiwan at £50 each. The consignment was for 500 widgets and A Ltd sold 300 before the year end stock take when the 200 were counted. From the price B Ltd allowed a 20% trade discount. A Ltd had to pay £2,000 carriage from Taiwan. On arrival the widgets were painted with A Ltd's Logo at a cost of £2 each and packaged at a cost of £3 each.

   b. 100 Things purchased by D Wholesale Ltd from E Ltd at £20 each. E Ltd gave a 15% trade discount and D took advantage of a 5% settlement discount.

   c. 50 Grombles manufactured by G Ltd. The cost of manufacture of each Gromble was:

	£
Materials and components	6
Direct Labour	4
Works overheads – estimated at 1.5 × prime cost	

   d. A stock of 8 houses built by H PLC in the hope of selling them. Each house was planned to cost:

   Land the houses will almost fill one acre which cost £270,000. There is room for one more house.

   Site works i. before building. The whole site is now complete as to these which cost £90,000

   ii. after build. These will cost £120,000 but have not yet been commenced.

   Professional fees. Architects (already paid) £1,000 a house

   Construction costs (all sub-contracted) £60,000 a house. The houses are estimated to be just half complete. (note that in practice this would be determined more precisely)

   Selling and conveyance costs £1,000 a house. (not yet spent)

*3. How would the following stock items be valued?

   a. 4 gubbins in the stock of J Ltd which are the obsolete mark 2 model. They cost £60 each but can now be sold at 2/3 of the normal selling price of £105. Each sale will cost J Ltd 10% sales commission and £10 delivery costs

   b. Stubby Homes plc have sold an estate of new houses but have in stock just one second hand home which they took in part exchange. The part exchange price was £40,000 but the agent reckons:

   i. it will require £4,000 repair expenditure before sale.

   ii. it will sell for only £38,000.

   iii. the sale will cost £1,000 in professional fees.

4. K Ltd deal in car spares. Among these are exhausts for the Rocket mark 1. His transactions in these items in the year 19x2 are:

1 Jan	In stock 15 at cost £20 each
3 Feb	Purchase 23 at £18 each
4 Mar	Sell 8 at £40 each
5 Apr	Sell 25 at £45 each
6 May	Purchase 9 at £26 each
7 Aug	Purchase 10 at £30 each
8 Oct	Sold 3 at £40 each
9 Dec	Sold 9 at £42 each

How should the stock be valued at 31 December 19x2 based on i. FIFO ii. Average Cost iii. LIFO?

*5. Liz's gift shop stocks, among many other things, a line of identical alpine paintings. Her deals in 19x2 in these were:

4 Feb	Purchase 40 at 10
6 Mar	Purchase 20 at 12
8 May	Sold 22 at 30
9 Oct	Purchase 10 at 15
1 Dec	Sold 35 at 28

a. How should the stock of paintings be valued at 31 December 19x2 based on i. LIFO ii. FIFO iii. AVCO?

b. One painting in stock at 31 December 19x2 is damaged and can only be sold for £5. How should this be valued and why is this value adopted?

Assignment 1

Eli formed his company Eli Ltd to manufacture specialised machinery which it makes for stock and then sells overseas. His first (19x2) year expenditure was:

	£
Materials and components	100,000
Direct Labour	75,000
General Works overheads	160,000
General Overheads	71,000
Interest	15,000
Plant and Machinery	140,000
Vehicles	60,000

Sales in the year were £346,000

His stocks on 31 December 19x2 were:

Raw materials and components valued at £15,000 (FIFO) or £8,000 (AVCO)
Finished goods valued at prime cost £24,000 + works overheads

He calculated his profit as:

Raw Materials and components	x	
Less Stocks	x	x
Direct Labour		x
Prime cost		x
Works Overheads:		
General	x	
Depreciation of Plant	x	x
Total Works inputs		x
Less Finished goods stocks		x
Cost of goods sold		x
Sales		x
Gross Profit		x
General Overheads	x	
Interest	x	
Vehicle depreciation	x	x
Net Profit		x

The Plant and Machinery is expected to last 4 years and have a salvage value of £32,000. The depreciation rate on the reducing balance method would be 30%.

The vehicles are expected to last 3 years and have a salvage value of £12,000. The depreciation rate on the reducing instalment method would be 40%.

The works overheads to be included in the valuation of finished goods stocks is that proportion of the total works overheads as the prime cost of the stock bears to the total prime cost.

Required:

a. Calculate the profit using alternative accounting policies for stock valuation (FIFO or AVCO) and depreciation (Straight line or reducing balance)

    Note that both types of fixed asset should be subject to the same depreciation method because of the consistency convention.

b. Eli Ltd had a large overdraft from the bank to fund the company initially. This is possibly renewable and the survival of the company depends upon its renewal. Eli knows that the bank is not expecting large profits in the early years of the company but is very wary of a loss making company. In view of this:

    i.   Recommend which accounting policies should be adopted.

    ii. Discuss the impact of the alternative accounting policies on subsequent annual profits/losses.

c. Describe the circumstances in which the valuation of raw material stocks can be so different on the two methods. Discuss the effect of the two alternative methods on future profits.

Assignment 2

Grape Ltd manufacture specialised plant to order. A substantial part of the plant items made is a component of which Grape stock about 200 varieties. The input cost of these varies substantially as they are partly made from a rare metal for which demand fluctuates widely.

Customers usually send a specification for a piece of plant to Grape and other suppliers. Grape's estimator then draws up a cost schedule for manufacture, adds a profit margin and quotes a price to the customer.

The stocks of the component are recorded, in quantities only, on a computer system and the estimator obtains his costs from a file of invoices. This system is unsatisfactory and it is proposed to incorporate values into the stock recording system.

The systems analyst has asked the company whether she should value the stocks on:

> FIFO or LIFO or AVCO.

The estimator also wonders if it would help him if information could be incorporated on:

The highest input price in the previous six months

The current price charged by suppliers

The price of the most recent purchase

Required:

a. Discuss the price that the estimator might include in his cost schedule when preparing a quotation for a customer.

b. The computed values must be used for stock valuation purposes in the annual accounts. Discuss the constraints this may make on the choice of values used by the systems analyst.

Further development

The effects of stock valuation on profit measurement

Stocks are often very large in relation to profit and the method of valuing stocks has a considerable impact on the actual profit measured and reported.

Drake commenced business on 1st January 19x1 as a builder of a standard type of car budgeted his production costs as:

	£
Materials	8,000
Direct Labour	6,000
Manufacturing Overheads	9,000
	23,000

Note:

Total manufacturing overheads are budgeted at £180,000 and Drake expects to make 20 boats in the year. Therefore the manufacturing cost of each boat includes £180,000/ 20 = £9,000 for manufacturing overheads.

In 19x1 the actual results were measured as:

Sales	17 boats at £30,000		510,000
Less cost of goods sold:			
Manufacturing Cost 23 boats:			
Materials		190,900	
Direct Wages		156,400	
Manufacturing Overheads		184,000	
		531,300	
Less Stock 6 boats		138,000	393,300
Gross Profit			116,700
Non-Manufacturing Overheads			86,000
Net Profit			30,700

a. How has the stock been valued?

b. Calculate and discuss the profit if:

   i.   only 15 boats had been sold and 8 were in stock

   ii. 20 boats had been sold and only 3 were in stock

   iii. all 23 boats had been sold

c. Statement of Standard Accounting Practice Number 9 on Stocks (which all accounts should follow) says:

   "In order to match costs and revenue, 'cost' of stocks should comprise that expenditure which has been incurred in the *normal* course of business in bringing the product or service to its present location and condition. Such cost will include all related production overheads, even though these may accrue on a time basis."

   "Production overheads are: overheads incurred in respect of materials, labour or services for production, based on the *normal level* of *activity*, taking one year with another. For this purpose each overhead should be classified according to function (eg, production, selling or administration) so as to ensure the inclusion, in cost of conversion, of those overheads (including depreciation) which relate to production, notwithstanding that these may accrue wholly or partly on a time basis."

   Has Drake complied with these requirements? What difference might strict compliance make to profit?

d. Drake notes that he has included £20,700, the salaries of his accountant and his general handyman, in non-manufacturing overheads. He reckons that his accountant whose salary is £13,800 a year spends 3/4 of his time on management accounting and paying the production workers. The general handyman spends 2/3 of his time in the works.

   What effect will these facts have on the value of stocks and the measurement of profit?

5 | Manufacturing accounts

Exercises

*1. The following sums are relevant to the measurement of profit for Stubby Furniture Manufacturing Co Ltd:

(all figures are in £'000)

	19x1	19x2	19x3	19x4
Assets at 31 December (the year end)				
Raw Material stocks	132	144	156	180
Work in Progress	89	201	128	145
Finished Goods stocks	360	380	529	602
Plant and Machinery at cost	1,680	1,680	2,450	2,480
Delivery vehicles at cost	240	280	350	350
Expenditure in the year				
Raw Materials	520	540	602	
Factory direct wages	720	730	702	
Royalties payable on manufacture	74	68	170	
Production Overheads	530	489	470	
Rates (2/3 Works,				
1/6 Office, 1/6 Distribution)	294	330	384	
Administration Costs	332	370	290	
Selling and distribution costs	448	502	540	
Financial Charges	39	80	140	
Revenues in the year:				
Sales	2,800	2,950	3,420	

Note: Depreciation is 10% per annum on the cost of the Plant and Machinery held at the year end (straight line method) and 20% on the cost of the vehicles held at the year end.

a. Prepare manufacturing, trading and profit and loss accounts for the years ending 19x2, 19x3 and 19x4.

b. After the preparation of the accounts of these years, the following errors were found:

   i. The raw material stock at 31 December 19x2 omitted some components which had cost £24,000

   ii. The finished goods stock at 31 December 19x3 included some tables which had been valued at materials only instead of at prime cost + works overheads. The difference is £38,000.

   iii. A royalty payable on the sale of some desks in 19x3 was not recognised (and therefore not included in the accounts) until 19x5 when a court case was settled. The amount involved is £16,000.

   iv. Sales of £17,000 were made in December 19x2 but due to holidays the invoices were not typed until January 19x3 and as the wrong dating was not spotted the sales were actually included in the 19x3 accounts.

   v. A fire insurance premium for the year ending 30 April 19x4 £12,000 was entirely included in the accounts for 19x3. The corresponding premiums for other years were correctly treated.

   The accounts cannot normally be altered retrospectively but you are required to state the effect on individual figures and the net profit of each year for each of these items.

c. The company sells its products to retailers and guarantees its products for one year after sale by the retailer. The average retailer holds in stock furniture bought from Stubby for an average of four months. Any item returned is normally replaced from finished goods stock free of charge and the returned items re-used in the manufacturing process if possible.

Stubby do not make a provision for expected returns at each year end so that the cost of replacing a faulty item falls into the year when the return is made instead of in the year when the item was originally sold.

Calculate the effect on profits for the years 19x2 to 19x4 of making a provision so that the cost of replacing faulty furniture falls in the year of sale. You can assume that 2% of sales are returned as faulty and that the cost of replacement (less re-usable parts) is 1/3 of the selling price from Stubby to its customers.

Which of these two alternative accounting policies do you think is most appropriate?

d. Look at the following items in the three years of Stubby's activities and suggest a plausible explanation of changes between the years:

Work in progress	Production Overheads
Finished goods stocks	Administration costs
Plant and Machinery	Selling and Distribution costs
Factory Direct Wages	Financial Charges
Royalties	

Case Study

Keith is the newly appointed managing director of Stubby Widgets Ltd a subsidiary of a major group. The company make a range of three widgets – the deluxe, the special and the super and they supply the European market. The company accountant has produced a manufacturing, trading and profit and loss account for the year just ended and this shows a loss. It is Keith's primary job to make the factory more efficient and he is looking for ways of achieving this. With this in mind he has been able to obtain a copy of the accounts of a fellow subsidiary, Lee Widgets Ltd, which makes a similar range of products to sell in North America. This subsidiary is located in the Far East and is reputed to be extremely efficient. Below are the two sets of accounts:

	Stubby Ltd in £'000		Lee Ltd in local currency	
Raw Materials:				
Opening stock	146		103	
Purchases	541		870	
	687		973	
Closing Stock	171	516	99	874
Direct Labour		782		207
Prime cost		1,298		1,081
Works Overheads				
Rent, rates, insurance	480		280	
Plant Depreciation	32		180	
Energy	249		200	
Staff Salaries	521		320	
Other overheads	178	1,460	190	1,170
		2,758		2,251
Opening Work in Progress		212		46
		2,970		2,297
Closing Work in Progress		280		54
		2,690		2,243
Opening Finished Goods Stock		401		208
		3,091		2,451
Closing Finished Goods Stock		441		160
		2,650		2,291
Sales		3,100		3,900
Gross Profit		450		1,609

Administration Costs	390		340	
Selling Costs	270		360	
Warehousing Costs	246		90	
Distribution Costs	180	1,086	238	1,028
Net Profit (Loss)		(636)		581

Keith makes a few enquiries and finds that:

i. The raw material unit costs are similar for the two companies.

ii. Selling prices are higher in the European market as there is, as yet, less competition.

iii. Due to environmental and legal factors, the companies produce products of very marginally different specifications.

iv. There are no financial costs as Group supply all capital requirements (but require a commensurate profit to be earned on the use of the capital).

Required:

Write a report as from Keith to the Group Chief Executive:

i. Detailing the problems of the company.

ii. Giving proposals to turn the company round

You can make any reasonable assumptions but must state them.

Assignment

A summary of the manufacturing, trading and profit and loss account of Revpen Manufacturing Co Ltd for the year ending 31 December 19x2 is:

(All figures in £'000)

Raw Materials:		
Opening stock	56	
Purchases	345	
	401	
Closing Stock	36	365
Direct Labour		582
		947
Works Overheads		
Rent, rates, insurance	232	
Plant Depreciation	52	
Energy	180	
Staff Salaries	241	
Other overheads	103	808
		1,755
Opening Work in Progress		240
		1,995
Closing Work in Progress		379
		1,616
Opening Finished Goods Stock		180
		1,796
Closing Finished Goods Stock		193
		1,603
Sales		2,600
Gross Profit		997
Administration Costs	401	
Selling Costs	240	
Distribution Costs	49	690
Net Profit		307

Questions:

A. Note each statement is either true or false. Tick those that are true.

   1. Re Closing stock of raw materials:

      a. These are mostly valued at cost
      b. These are mostly valued at replacement price
      c. Some of these may be valued at below cost

   2. Re Purchases of raw materials:

      a. Goods purchased on 16.12.19x1 and paid for on 16.1.19x2 is included in this sum.
      b. Goods purchased on 30.6.19x2 (£4,100) and stolen on 18.7.19x2 are included in this sum
      c. Heating Oil purchased and paid for on 13.11.19x2 is included in this sum

   3. Re prime cost.

      a. Prime cost was   £947,000
      b. Prime cost was   £582,000
      c. prime cost was   £1,755,000

   4. Re Work in Progress:

      a. Work in progress was valued at cost
      b. Work in progress was valued at prime cost
      c. Work in progress was valued at a percentage of the selling price
      d. Work in progress was valued at Prime cost + an appropriate proportion of all overheads
      e. Work in progress was valued at Prime cost + an appropriate proportion of works overheads

   5. Re Rent, Rates and Insurance £232,000

      a. Rent for the quarter ending 31 March 19x3, paid on 27 December 19x2, is included in this sum
      b. Rates paid in October 19x1 for the half year ending 31 March 19x2 is included in full in this sum
      c. Insurance of the delivery vans is included in this sum.

   6. Re Plant Depreciation (note that the straight line method is used and items of plant are depreciated over 8 years.)

      a. Depreciation includes the total cost of a new machine purchased in the year
      b. Depreciation includes depreciation on a machine purchased ten years ago.
      c. Depreciation includes the loss on sale of a machine sold in the year.
      d. Depreciation includes depreciation on the sales director's secretary's word processor

   7. Re finished goods stock

      a. This is mostly valued at prime cost + an appropriate portion of works overheads
      b. This is mostly valued at selling price
      c. This is mostly valued at prime cost + an appropriate portion of all overheads
      d. This is valued at prime cost
      e. This may include some items valued at net realisable value.

   8. Re administration costs.

      a. This includes £2,000 paid in December 19x2 for stationery to be delivered in January 19x3.
      b. This includes the salary of the cost accountant
      c. This includes depreciation on the office photocopier
      d. This includes the cost of a new computer system acquired to record shareholdings.

   9. Re net profit

      a. This measures the increase in the company's bank account in the year
      b. This measures the net increase in net assets in the year from manufacturing and trading activity.

B. The manufacturing, trading and profit and loss account is a very detailed and comprehensive document. In fact the above document is somewhat summarised, as works and other overheads are divided into more categories in the original. (For example selling costs are categorised into advertising, reps' salaries, reps' expenses, selling overheads). Also the original contains the corresponding figures for the previous year. However the works manager says that the document is:

a. available only to senior management
b. not understood by all of them
c. useless as a diagnosis of what went well/wrong in the year.
d. useless as a guide to action

Comment on the works manager's views and suggest ways that these accounts could be made more useful to him and others.

Further development

Manufacturing companies are likely to have many different products. The Manufacturing, Trading and Profit and Loss Account summarises the performance of the whole enterprise and makes no attempt to break down the performance to determine the profits made by each product or the performance of each *department* or *manufacturing centre*.

Case study

a. Speckless Ltd makes different kinds of vacuum cleaners. Its Manufacturing, Trading and Profit and Loss Account for the years ending 31 December 19x2 and 19x3 showed:

(All figures in £'000)

Raw Materials:				
Opening stock	680		720	
Purchases	3,100		3,240	
	3,780		3,960	
Closing Stock	720	3,060	840	3,120
Direct Labour		3,580		2,900
		6,640		6,020
Works Overheads		5,700		7,100
		12,340		13,120
Opening Work in Progress		950		1,280
		13,290		14,400
Closing Work in Progress		1,280		1,350
		12,010		13,050
Opening Finished				
Goods Stock		2,040		1,950
		14,050		15,000
Closing Finished				
Goods Stock		1,950		2,200
		12,100		12,800
Sales		15,800		17,100
Gross Profit		3,700		4,300
Administration, Selling				
and Distribution Costs		2,480		2,750
Net Profit		1,220		1,550

You can assume that there was no inflation in the two years.

Review the performance of the company so far as you can from this data. Consider each figure in relation to the other figures and to the figure for the other year. Suggest reasons for changes between the years.

b. The management felt that the performance shown in the manufacturing accounts was satisfactory considering that trading was very competitive.

However Timothea, the Chief Executive asked for a breakdown of the figures over the four products. This produced this schedule:

	Giant		Large		Small		Special	
	19x1	19x2	19x1	19x2	19x1	19x2	19x1	19x2
Raw Materials								
Opening stock	128	132	152	146	230	250	170	192
Purchases	660	698	1,100	1,185	800	940	540	417
	788	830	1,252	1,331	1,030	1,190	710	609
Closing Stock	132	160	146	131	250	290	192	259
	656	670	1,106	1,200	780	900	518	350
Direct Labour	480	490	990	780	840	950	1,270	680
	1,136	1,160	2,096	1,980	1,620	1,850	1,788	1,030
Works Overheads	1,290	1,490	1,200	2,890	1,500	1,620	1,710	1,100
	2,426	2,650	3,296	4,870	3,120	3,470	3,498	2,130
Opening WIP	200	320	166	340	340	232	244	388
	2,626	2,970	3,462	5,210	3,460	3,702	3,742	2,518
Closing WIP	320	280	340	350	232	600	388	120
	2,306	2,690	3,022	4,860	3,328	3,102	3,354	2,398
Opening FGS	450	430	510	290	380	120	700	1,110
	2,756	3,120	3,532	5,150	3,708	3,222	4,054	3,508
Closing FGS	430	500	290	720	120	180	1,110	800
	2,326	2,620	3,242	4,430	3,588	3,042	2,944	2,708
Sales	2,560	2,940	5,200	6,300	5,200	4,960	2,840	2,900
Gross Profit	234	320	1,958	1,870	1,612	1,918	(104)	192

Review the schedule and make comments on the performance of each of the four products over the two years.

What changes might be made?

6 Company accounts

Exercises

*1. From the following data relating to two companies Cain Ltd and Abel Ltd, prepare profit and loss accounts and balance sheets. The relevant year is 19x2.

(All figures in £'000)	Cain	Abel
Sales	10,300	2,300
Distribution costs	620	120
Tangible Fixed Assets	4,108	1,030
Goodwill	560	200
Interim Dividend paid	70	25
Extraordinary items:		
Expenditure		28
Stocks	375	430
Trade creditors	680	213
Debtors	980	540
Prepayments	32	17
Cost of sales	7,800	1,240
Administration Expenses	790	135
Debenture loan at 12% payable 19x6	2,400	600
Interest	370	72
Corporation Tax on 19x2 profits	180	201
Taxation and social security due	134	39
Bank Overdraft	621	
Cash at bank		74
Cash in hand	12	18
Final Dividend proposed	140	50
Issued Ordinary share capital (20p shares)	700	250
Share Premium	280	80
Revaluation Reserve	239	75
Profit and loss account at 1.1.19x2	363	341
Minority Interests		31

2. From the following data relating to two companies Samantha Ltd and Damian Ltd, prepare profit and loss accounts and balance sheets. The relevant year is 19x2.

(All figures in £'000)	Samantha	Damian
Sales	26,000	1,400
Distribution costs	1,380	134
Tangible Fixed Assets	12,567	943
Goodwill, Patents and Trade Marks	500	320
Interim Dividend paid	460	30
Extraordinary items:		
Expenditure	1,200	
Income		23
Stocks	6,390	124
Trade creditors	3,870	67
Debtors	6,800	87
Cost of sales	20,100	470
Administration Expenses	2,512	98
9% Bonds payable 19x7	1,000	
8% Convertible loan 19x4/19x6		250

Interest	135	20
Corporation Tax on 19x2 profits	540	220
Taxation and social security due	967	86
Bank Overdraft	260	
Cash at bank		55
Final Dividend proposed – Ordinary	690	120
– Preference	70	
Issued Ordinary share capital		
(20p shares)	2,300	700
Share Premium	1,678	
Revaluation Reserve	239	
Profit and loss account at 1.1.19x2	14,230	(276)
7% Preference Shares of 1 each	1,000	
Minority Interests		31
Capital Redemption Reserve	500	

Note:

❏ *"Bonds"* is just another word for loans

❏ *Preference shares* are shares where the holders have different rights from the ordinary shareholders. Preference share rights normally include the right to a fixed rate of dividend (here it is 7% of the nominal value of the shares) which can only be paid if there are profits and the right to take preference over ordinary shareholders in a winding up (= liquidation) when they would be paid a maximum of the nominal value of the shares. The ordinary shareholders can only be given a dividend if one is also given to preference shareholders. Preference shareholders normally do not have a vote at meetings of the company.

❏ Many preference shares (and also some ordinary shares in special circumstances) are *redeemable* (= repayable). When they are redeemed part of the profit and loss balance is renamed *Capital Redemption Reserve*.

❏ *Convertible Loans* are loans where the lender has an *option* at specified times to convert his loan into ordinary shares at a specified rate.

Answer the following questions:

Samantha Ltd

a. Has the company made sufficient profits to cover its dividends relating to the year 19x2? If not, how is it able to pay dividends?

b. What are the rates of dividend per share on each dividend?

c. What are the earnings per ordinary share if earnings are defined as profits after tax and preference dividends but before extraordinary items?

d. Can you calculate the interest paid on the overdraft?

e. Have any of the preference shares been redeemed?

f. Are any of the fixed tangible assets valued by reference to a valuation?

Damian Ltd

a. What are the rates of dividend on the ordinary shares?

b. Can you calculate the earnings per share

c. Is the balance sheet that of a company or a group? If it is a group, does Damian Ltd own all the shares in its subsidiaries?

3. The Profit and Loss Accounts of Jephtha PLC for two years show:

Profit and Loss Account

(All figures in £'000)

	19x2	19x3
Turnover	6,300	7,400
Cost of Sales	4,200	4,600
Gross Profit	2,100	2,800
Distribution Costs	450	280
Administration Expenses	340	510
Operating Profit	1,310	2,010
Interest Payable	550	300
Profit on Ordinary activities before taxation	760	1,710
Taxation	230	510
Profit on ordinary activities after taxation	530	1,200
Extraordinary items	450	670
Profit of the year	80	530
Dividends	200	220
Retained profit for the year	(120)	310
Earnings per share	10.6p	16p

Required:

a. Comment on these two accounts in detail

b. How might your comments change when you know that:

❐ The extraordinary item in 19x2 is the closure costs of the loss making wholesale division of the company.

❐ The extraordinary item of 19x3 is the loss on disposal of the US subsidiary. This subsidiary made profits but the directors decided that as these were lower than expected when the company was bought, it should be sold again.

*4. Mixwell PLC have a Balance Sheet as follows at the end of 19x1:

(all figures in £'000)

Net Assets	6,900
Share Capital (50p shares)	2,000
Profit and Loss Account	4,900
	6,900

The company did the following things:

a. Made a bonus issue of 1 share for every 2 held.

b. Then made a rights issue of one share for every four shares held of the enlarged capital at £2.40 a share.

c. Revalued the property upwards by £6 million.

d. Made a profit of £1.6 million.

e. Paid a dividend of 4p a share.

Required:

a. Show the summary Balance Sheet after each thing.

c. Comment on the fact that the share price moved from £4.00 a share before the bonus issue to £2.70 immediately after the bonus issue.

d. Comment on the fact that the share price moved from £2.70 a share to £2.50 a share immediately after the rights issue.

5. Financial Chicanery PLC made a bonus issue at the end of 19x1, a profit in 19x2 and a rights issue at the end of 19x2. The company is divided into shares of 20p each. Its Balance Sheets at various dates were:

(all figures in £'000)	end 19x1 but pre bonus issue	end 19x1 post bonus issue	end 19x2 pre rights issue	end 19x2 post rights issue
Net Assets	1,900	a	2,400	3,300
Share Capital	800	1,000	1,000	1,400
Share Premium	500			
Profit and Loss Account	1,100	b	c	d
	e	f	g	h

a. Insert figures instead of the letters a to h.

b. How many extra shares were issued to a shareholder holding 800 shares as a result of the bonus issue?

c. How many shares were offered to a holder of 1,000 shares as a result of the rights issue? And at what price?

d. Before the bonus issue each share was quoted at 60p. What would you expect the price to be after the bonus issue?

e. Before the rights issue each share was quoted at 84p. What would you expect the price to be after the rights issue?

Assignment 1

The published accounts of Adam PLC, wholesalers of ladies wear for the two years 19x2 and 19x3 are:

Profit and Loss Account

(All figures in £'000)

	19x2	19x3
Turnover	6,700	9,300
Cost of Sales	4,500	6,100
Gross Profit	2,200	3,200
Distribution Costs	680	830
Administration Expenses	1,125	1,350
Operating Profit	395	1,020
Interest Payable	75	140
Profit on Ordinary activities before taxation	320	880
Taxation	80	256
Profit on ordinary activities after taxation	240	624
Extraordinary items	302	60
(Loss)/Profit of the year	(62)	564
Dividends	20	200
Retained profit for the year	(82)	364
Earnings per share	8p	10.4p

Balance sheet as at 31 December

	19x2	19x3
Fixed Assets		
Intangible assets		600
Tangible assets	<u>1,200</u>	<u>2,100</u>
	1,200	2,700
Current Assets		
Stocks	830	1,380
Debtors	1,200	1,590
Cash at bank and in hand	<u>180</u>	<u>20</u>
	2,210	2,990
Creditors:amounts falling due within one year		
Creditors	1,430	1,579
Bank Overdrafts		269
Taxation and Social Security	245	367
Corporation Tax	80	256
Dividends		<u>180</u>
	1,755	2,651
Net Current Assets	455	339
Total Assets less Current Liabilities	1,655	3,039
Creditors: amounts falling due after more than one year		
Bank and Other Loans	<u>500</u>	<u>770</u>
	1,155	2,269
Capital and Reserves		
Issued Share Capital (10p shares)	300	600
Share Premium		200
Revaluation Reserve		250
Profit and Loss Account	<u>855</u>	<u>1,219</u>
	1,155	2,269

Required:

Write a report explaining the happenings to Adam PLC in 19x2 and 19x3 as far as it is possible to do so from the accounts. You should deal with:

> Increase in business from 19x2 to 19x3
> Interest
> Extraordinary items (19x2 re closure of three branches) (19x3 re sale of a subsidiary company)
> Dividends
> Earnings per share
> Intangible assets
> Tangible fixed assets
> Cash at bank/Overdraft
> Bank and Other loans
> Share capital and share premium
> Revaluation
> Profit and loss account on the balance sheet

Assignment 2

Obtain a copy of the annual report and accounts of a public company (or preferably several) and write a report on the following matters:

Profit and Loss Account

i.   How much are the auditors paid?

ii. How much is the depreciation (and amortisation) charge?

iii. Are any research and development costs charged?

iv. How much interest is paid?

v. Is segmental information given on activities and geography?

vi. What is the rate of corporation tax?

vii. Are there any minority interests?

viii. Summarise the extraordinary items.

ix. What are the rates of interim and final dividend?

x. Relate the rates of dividend with the amounts payable and the share capital.

xi. How is the earnings per share calculated?

xii. What are the accounting policies on the valuation of stocks?

Group Balance Sheet

i. Are there any intangible assets?

ii. If yes, how are they valued?

iii. What are the categories of tangible fixed assets?

iv. Are land and buildings depreciated?

v. Are any tangible fixed assets at a valuation?

vi. Can you reconcile the depreciation to the profit and loss account figure?

vii. Are there any fixed asset investments?

viii. If yes, how are they valued?

ix. What are the categories of stocks?

x. Do debtors include any Advance corporation tax (this is a tax paid at 1/3 of the net dividend, when a dividend is paid. It is recoverable by deduction from later corporation tax payments.)

xi. What types (if any) of current asset investments are held?

xii. What are the categories of creditors due in less than twelve months?

xiii. Do they include advance corporation tax and obligations under finance leases (finance leases arise when the company leases equipment in such a way that the lease transfers substantially all the risks and rewards of ownership of assets to the lessee. They are in effect very similar to hire purchase contracts)

xiv. What are the names given to obligations included in creditors: amounts falling due after more than a year?

xv. What is the nominal value of one share? What is its present stock market value?

xiv. Have any new shares been issued in the past year? Do any issues relate to executive share option schemes, scrip dividends (many companies allow shareholders to take dividends in the form of new shares instead of cash), a bonus issue, a rights issue, an issue in connection with an acquisition of another company?

xvi. Is there a share premium account and has it changed in the year?

xvii. Is there a revaluation reserve?

xviii. Does the profit retained in the profit and loss account reconcile with the increase in profit and loss account on the balance sheet?

General:

i. How many directors are there? How many are non-executive? What is their total remuneration?

ii. How many shares in the company do the directors own? What proportion of the total share capital does this represent?

iii. Did the company make any charitable or political donations in the year?

iv.   How many people worked for the Group in the year and what was their total remuneration?

v.   Is there any qualification to the auditors' report?

vi.   Has the Group acquired or disposed of any companies in the year?

vii. What is the time of the Annual General Meeting?

viii. What are the items on the agenda?

ix.   Is there an election for directors?

x.   Can all the shareholders be accommodated in the venue of the AGM?

xi.   How many of the directors are under 50; female; non-executive?

Further development

Accounting Regulation

At the time of writing accounting and in particular company accounting is very highly regulated. We will now review some of the regulations

1. The Companies Act 1985 as amended by the Companies Act 1989.

    Accounting and reporting by companies to their shareholders in the form of a Profit and Loss Account and Balance Sheet have been subject to statutory regulation since the mid nineteenth century and successive Companies Acts have added to and refined the requirements ever since. The current Act is very detailed and I have covered some of its requirements in the Units on company accounting. Some points of note are:

a. All companies are required to comply in detail with the requirements of the Act as to the production of the Profit and Loss Account, Balance Sheet, Directors' Report and Auditors Report. This means that they have to be produced in the format required and with all the detailed information which is obligatory in the Act. The Profit and Loss Account and Balance Sheet also have to be audited and auditing is itself now highly regulated.

b. These accounts have to be laid before the shareholders at the Annual General Meeting and be filed at Companies House where they will be available to be seen by the public. However there are some exceptions which we will discuss below.

c. Private companies can, by elective resolution of the shareholders, dispense with the requirement to lay the Accounts before the members at a general meeting of shareholders but the accounts must still be sent to the individual shareholders so this exemption does not really save very much.

d. Small and medium sized companies need only file abbreviated accounts with the Registrar of Companies. A small and medium sized company is defined as one satisfying two of the three conditions:

	Small	Medium Size
Turnover not more than	£2million	£8million
Balance Sheet total not more than	£0.975m	£3.9m
Average number of employees not more than	50	250

Instead of filing all the accounts a Small company need only file an abbreviated Balance Sheet with reduced notes and need not file a Profit and Loss Account or Directors' Report. A medium sized company need only file a slightly abbreviated Profit and Loss Account but must file all the rest.

It is important to note that all accounts and reports must still be produced, audited and sent to shareholders so the saving is only that more limited information is made available to the public.

e. *Listed* public companies (companies quoted on the Stock Exchange) need not send their shareholders the full Report and Accounts but instead may send a summary financial statement. The content of the *summary financial statement* is prescribed by regulation. Any shareholder who wants the full set of Accounts can require that the company supply it to her.

The Financial Reporting Council

2. The financial reporting council is a company limited by guarantee so that in theory it is in the private sector but it was set up by the government who, with the Bank of England, appoint its Chairman and three Deputy Chairmen so that it has statutory backing. Its remit is to give support to its operational bodies and to encourage good financial reporting generally. It has two subsidiaries – the Accounting Standards Board (ABS) and the Financial Reporting Review Panel (FRRP).

   The Accounting Standards Board makes and amends and withdraws Accounting Standards. One of its first acts was to adopt the 22 extant Statements of Standard Accounting Practice which were approved by the professional accounting bodies. The previous system of creation of SSAPs by the Accounting Standards Committee and approval by the professional bodies has now been discontinued. The first new Financial Reporting Standard (FRS 1 – Cash Flow Statements) was issued in 1991 and a programme of new and amended standards is now under way. Before issuing a new Standard the ABS issues its proposals in the form of a *Financial Reporting Exposure Draft* (FRED) for public comment and sometimes before issuing a FRED it issues a *Discussion Paper*.

   Some industries need accounting standards for their particular purposes and they can produce *Statements of Recommended Practice* (SORPS). The ABS has a role in the approval of these by approving bodies who issue them rather than the SORPS themselves.

   The Accounting Standards Board has a sub-committee called the *Urgent Issues Task Force* (UITF). The work of the UITF is to assist the ABS in areas where an accounting standard or Companies Act provision exists but where unsatisfactory or conflicting interpretations have developed or seem likely to develop. A surprising number of matters have been subject to UITF pronouncements, most of them very technical.

Financial Reporting Review Panel

3. The FRRP is a subsidiary of the FRC. Its role is to examine departures from the accounting requirements of the Companies Act 1985 and if necessary to seek an order from the court to remedy them. As well as having detailed requirements on accounting the Companies Act requires all accounts to show a *true and fair view* and by implication to comply with the accounting standards. The panel does not seek out departures but acts on matters drawn to its attention directly or indirectly. The panels concerns are with the public companies and small and medium sized companies are outside its ambit.

Acts of Parliament

4. Many businesses are subject to the regulation of Specific acts of Parliament and the Acts also regulate the records to be kept and the reporting to shareholders and to regulatory bodies that must be done. Examples include Building Societies, Housing Associations, Solicitors, Friendly Societies and Financial Services companies. Many businesspeople now feel that the amount of regulation is unduly restrictive and expensive. It is often pointed out that legislation to deter rogues causes immense labour and expense for the honest businessperson without deterring the rogue at all.

Government Agencies

5. Adequate accounting and record keeping are needed by businesses to accord with the requirements of a number of government agencies. These include the Inland Revenue for income tax, corporation tax and PAYE purposes and by the Customs and Excise for Value Added Tax (VAT) purposes. Records re also required for Statutory Sick Pay purposes and National Insurance. The burden of complying with regulation is considerable on all businesses but is very good for accountants!

Case Study

Gedoutovit PLC is a listed company with a number of different activities. Among these are life assurance and pensions broking, speculative housebuilding and brewing. Turnover is around £20 million and total number of employees is about 300.

The company accountant is preparing the annual accounts for the year ending 31 December 19x2. He is not sure what do to about:

a.   The company advance substantial sums as interest free loans to organisations such as clubs to induce them to buy the company's beers to the exclusion of other brewers' beers. These are repayable immediately if the club goes into receivership or liquidation or if it revokes the agreement to buy exclusively from Gedoutovit. After 10 years of exclusivity the loans are written off. In recent years a significant number of clubs have failed and Gedoutovit has received almost nothing in the ensuing liquidations.

The present accounting treatment is to show all outstanding loans by including them in trade debtors in current assets i.e they are not shown as a separate item although they represent about 15% of trade debtors. When loans are written off either on the time expiry rule or because they are bad debts they are included in the Profit and Loss Account figure of cost of sales.

b.   The company have built 50 houses to sell and the average cost of these has been £75,000. Only 10 have been sold as the market has dried up and the agent reckons the houses will only sell at about £50,000. The company decided to let them instead and they have all been let to sound tenants at very modest rents. The company's intentions are to sell the houses when the market improves and the tenants leave.

The present accounting treatment is to transfer the houses from current assets to fixed assets at cost. No depreciation will be charged and they will be carried at cost.

Discussion:

a.   List the record keeping and financial reporting regulations that may apply to the company. It may help to consult friends who are involved in record keeping for companies and financial services companies.

b.   Comment on the accounting treatment of the loans and the houses and suggest alternative policies and the extent of disclosure. As a matter of record both of these issues were raised in UITF information sheet No 2 issued on 15 April 1992 without resolution.

Accounting for the effects of changing price levels

6.   Traditional accounting measures profit by comparing sales with cost of sales and overheads measured at their historical input cost. This method is objective and, in times of relatively stable prices, works very well. However in recent years inflation has been as high as 20% in the UK and even at rates as low as 4% or 5%, Accounts are distorted. As a result the accountancy profession has tried to introduce adjustments to accounts to counter the effects of inflation.

The major problem lies in the fact that dividends and taxation are based on profits measured using historical costs. The effect of this is that there is a possibility that operating assets will not be maintained and capital will be reduced. This is not easy to see so I will illustrate it in two examples:

		£
a.	A Ltd maintains a stock of 10 widgets at cost of £1 each	10
	They sell these for £1.50 each	15
	and make a profit in historical terms of	5
	This permits a dividend (ignoring tax) of	5
	But, prices are rising and A Ltd must replace the widgets at £1.20 each	12

If the historical cost profit (5) is distributed in full, it will not be possible to replace the ten widgets at £1.20 each since the operating capital is only £10. To stay in the same position of stocking 10 widgets, capital must be increased by £2.

b. B Ltd operate an ice cream van. This cost £4,000 and will last for four years.

Each year –	Sales		10,000
	Cost of sales	3,000	
	Depreciation	1,000	4,000
	Historical Cost Profit		6,000

If this profit is distributed in full as a dividend, then resources available to replace the van will be £4,000 – cash flow each year is Sales £10,000 – cost of sales £3,000 – dividend £6,000 = £1,000.

However because of inflation the cost of replacing the van after 4 years is £7,000. Capital has been maintained at £4,000 but £7,000 is needed so more capital has to be put into the business.

Benefits of historical cost accounting

There are limitations to historical cost accounting but there also considerable benefits. These include:

a. Book keeping is done by recording transactions. It is not really feasible to record transactions (eg the purchase of a good) in any way other than at its cost.

b. Financial statements are drawn up from the book keeping system. Any alternative to historical cost would require much manipulation of the data.

c. Historical cost accounting is *objective* and *verifiable*. The cost of an asset is clearly stated in the invoice and payment and this can be verified by the auditor. Any other value is inevitably subjective. Users of accounts know where they stand with historical cost accounts and can and do make mental adjustments.

d. The original raison d'etre of accounts was the report to owners as to "what has happened to our money?" Historical cost accounting answers this question fairly well. It is only relatively recently that persons other than owners are taking an interest in financial statements.

e. After many years of development, historical cost financial statements are well understood – this is a doubtful statement.

f. No acceptable alternative to historical cost has yet been found.

Limitations of historical cost

It is easy to pick out weaknesses in the measurement of income and capital under historical cost principles. Some of these are:

a. Fixed assets in a balance sheet and depreciation in a Profit and Loss Account bear no relation to real values. The requirement to depreciate buildings worsens this criticism but the tendency to revalue property lessens it.

b. Stock valued at £40,000 at cost may need £50,000 to replace and yet £40,000 is the value used in accounts.

c. The sum of values of assets in a Balance Sheet is a mixture of say 19x2, 19x3, 19x8 pounds etc and because of inflation these are not the same.

d. The capital (= capital and reserves in a company) purports to show the capital tied up in a business but this is nonsense when historical values are used.

e. In a Profit and Loss Account sales at current prices are matched with inputs which will include stocks purchased months earlier and depreciation of assets purchased years earlier when price levels were different.

f.   Holding gains are ignored. Inflation increases the money value of assets but this is ignored in Profit and Loss Accounts.

g.   The sum repayable on long term loans and debentures may be mush reduced in real terms but this is ignored in Profit and Loss Accounts.

h.   Dividends and drawings are based on historical value financial statements and may as a consequence be paid partly out of capital. We have already considered this point.

i.   Return on capital employed calculations are usually misleading:

   ❑   capital employed is distorted by using historical cost

   ❑   return (= profit) is distorted by using depreciation at historical cost

j.   Decision making on out of date values will be sub-optimal. As examples:

   ❑   X does not really know the profitability of his marginal branch in Darlaston and so does not know whether or not to close it down

   ❑   Y does not know if selling his product at prices based on historical cost costings is actually profitable

   ❑   Z, an investor, is unable to evaluate realistically the companies he has shares in.

Solutions to the problems of historical cost accounting

a.   One partial solution is to *revalue* assets and this approach is widely adopted but applies largely only to land and buildings.

b.   Another solution is more comprehensive and is called *Current Purchasing Price Accounting* (CPP). This complete system works by converting the historical figures to current purchasing power by an appropriate price index usually the Retail Price Index (RPI). CPP had a vogue in the 1970s but is not much considered now.

c.   The most regarded solution is *Current Cost Accounting* (CCA). This system is also comprehensive and is still found (for example in the Accounts of British Gas PLC).

The basic concepts are:

   ❑   Profit and Loss Account: the profit is adjusted by charging an extra item against profit. The extra item is the difference between the value to the business of assets consumed and the historical acquisition costs. Value to the business is generally taken as the replacement costs of the assets consumed. Four adjustments are taken in two stages:

Stage i.

a.   A depreciation adjustment

b.   A cost of sales adjustment being the difference between the value to the business of the stocks consumed and their historical input costs

c.   A monetary working capital adjustment to reflect the additional working capital (mainly debtors) required in times of rising prices. Additional resources are needed to finance any increase in debtors caused purely by inflation, less any part financed by increased creditors.

Stage ii.

The gearing adjustment. When part of the net operating assets are financed by long term debt, a proportional reduction of the stage i. adjustments is made to reflect the gain made by the company from borrowing which will be repaid at some future date in depreciated currency.

❑ the Balance Sheet: the Balance Sheet should contain:

i. Fixed Assets and stocks at their value to the business

ii. Other current assets and all liabilities at their historical cost

iii. Shareholders interests divided into

Share capital
Current Cost Reserve – the adjustments made
Other Reserves

CCA is very sophisticated at a detailed level but is not easy to grasp at an intuitive level and as a result has not really commanded the respect of the business community.

The search continues!

Case Study 1

Nomm PLC and Penn PLC are two rival companies of similar size in the widget trade.

Nomm is very long established and is financed largely by retained earnings. It has a net profit after tax to dividends ratio of 1.5. Its factories and plant are in good repair but not at all new. The factories are carried in the accounts at cost less depreciation of the buildings elements. Nomm carries significant stocks of raw materials and finished goods. Traditionally in the widget trade customers are slow in paying.

Penn is a young company with the very latest in factory design and modern plant. In order to finance the fixed assets, it is heavily geared with short, medium term and long term borrowings. Penn operates a just-in-time system for its raw materials and components and has a very sophisticated computerised system for keeping finished goods stocks as low as possible.

The main component in widgets is the metal Alanium which is traded in the commodity exchanges. Demand and supply fluctuates wildly and the price has varied from 20% to 290% of the mean price over the last five years. Prices of widgets have on the contrary varied little.

Discussion:

Both companies report profits and assets on historical cost principles. What would be the effect on profits and return on capital employed of using Current Cost Accounting principles instead?

Case Study 2

In 1968, Willenhall Metal Bashers Ltd was formed by a group of friends who subscribed at par for the £1 shares. A factory site was acquired and a factory building erected. The company depreciated the factory building over 50 years. Very little profit was made and small losses occurred in the final four years. Most of the profits were distributed as dividends.

In 1988 the factory was sold to a neighbouring company who demolished the factory building as it was in disrepair and obsolete for modern needs. The goodwill and other assets of the company were sold to the son of one of the founders.

As a result of the disposal of the substance of the company, the company was liquidated and the shareholders received £6 a share.

Discuss the relevance of historical cost accounting to the decisions of the directors and shareholders of this company.

Accounting conventions

Exercises

1. Edna, an heiress, has a boutique which does a large volume of business with very little actual stock. She rents the premises which needed little doing to them when she started the business. Paul has been shown her accounts so that he can be convinced that he should sell to her on credit. He sees that the business is profitable but that Edna makes drawings nearly equal to the profit. He also sees that due to her few fixed assets, her small stock and that all her customers pay cash, her capital account is actually negative.

    Comment on the utility of these accounts to Paul with especial consideration on the entity convention.

2. Shankar is considering buying some shares in a company, AmalConsInternat PLC, which have been recommended by a friend. He obtains a copy of the accounts and finds that they are in the form of Group accounts.

    Comment on the entity convention in relation to Group Accounts and what further information in the small print might help Shankar evaluate the past, present and future of the Group.

*3. Gogg, the manager of the local branch of the ESP Bank, is perusing the accounts of Wilco Ltd with a view to lending the company money for expansion. He has been told by the company that it has just obtained a contract for the sole importing rights of a new American electronic product. The company also told him that it has full order books at last for its major product and would not after all have to lay off its 20 strong workforce most of whom have been with the company for twenty years or more. The company is offering as security its old factory which it bought many years ago and which is sited on an estate which has been used for a century or more for heavy industry and which is gradually being developed by the Midlands Development Board.

    How much of the information given above will be ignored in the accounts because of the conventions of accounting?

4. Fir Ltd is a public relations consultant and does work for major companies on an ongoing basis. He complains that his clients usually take six months to pay after he has issued them with invoices and that they then quibble about his charges and he has to knock anything up to 40% off to get payment.

    Acacia Ltd sells reconditioned copiers to small companies giving them interest free extended credit. He always gets his customers to sign a contract of supply with a Romalpa clause.

    Euphorbia Ltd sell furniture from examples in their showroom. Each customer pays in full with the order and then the goods are obtained from the manufacturer and delivered to the customers. There is usually a 6 to 12 weeks gap between order and delivery.

    Comment on the appropriateness of the realisation convention in these three cases.

5. Angelica works for an accountant and she is currently preparing the annual accounts of Jagworth Ltd. a motor car main dealer. She is going through the expenses preparing a schedule of prepayments and accruals. She has apportioned the telephone bills, the electricity, the rents, the rates, the insurances, the subscriptions to the Chamber of Commerce etc, the advertising, the stationery, the wages and many others.

    At the same time, Angelo is calculating the depreciation on the fixed assets and trying to make sense of the valuations put by the company on the enormous second hand car stock.

    In the light of the above, comment on the accruals convention.

6. Twill Ltd has a business installing central heating systems and the first accounts are in course of preparation. Three problems have arisen:

   ❏ the company guarantees its systems with a full parts and labour guarantee for twelve months.

   ❏ the company's estimator has just left after a nervous breakdown and Twill (the sole director) knows that several contracts for supply in the new year have been signed recently and that a number of these will work out at a loss.

   The company have overbought and now have a large stock of components some of which are obsolete.

   How should these problem areas be solved using the accounting conventions?

*7. Cowboy Construction Ltd is a firm of civil engineers specialising in site works and roads. Their balance sheet at 31 December 19x2 showed:

(figures in £'000)

Fixed Assets		
Plant at cost	684	
Less Depreciation	435	249
Premises at cost	400	
Less depreciation	102	298
		547
Current Assets		
Stock of materials etc	231	
Approved current contract work awaiting payment	542	
Retentions	358	
Current contract work in progress	870	
Prepayments	104	
	2,105	
Liabilities: amounts due in less than twelve months		
Creditors	987	
Overdraft	710	
Taxation	651	
Proposed dividend	200	
	2,548	
Net current liabilities		(443)
Total assets less current liabilities		104
16% Debenture payable in 19x8		100
		4
Share Capital		1
Profit and Loss account		3
		4

This balance sheet has been drawn up on the going concern basis. Discuss in detail how it might look if the company was forced to close and go into liquidation immediately.

8. Lilac Ltd manufacture special equipment for fire services. In 19x2, the company recognised a niche in the market for a special high powered pump and set about designing and developing the pump. All of the workforce spent at least some time in the year on the project. By the end of the year a prototype pump was ready but did not work effectively. The company recognise that the market still wants the pump but that another year of development will be necessary before manufacture can begin.

It is estimated that in 19x2 some 5,000 man hours at an average cost of £8 an hour have been spent on the project together with about £20,000 in materials (you can ignore overheads associated with these costs).

Required:

a. Describe the possible accounting treatments that could be used for the project in the 19x2 accounts.

b. Which would you recommend in these two separate circumstances:

   i. The company is small and is heavily indebted to the bank who are being asked to renew overdraft facilities.

   ii. The company is very profitable and the Board are anxious to pay as little tax as possible.

9. You are an executive of the Mercia Software Association and are setting up a scheme for interfirm comparison of the performance (as revealed by the annual accounts) of member companies. The members are all small firms developing software for clients. What problems of comparability are likely to arise which will have to be resolved if interfirm comparison is to be useful?

10. The accounts for the two years ending 31 December 19x2 and 19x3 of the Stubby Social Club include a bar trading account as:

	19x2	19x3
Sales	24,000	31,000
Cost of goods sold	15,000	20,398
Gross Profit	9,000	10,602
Gross Profit as a %age of sales	37.5	34.2

Required:

a. What might the members of the club conclude from an examination of these figures?

b. Would their reading be different if the following facts were revealed:

   ❐ a burglary in the night of 14 February 19x3 led to an uninsured loss of £1,200 worth of stock

   ❐ a temporary barman was dismissed in November 19x2 after a shortage of £105 was found in his till. This loss was uninsured.

   ❐ the club started to do wedding receptions in March 19x3 and a reception was held nearly every Saturday in the summer with a cash bar at each.

11. Fidelio Transport (19x3) Ltd is a bus company which operates a number of scheduled routes. It had previously failed and had been reconstructed with a staff buyout at the beginning of 19x3. The buy out has been supported by the Bank which has a guarantee of its loan from each member of staff. Trading is still difficult.

How frequently and in what measure of detail should accounts be produced?

Case Study

The annual accounts of Hoopoe Ltd for the year ending 31 December 19x2:

Profit and Loss Account

(all figures in £'000)

Turnover		12,300
Cost of sales		8,380
Gross Profit		3,920
Distribution costs	654	
Administration expenses	342	996
		2,924
Net Income from hire purchase financing		480
Income from shares in group companies		1,200
		4,604
Interest payable		730
Profit on ordinary activities before taxation		3,874
Tax on profits		1,404
Profit on ordinary activities after taxation		2,470
Extraordinary charges	180	
Tax on extraordinary charges	35	145
Profit for the financial year		2,325
Proposed dividend		800
Retained profit for the year		1,525

Balance sheet

Fixed Assets		
Tangible		9,456
Intangible		2,100
Investments		8,650
		20,206
Current Assets		
Stocks	1,900	
Debtors	2,390	
Prepayments	250	
Cash at Bank	180	
	4,720	
Creditors: amounts falling due within one year		
Creditors	730	
Leasing Obligations	240	
Taxation	1,790	
Bank Overdraft	781	
Dividend	800	
	4,341	
Net current assets		379
Total assets less current liabilities		20,585
Capital and Reserves		
Called up Share Capital		8,000
Share Premium		4,700
Revaluation Reserve		4,200
Profit and Loss Account		3,685
		20,585

Required:

List the accounting conventions used in preparing these accounts and explain how each convention may have affected figures in these accounts. Alternative accounting conventions can be suggested with an indication of how the accounts would change if they were adopted.

Further development

Escaping from the conventions of accounting

Financial statements offer limited information and are historical in nature. In recent years more people have found a use for them – customers, suppliers, all sorts of government agencies including the tax authorities, banks and other suppliers of finance, employees, managers, buyers of businesses, investors etc. More people now have some understanding of accounting as a consequence of the proliferation of courses in business and management studies.

The limitations of convention bound accounting have become more evident to more people. However no radical attempt to reform accounting to make it more informative has yet appeared. Some suggestions that have been made are:

a. valuing goodwill, especially the value of brands

b. valuing the people who are employed by the business

c. requiring a profit forecast with each set of financial statements

d. listing statistics like orders on hand

e. a review of products and research and development into new products

f. review of ecological progress by the company

g. review of employment practices and health and safety

h. listing of exporting and importing undertaken

i. provision of accurately calculated and detailed ratios

j. a commentary on each line of the accounts with explanations of changes from the previous year.

k. a summary of significant activities and contracts affecting the company.

All of these things seem a good idea but have practical difficulties. For example c. requires the directors to put their necks upon the block. Forecasting is very difficult and the directors may be afraid of litigation if their forecasts were not fulfilled.

Assignment:

Consider the suggestions and summarise the practical and legal difficulties that may occur to you.

8 | Ratio analysis

Exercises

1. The trading account of two companies for the years 19x1, 19x2 and 19x3 showed: (in '£000)

	19x1	**19x2**	**19x3**
Company A			
Turnover	8,800	9,700	10,100
Cost of goods sold	6,130	6,596	6,717
Gross profit	2,670	3,104	3,383

    Inflation in 19x2 was 6% and in 19x3 8%.

	19x1	**19x2**	**19x3**
Company B			
Turnover	4,400	5,250	6,015
Cost of goods sold	3,000	3,702	4,331
Gross Profit	1.400	1,548	1,684

    Comment on all these figures using ratios.

2. The summarised profit and loss accounts of two companies for 19x2, their budgeted figures for the same year and the average for the industry are:

    (in £'000)

	Company C		**Company D**		**Industry**
	Actual	**Budget**	**Actual**	**Budget**	**%age of sales**
Sales	240	230	280	320	100
Gross Profit	91	92	104	128	41
Selling and					
Distribution	23	27	26	22	6
Admin	31	30	35	39	10
Net Profit	37	35	43	67	25

    Comment on the figures using ratios.

3. Some figures from the accounts of two similar chemical companies, one in the UK and one in another European country:

	UK Company in £'000	**European in currency**
Turnover	86,000	145,000
Net Profit	6,400	18,400
Land and Buildings	33,700	33,100
Plant and Equipment	18,400	27,000
Current Assets	22,100	34,500
Current Liabilities	19,400	18,200
Long term liabilities	2,000	21,000

    a. Comment on these figures using ratios including an asset utilisation ratio and a measure of return on capital employed.

    b. Comment further in the light of knowledge that:

        i. The British company recently revalued upwards all its land and buildings. The European company values all its land at buildings simply at cost without depreciation.

        ii. The British company has financed its recent acquisitions of plant with the aid of bank overdrafts with the intention of replacing the overdrafts with long term loans shortly. Note that replacing short term loans with long term loans is known as funding the short term debt. The European company has access to very long term bank finance.

*4. The accounts of three companies for the year ending 31 December 19x2 show: (in '000)

	K	L	M
Turnover	35,800	21,000	34,000
Gross Profit	8,700	4,800	6,000
Net Profit	2,400	1,200	1,540
Property	1,600	2,800	10,400
Plant etc	3,520	1,400	8,600
Stocks	1,100	1,800	6,300
Work in Progress	–	720	2,300
Debtors	340	3,200	4,200
Cash at bank	2,890		
Creditors	3,100	1,400	2,430
Bank Overdraft		2,180	5,900

Required:

a. For each company calculate:

Return on capital employed
Asset utilisation ratio
Debtors payment period
Net profit to sales ratio

Stock turnover

Which, if any, of these ratios are meaningful?

b. One of the companies is a supermarket chain, one is a textile manufacturer and the other is a company in heavy industry making process plant. Which company is which and how do you know?

5. Here are some data about three companies, all of whom are in the wholesale widget business:

	S		T		U	
(all in £'000)						
For 19x2:						
Sales		8,200		6,200		9,500
Opening stock	1,450		900		1,480	
Purchases	6.170		4.568		5.840	
	7,620		5,468		7,320	
Closing stock	1.820	5.800	880	4.588	960	6.360
Gross Profit		2,400		1,612		3,140
At 31.12.19x2						
Debtors		2,220		1,020		2,980
Trade creditors		1,678		730		930

Required:

a. Calculate ratios which might enable you to compare the performance of these three companies.

b. Comment on the ratios and suggest to each management where improvements in performance may be possible.

c. Would your commentary be different if you knew:

☐ that company U had an exceptionally large turnover in December 19x2

☐ company S purchased a specially large amount in December 19x2 at a very advantageous price?

6. The following are the profits after tax and the dividends for four successive years for two companies Zig PLC and Zag PLC:

   (all in £'000)

	Zig				Zag			
year	1	2	3	4	1	2	3	4
Profits	6,700	7,100	2,800	8,600	4,500	4,700	6,200	6,600
Dividend	2,400	2,500	2,500	2,900	1,300	1,350	1,650	1,750

   Required:

   a. Calculate the dividend cover for all years.

   b. Comment on the change in cover over the years, suggesting reasons for any change.

   c. Would your commentary be different if you had known that Zag PLC had a large rights issue in year 2?

   d. Which company would you expect to grow the fastest? Justify your opinion.

7. The accounts for the year ending 31 December 19x2 of Hyde Ltd are shrouded in mystery. Certain facts only are known. These include:

   Gross Profit £1,000,000
   Gross Profit to sales ratio 40%
   Stock 31.12.19x1 £300,000
   Creditors £270,000
   Creditors are paid after two months
   Overheads 20% of sales
   Debenture Interest £100,000
   Debentures carry interest at 10%
   Corporation Tax 25% of profits
   Dividend   1/3 of post tax profits
   Fixed assets at 31.12.19x1 at cost £1,200,000 less
        depreciation of £800,000
   Depreciation is at 25% reducing balance method
   Debtors take 50 days to pay (use round £'000)
   Dividend is 25p per £1 share
   Profit and Loss balance at 31 December 19x1 was £312,000

   Required:

   a. Reconstruct the accounts

   b. Calculate return on capital employed and return on shareholders funds.

8. The accounts for the year ended 31 December 19x2 of Cache Ltd are also very mysterious but some information is available:

   Sales   £2,000,000
   Gross Profit to sales ratio 45%
   Stock 31.12.19x2 £400,000
   Stock 31.12.19x1 £300,000
   Creditors are paid after three months
   Overheads 10% of sales
   20% Debentures £1,800,000 are payable in 19x5
   Corporation Tax 25% of profits
   Dividend   1/3 of post tax profits
   Fixed assets at 31.12.19x1 at cost £2,100,000 less
        depreciation of £900,000
   Depreciation is at 10% straight line method
   Half the sales are for cash, the remainder pay after three months
   Dividend is 10p per 20p share and takes 1/2 of post tax profits
   Profit and Loss balance at 31 December 19x1 was £205,000

Required:

a. Reconstruct the accounts

b. Calculate return on capital employed and shareholders funds.

*9.   Some extracts from the accounts of four companies for 19x2:

(all figures in £'000)

	A	B	C	D
Net profit before interest	168	240	398	231
Interest	93	25	120	68
Corporation Tax	18	62	106	45
Share capital	54	200	530	89
Profit and loss balance	728	480	790	180
Long term Finance	800	170	640	480

Required:

a. Calculate for each company: gearing, return on total capital employed and return on shareholders funds.

b. Comment on the ratios including a commentary on each company's performance and the risks to lenders and shareholders.

10.   Some extracts from the accounts of four companies for 19x2:

(all figures in £'000)

	E	F	G	H
Net profit before interest	657	813	923	475
Interest	320	64	320	380
Corporation Tax	84	160	144	23
Share capital	1,200	900	2,900	1,700
Profit and loss balance	780	733	540	2,300
Long term Finance	2,000	390	1,800	1,750

Required:

a. Calculate for each company: gearing, return on total capital employed and return on shareholders funds.

b. Comment on the ratios including a commentary on each company's performance and the risks to lenders and shareholders.

c. Would your remarks be different if you knew that H had a property valued at cost less depreciation at £2,300,000 when its market value is about £6,000,000.

d. Would your remarks be different if you know that:

❏   company E is a brewery that has just spent large sums on doing up its houses.

❏   company F is a manufacturer of motor components which is moving into the European market.

❏   company G is a construction company

❏   company H is a hotel

11. The following are data about four quoted companies:

	I	J	K	L
(all figures in £'000)				
Profit after tax	2,700	12,500	870	2,800
Interim Dividend	400	3,700	45	600
Final Dividend	800	5,800	47	1,400
Total Share capital	2,000	40,000	900	12,000

(figures in pence)	I	J	K	L
Nominal value of one share	20	25	10	100
Quoted Share Price	280	56	170	300

Required:

a. For each company calculate: earnings per share, PE ratio, dividends per share, dividend cover, dividend yield.

b. Comment on each set of ratios.

12. The following statistics are available for these four companies for the year ending 31 December 19x2

(all figures in £'000)

	P	Q	R	S
Profit after tax	3,900	320	2,400	15,900
Interim Dividend	500	200	–	7,000
Final Dividend	600	250	1,000	–
Total Share capital	2,000	900	13,000	77,000
Total Reserves	18,500	450	32,000	4,500

(figures in pence)				
Nominal value of one share	50	10	25	20
Quoted Share Price	1,250	70	70	19

Required:

a. For each company calculate: earnings per share, PE ratio, dividends per share, dividend cover, dividend yield, net assets per share, return on shareholders funds.

    (note that net assets per share is calculated by net assets divided by the number of shares or as net assets = share capital + reserves by share capital + reserves divided by the number of shares)

b. Comment on each set of ratios.

c. Would your comments be different if you knew that:

    ❏ P's directors have announced that earnings in 19x3 will be much reduced from those in 19x2.

    ❏ Q's directors have announced that following a scheme of cost reduction the company will return to its normal productivity and make in the region of £900,000 in 19x3.

    ❏ the City are expecting a takeover bid for R

    ❏ S is highly geared and is having liquidity problems.

Case Study

The following are the accounts of Ketone Ltd, who retail commercial vehicle components, for the two years ending 31 December 19x1 and 19x2. The company are members of a trade association which operate an interfirm comparison scheme and the percentages which have been obtained from this scheme are also given. In addition the company operate a budgetary control scheme and produced a forecast set of accounts for 19x2 at the beginning of that year and these are shown also.

Trading and Profit and Loss Account

(all figures in £'000)

	19x1	19x2	Budget 19x2	Inter Firm %age sales
Sales	2,450	2,970	3,200	100
Cost of goods sold	1,470	1,841	1,920	58
Gross Profit	980	1,129	1,280	42
Occupancy Costs	140	156	160	3.5
Employee Costs	270	280	240	6.8
Advertising	135	158	150	6.2
Administrative costs	234	220	200	5.5
Directors Salaries	80	80	80	4.0
Depreciation	74	104	110	4.1
	933	998	940	30.1
Net Profit before interest	47	131	340	11.9
Interest	31	50	40	1.1
Net Profit after interest	16	81	300	10.8
Corporation Tax	4	19	75	2.6
Net Profit after Tax	12	62	225	8.2
Dividends	–	10	50	4.0
Retained profit for the year	12	52	175	4.2

Balance Sheet

	19x1	19x2	Budget 19x2	Inter Firm %age sales
Plant and vehicles at cost	434	502	500	20.6
less Depreciation	306	108	106	5.4
	128	394	394	15.2
Current Assets				
Stocks	420	410	350	8.4
Debtors	590	730	650	21.2
	1,010	1,140	1,000	
Creditors: amounts falling due within one year				
Creditors	330	370	300	14.8
Overdraft	146	122	20	6.2
Corporation Tax	4	19	75	2.6
VAT and PAYE	20	23	27	.8
Dividend	–	10	59	4.0
	500	544	481	
Net Current Assets	510	596	519	
Total Assets less current liabilities	638	990	913	
Creditors: amounts falling due after more than one year				2.0
Bank Loan	–	100	100	
	638	890	813	
Capital and Reserves				
Called Up share capital (20p shares)	100	200	100	
Share Premium		100		
Profit and Loss Account	538	590	713	
	638	890	813	14.4

Required:

Write a report:

a. Summarising the events of 19x2 in relation to fixed assets, borrowings and share capital.

b. Preparing a list of ratios for 19x1, 19x2 and the forecasted 19x2.

c. Commenting on the performance of the company in 19x1, and 19x2 in relation to the forecast and the interfirm comparison.

Further development

Misleading ratio analysis

Things are rarely what they seem to be. Consider the accounts of two companies:

Profit and Loss Account

(all figures in £'000)	Matthew	Mark
Turnover	6,800	4,000
Cost of goods sold	5,200	3,000
Net Profit	568	432
Fixed Assets	500	550
Stocks	1,400	460
Debtors	900	34
Cash at Bank	–	90
Creditors	1,300	680
Overdraft	900	330
Capital and Reserves	600	124

a. Calculate for each company:

> Return on capital employed
> Asset utilisation ratio
> Net Profit to sales ratio
> Debtors turnover in days
> Creditors turnover in days
> Stock Turnover
> Current Ratio
> Liquidity ratio

b. Try to draw some conclusions about these companies and their performance and liquidity.

Before jumping to conclusions some further information would have been helpful:

Matthew: This is a construction company and it occupies its own headquarters building which is valued at £2,400,000 although it is in the Balance Sheet at cost less depreciation.

Stocks are of raw materials and of work in progress including a property which has since been sold at a good profit.

The overdraft is secured on the property and is for normal operational requirements + £550,000 for the property mentioned above.

Creditors include £300,000 tax not payable for nine months and £200,000 dividend not payable for six months.

Mark: This company is a retailer of babywear with several branches. Sales are for the most part for cash.

The fixed assets are mostly leasehold properties which were recently acquired.

The company are expanding fast and have agreed an overdraft facility of £500,000

How does the view given by the ratios now appear?

9 Cash flow statements

Exercises

1. Here is the Cash Flow Statement for 19x3 for Haggai PLC, a manufacturing company:

(all figures in £'000)

Net Cash Inflow from operating activities (Note 1)		458
Returns on Investments and servicing of finance		
Interest Received	12	
Interest Paid	(109)	
Dividends Paid	(65)	
Net cash inflow from returns on investments and servicing of finance		(162)
Taxation		
Corporation Tax paid		(43)
Net Revenue cash inflow		253
Investing Activities		
Payments to acquire intangible fixed assets	(145)	
Payments to acquire tangible fixed assets	(265)	
Receipts from sales of tangible fixed assets	15	
Net cash outflow from investing activities		(395)
Net cash outflow before financing		(142)
Financing		
Issue of ordinary share capital	80	
Issue of 12% Unsecured Notes 19x7-19x9	50	
Expenses paid in connection with share issue	(3)	
Expenses paid in connection with Notes issue	(2)	
Net Inflow from financing		125
Decrease in cash and cash equivalents (Note 2)		(17)

Notes to the cash flow statement

1. Reconciliation of operating profit to net cash inflow from operating activities.

Operating profit	454
Depreciation Charges	68
Loss on sale of tangible fixed assets	4
Increase in Stocks	(35)
Increase in Debtors	(51)
Increase in creditors	18
Net cash inflow from operating activities	458

2. Analysis of changes in cash and cash equivalents during the year.

Balance at 1 January 19x3	(143)
Net Cash outflow	(17)
Balance at 31 December 19x3	(160)

3. Cash and Cash equivalents as shown in the Balance Sheet.

	19x2	19x3	Change in year
Cash at Bank and in hand	12	18	6
Short term Investments	72	–	(72)
Bank Overdrafts	(227)	(178)	49
	(143)	(160)	(17)

Required: Explain what the company has done during 19x3 as far as can be discerned from the statement.

*2. The Balance Sheets of three companies at one year intervals are:

(all figures in £'000)	Jonah 19x1	Jonah 19x2	Micah 19x1	Micah 19x2	Nahum 19x1	Nahum 19x2
Fixed Assets						
at cost or valuation	87	102	97	151	34	76
Depreciation	21	39	63	78	10	22
	66	63	34	73	24	54
Current Assets						
Stock	20	24	45	43	16	19
Debtors	31	38	23	27	18	15
Bank and Cash	–	12	21	–	–	–
Current Liabilities						
Trade Creditors	15	31	54	46	11	10
Overdraft	2	–	–	4	2	6
Taxation	5	8	12	14	10	8
Dividend	5	6	13	11	14	17
Net Current Assets	24	29	10	(5)	(3)	(7)
Total Assets less Current						
Liabilities	90	92	44	68	21	47
15% Debentures	30	20	–	10	12	–
	60	72	44	58	9	47
Capital and Reserves						
Share Capital	20	25	12	18	6	9
Share Premium	5	10	–	6	1	7
Revaluation Reserve	–	–	–	–	–	30
Profit and Loss Account	35	37	32	34	2	1
	60	72	44	58	9	47

Profit and loss Accounts for 19x2 for the three companies showed:

	Jonah	Micah	Nahum
Net Profit	24	29	29
Interest	4	2	2
Net Profit after Interest	20	27	27
Taxation	8	14	8
	12	13	19
Dividends	10	11	20
Retained	2	2	(1)

Note:

Jonah: Fixed Assets costing £16,000 (Net Book Value – £11,000) were sold for £7,000.

Micah: Fixed Assets at cost £12,000 less depreciation £7,000 were sold for £8,000.

Nahum: No fixed Assets were sold but the property (Cost £20,000 less Depreciation £4,000 was revalued to £46,000).

Required:

Prepare a cash flow statement for each company for 19x2.

Further development

Ratio analysis and cashflow statements

Ratio analysis of Profit and Loss Accounts and Balance Sheets has been developed over a century or more and used with care much useful information can be deduced about a company or at least it is possible to determine the pertinent *questions to ask*.

Ratio analysis of Cash flow statements can also be very revealing and a number of ratios can be produced and compared with previous years, with other companies and with industry averages.

Since Cash Flow Statements only commenced in the UK in 1992 (and only in 1988 in the USA) ratio analysis of Cash Flow Statements as an art or science is in its infancy and will no doubt develop over the next few years.

It is considered that Cash Flow Statements may be of use to investors, creditors and others in assessing:

❏ the company's ability to generate future positive net cash flows

❏ a company's ability to meet its obligations and pay dividends

❏ a company's needs for external financing

❏ the reasons for differences between Profit and Loss Account income and associated cash receipts and payments

❏ the effects of a company's investing and financing activities on its financial position.

Some of the ratios that might be seen as tools to assist assessment are given below and to help you understand them we will use an example:

ABC Manufacturing Company PLC

Cash Flow Statement for 19x3

(all figures in £ million)

Net Cash Inflow from operating activities (Note 1)		8.9
Returns on Investments and servicing of finance		
Interest Paid	(2.6)	
Dividends Paid	(2.1)	
Net cash outflow from returns on investments and servicing of finance		(4.7)
Taxation		
Corporation Tax paid		(1.9)
Net Revenue Cash flow		2.3
Investing Activities		
Payments to acquire tangible fixed assets	(12.5)	
Receipts from sales of tangible fixed assets	0.8	
Net cash outflow from investing activities		(11.7)
Net cash outflow before financing		(9.4)
Financing		
Issue of 14% Loan 19y9-19z1		5.0
Decrease in cash and cash equivalents (Note 2)		(4.4)

Notes to the cash flow statement

1. Reconciliation of operating profit to net cash inflow from operating activities.

Operating profit	11.7
Depreciation Charges	3.6
Loss on sale of tangible fixed assets	0.4
Increase in Stocks	(2.6)
Increase in Debtors	(4.1)
Increase in creditors	2.8
Net cash inflow from operating activities before exceptional item	11.8
Net Cash outflow in respect of exceptional item	(2.9)
Net cash inflow in respect of operating income	8.9

2. Analysis of changes in cash and cash equivalents during the year.

Balance at 1 January 19x3	(3.6)
Net Cash outflow	(4.4)
Balance at 31 December 19x3	(8.0)

3. Cash and Cash equivalents as shown in the Balance Sheet.

	19x2	19x3	Change in year
Cash at Bank and in hand	0.7	0.8	0.1
Bank Overdrafts	(4.3)	(8.8)	(4.5)
	(3.6)	(8.0)	(4.4)

To assist the analysis we have obtained the industry averages and we will compare these with the ratios of ABC.

Some ratios that might assist the analysis are:

a. Normal Operating Cash Flows against exceptional cash flows.

In this case exceptional items (the notes pointed out that these were redundancy and other costs in connection with the restructuring of a continuing business segment) £2.9M took 24.6% of Cash Flow From Operations (CFFO). Industry average was 10.1% so ABC suffered badly in cash terms in this year.

It would also be helpful to see how much CFFO came from the different segments of the company's operations. However such cash flows are not likely to be revealed although there will be a segmental analysis of profit.

b. Cash Interest coverage. This shows the size of CFFO as against interest payments. The calculation is:

$$\frac{\text{CFFO}}{\text{Interest}} = \frac{11.8}{2.6} \text{ 4.5 times}$$

The industry average is 6.3 times so that ABC appears as relatively highly geared.

c. *Cash Flow to Debt.*

This measures the retained cash flows in relation to total debt.

Total debt can be defined as all long term debt plus short term debt such as lease obligations and overdrafts. Suppose ABC's total debt is £19M then the ratio is:

Retained cash flows are CFFO – Interest – tax – dividends = £5.2M

So the calculation is:

$$\frac{19.0}{5.2} = 3.65$$

Repayment of existing debt would take 3.65 years retained operating cash flows. The industry average is 1.42 so ABC is confirmed as highly geared. It is possible to suggest that this may have a bearing on ABC's ability to remain as a going concern. However much depends on the timing of repayments which include some very long term debt repayments.

d. *Cash Dividend cover*

This measures the ability of the company to generate enough cash to pay dividends.

The calculation is:

$$\frac{\text{CFFO} - \text{tax} - \text{Interest}}{\text{Dividends}} = \frac{11.8 - 1.9 - 2.6}{2.1} = 3.48$$

The industry average is 6.1 so ABC is absorbing a higher proportion of CFFO than industry average in dividends.

e. *Quality of Income.*

This ratio compares CFFO with Income as measured in the Profit and Loss Account.

We will take both figures gross of the exceptional items.

The ratio can be calculated as:

$$\frac{\text{CFFO}}{\text{operating income}} = \frac{11.8 \times 100}{11.7 + 2.9} = 81\%$$

The industry average is 102% so the quality of ABC's earnings is low. What is meant by this is that a given Income yields a lower CFFO because of the greater effect of increases in working capital items relative to depreciation and other non-cash items in the Profit and Loss Account.

f. *Capital Expenditure.*

It is desirable to see a company's ability to maintain and develop its fixed assets base from CFFO. Ideally the capital expenditure would be divided into that part which maintained productive capacity and that part which improved productive capacity. However this is subjective and is in any case not normally revealed.

Possible ratios are:

i. $\dfrac{\text{Retained operating cash flows}}{\text{Investing cash flows}} = \dfrac{11.8 - 4.7 - 1.9}{11.7} \times 100 = 44\%$

This shows that ABC cannot finance is capital expenditure from current operating cash flows and is reliant on external finance. Of course if the capital expenditure includes a substantial amount of new developments then that is not unreasonable although we should bear in mind ABC's high gearing and need to generate cash to repay debt.

Industry average is 76%.

ii. $\dfrac{\text{Net cash flows for investing}}{\text{Net cash flows from financing}} = \dfrac{11.7}{5.0} = 2.34$

This shows that ABC financed only 43% of its capital expenditure from external financing as against an industry average of 47%.

This is somewhat misleading as some of the bank overdraft finance may be repayable on demand but will in practice be renewed so that it is virtually long term.

g. Cash return from gross assets.

This is comparable to the much vaunted return on capital employed.

It is calculated by:

$$\frac{\text{CFFO}}{\text{Total assets}} = \frac{11.8}{41.2} \times 100 = 28.6\%$$

I have assumed that total assets are £41.2M. Industry average is 15.9% so ABC seems to be doing very well. This seems to me to be a useful ratio as it measures the ability of the company to generate cash from using its gross assets.

Overview of cash flow ratios

❏ Firstly no real experience has been gained in using these ratios and time will tell which ratios are good indicators of malaise or well being or good or bad prognosis for the company.

❏ Secondly taking a single year by itself is generally misleading. Calculating ratios using several years figures would be better. For example a long term inability to generate retained cash flows sufficient to maintain fixed assets may be serious but a single year may give false signals as it may be an unusually heavy year for capital expenditure.

Cash Flow ratios should be used in conjunction with the conventional ratios applied to financial statements.

Case Study

The Financial Statements of Wednesfield Wholesale and Importing PLC for the two years 19x2 and 19x3 show:

Profit and Loss Accounts

(All figures in £'000)

	19x2	19x3
Turnover	14,500	16,800
Cost of Sales	7,900	9,350
Gross Profit	6,600	7,450
Distribution Costs	2,100	2,160
Administration Expenses	2,870	3,260
Operating Profit	1,630	2,030
Interest Payable	620	850
Profit on Ordinary activities before taxation	1,010	1,180
Taxation	300	360
Profit on ordinary activities	710	820
Dividends	350	550
Retained profit for the year	360	270
Earnings per share	1.04p	1.21p

Balance sheet as at 31 December

	19x2	19x3
Fixed Assets		
Tangible assets	10,300	13,510
Current Assets		
Stocks	2,400	2,900
Debtors	2,100	2,570
	4,500	5,470
Creditors:amounts falling due within		
Creditors	1,200	1,430
Bank Overdrafts	340	760
Corporation Tax	300	360
Dividends	250	450
	2,090	3,000
Net Current Assets	2,410	2,470
Total Assets		
less Current Liabilities	12,710	15,980
Creditors: amounts falling due after more than one year		
15% Debenture 19x5	2,200	2,200
13% Debenture 19y3		3,000
	10,510	10,780
Capital and Reserves		
Issued Share Capital (10p shares)	6,800	6,800
Share Premium	500	500
Profit and Loss Account	3,210	3,480
	10,510	10,780

Notes to Profit and Loss Account and Balance Sheet

1. Fixed Assets

	Land	Buildings	Plant	Total
Cost at 31.12.19x2	3,000	5,500	4,970	13,470
Disposals at cost			850	850
Additions at cost		800	4,250	5,050
Cost at 31.12.19x3	3,000	6,300	8,370	17,670
Depreciation to 31.12.19x2		1,690	1,480	3,170
Depreciation on disposals			470	470
Depreciation in year		210	1,250	1,460
Total Depreciation at 31.12.19x3		1,900	2,260	4,160
Book Value 31.12.19x3	3,000	4,400	6,110	13,510

2. The 15% Debenture is secured on the company's freehold properties. The 13% Debenture is secured by a second mortgage on the properties. The directors estimate that the open market value in existing use of the properties is about £10 Million.

Cash Flow Statement 19x3

(all figures in £'000)

Net Cash Inflow from operating activities (Note 1)		2,800
Returns on Investments and servicing of finance		
Interest Paid	(850)	
Dividends Paid	(350)	
Net cash outflow from returns on investments and servicing of finance		(1,200)
Taxation		
Corporation Tax paid		(300)
Net Revenue Cash Inflow		1,300
Investing Activities		
Payments to acquire tangible fixed assets	(5,050)	
Receipts from sales of tangible fixed assets	330	
Net cash outflow from investing activities		(4,720)
Net cash outflow before financing		(3,420)
Financing		
Issue of 13% Debenture repayable in 10 years time		3,000
Decrease in cash and cash equivalents (Note 2)		(420)

Notes to the cash flow statement

1. Reconciliation of operating profit to net cash inflow from operating activities.

Operating profit	2,030
Depreciation Charges	1,460
Loss on sale of tangible fixed assets	50
Increase in Stocks	(500)
Increase in Debtors	(470)
Increase in creditors	230
Net cash inflow from operating activities	2,800

Notes:

1. The plant that was sold was an obsolete production line. This was replaced with new plant costing £1,600,000. The remaining capital expenditure was on a new building on the old sports field with plant designed to produce an entirely new product.

2. One share in the company is quoted at 16p.

Required:

Write a report on the company including:

a. What occurred in 19x3

b. Performance ratios

c. Liquidity ratios

d. Cash ratios

e. Investment ratios

10 Total absorption costing

Exercises

1. Codd makes filing cabinets. Divide the following costs, firstly, into materials, labour and services and secondly into direct costs and indirect costs:

Steel sheet	Maintenance wages
Paint	Window cleaning
Letterheads	Depreciation of a fax machine
Drawer handles	Van spares
Advertising	Cost accountant's salary
Bank Interest	Cleaning contract
Debt collection fees	Sheet metal workers' wages
Packers' wages	Heating Oil

Finally attempt to divide the overheads between production and non-production.

2. Haddock Brothers have an architectural practice. divide the following costs, firstly into materials, labour and services and then into direct costs and indirect costs:

Drawing paper	Technicians' salaries
Advertising	Accountants' fee
Textbooks	Travelling expenses
Repairs to partner's car	Telephone
Subcontract work	Computer software
Repairs to office building	Professional Indemnity Insurance
Pension scheme re employees	Typist's salary
Donation to Client's favourite charity	

*3. Munday has a business making a single product – a widget. His costs are forecast for 19x3 as:

	£
Materials	134,000
Direct labour	160,000
Production Overheads	100,000
Administration Costs	60,000
Selling and distribution	90,000

Output from these costs is forecast at 20,000 units.

Required:

a. What is the forecast total prime cost?

b. What is the prime cost per unit?

c. What are the total manufacturing costs?

d. What are the manufacturing cost per unit?

e. If selling price is £30 what should be the profit?

4. Same figures as in question 3 but Munday makes a range of widgets. He recognises that the cost of production is prime cost + manufacturing overheads.

Required:

a. Munday reckons that the overheads to be added for any given widget will be a percentage on prime cost. Calculate a suitable percentage and calculate a manufacturing cost for a widget whose prime costs are materials £30 and Direct Labour £15.

b. Munday requires a rule of thumb approach to pricing his widgets and to that end would like to have a price which was calculated as:

Prime cost
+   manufacturing overheads
=   manufacturing cost
+   a percentage on manufacturing cost to give him a profit
      equal to 10% of total cost.

Give him a formula to find the selling price for his products.

Note that selling prices arrived at in this way are usually regarded as a first guess. The company then have to assess the customer to determine if more or less can be obtained from the customer.

c.   Same facts as in b. but Munday wants his profit to be 10% of his selling price. Now find a formula.

5.   Tuesday has a has a business making bespoke chemicals for the cleaning industry. Her costs for 19x3 are forecast as:

	£
Materials	230,000
Direct labour	345,000
Production Overheads	260,000
Other Overheads	180,000

She prices her chemicals on the basis of:

Prime cost
+   a percentage for production overheads
=   production cost
+   a percentage on production cost for other overheads
=   total absorption cost
+   20% for profit
=   selling price

Required:

a.   Calculate the selling price for chemical XY which cost: materials £80 and Direct labour £45.

b.   She meets a competitor at a conference who tells her that he prices his products on the basis of material cost + various percentages for the other costs. Calculate the selling price of XY on this alternative basis.

c.   Explore the effect of Tuesday determining her selling prices differently from her competitors in terms of getting sales and making profits.

6.   Wedd makes mass produced machine parts by sophisticated machinery. The principal costs are the overheads associated with the machines except in the packing shop which is largely labour oriented. All the workers in the machine departments are regarded as indirect but most in the packing department are direct. There are 3 manufacturing departments and information about them is:

	Machine 1	Machine 2	Packing
Floor area (Sq M.)	400	300	400
Number of workers	30	12	60
Value of machinery	£400,000	£150,000	£25,000

Overheads expected in 19x2 (in £'000) to be apportioned to departments:

Rates	£240
Property Insurance	£60
Works management Costs	£300
Power	£180
Depreciation	10% of value

Overheads (in £'000) to be allocated to specific departments:

	Machine 1	Machine 2	Packing
Indirect labour	£320	£160	£60
Machine Spares	£34	£40	£4

Required:

a. Prepare an overhead schedule to determine the total overheads for each department.

b. Budgeted machine hours in 19x2 are:

> in Machine 1 dept 4000
> in Machine 2 dept 6000

Budgeted direct labour hours for the packing department are 100,000.

Calculate overhead absorption rates for the three departments.

c. Use these rates to produce a cost for a batch of machine parts which will consume:

Material costs	£600
Direct labour packing	£400
Machine 1 hours	30
Machine 2 hours	25
Packing Labour hours	60

d. Calculate a price for the batch on the basis that Wedd expects a profit of 20% of the sales price.

e. Calculate the under recovery of overheads assuming that actual production consumed only:

Machine 1	3,600 hours
Machine 2	5,500 hours
Packing	90,000 hours

*7. Thor is a manufacturer of shelving to order. Budgeted data for period 6 are:

	£
Direct materials	30,000
Direct Labour 10,000 hours at £6 an hour	
Rates	20,000
Machinery Depreciation	14,000
Electric Power	30,000
Supervision	22,000

Statistics about the three manufacturing departments (Cutting, Making, Finishing) are:

	Cutting	Making	Finishing
Area in square metres	100	200	160
Machinery value	£60,000	£30,000	£10,000
Number of employees	10	20	25
Machine hours	600	300	100

Required:

a. prepare an overhead apportionment schedule for the three production cost centres.

b. calculate absorption rates (machine hour rates) for the three departments.

c. calculate an alternative absorption rate (a labour hour rate) for the finishing department using labour hours – budgeted at 4,500 hours.

d. calculate a selling price for a product whose estimated costs are:

Materials	£300
Direct Labour	
Cutting	30 hours
Making	12 hours
Finishing	36 hours
Machine hours	
Cutting	12 hours
Making	6 hours
Finishing	22 hours

Profit margin should be 25% on cost.

Initially you should use machine hours for all departments and then use a labour hour rate for the Finishing department.

e. How might a manager decide on whether a labour hour rate or a machine hour rate (or some other method) might be most appropriate for his department?

8. Fry makes cakes for the retail trade. His costs are budgeted for period 8 as:

Materials	£10,000
Direct Labour	£30,000
Overheads	£36,000

He makes a wide variety and is continually trying out new recipes. All cakes are made in batches in one single cost centre.

He has to fix a selling price for each batch of cakes and finds he can determine the materials and direct labour cost of each batch but is unsure of how to include overheads in the cost calculation. Suggestions include:

- ❐ a perceantage on material cost

- ❐ a percentage on labour cost

- ❐ a percentge on prime cost

- ❐ a baking hour rate

The last would depend on the total baking hours available which are estimated for period 8 at 4,000 – there are various ovens of different sizes.

Required:

a. Calculate a cost for batch AX using each method assuming costs will be:

Materials	£50
Labour Hours	£200
Baking hours	25 hours

b. Discuss which method might be most appropriate.
c. Calculate a selling price on the basis of:

- ❐ Profit is 25% on cost

- ❐ Profit is 20% of selling price

d. Discuss the viability of fixing a selling price based on total cost + a percentage for profit. What alternative pricing methods might be adopted? If cost + is not used, is there any purpose in calculating cost?

Further development

Service Departments

The principle of allocating and apportioning costs to cost centres is defensible and practical if arbitrary but there can be complications. One of these is the problem of service departments. In Saturn's factory there are 5 departments and here is a list of them with some statistics:

	Prod 1	Prod 2	Stores	Maint'nce	Canteen
Area (Sq M)	300	250	80	24	120
Number of employees	30	20	8	10	6
Machine Hours	4,000	2,000			

Overheads budgeted are allocable:

	£	£	£	£	£
Depreciation	8,000	5,000	1,000	2,000	2,500
Indirect costs	28,000	9,000	7,000	8,000	16,000

Overheads to be apportioned are:

Rent, rates etc	£46,440
Management	£29,600

There would be more expense headings and probably many more departments in a real situation but the principle is illustrated with just a few.

So, overheads can be summarised as:

Overhead apportionment schedule

	Prod 1 £	Prod 2 £	Stores £	Maint'nce £	Canteen £	Total £
Depreciation	8,000	5,000	1,000	2,000	2,500	18,500
Indirect	28,000	9,000	7,000	8,000	16,000	68,000
Rent, Rates	18,000	15,000	4,800	1,440	7,200	46,440
Management	12,000	8,000	3,200	4,000	2,400	29,600
	66,000	37,000	16,000	15,440	28,100	162,540

You will notice that the rent and rates have been apportioned on floor area and management on number of employees.

So far we have produced a schedule in much the same way as before but at this point we have to realise that although the total overheads are £162,540 only £103,000 have been apportioned to production departments. And it is from production departments that products absorb overheads. Consequently the next step is to apportion the overheads of the three service departments to the two production departments. We will do this as:

❑ Stores in proportion to usage as evidenced by numbers of stores requisitions which are 960 to 1 and 640 to 2.

❑ Maintenance in proportion to depreciation

❑ Canteen in proportion to number of employees

Thus:

	Production 1	Production 2	Total
	£	£	£
brought forward	66,000	37,000	103,000
Stores	9,600	6,400	16,000
Maintenance	9,502	5,938	15,440
Canteen	16,860	11,240	28,100
	101,962	60,578	162,540

All the overheads have been effectively located in the two production departments and we can now derive an absorption basis. Suppose we use machine hour rates, then the machine hour rates will be:

❑   Production 1 $\dfrac{£101,962}{4,000} = £25.50$

❑   Production 2 $\dfrac{£60,578}{2,000} = £30.30$

Management are often led into thinking that the £25.50 is a scientifically accurate measure. The process, as you have seen, is full of assumptions (for example, that maintenance expenditure is proportional to machine depreciation) and guesses (for example, that machine hours in Department 1 will be 4,000). So the figure is a practical usable sum and the true cost cannot actually be measured except after the event and even then only with the assumptions.

You may also have noticed that the stores department overheads were apportioned just between the two production departments whereas in practice they should be divided up into the production and the other service departments. The same applies to the other two service departments. The problem can be that having apportioned the stores, stores acquires new overheads from an apportionment of the canteen. The canteen then has an apportionment of this from maintenance. The problem is called the *reciprocal service department problem*. We need not detain ourselves with it.

Exercise

9.   Davina has a factory making a wide variety of jars of molluscs. There are four departments in the process: preparation, steam cooking, steam production, stores. Statistics are:

	Preparation	Cook	Steam	Stores
Employees	10	6	4	3
Floor area (m²)	30	15	6	12
Value of Plant (£'000)	4	6	6	2
For period 12 overheads allocated are:	£4,200	£2,900	£3,800	£3,000

Overheads to be apportioned are:

	£
Rent, Rates	24,800
Supervision	36,000
Repairs and Maintenance	12,000

Required:

a. Prepare an overhead apportionment schedule four the four departments and then reduce it to the two production departments.

b. Preparation is a largely manual process although the staff do use machines. In period ten 2,000 hours will be available. Steam cooking is largely a machine operation although much direct labour is involved. Machine hours in the period will be 800. Calculate suitable absorption rates.

c. A batch of mollusc jars is to be produced. Costs will probably be:

Materials   £180
Direct Labour
       Prep 18 hours at £4
       Cook 10 hours at £5
Machine hours – 12

Calculate a cost and also a selling price if profit is to be 15% on Cost.

Assignment

Upmarket Stores PLC have paid a premium on a 21 year lease on a department store in a newish development in a county town. The intention is to spend a considerable sum on a new shop front and on complete redecoration and refurbishment. The store will hold a number of departments operated by Upmarket and will let some parts as concessions to a number of interested firms.

Required:

a. In the context of the store explain the difference between direct and indirect costs.

The Chief Executive has a provisional idea on which parts of the store to put each department and where to place the concessions. He now wants to know the costs associated with each area.

b. Explain why it is desirable to know the costs of each area.

c. Explain in detail how the costs could be calculated.

d. Explain the consequences of getting the calculations in c. wrong.

11 Cost behaviour, marginal costing and breakeven charts

Exercises

1. Describe the behaviour of the following costs at different levels of output in a foundry which melts iron in an electric furnace and makes a variety of iron castings to meet customers' individual wants:

Iron	Telephone
Sales representatives	Foundry workers (piecework)
Sand	Rates
Product Liability Insurance	Tools
Protective clothing	Stationery
Electricity	Refractory materials
Building repairs	Dust extraction Equipment
First Aid Materials	Wooden Pallets
Wages Office Salaries	Wood patterns

    State any assumptions you make.

2. The Cut Railway Co PLC run a steam railway both as a service to the local population and as a tourist attraction. All staff are paid professionals.

    a. Describe the behaviour of the following costs at different levels of output:

Coal	Depreciation of rolling stock
Track repair materials	Wages of Drivers
Wages of booking office staff	Advertising
Electricity	Public Liability Insurance
Weedkiller	Paint
Sponsorship of local arts festival	Oil and Grease
	Interest on Loans
	Bank Charges

    State any assumptions you make.

    b. What is meant by output in this case? How might output be measured?

    c. How might the knowledge of cost behaviour assist management in this case? What decisions might be assisted?

*3. Willa has discovered that the cost of raw cloth in her textile factory is a function of quantity bought which in turn is very closely correlated with usage as little stock is carried. Usage is measured in square metres. She finds that the average cost per square metre is not linear with usage but is given by the formula:

    Cost per metre = $(0.6 * U - (0.01 * U)^2)/1{,}000$

    where U = number of batch purchases. Each batch is 1,000 square metres.

    This is over the relevant range of 400 to 1,200 batches.

    She also discovers that the cost of preparing the cloth for processing is 10p a square metre as all the cost is outwork which is paid on a piecework basis.

    The annual cost of buying and storing the cloth is £200,000 which consists of rent, rates, heating etc and the salaries of staff.

    Required:

    a. Calculate the total cost and the cost per square metre of

    i.   600,000 square metres and

    ii. 1,200,000 square metres.

    b. Comment on these figures.

4. Edwige operates an introductions bureau. Her modus operandi is to invite enquirers to a dinner party at a hotel.

    Her costs are estimated to be:

Hire of dining suite	£200
Flowers, print costs etc	£50
Meal and wines	£20 a head

    Maximum numbers are 30 per party and minimum 20.

    Required:

    a. Calculate total cost of a party and cost per person if i. 20 people attend and ii. if 30 people attend.
    b. How might Edwige use these figures in her decision making?

5. Calculate the contribution in the following cases:

    a. Joe's wine bar: cost of a case of six bottles of Chateau Bilston £12.40, selling price per bottle £5.80.

    b. Krishan's restaurant: Materials for set meal A £2.10, selling price £8.00

    c. Ram's sari factory: cost of sari type B, materials £5.60, direct piecework labour £4, selling price £15.20.

    d. Lewis's curtain contracting: cost of Job C Materials £194, Direct Labour 16 hours at £7 an hour, sales commission 10% on selling price, selling price £400

*6. The following sets of figures relate to a a number of businesses:

    Fred's snooker club:

Fixed Overheads	£26,000
Selling Price	60p per person per game

    Based on previous years, Fred expects a minimum of 400 persons a week with each playing an average of 2 games and a maximum of 600 persons a week. Most likely average is 500 persons per week.

    Ken's lollipop factory:

Fixed Overheads	£40,000
Variable overheads	£30 a batch
Selling price	£50 a batch
Maximum output	4,000 batches
Sales budget	2,500 batches

    Lila's delicatessen:

    Fixed Overheads £18,000 but she will have to take on an additional assistant at a cost of £6,000 a year if turnover exceeds £38,000

    Gross Profit to sales ratio averages 60%

    Turnover last year was £39,000 but she expects an increase of 10%.

    Rufus's one man driving school:

Fixed Overheads	£6,000
Variable overheads	£1.50 a lesson
Selling Price	£9.00 a lesson

    Rufus has been offered a job as an instructor for a large firm at a salary of £10,000 a year.

    He reckons to do 2,200 lessons a year.

Todd's wholesale stationery business:

Fixed Overheads increase at various turnover points because of the need for extra accommodation and staff. Probable points are:

Turnover (in £'000)	600	700	800	1,000
Fixed Costs (£'000)	200	220	260	320

Gross Profit to turnover ratio is 30%

Required:

a. In each case calculate where possible:

   ❑ breakeven point(s)

   ❑ relevant range

   ❑ margin of safety

   ❑ some easily measurable statistic to assist the proprietor in knowing how the business is faring.

b. Draw a breakeven chart for each business.

7. Liz intends to start a gift shop. She estimates her annual fixed costs at £10,000. Her gross profit margin is 40%. Calculate her break even sales and draw a break even chart.

8. Hugh makes widgets. His annual fixed costs are £50,000 up to 10,000 units and £70,000 up to a maximum of 15,000 units. The sale price of a widget is £12.50 and the variable costs are £6.50. Expected sales are 11,000 units but he guesses that they will fall between 8,000 and 14,000 units.

Calculate and show on a breakeven chart the breakeven points, the relevant range and the margin of safety.

Further development

Effects of sales mix on breakeven

Jacob sells two types of garden shed: the standard and the special.

Variable costs are £100 for the standard and £180 for the special. Selling prices are £200 for the standard and £430 for the special. His fixed costs for the year are expected to be £60,000. His budget for 19x2 shows:

	Standard	Special	Total
Sales volume (units)	600	80	
Sales	£120,000	£34,400	£154,400
Variable costs	£60,000	£14,400	£74,400
Contribution	£60,000	£20,000	£80,000
Fixed costs			£60,000
Net Profit			£20,000

Is it possible to calculate a breakeven volume? If we assume that the sales mix remains constant then we can using the following reasoning:

At breakeven contribution = fixed costs =£60,000.

Turnover in £'s is 154,400/ 80,000 * Contribution.

At breakeven sales in £'s will therefore be 154,800/80,000 * 60,000 = £116,100.

If sales mix remains the same then breakeven sales will be: Standard £90,233 and Special £25,867.

In quantity terms that is 451 standard and 60 special.

Suppose however that sales of standard are likely only to be 360 units due to competition but the sales of specials are likely to soar as up market sheds have become more in demand. What would be the breakeven sales of Specials in these circumstances?

This chain of reasoning may be useful:

Breakeven total contribution must be £60,000

Contribution from standards is 360 * £100 = £36,000

Therefore contribution from Specials must be £24,000.

At £250 contribution per special the sales must be 96 units or £41,280 in money terms.

Exercise

9. Lily manufacture two types of bicycle – the de Luxe and the super. Costs and selling prices are:

		de Luxe	Super
Fixed Costs	£70,000		
Variable costs (per unit)		£123	£185
Selling Price (per unit)		£220	£400

    The company has budgeted to sell 500 de Luxe in 19x2 and 200 super.

    Required:

    a. Prepare a budgeted profit and loss account in marginal costing form.

    b. Assuming that sales mix remains the same, calculate the breakeven point and the margin of safety.

    c. Draw a breakeven chart of (b).

    d. Sales of Super may prove difficult and the sales director fears that only 100 will be sold. How many de Luxe need to be sold to achieve the same profit as that forecast in the budget?

Case Study

Tangerine Ltd is a wholesaler and importer of a wide range of computer hardware, peripherals and software packages. The Chief Executive has produced a breakeven chart and intends to present it to the sales force at a sales conference.

a. Design a suitable chart and prepare a speech for the Chief explaining the chart and its significance.

b. Summarise the assumptions underlying the chart.

c. Two of the company's best sellers are the Quick X Printer which sells for £150 and the Rapid Y Printer which sells for £200. These prices enable the company to just undercut rival products from other suppliers. The company buys these printers in Taiwan for £100 and £150 respectively.

    The company pays a commission to its salespersons of 10% of the sales price. Discuss whether the company might do better to have commission rates which vary from product to product.

12 Uses of marginal costing

Exercises

1. Legge makes Wotsits. His budget for 19x2 is:

Selling price	£20 each
Variable cost	£8 each
Fixed costs	£42,000

Required:

  a. Calculate contribution per item

  b. Calculate breakeven point in units and total sales revenue

  c. If his expected sales are 4,000 calculate his margin of safety.

2. Costas is considering opening a new fish and chip shop in a new shopping parade in the suburbs. He envisages that his costs would be:

Fixed costs £27,000

Variable costs (materials etc) 40% of sales

  a. What costs might be included in the fixed costs?

  b. Calculate the weekly takings that would enable the shop to break even.

3. Ludwig is considering sinking his savings into a shop which would sell music/instruments/tapes and discs etc.

He has £70,000 in a building society earning 11% Gross. The shop he wants is freehold and would cost £50,000. He would spend a further £10,000 on a shop front and general repairs to the shop. The remaining £10,000 would form his working capital (roughly = stock at cost less creditors).

He currently earns £12,000 a year as a clerk, a job he has held for two years.

He reckons the fixed costs of running the shop (rates, insurance, part time staff wages, telephone, electricity etc) are likely to be about £15,000 a year.

He knows that he will make an average gross profit to sales ratio of about 40%.

Required:

  a. Calculate the weekly turnover that would make the project worthwhile.

  b. Summarise the other factors that Ludwig should take into account in deciding on whether or not to take the plunge. Bear risk in mind as a major factor.

*4. Fiona is considering setting up as a self employed computer systems consultant. She would need to borrow about £10,000 from the bank at 20% interest to pay for equipment and for working capital. She would have to give up her part time job as an analyst with its salary of £8,000 a year.

Her mode of operation would be to obtain commissions from clients and analyse the systems required. Actual programs would be written by a friend who would be paid 20% of the sales price in advance.

She estimates that fixed costs (depreciation of equipment, motor expenses, advertising, etc) would cost no more than £6,000 a year.

Required:

  a. Why would she need a sum for working capital?

  b. Calculate the annual turnover she would need i. to simply break even and ii. to make the project viable.

  c. Assess any other factors that may influence her decision to go it alone.

5. Megan makes souvenirs. One of her products is a gift marked "a present from Wolverhampton". Currently each of these costs:

Variable costs	£5
Fixed costs	£4

She is considering sub-contracting the manufacture of this item to Dilys who has quoted £7 an item. Currently output of the product is 3,000 a year and if she ceases manufacture Megan would save £3,000 of fixed costs.

Should Megan make or buy? how would your answer differ if fixed costs saved were £8,000?

6. Dill supplies quaggles to the leather trade. His budget for 19x2 is:

	£
Sales	50,000
Cost of goods sold	30,000
Contribution	20,000
Fixed Costs	7,000
Net Profit	13,000

He considers the profit very low for the effort he puts in and the needs of his family and is planning changes. He currently buys in all the quaggles from a variety of sources but reckons he can make them more cheaply in a rented corner of his brother's factory.

If he did this he reckons:

- ❑ £4,000 of his budgeted fixed costs would still be spent
- ❑ materials would cost him £12,000
- ❑ part time machine operatives would cost him £7,000
- ❑ he would need to spend £15,000 on a machine that would last him 5 years and have a scrap value at the end of its life of £5,000.
- ❑ he would borrow the money to buy the machine from the bank. Interest would be at 15%

Required:

a. Produce a revised budget assuming he goes ahead with manufacture.

b. Calculate the breakeven sales under both alternatives

c. Suggest some other factors that he might take into account in making his decision

d. Discuss the risk factors involved.

*7. Cressage Ltd has developed a new product – a household electrical appliance. The company can make the product in their factory or buy it in from a Czech manufacturer. They have collected some data to assist in deciding which course of action to take:

❑ at a selling price of	£300	£320
sales would be (units)	5,000	4,500
❑ costs would be:		

	Fixed	Variable
if made in own factory	£600,000	£130 each
if made abroad	£200,000	£200 each

Required:

a. Produce forecast profit and loss accounts showing the net profit on each of the four alternatives.

b. Which alternative gives the highest profit ? Suggest reasons why Cressage may not opt for the best alternative.

8. Rosemary makes a component for its main product and the cost accountant has produced a cost statement of the cost of manufacture of this component as:

Costs of component CJ	£
Materials	15.00
Labour	17.00
Variable overheads	4.00
Fixed Overheads	<u>24.50</u>
	60.50

The fixed overheads are absorbed by the component on a labour hour rate.

A company in Turkey has offered to make the component for £48.00.

Currently the company makes 5,000 of the components a year.

If manufacture was discontinued then fixed costs would reduce by £40,000.

Required:

a. What are the total fixed overheads currently absorbed by the component?

b. Why would this sum only reduce by £40,000 if manufacture was discontinued?

c. Should Rosemary continue to make the component or buy it in Turkey?

d. What is the lowest Turkish price that would make it just favourable to buy the component from the Turkish supplier?

e. Discuss reasons why the Turkish supplier can make the component more cheaply than Rosemary.

9. Olly makes a product which he sells using his sales force of 10 full time representatives. Each representative costs £20,000 a year in salary and expenses. Each representative is also paid a commission of 2% of the sales he makes. The budgeted sales of the product for 19x2 are £3,000,000. All of the representatives are relatively recent appointments and turnover of reps is high.

Olly is considering making his representatives into self employed agents and paying them a straight 10% commission.

Required:

a. On financial grounds should Olly employ reps or agents?

b. At what level of sales would employment of agents cost the same as employment of reps?

c. Discuss other factors that may be relevant to the decision.

10. Michelle makes and sells jewellery exclusively for the American market. A French firm have offered to buy 100 units of her standard line at a maximum price of £20. Her usual price to the USA is £35. She can make the extra 100 units at a cost of:

Materials	£10 each
Labour	£12
Additional overheads	£600

Should she accept the order?

11. Sage manufactures a range of products for export. One of these has an expected profitability as:

	£	£
Selling Price		50
Variable Manufacturing cost	26	
Fixed Manufacturing cost	8	
Variable selling cost	4	
Fixed selling cost	<u>6</u>	<u>44</u>
Net Profit		6

These figures are based on a turnover of 5,000 units.

Sage has been asked by a manufacturer on the same trading estate to supply him with 500 units at a price of £35 each. Sage has the capacity to do this.

Required:

a. Should Sage sell him the products at this price?

b. What is the lowest price that Sage could sell them at and still make a positive contribution?

c. What other factors may Sage consider?

12. Thyme makes and sells car kits in the home (UK) market. She sells direct to consumers through specialist magazines Her budget for 19x2 shows:

	£	£
Sales (100 units)		200,000
Materials	50,000	
Direct Labour	30,000	
Variable Overheads	5,000	
Fixed Production costs	35,000	
Fixed Admin cost	23,000	
Fixed Selling costs	18,000	161,000
Net Profit		39,000

Thyme has been approached by a dealer in Belgium who reckons she can sell 20 units a year. However she is only willing to pay £1,200 a unit.

Thyme reckons that if she accepts the order from Belgium she will:

❏ Spend 5% less on all her materials as she can buy larger quantities.

❏ Increase fixed production cost by 10% and admin costs by £2,000.

Required:

a. Calculate the breakeven volume implied by the original budget.

b. Recast the budget on the assumption that she accepts the Belgian order.

c. Should she accept the Belgium order?

d. If you ran the company what initiatives would you take?

One year later:

Thyme accepted the order and in fact sold 40 units in the first year to the Belgian. The Belgian dealer sells them for £1,700 in Belgium and also in Holland.

Thyme has heard that several of the units were in fact sold by the Belgian dealer to British customers.

e. What should Thyme do about the sales from Belgium to the UK?

13. Webb is a manufacturer of domestic kettles for sale in the UK and EEC. He has spent a great deal on installing automatic plant which produces the kettles almost without human intervention.

His budget for 19x2 is:
(all figures in £'000)

	£	£
Sales		4,000
Variable costs:		
Production	1,200	
Selling	300	
Fixed Costs:		
Production	1,800	
Admin	400	
Selling	600	4,300
Net Loss		(300)

Output achievable from his plant without any increase in fixed costs is actually 2 1/2 times the output implied by his budget but his salesmen tell him that at his prices these are the maximum sales attainable. He is considering two strategies:

i.   Reducing prices by 15% which should increase sales by 50% and reduce variable unit material costs by 5%

ii. Selling his kettles in North America at a price 30% below his UK price. This should enable him to double his unit sales and reduce unit material cost by 5%.

Required:

a.   Calculate the breakeven sales on his original budget.

b.   Discuss his two additional strategies and make recommendations.

*14.   Lily makes three types of model. Statistics are:

Type	A	B	C
Sales price	£8	£10	£12
Variable cost	£3	£4	£5
maximum Sales in period 1	4,200	3,000	2,700
Usage of machine W time (minutes)	5	2	6

What should be made if production should not exceed sales and time on machine W in period 1 is restricted to 600 hours.

15. Cohen makes three types of widget – statistics re these are:

	X	Y	Z
Selling Price	£50	£40	£23
Variable costs	£35	£23	£8
Maximum sales in period 1 (units)	1,000	2,100	2,500
Usage of Machine M (minutes)	12	20	15
Usage of Skilled Labour (minutes)	10	8	5

Required:

a.   Assuming that usage of Machine M is restricted to 1,000 hours and that the company will not make more than can be sold, what and how many widgets should be made in period 1, to maximise profit? There is unlimited skilled labour available in this period.

b.   How much profit would then be made?

c.   How much more profit would be made if the restriction could be removed?

d.   Assume that the figures are the same in period 2 except that maximum sales of Z will be only 2,400 and once again that the company do not wish to make widgets they cannot sell. In period two there is no restriction on the use of Machine M but skilled labour is limited to 500 hours. What types should be made and in what quantities to maximise profit?

e.   How much profit will then be made?

16. Kaur makes suits of three patterns:

Details of these are:	Check	Spotted	Striped
Selling price	£80	£85	£100
Variable costs	£30	£40	£52
Maximum Sales (Units)	500	300	270
Time on special machine (minutes)	30	40	40
Usage of special buttons	10	12	6

Required:

a.   Assume that the maximum time available on the special machine in period 3 is 400 hours and that unlimited buttons are available and that output should not exceed sales, what should be produced in period 3 to maximise profit?

b.   What profit will then be made?

c. Assume the same data in period 4 but that machine time is unlimited but supply of special buttons is limited to 7,000 in the period. What types and in what quantities should be made in period 4 to maximise profit? Again, output should not exceed sales.

d. What profit should be earned?

e. In period 4 a supply of buttons can be made available but from a source which charges £3 a button more than the usual supplier. Should these be purchased?

17. Oldfash Ltd produces its budget on total absorption accounting principles as this one, for 19x2: (all figures in £'000)

Product	Big £	Bigger £	Biggest £	Total £
Sales	240	180	70	490
Variable costs	120	100	35	255
Fixed Costs	85	60	45	190
Profit (Loss)	35	20	(10)	45

The Board consider this and decide to discontinue the manufacture of Biggest which they see as making a loss.

Before doing so they fortunately ask Len, a bright young manager, to look further into the matter. Len discovers that if manufacture of Biggest were discontinued, fixed costs would reduce from £190,000 to £170,000 only. What should the decision be on financial grounds.

18. Swade operates bus routes. He runs 10 buses and 4 routes and his revenues and costs are:

(all figures in £'000)

Route	1	2	3	4
Revenues	30,000	36,000	23,000	18,000
Variable costs	12,000	14,000	10,500	11,000
Fixed costs	10,000	10,000	10,000	10,000

Swade thinks that he should drop route 4.

Required:

a. What costs might be included in variable costs?

b. What costs might be included in fixed costs?

c. How has his accountant distributed the fixed costs over the four routes?

d. Might this be justifiable?

e. If Route 4 is discontinued, fixed costs would be reduce by $\frac{1}{8}$ only. Would discontinuance increase profits?

f. What actions do you think Swade might take to increase profit on route 4?

Further development

Opportunity Cost and Relevant Cost

Two important concepts in costing that are very significant in decision making are opportunity cost and relevant costs.

Opportunity cost can be defined as the value of a benefit sacrificed in favour of an alternative course of action.

An example: Onions has 20 square metres of his warehouse unused at present. He considers that it is costing him nothing so that using it for skin packing some of his products, instead of sub-contracting the skin packing to another firm, will be worth while as he will save £30 a week by so doing. In fact he could let the spare space for £100 a week to another firm. In considering the implementation of skin packing he needs to see the opportunity cost (£100 a week) as a real cost.

Relevant cost can be defined as any costs appropriate to a specific management decision.

An example: Horace is considering repairing and then selling a redundant machine. Business is slack and his fixed salary foreman is not fully busy. Horace reckons he could use one day of the foreman's time (cost £60 + a proportion of fixed overheads) to install the spare sprogget which he has in stock and which cost £80, five years ago. The machine can then be sold for £200. Alternatively he can sell the spare sprogget for £100 and sell the unrepaired machine for scrap for £5. What should he do?

He has two alternatives: repair the machine, do not repair the machine. Relevant cost data are:

	Repair:	Do not repair
Revenue	£200	£105

The cost of the foreman's time is irrelevant since his salary and overheads will be spent anyway. The cost of the sprogget is irrelevant since it is a past or sunk cost which cannot be changed.

19. Anthea buys scrap from metal processes and reprocesses it to extract the valuable metals which she then sells. She has some scrap materials which she bought some time ago for £100. She can process it at a cost of:

Electricity	£30
Water	£5
Labour	£10
Overheads	£30

and then sell the metal for £40 or resell it unprocessed for £20 or deposit in the town dump at a cost of £5.

What should she do, assuming that the overheads are all fixed and that alternatively:

i. The labour is overtime which would not otherwise be spent; or

ii. The labour is of the full time workforce that are underemployed at present?

20. Nat purchased a machine for use in his toymaking factory in 19x2 for £20,000 and determined his straight line depreciation policy on the assumption the machine would last 5 years and have a zero scrap value at the end of that time. In mid 19x3 he discovers that there is a new machine on the market that will do exactly the same things as the old machine but will save £10,000 a year in wages, materials and energy. The new machine will cost £18,000 and the suppliers will take the old machine in part exchange for £2,000. What should Nat do?

21. Owain makes special order engineering products. he has received an enquiry from a customer for a Thingum and has costed it as follows:

Materials:	Material A 10 Kg. He has some 15 Kg of this in stock which cost £13 a Kg. Buying it was a mistake and he cannot now use except on the order for the Thingum. He could however sell it as scrap for £40 the lot.
	Material B 5 Kg. This material is regularly used and he has 20 Kg in stock which cost £25 a Kg. The current price is now £35 a Kg.
	Material C 20 Kg. This material is also regularly used and there is a stock amounting to 30 Kg which cost £4 a Kg. The material can now be bought for £2.50 a Kg.
Labour:	David 12 hours at £5 an hour. David is paid by the hour.
	Frank 8 hours at £6 an hour. Frank is skilled and if he is used on this job he will have to be taken off the manufacture of Job 23 and Jeb brought in at a cost of £100 to finish Job 23.
	Lewis 4 hours. Lewis is also skilled and if he works on the Thingum he will need to be paid in overtime at time and one half as he is currently fully occupied. His normal rate is £9 an hour.

Overheads: Plans – £50 commissioned for XY Ltd

Royalty for use of patent process – 10% of selling price.

Variable overheads (energy etc) – £120

Fixed Overheads – usual recovery rate is 60% on prime cost.

What is the lowest price that Owain can quote to just make a profit on the Thingum?

Differential/ Incremental Costs and Revenues

In essence this whole chapter is about these concepts but we will look at a few **special situations** where the words have special relevance. Firstly we can define the words as the **difference** in revenues and costs if we do something as opposed to not doing it.

Suppose I am running a fund raising dinner for a charity. I have capacity for 100 guests and am charging £20 a head. I have sold only 90 tickets and Mr and Mrs Pore have asked to go but can only pay £12 a head each. The cost of supplying two more meals is calculated at only £4 each. Should I sell them the tickets at £12 each?

Marginal revenue is £24 and marginal cost is only £8 so it clearly makes sense to sell them the tickets. However nothing is simple and I might consider:

❑ revenue may be greater as they will buy drinks at a profit for the charity

❑ other guests may insist on having a cheaper price if they know the Pores have been sold cheap tickets.

❑ there may be a last minute demand for 10 tickets at full price.

22. Fiona makes wedding cakes to order. She has made one for £25 but the groom has been killed in an accident and she is unable to collect the £25 but she still has the cake. Another bride, hearing this has offered £10 for the cake. Fiona will have to rework the words in icing sugar. This will cost £5 and she will also have to refuse an order for a small birthday cake on which she would make a profit of £3. Discuss the problem.

Case Study

Marigold Ltd was set up five years ago to manufacture and market a caravan security system. The company has had an annual 5% increase in sales in real terms since its start but is now reaching the limits of manufacturing capacity at its present freehold factory in Wednesfield.

The board are meeting in order to determine action for the future and each directors expresses his opinion on what should be done:

Alan, the accountant says that the company will make a profit of £100,000 this year which after tax will enable the company to pay a dividend of 5p a share on its share capital and still leave a third of its after tax profits available to fund updating of its plant. In his opinion increases in sales next year are by no means certain and doing the same turnover as the current year would seem very satisfactory. He knew that Bryn was expecting a 5% increase in unit sales next year but he felt that by increasing the unit selling price by 5% to £105 sales would remain the same as this year but with extra profit.

Bryn, the marketing man points out that they have a leading market position and that further expansion is the only way to success. He personally enjoys a good standard of living but would like more dividends to help pay for his children's expensive education. He has 10% of the 1,000,000 10p shares. Expansion should take place on a new site, which could be funded by the sale of the current factory and by a rights issue of new shares. He could borrow from his father in law to subscribe for them.

Carl, the personnel person suggested that a way of increasing output would be to rent a new small factory in Telford, 20 miles away, where part of the manufacture could take place and would enable any increase in demand to be met.

Della, the engineer suggests that she could squeeze 5% or 10% more output from the existing plant by paying overtime. This would push the variable costs up by 10%. But even then variable costs would only be 55% of sales revenue. she thought a 10% increase in turnover could be achieved by spending £30,000 more on advertising. She agreed that losing market share was in the long run disastrous.

Eleni, the non- executive director suggested that the extra output could be obtained by sub-contracting part of the manufacture to a firm in Athens known to her. This would mean no increase in the current £400,000 total fixed costs which she saw as a good thing.

At the end of the meeting each of the directors agreed to obtain some figures to back up their suggestions and to give them to Alan who would summarise the data and make a written report to the Board for final decision at the next meeting.

Alan's subsequent activities were as follows:

i. He summarised this year in his usual statement like this:

> Sales ... units at ...
> Variable costs
> Contribution
> Fixed Costs
> Net Profit
> Taxation at ... %
> Profit after Tax
> Dividend ... p per share
> Retained Profit

ii. Bryn's suggestion of an entirely new factory was more difficult to cost but opportunity would be taken to modernise the plant and variable costs would probably come down to 40% of turnover and fixed costs go up by 25% including the extra depreciation and the extra advertising to ensure that turnover increase was 10%. It would be necessary to issue a further 1,000,000 shares to finance the move.

iii. If the factory at Telford was rented, fixed costs would go up by £30,000 but variable costs as a percentage of turnover would be the same. The factory would enable an increase in output of up to 30%

iv. The Athens firm were willing to produce a products equivalent to 5% or 10% of current turnover at a price of £60 a unit. They were willing to take over all of Marigold's production so freeing Marigold to be a purely marketing company. Alan felt it politic to postpone exploring this idea until next year.

Required:

a. Prepare Alan's report to the Board. This should include: a completed statement of this years activities, a calculation of the profit from each alternative suggestion (at 5% and 10% growth).

b. Evaluate each of the propositions from the point of view of short and long term profitability and risk.

c. Stating any assumptions you make, suggest some other strategies that the company may adopt.

13 Budgeting

Exercises

1. Stubby Air Systems PLC are manufacturers of highly sophisticated components for the aircraft industry and they are currently preparing their 19x4 budget. They have about 1,000 employees in total. The following facts have been identified as being relevant to the budget:

   ❏ demand will be 10% less than in 19x3 due to a recession in the aircraft industry.

   ❏ updating of plant and manufacturing systems must continue during the year

   ❏ systems of "just in time" supply of parts will be extended in 19x4

   ❏ elimination of the last remaining old Spanish customs among the skilled workers is a top priority

   ❏ constant change in recent years has caused a loss of morale among some managers and other staff, particularly as hierarchical systems have become more democratic. Good morale is seen as essential to the company

   ❏ the company faces a difficult year and a fear of takeover if results are poor worries top management.

   ❏ the work force needs to be reduced to about 800.

   Required:

   a. Discuss the relevance of each of these thoughts to the budgeting process and how the budgeting process can be useful in achieving the aims of the company.

   b. Consider what budgets and sub-budgets might be required and who might be responsible for their production.

*2. Ape Ltd supply copying machines to businesses. All machines are subject to a service agreement and the servicing of the copiers is the responsibility of Margaret. The sales budget has specified the expectations of the company in terms of the number of copier service agreements extant in 19x3. Margaret has constructed a budget of the costs to maintain the level of service required:

		£
Salaries and National insurance of 8 staff		104,000
to provide:	1,800 hours each of service work	
	100 hours of sick leave	
	100 hours of training	
Clerk to control activities		8,500
Margaret's own salary		18,000
to provide	1,000 hours of service work	
	900 hours of management	
	100 hours of training	
Courses and other training costs		5,000
Vehicle running costs		18,000
Changing 3 vans (now 4 years old)		24,000
Stationery		3,000
Tools etc		2,000

The budget officer (who is the company chief accountant) has told her that the company must be leaner and fitter to make a profit in 19x3 and that she must take 10% of her total budget claim.

Required:

a. Discuss how she might prune her budget.

b. Discuss the firm's approach to budgeting revealed in this scenario.

3. Here are some data re expectations of VG Ltd for January 19x6:

	Product	Quantity	Price
Sales:			
	Size 1	5,000	£230
	Size 2	3,000	£370

Materials used in producing one unit of these products are:

	Metal	Component A	Packaging
Size 1	10 Kg	4	1 set
Size 2	14 Kg	6	2 sets

Metal is £3 a Kg, Component A can be bought for £10 in January, and one set of packaging cost £15.

Stocks at 1 January are:

Size 1	Size 2	Metal	Comp A	Packaging Sets
2,000	400	2,000 Kg	18,000	2,500

Stocks projected for 31 January:

Size 1	Size 2	Metal	Comp A	Packaging Sets
1,500	1,200	6,000 Kg	10,000	2,000

Required:

a. Prepare: a sales budget in quantity and value
   a production budget showing quantities to be produced
   a material usage budget
   a purchases budget in quantity and value

b. State what is the principal budget factor here.

c. Explain the wide fluctuations in stock levels and expectations.

d. Rework the problem on the basis that 10% of all production will be rejected and that all the metal in the rejected production will be scrapped along with 50% of component As. No packaging sets are used on rejected production.

4. The hands on staff of Chicory Ltd comprise:

   12 Skilled staff
   8 semi – skilled staff
   8 unskilled staff

In period 8 a skilled person can work 480 hours, a semi-skilled person 440 hours and an unskilled person 500 hours. These hours can be boosted by 10% by working overtime at time and one half.

Production requirements for period 8 are budgeted at 1,600 units. Each unit will require:

   5 skilled man hours
   3 semi-skilled man hours
   2 unskilled man hours

Required:

a. Calculate the availability of labour in the period.

b. Calculate the demand for labour in the period.

c. Suggest and discuss various solutions to the mismatch.

d. Discuss how the mismatch might have come about.

5. The Income statement for 19x2 for St Chad's Hall is:

	£	£
Lettings 1,400 hours at £14 an hour		19,600
Administrative staff 400 hours at £3 an hour	1,200	
Electricity	6,800	
Planned Maintenance	2,000	
Repairs	2,600	
Caretaker – salary	2,000	
Cleaning Staff 2,000 hours at £2.50	5,000	
Sundry expenses	900	20,500
Loss		900

The honorary treasurer is preparing his budget for 19x3 and will take into account:

- ❑ the administrator needs a pay rise of 10%

- ❑ Electricity is to rise in price by 8%

- ❑ Planned maintenance is not sufficient and the committee wish to raise the provision to £2,500

- ❑ Repairs will cost about the same

- ❑ The caretaker will accept the same salary but needs a deputy at a cost of £400 a year

- ❑ complaints about cleaning have led the committee to up the cleaning hours to 2,400.

- ❑ sundries will rise by about 5%

- ❑ a necessary structural alteration to meet environmental requirements has led to the borrowing of £5,000. The interest on this is at 12% and repayments will be by equal annual instalments over 5 years beginning at the end of 19x3.

Required:

a. Prepare a budget for 19x3 such that lettings of 1,400 hours will just cover all outgoings.

b. The required letting fee rise is unacceptable to many users and the committee have decided to have a differential fee policy:

    day time use 800 hours at 5% above 19x2 rates

    evening use 600 hours at a rate to provide the rest of the required revenue.

    What should the evening rate be?

c. A keep fit group have asked to use the hall in the early mornings when the hall is not in use. They are prepared to pay only £8 an hour for about 200 hours use a year. The associated outgoings are only caretaking at 1 an hour. Should the committee accept the booking?

Case Study

Kale manufactures tents. He has two types: the Orange and the Green. His budgeted sales for 19x5 are; Orange 5,000 at £160 and Green 3,000 at £130.

His stocks at the beginning of the year are 1,500 Orange and 100 Green. By the year end he hopes to change that to 500 Orange and 300 Green. His stocks of finished tents were valued at 31 December 19x4 at £158,000 at prime cost.

He has in stock 30,000 metres of canvas and hopes to get the stock down to 20,000 metres by the year end. Each Orange uses 30 square metres and each Green 22 metres. He has a long term contract with his canvas supplier for supply at £1 a metre.

He has in stock £20,000 of other direct materials and components. He intends to increase the stock to £25,000 by the year end. Each Orange uses £25 worth and each Green £19 worth.

Direct labour is all piecework and costs £50 an Orange and £40 a Green.

Overheads can be assumed to be all fixed and amount to in 19x5:

	£
Factory	200,000
Administrative	100,000
Selling and Distribution	100.000

Required:

a. Prepare:

- ❑ a sales budget in quantity and money terms
- ❑ a production budget in quantity terms
- ❑ a materials budget in quantity and money terms
- ❑ a direct wages budget

b. Kale produces his master budget using a template as:

Budgeted Manufacturing, Trading and Profit and loss Account for the year ending 31 December 19x5

Materials:	Canvas	Other	£
Opening Stock			
Purchases			
Closing Stock			
Consumed			
Direct labour			
Prime cost			
Opening Stock of Finished Goods			
Closing Stock of Finished Goods			
Cost of Goods Sold			
Sales			
Contribution			
Production Overheads			
Gross Profit			
Administration Costs			
Selling and Distribution Costs			
Net Profit			

Complete the template for 19x5. Note that closing stock of finished goods should be valued at prime cost.

c. In the budget, stocks are valued at prime cost. For the final accounts stock must be valued at total absorption cost. How can Kale convert prime cost into total absorption cost? Answer in detail.

d. Would the results be different if stocks were valued at total absorption cost instead of prime cost in 19x5?

e. Explain how the reduction in stocks of Orange will ease Kale's cash position.

f. Kale is dissatisfied with the budgeted profit. Suggest some possible changes he could make to increase profit. State any assumptions you make.

g. Might the budget be different if Kale paid strict attention to all the objectives of budgeting outlined in Section 2 of this book?

Further development

Zero Based Budgeting

Much budgeting works on the basis of taking last years expenditure and adding on a few percent for inflation and making any necessary changes for changed circumstances. This applies very much in local authorities and public bodies such as the Health Service but it also applies in the private sector. In a manufacturing firm, the running of a department may involve expenditure on staff, energy, maintenance, dust extraction etc. Here the manager might simply start with last years expenditure and add on 6% for pay rises and other inflation caused extra costs and then add £X,000 for an additional person to assist in monitoring pollution control within the department.

The point is that last years expenditure is considered satisfactory and argument and negotiation centres around changes.

An alternative is to adopt zero based budgeting. This approach starts with a base of nil expenditure, a clean slate, it requires the manager to justify everything he puts in his budget. This has the effect of enlarging and prolonging the budgetary process as arguments and negotiations apply to the whole budget and not just to changes.

Many organisations apply normal budgetary processes but select particular activities or departments for zero based budgeting.

An example of zero based budgeting in a local authority may be in a day centre for the elderly and handicapped. The manager might be asked in a normal budgeting process to start with last year and add so much for inflation and proposed changes. In a zero based budget, he might be asked to produce a package each year:

- ❏ setting out the objectives and justification for the centre
- ❏ setting out and justifying the proposed means of meeting the objectives
- ❏ costing the means

Alternative packages with different approaches and costs may also be produced.

It is then up to the local authority to approve, select or reject or negotiate on the package.

*6. Contrast the responses of a public relations department of a manufacturing firm under conventional budgeting approach and a zero based budgeting approach.

7. Outline a zero based budgeting approach to the pathology department of a private hospital.

Flexible budgeting

Most budgets are produced on an assumption of a particular level of output or activity. For example, the lathe turning department of Rake's metal parts factory has a budget for period 21 as:

Output   3,000 standard hours.

	£
Direct Labour	3,600
Supervision	1,100
Consumable stores	1,000
Energy	600
	6,300

The department processes a wide range of products and output is expressed in terms of standard output from an hour of lathe turning..

In practice the output is not likely to be exactly 3,000 standard hours for any number of reasons – work availability, machine breakdown, labour sicknesses etc. For *control* purposes it is important to know the budgeted costs at any level of output within the relevant range. The actual costs can then be compared with the budgeted costs at that level.

To do this a flexible budget is required. Suppose that costs would vary as: (x is the level of output in standard hours)

Direct Labour	$£2,600 + \dfrac{x}{3}$
Supervision	$£1,100 \left(+ \dfrac{x - 3,000}{10} \text{ if x is greater than 3,500} \right)$
Consumable stores	$\dfrac{x}{3}$
Energy	$£100 + \dfrac{x}{6}$

Then it is possible to calculate the budgeted expenditure at this level.
At an output of 3,600 hours expenditure is budgeted at:

	£
Direct Labour	3,800
Supervision	1,160
Consumable stores	1,200
Energy	700
	6,860

8.   The actual results for periods 21 and 22 were:

Period	21	22
Standard hours	2,800	3,800
Direct Labour	£3,600	£,780
Supervision	£1,150	£1,150
Consumable stores	£947	£1,240
Energy	£602	£786

Flex the budget, contrast it with *actual* and comment on the *variances* found, suggesting possible reasons for them.

Further development

Budgeting and Behaviour

Much has been written about the behavioural effects of the budgeting process and this introductory book is not the place for an exhaustive treatise on the subject. However it is possible to summarise some of the benefits, which are largely behavioural, of involving managers and other staff in the budget setting process. These include:

a.   Managers and staff have detailed knowledge which the budget makers ought to draw on. Solution to problems are often produced by management or consultants without reference to the immense body of knowledge held by people on the ground. It is to the organisation's benefit to draw on the ideas and creativity of the employees.

b.   Budgets produced in collaboration with staff are usually felt to be owned by the staff who then feel responsible for them. This ensures a greater level of commitment to the budgets by the staff.

c.   In most firms there is a tendency to a lack of goal congruence by staff. Budgets drawn up in collaboration with staff enable the different goals to be verbalised and common goals agreed.

d. The exercise of collaborative budgeting makes staff more aware of corporate aims and also of the difficulties and problems of colleagues in other departments of the organisation. This tends to build corporate morale and identification with the employer.

e. Conflicts of interest between departments (eg on allocation of resources or responsibilies) are brought into the open and resolved by agreement.

f. A thorough understanding of the budget is gained by more members of staff and this enables greater delegation.

g. Staff are much more motivated.

h. Corrective behaviour required as a response to variances is easier to orchestrate when the staff own the budget.

i. Staff are more willing to be judged, evaluated or assessed in relation to a budget which they had a hand in producing.

k. Necessary changes to plans required by changed circumstances are recognised by staff more quickly when they fully understand the budget.

l. When staff more fully recognise the purposes of budgeting they are less likely to engage in practices like building in budgetary slack and overspending just because a budget allows it.

Case Study

The maintenance department of Stubby Metal Bashing PLC provide a service to the company's large factory which includes maintenance and repair of machinery and buildings including office equipment. The service is on a planned and preventative maintenance and an emergency repair and breakdown basis. The department currently has twelve employees who work shifts.

The company's cost accounting staff have produced the 19x2 budget for the department on the basis of the 19x1 expenditure on personnel, tools, training and office support + 5% when inflation would require 10%. The factory has also increased about 8% in activity. The staff of the department are furious and the department head is trying to find ways of making the necessary economies.

Discuss an approach to the departmental budget which might have benefited the company more than the top down axe approach currently employed.

14 Standard costing

Problems

1. Jerry Boam PLC are manufacturers of electronically controlled robotic manufacturing systems to special order. Most systems are composed of a selection of discrete components drawn from an extensive selection kept in the warehouse. Some are made in the factory and some are bought in. Enquiries are received from potential customers and specifications are drawn up by the design department. The actual price quoted to the customer is estimated by the estimation department. The company have full order books and have achieved record turnover but return on capital employed has been disappointing. The company currently measure profit only twice a year owing to the difficulty of determining stocks of components, work in progress and finished goods.

    How might the adoption of a system of standard costing assist the company?

2. The standard material cost of one of Moises's widgets is:

    > 30 grams of Green Metal at £12 a gram
    > 10 grams of Epson's salts at £500 a kilo

    In period 1,260 widgets were made. The material used was:

    > 7,500 grams of Green Metal at £13 a gram
    > 2,700 grams of Epson's salts at £496 a kilo

    a. Calculate material usage and price variances for period 1.

    b. Suggest possible causes for the variances

    c. Might the variances be related?

*3. The standard material cost of one of Jaime's costumes is:

    > 12 yards of cloth at £2 a yard
    > 20 buttons at 30p each

    In period 2, 300 costumes were made. The material used was:

    > 4,000 yards of cloth at £1.89 a yard
    > 6,400 buttons at 35p each

    a. Calculate the total variance and the material usage and price variances for period 2.

    b. Suggest possible causes for the variances.

    c Might the variances be connected?

    d. What might the works manager do about the variances?

4. The standard direct wage cost of making one of Davis's wooden souvenirs is:

    > 6 skilled worker hours at £6.50 an hour
    > 4 unskilled worker hours at £4.20 an hour

    In period 3, 800 souvenirs were produced costing:

    > 4,500 skilled hours at £6.40
    > 3,500 unskilled hours at £4.50

    a. Calculate rate and efficiency variances for period 3.

    b. Suggest possible causes for the variances.

    c Might the variances be connected?

    d. What might the works manager do about the variances?

5. The standard direct wage cost of making one of Chip's chairs is:

    > 3.5 skilled worker hours at £5.50 an hour
    > 4 unskilled worker hours at £4.70 an hour

In period 3,420 chairs were produced costing:

> 1,300 skilled hours at £5.40
> 1,500 unskilled hours at £4.50

a. Calculate total, rate and efficiency variances for period 3.

b. Suggest possible causes for the variances.

c   Might the variances be connected?

d. What might the works manager do about the variances?

*6. Pip produces plastic components in his factory. The budget and actual for **period 1 is:**

	Budget	**Actual**
Variable overheads	£20,400	£23,900
Direct labour Hours	4,500	4,650
Units of output	13,500	13,100

Variable overheads are direct labour hour driven.

Required:

a. Calculate variable overhead efficiency and expenditure variances.
b. Suggest reasons for the variances.

7. Pippa produces dresses in her factory. The budget and actual for period 1 is:

	Budget	**Actual**
Variable overheads	£18,600	£17,300
Direct labour Hours	3,000	2,900
Units of output	7,000	7,600

Variable overheads are direct labour hour driven.

Required:

a. Calculate variable overhead total, efficiency and expenditure variances.
b. Suggest reasons for the variances.

*8. Don produces floral displays in his workshop. Part of his budget and actual **for period 4:**

	Budget	**Actual**
Fixed Overheads	£10,000	£11,050
Output	4,000	3,870

Required:

a. Calculate fixed overhead expenditure and volume variances.
b. Suggest reasons for them.
c. What might Don do about them.

9. Donna delivers parcels in vans for customers.

Part of her budget and actual statistics for period 5 are:

	Budget	**Actual**
Fixed Overheads	£23,000	£21,600
Parcels delivered	4,600	4,920

Required:

a. Calculate fixed overhead expenditure and volume variances.
b. Suggest reasons for them.
c. Does this calculation seem to you to be informative?
d. What might Donna do about them.

10. Washington sells new cars. He has only two models to sell – the Amazing **and the Fab.**

Budgeted and actual sales for period 7 were:

	Budget		Actual	
	Amazing	**Fab**	**Amazing**	**Fab**
Unit sales	40	15	46	13
Sales Price	£10,200	£15,100	£9,600	£13,000
Standard Cost	£8,300	£12,750		

Required:

a. Calculate total, sales margin and volume variances for period 7.

b. Suggest explanations for them.

c. Do you think:

   ❑ this is a very realistic problem?

   ❑ the sales margin variances provide a useful explanation of why Washington's profit is different from budget?

11. The budget for the furniture department of Randolph's department store and actual performance in period 11 were:

	Budget	Actual
Unit Sales	80	70
Sales price	£210	£190
Standard Cost	£140	

Required:

a. Calculate total, sales margin and volume variances for period 11.

b. Suggest reasons for them.

c. Do you think the variances might be connected?

d. Why is standard cost and not actual cost used in calculating these variances.

Case Study 1

Mack makes a single type of widget in his small factory.

His budget for period 1 was:

	£	£
Sales 2,000 widgets at £60		120,000
Materials 4,000 Kg at £6	24,000	
Direct Labour 6,000 hours at £5	30,000	
Variable overheads	18,000	72,000
Contribution		48,000
Fixed Overheads		28,000
Net Profit		20,000

The actual outturn in period 1 was:

Sales	2,400 at £58	
Materials	5,000 Kg at £6.20	
Direct Labour	7,000 hours at £5.60	
Variable Overheads		£22,780
Fixed Overheads		£30,210

Required:

a. Produce an actual profit and loss account for period 1 in the same format as the budget

b. Prepare a reconciliation of the budgeted profit and the actual profit showing all the standard variances.

c. Prepare a report to Mack explaining the reconciliation giving imagined but plausible explanations for each variance.

Case Study 2

The standard cost of producing one of Eddy's wheelbarrows is:

Galvanised steel 2 yards at £1 a yard
Bought in components £3
Consumable stores £1
Direct labour 2 hours at £4.50
Variable overheads   £4
Fixed Overheads £2.50

Budgeted output is 2,000 units.
Selling price is £24

Actual results for period 2 were:

Output and sales 2,200 units at £26 (average)
Galvanised steel used 4,500 yards at £1.20 a yard
Bought in components used £6,700
Consumable stores used £2,170
Direct Labour 4,700 hours at £4.80 (average)
Variable overheads £9,800
Fixed Overheads £4,950

Required:

a. Calculate and comment on variances.

b. Prepare a statement of budgeted and actual profit.

c. Variances have been similar for several periods.

Eddy is very concerned and has asked you to suggest actions he could take to ensure that variances are minimised. Write him a report.

Further development

Planning and Operating variances

The causes of variances can be divided into planning variances and operating variances. For example, standard labour cost of one of Jon's widgets is:

$$4.5 \text{ hours at } £5.00 = £22.50$$

In period 12, output was 2,000 widgets and labour cost was 10,000 hours at £5.60. Standard variances are:

Rate	$10,000 \times 60p$	$= £6,000$ ADV
Efficiency	$(10,000 - 9,000) \times 5$	$= £5,000$ ADV

On investigation of the variances it was discovered:

☐ all workers were given a 10% wage rise at the beginning of period 12.

☐ workers are now required to wear protective clothing and this is estimated to cause then to be 15% longer on the operations.

If we see these as planning variances we can subdivide the variances as:

Planning:	Rate	$10,000 \times 50p$	$= £5,000$ ADV
	Efficiency	$9,000 \times .15 \times £5$	$= £6,750$ ADV

This explains most of the variances but operational variances remain:

Rate 10,000 ×   10p   £1,000 ADV
Efficiency (10,350 − 10,000) × 5   £1,750 FAV

Effectively, the view that can be taken over planning variances is:

- ❏ the standard costs are incorrect. For example standard wage rate should be £5.50 after the pay increase.
- ❏ they obscure the message of the true operating variances.

In this case the operating variances need some explaining. Perhaps the mix of labour was unnecessarily at the expensive end or some overtime was worked. Efficiency is in fact very favourable. This suggests that the standard usage is still not right.

Calculation of planning variances when standard costs have not been updated is useful in explaining the effects and costs of changes in circumstances.

12. The standard cost of wool in Jane's tapestry kits is 100 grams at 2p a gram.

   In period 13 she made 400 kits and used 43.1 kilograms of wool at 1.93p a gram.

   She knows that:

   - ❏ she has negotiated a special price for her wool with a Greek supplier at 1.9p a gram.
   - ❏ she now puts slightly longer cuts of wool in her kits as a response to customer criticism. The average amount included in a kit is now 102 grams.

   Calculate planning and operational variances. Suggest reasons for the operational variances.

Standard Marginal Costing

Most standard cost systems use the total absorption production costs as I have done in this section. However some systems omit the fixed costs and are then called standard marginal costing systems. The main differences are that fixed overheads are omitted and the sales margin variance becomes the sales contribution variance.

Other standard cost variances

Sales mix variances

Suppose the budgeted sales for X and Y components Ltd were:

	Product X	Product X
Unit Selling price	£100	£160
Unit Standard Cost	£80	£100
Unit Margin	£20	£60

Budgeted sales are 400 X and 200 Y giving total sales of £72,000 and a gross margin of £8,000 + £12,000 = £20,000.

Actual sales were 480 X and 150 Y giving total sales of £48,000 + £24,000 = £72,000 (as budgeted) but sales margin was only £9,600 + £9,000 = £18,600.

The loss of margin and profit comes, not from a drop in turnover, but in a change of sales mix with more of the lower margin X and less of the higher margin Y. The calculation of sales mix variances is best left to cost accountants but you will appreciate that they are very important in practice.

13. Lolling sells a range of garden furniture through reps to DIY sheds and caravan shops. There is a range of high margin De Luxe furniture and a range of lower margin standard furniture. Higher prices are obtained from the caravan shops than from the DIY sheds.

    Explain the information that could be obtained from a calculation of sales margin variances.

    In view of the different margins described, how might you reward the reps?

Mix and yield variances

Some processes require a mixture of material inputs. Examples are cake making and alloy making. In such processes the mix can vary a little and sometimes quite a lot. If some constituents are more expensive than others then a tendency to reduce dear inputs and increase cheap inputs to the mix will lower costs. A mix variance will measure the effect of non-standard mix on costs.

Some processes take a particular quantity of inputs and produce a particular (lower) quantity of outputs. Examples are steelmaking or pharmaceutical manufacture. Yields vary and a yield variance measures the extent of variation from a standard yield.

14. Martin is entertaining his friend Amar who sells a variety of cakes to the freezer trade and is telling the friend of his experiments with standard costing. The friend counters this by telling him that he has a very sophisticated system of standard costing in his bakery.

    In fact he shows Martin a list of variances which include:

    Production of type 11 cakes on 24th June:

Yield variance	£34 ADV

    Sales of cakes in week 25:

Mix variance	£131 FAV

    Martin is intrigued by these but needs to have them explained by his friend.

    Explain the meaning of these variances and why they are useful to Amar.

Fixed Overhead variances

Some systems calculate three fixed overhead variances. The expenditure variance is as shown in our two variance system. However the volume variance is divided into two – a capacity variance and an efficiency variance.

As an example in Len's knife factory:

Expenditure variance	£3,700 ADV
Capacity variance	£2,000 FAV
Efficiency variance	£1,400 ADV

The interpretation of these is:

Expenditure: fixed overhead is not a function of output but should be as budgeted. In fact it was £3,700 more than budget as, perhaps, repairs were more than expected or cold weather required more heating.

Capacity: Recovery of fixed overheads may be more or less than budget depending on output. If more time (labour hours) is spent on output then output should be larger and a greater recovery made. This extra recovery possible is this variance.

Efficiency: despite the greater time spent on production, actual output was less than expected due to inefficiency.

Activity Based Costing

Product costing systems have generally been of two types – total absorption costing and marginal costing. Total absorption costing is required for determining the cost of inventory in preparing the annual financial statements and it is used in long run pricing decisions and in control and evaluation in budgetary control and standard costing systems. Marginal costing tends to find its uses in short term decision making.

A new concept of product cost which is really a new approach to total absorption costing has been developed in recent years and this is activity based costing (ABC).

The system is based on the following set of ideas:

- ❐ the decision to manufacture a product is a seen as a long term commitment which should take into account all costs both fixed and variable.

- ❐ in modern manufacturing variable costs are a decreasing proportion of total costs

- ❐ methods of absorbing overheads onto products by labour hour rates (which is the commonest way) are inequitable as direct labour forms only a small proportion of total cost. Machine time is a more appropriate method but has many limitations for some categories of overheads.

- ❐ ABC concentrates on what causes overhead expenditure

- ❐ ABC views all costs as variable, that is they vary with some measure of activity.

- ❐ even traditional long term costs, usually regarded as fixed are in fact variable with some measure of activity although changes are not usually immediate. As an example quality control inspectors are not going to vary in number and hence cost with short term changes in output but in the long term numbers will be a function of output.

- ❐ ABC tries to relate costs to products by understanding the forces which cause costs – the so-called cost drivers. Examples include material handling costs being driven by the number of parts in a product, packing costs being driven by the number of orders, machine maintenance by machine hours.

- ❐ many cost drivers are transaction based. For example, material handling, packing, inspection, set-up costs for machines.

- ❐ product costs should be measured using absorption methods which take account of cost drivers.

A simple example of Activity Based Costing

Tops Ltd assemble two products from bought-in components – the A and the B. details of manufacture are:

	A	B
Output in units	10,000	15,000
Component numbers	8	4
Components cost (£)	4.5	3.6
Number of production runs	200	50
Machine hours per 100 units	2.6	5.3
Items packed in cartons of	10 units	50 units

You will notice that output of A is smaller but that it has more components, is produced in relatively frequent production runs with small numbers per production run and is packed in relatively small numbers per carton.

Overhead costs are budgeted at:

	£
Component purchasing and handling	14,000
Production control	18,000
Machine set-up costs	25,000
Machine running costs	64,355
Packing	31,200

Calculation of overhead rates:

Component purchasing and handling (driven by component numbers)

$$\frac{£14,000}{(8 \times 10,000 + 4 \times 15,000)} = 10\text{p per component}$$

Production control (driven by number of production runs)

$$\frac{£18,000}{(200 + 50)} = £72 \text{ per production run}$$

Machine set-up costs (also driven by number of production runs)

$$\frac{£25,000}{(200 + 50)} = £100 \text{ per production run}$$

Machine running costs (driven by machine hours)

$$\frac{£64}{355 / (2.6 \times 100 + 5.3 \times 150)} = £61 \text{ per machine hour}$$

Packing (driven by number of cartons packed)

$$\frac{£31}{200 / (1,000 + 300)} = £24 \text{ per carton}$$

Thus the cost of manufacture of the two items:

	A £	A £
Direct Materials (components)	4.50	3.60
Purchasing and handling	0.80	0.40
Production control (i)	1.44	0.24
Machine set-up	2.00	0.33
Machine running (ii)	1.59	3.23
Packing (iii)	2.40	0.48
Total	12.73	8.28

(i) $\frac{10,000}{200} = 50$ are made per production run. Therefore the cost per item is $\frac{£72}{50} = £1.44$

(ii) $\frac{2.6}{100 \text{ hours}} \times £61 = £1.59$

(iii) 10 units in a carton Therefore cost is $\frac{24}{10} = £2.40$

Note:

❑ Overheads are a mixture of conventional fixed and variable costs but will vary in the long term with cost drivers.

❑ this example is simplified. For example the cost driver for component purchasing and handling should include size of components and size of orders

❑ this example illustrates that long runs do not drive overheads as much as short runs. For example A is run more often than B and consequently costs per unit such as production control and machine set-up are higher.

□ costs are very much transaction driven as you can see from purchasing and handling, production control, set-up and packing.

□ the overhead absorption system still has two stages:

allocating and apportioning costs to cost centres
finding absorption methods

An ABC system is likely to be expensive to set up but will produce more appropriate product costs which in a competitive market will give a firm an edge in its pricing and product mix policies. Further, knowing the underlying driving force behind costs enables management to anticipate the cost change effects of decisions and hence enables them to make better decisions.

Case Study

Stubbee PLC manufacture widgets. They have three major products, A, B, and C. Some data about manufacture are:

	A	B	C
Annual number of production runs	50	20	30
Component numbers	3	10	12
X Type Machine hours	4	2	9
Y type Machine hours	9	7	2
Manual Polishing time in hours	8	4	8
Packing – units in each carton	12	24	6
Cartons per lorry	20	25	30
Number of customers	6	150	200

All products are delivered to customers in the company's own vans.

The X type machine is much more expensive to set-up and run than the Y type.

The company have been hit by competition and are considering introducing a small range of additional products using small production runs but with the products tailored to the needs of specific customers. The company currently work 5 daily shifts and the additional products would require 2 night time shifts.

Discussion

The company currently use a simple Total absorption costing system based on manufacturing overhead recovery by machine hour rates and labour hour rates. How might an ABC system assist the company in formulating a pricing policy for their existing and proposed products which might assist it to compete more strongly in the widget market?

15 Cash flow forecasting

Exercises

1. Willa intends to start her catering business from 1 January 19x2:

   Her forecast is:

   ❑ she will put £2,000 into a business bank account from her savings.

   ❑ she will rent a small workshop at a rent of £3,000 a year payable on the usual quarter days in arrear.

   ❑ she will have to pay rates of £1,200 payable £380

   in March and £820 in September.

   ❑ she will equip the workshop at a cost of £6,400 payable in February

   ❑ she hopes to make cash sales and credit sales of:

Quarter	March	June	Sept	Dec
	£	£	£	£
Cash	3,000	4,000	5,000	7,000
Credit	6,000	8,000	9,000	10,000

   She expects 30% of credit sales in a quarter to be outstanding at the end of a quarter.

   ❑ materials will cost 30% of the sales in a quarter. She expects to still owe 25% of her purchases in a quarter at the end of the quarter.

   ❑ labour will cost £1,200 a month

   ❑ she will draw £400 a month

   ❑ she will spend about £300 a month on other expenses (advertising, energy etc)

   ❑ she will buy an estate car to use in the business. This will cost £6,000 and will be financed by trading in her old car at £2,000 and the rest by hire purchase with instalments at £165 a month beginning in February.

   Required:

   a. Prepare a cash flow forecast for Willa for the four quarters of 19x2.

   b. Should she ask her bank for an overdraft or a long term loan?

   c. Prepare a forecast profit and loss account for the year.

*2. Giles has been made redundant from his job as a driver with a local firm of agricultural wholesalers and intends to start a business buying produce from local farmers and selling it to supermarkets. He intends to start on 1 January 19x3 with £2,500 of his savings and his van worth £2,000.

   ❑ He will sell on credit to the supermarkets who will, he hopes, pay him 50% in the month following a sale and 50% in the month after that.

   ❑ He will have to pay cash to the farmers

   ❑ He will add 50% to the cost of purchases in fixing his selling prices to supermarkets..

   ❑ He does not intend to carry any stock.

   Expected income and expenditure for the first six months are:

	Jan £	Feb £	Mar £	Apr £	May £	Jun £
Sales	4,000	6,000	8,000	9,000	9,000	9,000
Wages	840	840	900	900	1,050	1,050
Drawings	700	700	700	700	700	700
Advertising	500	500	500	200	200	200
Motor Expenses	300	400	300	750	300	300
Other expenses	200	250	250	250	300	300

Note that wages is gross + employers national insurance contributions. You can assume that 1/3 of the cost will be paid in the month after the wages are earned.

Ignore VAT

Required:

a. Prepare a cash flow forecast for the first six months.

b. How much overdraft should Giles ask for?

c. What evidence might the bank manager ask for to demonstrate that the business is a viable one.

d. Giles is considering trading as a limited company. How might this affect the attitude of the bank manager?

e. Is the business expected to be adequately profitable?

f. Comment on the trend of cash flows

3. Carteclo Ltd are expanding fast in selling their range of industrial solvents and have appointed a new rep and increased advertising expenditure to take advantage of the popularity of the products.

At 31 December 19x2 the balance sheet included:

Debtors:	£59,800
Creditors	£25,200
Stock	£34,000
Bank Overdraft	£2,700

Sales for the last three months of 19x2 were

October	November	December
£28,000	£32,000	£35,000

Sales in 19x3 are expected to be £36,000 in January and then increase at a compound rate of 5% until June. Sales will then level out and July is expected to be the same as June.

Customers generally pay: 2/5 in the month following the sales, 2/5 in the month following that and 1/5 in the month after that.

Gross profit is expected to be 30% of the sale price.

The company buy in any month sufficient goods to meet the sales of the following month. This they will do in 19x3 except that they will buy an additional £1,000 at cost in each of the first six months to increase stock to offer a better service to customers.

Carteclo pay their suppliers in the month following the purchase.

Costs other than purchases of goods for resale in the first six months will be:

Wages £5,000 a month (assume all paid in each month)
Overheads £3,300 a month also paid as incurred.
Loan Instalment £6,000 and Interest £2,000, both payable in March 19x3.
Fixed Asset purchases payable £7,000 in February and £12,000 in May.
Corporation tax payable in January 19x3 £4,100
Depreciation is £4,800 a year

Required:

a. Prepare a cash flow forecast for the first six months of 19x3.

b. What overdraft facility should Carteclo ask for? How might the overdraft requirement be modified?

c. If sales become stabilised from July onwards, what do you think would happen to the overdraft?

d. Prepare a profit and loss forecast in this form:

Forecast trading and profit and loss account for the six months January to June 19x3

	£	£
Sales		x
Less Cost of goods sold:		
Stock 1 January	x	
Purchases	x	
	x	
Less Stock 30 June	x	x
Gross Profit		x
Wages	x	
Overheads	x	
Loan Interest	x	
Depreciation	x	x
Net Profit		x

e. Evaluate the decision to appoint a new rep and increase advertising expenditure in terms of profitability and risk.

4. Champ commenced in business on January 1 19x2 to trade in widgets. She prepared a cash flow forecast for the first six months for the bank and recorded the actual outcome. The forecast and actual are:

Forecast:

	Jan £	Feb £	Mar £	Apr £	May £	Jun £
Receipts:						
Introduced	6,000					
Customers		2,500	5,500	7,000	9,000	10,000
Payments:						
Suppliers		6,500	4,000	5,000	5,000	5,000
Overheads	2,000	2,000	2,000	2,000	2,000	2,000
Fixed Assets	10,000					
Overdraft:						
Beginning		6,000	12,000	12,500	12,500	10,500
End	6,000	12,000	12,500	12,500	10,500	7,500

Champ agreed an overdraft limit at £14,000 with her bank manager.

The actual outcome was:

	Jan £	Feb £	Mar £	Apr £	May £	Jun £
Receipts:						
Introducd	6,000					
Customers		2,000	5,000	7,500	8,500	11,000
Payments:						
Suppliers		7,000	3,300	2,200	5,600	7,800
Overheads	2,200	1,900	2,600	3,100	2,900	3,200
Fixed Assets	10,000			2,200		
Overdraft:						
Beginning		6,200	13,100	14,000	14,000	14,000
End	6,200	13,100	14,000	14,000	14,000	14,000

The forecast was based on sales and purchases as:

Sales	5,000	6,000	8,000	10,000	10,000	10,000
Purchases	6,500	4,000	5,000	5,000	5,000	5,000

The actual sales and purchases were:

Sales	5,000	7,000	8,500	12,000	13,000	16,000
Purchases	7,000	4,000	6,200	6,000	8,000	5,500

Champ expects to make a gross profit of 50% of sales.

Required:

a. Deduce the assumptions Champ made in preparing the cash flow forecast.

b. Write a report detailing why the actual turned out to be different from the forecast.

c. Assess the difficulties of cash flow forecasting and how well Champ succeeded in her forecasting.

Further development

Feedback on cash flow forecasting.

Virtually all new businesses prepare a cash flow forecast on a monthly basis for the first year's trading. They do this primarily because the bank require it before granting loan or overdraft facilities. Subsequently the bank monitor the state of the overdraft by simply ensuring that the amount overdrawn does not exceed the facility. The bank will also required financial statements in the form of a trading and profit and loss account and balance sheet. Usually annual accounts are sufficient but in some cases quarterly or half yearly accounts are required. Existing businesses are also usually required by their bankers to produce cash flow forecasts when negotiating a renewal or an increase in an overdraft facility.

The firm may also prepare a forecast for its own purposes and this is now more commonly done as businessmen play with spreadsheets on their personal computers. Spreadsheets seem to be designed for the purpose of doing cash flow forecasts.

An obvious requirement of a forecast is that it is reasonably accurate. The ability to do anything is much enhanced by having *feedback* on actual performance and forecasting is no exception. A cash flow forecaster who is given detailed feedback on actual outcomes can determine where the forecast was wrong and why. Hopefully she will learn by this to forecast better and her next attempt will be more reliable.

A problem in practice is that *feedback* is not normally given to forecasters. The reason is that data necessary to verify the assumptions of the forecast are not collected by the bookkeeping systems of most firms. For example:

☐ cash collected from customers is recorded but is not related to particular months' sales. Consequently no feedback is available on the pattern of payment by customers.

☐ cash paid to suppliers is recorded but is not related to particular months' purchases. Consequently no feedback is available on the pattern of payments to suppliers. In practice the timing of payments to suppliers is a complex business and account is usually taken of: the state of the overdraft, the availability of settlement discounts, the degree of pressure applied by a supplier and other factors.

☐ the relationship of sales, purchases and stocks is often obscure and the bookkeeping system certainly does not keep information which would give any enlightenment.

In 1991 a new Financial Reporting Standard was issued. This is FRS 1 on Cash Flow Statements. This does not require but recommends collection and reporting of:

Cash received from customers

Cash payments to suppliers

Cash paid to and on behalf of employees

Other cash payments relating to operating activities

If companies adopt this recommendation then at least some extra feedback may be available to cash flow forecasters.

Exercise

5. Dymphna has a business buying and selling special steels. She runs a large overdraft and is regularly required to provide a cash flow forecast when her overdraft facility comes up for renewal each year. She has half yearly accounts produced and sends copies to the bank for them to review.

    Required:

    a. What is meant by cash in cash flow forecasting?

    b. In what ways do cash flows differ from flows recorded in profit and loss accounts?

    c. Summarise the data that might be recorded in Dymphna's bookkeeping system to give her feedback on her ability to forecast.

Case Study

Lionel has a business wholesaling souvenirs and has had an overdraft for the five years of the life of the business. Each year he negotiates an increased facility with the bank but always finds that he has to pay his suppliers later than he (or they) would like. At each renewal he produces a cash flow forecast.

He feels that his forecast cannot be accurate and worries that the bank will realise this and consequently not grant him his renewal.

Suggest reasons why his forecasts are never accurate and how feedback might improve his forecasting ability.

16 Investment appraisal

Exercises

*1. At the beginning of 19x2, Buggins Ltd are considering 5 investments in replacement plant:

Reference	Net Cost	Savings in year: 1	2	3	4	5
	£	£	£	£	£	£
A	40,000	5,000	8,000	12,000	18,000	16,000
B	20,000	8,000	8,000	5,000	4,000	2,000
C	29,000	1,000	12,000	23,000	nil	3,000
D	29,000	24,000	6,000	1,000	1,000	1,000
E	30,000	nil	nil	nil	nil	45,000

You can assume that the returns in year 5 include the proceeds of disposal of the plant and that all the projects have 5 year lives.

Required:

a. Calculate payback period for each project

b. Calculate net present value for each project at

i. 10% ii. 12% iii. 16% cost of capital

c. Calculate the profitability index for each project

d. Make reasoned recommendations on acceptance or rejection of each project.

e. Using these projects, discuss the utility of the capital investment appraisal process.

f. Calculate the internal rate of return for each project.

2. Yogg Gurt Ltd have a chain of shops selling dairy produce. They are considering opening a branch in Wednesfield and the marketing director with the help of the finance director has produced the following forecasts for the proposal:

Cost of initial ingoing (lease, shop front, fittings, equipment etc)	£25,000
Initial working capital	£4,000
Annual outgoings (rent, wages, rates, heating etc)	£24,000

Annual sales:

year	1	2	3	4	5
(all figures in £'000)	60	90	100	100	100

Gross profit to sales ratio 50%

The branch will sell retail and also supply local businesses on credit.

At the end of the lease (after 5 years) the shop will either close and Yogg will get back their initial investment in working capital only or they can continue with a further investment in a new lease etc.

Required:

a. Calculate the payback period for the project

b. Calculate the net present value and profitability index at 14% the cost of capital.

c. Calculate the internal rate of return

d. Should the company go ahead?

e. Recalculate a. and b. if:

i. Initial ingoing was £27,000

    ii.   Annual outgoings were 5% more or 5% less than forecast

    iii. Annual sales were 5% more or 5% less than forecast

    iv. Gross Profit ratio was 45% or 55%

  f.   Explain the investment in working capital and why it will be returned at the end of the project

  g. What should the company do at the end of the lease?

3.   Dream Ltd, a manufacturer of special beds, are considering the purchase of a rival company Reverie Ltd. If the company is purchased, Dream Ltd will close it down and realise about £200,000 from the sale of the assets less the settlement of liabilities including redundancy pay. It is estimated that this will take about a year.

Dream reckon that they will make extra sales as follows as a consequence of this purchase:

Year	1	2	3	4
	£180,000	£140,000	£80,000	£40,000

They make a gross profit of 60% on all sales. They estimate that fixed costs will remain unchanged despite the increase in turnover.

Required:

  a. What is the minimum price that Dream could pay to make the purchase of Reverie worth while if cost of capital is i. 14% ii. 20% ?

  b. Discuss this question from an ethical and public policy point of view.

*4. Doreen is considering the purchase of a new and better machine for her hardwood business. She already has a machine which does the job. She bought the machine in 19x2 for £50,000 and it will work well for at least 5 years. She could sell it now for about £10,000. However the new machine is much more efficient and would save her £6,000 a year in wages and materials over the next 6 years, the life of the machine. In addition the new machine will do some work the present machine will not do and this will bring in a contribution of £6,000 a year.

The new machine will cost £50,000 and like the present one will have no value at the end of its life.

Required:

  a. Should she buy the new machine if her cost of capital is i. 14%   ii. 22% ?

  b. At what rate of interest is the purchase of the new machine just viable ?

  c. Assuming a straight line method of depreciation, calculate the depreciation in the accounts if:

    i.   the new machine is purchased
    ii. the new machine is not purchased

  d. The extra contribution of £6,000 mentioned above is not certain. How much actual contribution is required to make the project just viable at 14%?

5.   Labey is considering two investments offered by a financial institution:
  a. An investment now of £20,000 with guaranteed payment of £35,000 in 5 years time.

  b. An investment now of £20,000 with annual interest payments of £2,200 + a guaranteed return of £24,000 in 5 years time.

Required:

  a. Which investment offers the best return?

  b. Which should Labey invest in if A. also offers the guaranteed sum on the death of Labey at any time before the end of the five years if:

    i.   Labey is 60 and has no dependants

    ii. Labey is 40, is in work, is married and has 3 young children.

Case Study

Things PLC are in a very competitive industry making parts for the motor industry. They are considering the replacement of one production line with a more modern one. Indications are that the cost of the new line less the scrap value obtained from the present one will be £450,000. This figure is fairly certain but the changeover will have substantial costs and these have been estimated as between £50,000 and £150,000. The engineer cannot be more precise than this.

The new line will last 5 years and estimated savings in production costs over the old line are:

Year	1	2	3	4	5
(all figures in £'000)	150	150	150	200	250

The higher savings in later years are because the old line would be costing substantial sums in repairs by then and may well be unreliable.

The company fears a takeover bid from a larger company and the chairman has a issued a rather optimistic profit forecast which he is very anxious to adhere to in the short term.

The financial director is uncertain as to the cost of capital but accepts that the current figure is about 14% but fears it may rise to 15% if they need to borrow in the near future.

The marketing director is a natural optimist and considers that the new production line will enable higher production levels in the future should the increased sales which he expects actually happen. Currently sales are running at about 80% of capacity.

Required:

Write a report to the Board

a. Detailing the methods which might be used to evaluate the proposal.

b. Assess the proposal using these methods.

c. Express an opinion on the proposal and make a case for your opinion.

Further development

More advanced capital investment appraisal

Capital investment appraisal techniques such as payback and net present value have been much criticised as being based upon exceedingly unreliable estimates. For example James owns a very successful chain of menswear shops. He is considering opening a new shop in Walsall. To use the proper appraisal techniques, he should estimate the cost of setting up the shop and then estimate likely sales and overheads. The overheads can be estimated fairly readily but likely sales can really only be a guess.

In this case James is a successful entrepreneur and will rely on his own flair in deciding whether to go ahead or not.

In a case where the company is a large corporation and local management want to open the new shop then the company might require that the local management make out a good case. They can do this by:

- ❏ estimating costs and expenses by getting estimates from suppliers and considering costs levels at other shops

- ❏ estimate sales by considering comparable existing shops, assessing competition, market research etc. In other words they will have to do their homework and perhaps the benefit of capital investment appraisal lies in the homework rather than in the mathematics.

There are a number of more advanced techniques and we will review some of them.

Mutually exclusive projects

Jayne can use the first floor of their hairdressing salon for either:

A. Starting a beauty business

or   B. Starting a dressmaking business

The capital costs would be   A. £7,000

B. £3,200

and the sales less expenses would be: A. £3,000 a year

B. £1,500 a year

The business can only last the remainder of the lease – 4 years and we will assume a nil scrap value.

Cost of capital is 20%.

The net present values and profitability indeces are:

a. $(£3,000 \times 2.58) - £7,000 = £740: \dfrac{£7,740}{£7,000} = 1.1$

b. $(£1,500 \times 2.58) - £3,200 = £670: \dfrac{£3,870}{£3,200} = 1.2$

Note that 2.58 = the sum of the discount rates for four years at 20%.

Jayne cannot undertake both projects. She has to choose. The criterion is to select the project offering the highest net present value. Thus in this case she should adopt project A even though project B has a higher profitability index. This is because the higher NPV enriches the firm the most.

6.   Stoo can use a field at the back of his leisure complex for either A. a crazy golf course or B. a model boating lake. Estimated figures are:

	A	B
Capital costs	£100,000	£200,000
Annual Profits	£40,000	£70,000

Cost of capital is 18% and Stoo only considers returns for a maximum of 5 years. You can ignore any salvage value to the expenditure.

Which should he choose?

7.   Phyllis is considering building on the plot of land next to her house. There is planning permission for commercial use and she is considering:

a.   Building a bingo club and letting it on a seven year lease to an operating company (not connected to her) at £10,000 a year.

b.   Building an office block and letting it in small units on 7 year leases for a total rent of £7,000 a year.

c.   Building a showroom and opening a piano shop of her own. She estimates she will make £20,000 a year for the 7 years before she retires and will have to give up her job as an insurance clerk at £11,000 a year.

Cost of capital is 12% .

At the end of seven years, the whole site will be compulsorily purchased by the development corporation for redevelopment. Site value only will be paid.

Construction costs would be:

A. £40,000   B. £35,000   C. £30,000

Required:

a.   Which should she adopt?

b.   Discuss any other factors that she may wish to take into account.

Capital Rationing

In theory, any project that gives a prospective positive net present value should be undertaken. However if a company has a very large number of such projects (it would be very fortunate if it had) infinite capital may not be available to finance all the projects. In theory finance should be available as banks should be willing to finance any project with a positive NPV but in practice infinite finance is not available. Where limited capital is available and all positive NPV projects cannot be undertaken then a capital rationing situation is said to exist.

Other capital rationing situations exist where:

❑ all projects cannot be undertaken due to limited entrepreneurial energy or limited management time

❑ groups restrict capital available to subsidiaries.

Suppose Lal Ltd have identified the following projects:

	Outlay	Net Present Value
(all figures in £'000)		
A.	34	8.1
B.	20	4.3
C.	15	2.8
D.	47	8.8
E.	12	1.6

If capital is limited to £50,000, which should be chosen? The answer is to choose the combination of projects which maximises NPV. In theory every possible combination should be considered but in practice it is usually possible to work out the best combination fairly easily by trial and error. I think the answer is A. + C.

*8. Chall is considering six projects:

	Initial Outlay	Net Present Value
(all figures in £'000)		
A.	90	4
B.	30	11
C.	52	7
D.	32	6
E	120	19
F.	21	7

Capital is limited to £150,000

Which projects should be undertaken?

9. Bjorn is considering six projects:

	Outlay	Net Present Value
(all figures in £'000)		
A.	102	12.1
B.	55	4.3
C.	32	9.8
D.	120	14.1
E.	60	3.1
F.	80	5.0

If capital is limited to £210,000, which projects should be undertaken if:

a. Each project must be undertaken in full or not at all;

or

b. Each project can be scaled down as much as is necessary (in this case the criteria for selection is profitability index).

Taxation

In the real world taxation is a fact of life and must be taken into account in all decisions where it has an impact – it has an impact on most decisions. Taking tax into account in NPV calculations can be quite complicated. Here is an example:

Mary is considering buying a machine at the beginning of 19x2 which will cost her £20,000 and bring savings of £6,000 a year for 4 years before the machine is sold for £5,000.

She pays corporation tax on her profits at 25% and this is paid one year after earning the profit ie tax on 19x2 profits are paid in 19x3.

For tax purposes, instead of depreciation, there are *capital allowances* as:

Cost	20,000	
19x2	5,000*	
	15,000	* These are 25% of
19x3	3,750*	written down value
	11,250	and are called writing
19x4	2,812*	down allowances.
	8,438	
19x5 sold	5,000	
19x5	3,438~	~ Balancing Allowance

Extra tax will thus be 25% on:

Year	Savings	Capital Allowances	Net	Tax	Payable
19x2	6,000	5,000	1,000	250	19x3
19x3	6,000	3,750	2,250	562	19x4
19x4	6,000	2,812	3,188	797	19x5
19x5	6,000	3,438	2,562	640	19x6

Thus the net present value calculation is:

Year	0	1	2	3	4	5
Outlay	−20,000					
Inflow		6,000	6,000	6,000	11,000	
Tax			−250	−562	−797	−640
Net	−20,000	6,000	5,750	5,438	10,203	−640
Discount Factor		.92	.86	.79	.73	.68
Discounted	−20,000	5,520	4,945	4,296	7,448	−435

Net Present Value = £21,774 – project is viable.

I have take the after tax cost of capital as 8%.

10. Tau intends to buy a machine for £10,000. This will last five years and attract capital allowances of 25%. At the end of 5 years he will sell the machine for £3,000.

During the five years savings made by using the machine will be:

Year (all figures in £'000)	1	2	3	4	5
Savings	4	4.5	3.9	2.8	2.7

Cost of capital is 8% net of tax.

Tau pays tax at a marginal rate of 40%.

Is the project viable?

Risk

In choosing projects an appraiser ought to bear in mind risk. Risk in this context can be equated to uncertainty. A project which is more risky than the average run of projects undertaken will increase the overall risk profile of the company and should in theory therefore increase the cost of capital. Therefore the discount rate used in calculating net present value for such a project should be higher than for ordinary risk projects. Similarly, choosing between mutually exclusive projects a manager should take into account risk.

There are several complex methods of taking into account risk and I cannot really cover these in this non-specialist book. However here is one idea:

Loopy is considering a project which will cost £20,000 and last for two years. Returns are uncertain but the sales manager has forecast the following.

	Year 1		Year 2	Cumulative Probability
			9,000 (50%p)	.25
Profit	10,000 (50% p)	<		
			11,000 (50%p)	.25
			13,000 (50%p)	.125
Profit	15,000 (25% p)	<		
			16,000 (50%p)	.125
			17,000 (50%p)	.125
Profit	20,000 (25% p)	<		
			21,000 (50%p)	.125

The outcome of year 2 is assumed to be dependent on the outcome of year 1. Thus if profit in year 1 is £10,000 then it will be £9,000 or £11,000 in year 2.

p is the probability of something occurring. So the probability of profit in year 1 being 15,000 followed by 16,000 in year 2 is .125 or one chance in eight.

Applying a discount rate of 10% we find:

	Year 1	Year 2	Cumulative p	Present Value
Profit	9,090	7,434	.25	4,131
		9,086	.25	4,544
Profit	13,635	10,738	.125	3,046
		13,216	.125	3,356
Profit	18,180	14,042	.125	4,027
		17,346	.125	4,440
				23,544

You will deduce how the net present value is calculated.

It is £23,544 – £20,000. It is called the expected value.

You will realise that the present values of inflows can vary between (£9,090 + £7,434) £16,524 and (£18,180 + £17,346) £35,526. The degree of variation can be measured by calculating the standard deviation. We will leave this to the statisticians.

11. Sceepa has three possible uses for an unused part of his factory. These are

	Initial Outlay	Expected Net Present Value	Standard Deviation
	£	£	£
A.	8,000	1,790	2,180
B.	7,000	850	103
C.	7,500	1,500	670

Discuss which he might choose.

17 Sources of finance

1. Financial Chicanery PLC have a balance sheet at 31 December 19x1 as:

(all figures in £'000)

Fixed Assets			
Land and Buildings			830
Plant etc			<u>945</u>
			1,775
Current Assets			
Stock		1,250	
Debtors		<u>643</u>	
		<u>1,893</u>	
Creditors: amounts falling due within one year			
Creditors		436	
Midwest Factors Ltd		583	
Bills Payable		120	
Bank Overdraft		371	
Obligations under leases		168	
Corporation Tax		124	
Dividends		60	
Taxation and Social Security		238	
Hire Purchase Commitments		<u>89</u>	
		<u>2,189</u>	
Net Current Liabilities			<u>(296)</u>
Total Assets less Current Liabilities			1,479
Creditors: amounts falling due after more than one year			
15% Unsecured Loan Stock 19x6-7		200	
11% Mortgage Debentures 20x4		600	
10% Convertible Loan Stock		100	
Floating Rate French Franc Loan 19x9		<u>100</u>	<u>1,000</u>
			479
Capital and Reserves			
Ordinary Share Capital (20p shares)			54
10% Cumulative Redeemable Preference Shares of £1 each			60
Share Premium Account			27
Capital Redemption Reserve			100
Profit and Loss Account			<u>238</u>
			<u>479</u>

Notes:

1. The bank overdraft is secured on a floating charge on all the assets.

2. The mortgage debentures are secured by a fixed charge on the freehold property.

3. The unsecured loan stock is redeemable at a premium of 10%

Required:

a. Assuming no interim dividends are paid, what rate of dividend is paid on the ordinary shares?

b. What was the original amount of preference shares issued, assuming all were issued at par?

c. All the ordinary shares were issued at one go and one price. What was the price?

d. What is the maximum dividend per share that the company could, in law, pay in addition to the dividend already proposed? Why could this not be paid in practice.

e. The company have agreed a maximum overdraft facility. Can you see how much this is?

f. If the company failed and the freehold property was sold for £550,000, would the mortgage debenture holders be paid in full?

g. The French Franc Loan is for 1,000,000 francs. What would happen to the loan if the pound fell against the franc?

h. The convertible loan is convertible into ordinary shares at a rate of 1 share for each £1 of stock in 19x7. If all the loan stock was converted what would be the amount in the balance sheet of:

   Convertible Loan Stock

   Ordinary Shares

   Share Premium

i. How much interest does a holder of £100 nominal of the unsecured loan stock receive in a year and when will she be repaid the loan? How much will she receive?

j. List and explain all the sources of finance used by the company.

2. The balance sheet of Simple Sid Ltd at 31 December 19x2 showed: (all figures in £'000)

Fixed Assets		
Premises		875
Plant etc		660
		1,535
Current Assets		
Stock	546	
Debtors	1,650	
Cash at Bank	132	
	2,328	
Creditors: amounts falling due within one year		
Creditors	430	
Dividends	100	
Corporation Tax	230	
Taxation and Social Security	134	
	894	
Net Current Assets		1,434
Total Assets less current Liabilities		2,969
Capital and Reserves		
Ordinary 20p shares		500
Share Premium		1,200
Profit and Loss Account		1,269
		2,969

Required:

a. Assuming no interim dividend is paid, what rate of dividend per share is paid?

b. The company originally started with £500,000 shares of 20p each issued at par. These shareholders were later given a bonus issue of one for one. Later still there was a rights issue. At what price were those shares sold for?

c. The company now wish to expand rapidly by acquiring new premises, vehicles and plant and doubling sales. The existing shareholders have no resources available for new investment in the company but wish to retain control at least in the short term. Review and suggest possible sources of finance for the expansion.

*3. Livy PLC have a summarised balance sheet as:

(all figures in £'000)

Fixed Assets		
Freehold Premises at recent valuation		900
Plant etc		700
		1,600
Current Assets		
Stock	1,280	
Debtors	1,220	
	2,500	
Creditors: amounts falling due within one year		
6% Unsecured Loan Stock	1,000	
Bank Overdraft	940	
Creditors	760	
Corporation Tax	130	
Taxation and Social Security	178	
	3,008	
Net Current Liabilities		(608)
Total Assets less Current Liabilities		992
Capital and Reserves		
Share Capital: 10p shares		100
Profit and Loss Account		892
		992

Note that the bank overdraft is secured by a floating charge on all the company's assets.

Required:

a. Explain why you think the company is profitable.

b. Explain why the company did not propose a dividend.

c. The company have a financial problem. What is it?

d. The bank have indicated that they do not wish to advance any further sums to the company.

e. Review possible sources of finance to allow the company to continue and prosper.

f. The company is listed on the stock exchange and its shares are quoted at 56p. Comment on this value.

Assignment 1

Orgkem Ltd sells special chemicals to industry. Some of these it imports, some are bought in the UK and some are made in the company's modern factory. It distributes the chemicals in its own vans in order to offer a very rapid service. Opportunities for expansion have occurred and the company is looking for finance for:

an extension to the factory
new plant
new vehicles
increased turnover

The company is owned by the extended Jones family who lack the resources to further finance the company. The directors are considering:

leasing
HP
a mortgage
bank loans and overdrafts
factoring
any other sources

Required:

a. Approach financing institutions to find out the terms of issue and the interest rates payable on the various sources of money available to the company.

b. Write a report to the directors reviewing the possible sources of finance.

Further development

Risk in Investment in Companies

Investment in companies carries risk. A shareholder in XY Construction PLC may find the company goes into receivership and then liquidation and that his shares are worthless. The investor takes this risk because there is also the possibility of gain. He may buy his shares at 15p each and sell them a year or two later at 100p each as the company has prospered.

Investors can invest not only in ordinary shares but also in other securities. Here are some of the securities and the risks attached both downside and upside:

Loans secured on fixed assets (usually land and buildings)

Upside	**Downside**
Cannot lose unless company goes bust and property sells for less than loan. Interest very unlikely to be unpaid. Eventual repayment.	Modest interest rate No chance of capital gain. Boring.

Loans secured on floating charges

Upside	**Downside**
Cannot lose unless company goes bust and all assets sell for less than amount of loan and unpaid interest. Interest very unlikely to be passed. Eventual repayment	Modest interest rate No chance of capital gain. Dull

Unsecured loans

Upside	**Downside**
Regular interest. Interest rate slightly better than secured loans. Eventual repayment	No chance of capital gain. Modest interest rate. Chance of losing money if company goes bust. Dreary

Convertible loans

Upside	**Downside**
Regular interest. Chance of capital gain if shares do well. Eventual repayment if not converted Interesting	No capital gain unless shares do well. Low interest rate. Chance of losing money if company goes bust.

Preference shares

Upside	**Downside**
Dividend payable before ordinary dividend.	No capital gain.
	Low rate of dividend
Usually cumulative.	Chance of losing money if company
Usually redeemable	goes bust.

I have suggested that there is no chance of making a capital gain on these securities. This is not quite true. Suppose prevailing interest rates are 12% on company loans. AB PLC issue a loan in 19x2 at that rate for repayment in 20 years. In effect the investor in £100 worth gets assured interest of £12 a year for twenty years and then his money back. Suppose in 19x3 interest rates have fallen to 8%. If he wishes to sell his loan stock, another investor may see £12 a year and looking for an investment paying 8% may be willing to pay £150 for a £100 worth. This gives him $\frac{12}{150} \times 100 = 8\%$. In practice he will pay slightly less than £150 as he will ultimately be repaid only £100.

Of course if interest rates rise then the £100 nominal may fetch less than £100.

Assignment 2

Fortune has been left a more than modest sum by an aunt. He wants to invest this in company securities.

Required:

a. Explore the rates of interest (both flat and redemption yield) offered by different types of company securities. This information can most easily obtained by consulting a stockbroker or your high street bank.

b. Write a report contrasting the risks and rewards of these different types of security and contrasting them with the risk and rewards offered by investing in High Street financial institutions.

Business Risk and Financial Risk

The risk accepted by investors in companies can be considered as coming from two sources:

❑ Business Risk

This is simply the risk that the company may trade profitably or unprofitably. One particular risk is called operating gearing. Suppose FA PLC makes and sells a particular building material. Each batch of the material gives a contribution of £2,000 and fixed costs in its highly capital intensive process are £10,000,000 a year.

If the company sells 6,000 batches the company makes £2,000,000 profit and gives record dividends. But if the company sells only 4,000 batches it loses £2,000,000 and goes bust.

❑ Financial Risk

This is the risk that arises when companies are highly geared. Suppose part of the balance sheet of C PLC showed:

(all figures in £'000)

Share capital 20p shares	4,000
Profit and Loss Account	1,560
Loans at 15%	5,000

If profit before interest is £1,000,000 then interest takes £750,000 and the shareholders have a good dividend. But if the profit before interest is only £500,000 the company has lost £250,000 and may run into difficulty in paying its creditors.

Further if the company has to repay the loans it can only do so by borrowing a similar amount but it cannot do so if it is unprofitable.

Gearing confers benefits on a company that can earn business returns on capital greater than the interest paid on loans. But gearing can be very risky and even disastrous.

Assignment 3

Scan the city pages of the newspapers for reference to borrowings, gearing, refinancing packages and the like.

Write a report on your findings incorporating information on why companies get themselves into difficulties and how they attempt to get out of them.

Case Study

Some extracts from the Profit and Loss Accounts of four companies and from their Balance Sheets are:

(all figures in £'000)	A	B	C	D
Profit before interest	5,560	3,240	6,400	8,100
Interest	360	2,950		3,600
Shareholders funds	21,000	8,000	32,000	24,000
12% Debentures	3,000	20,000	–	30,000

Required:

a. Comment on the interest paid by B

b. Comment on the risks borne by the Debentureholders and the shareholders

c. Comment on the degree of gearing of each company

d. What might B do about its financial problem?

e. How might D raise more money for expansion?

18 Working capital

Exercises

1. Some extracts from the annual accounts of AHM Trading are:

   Balance sheet at 31.12.19x2:

		£			£
	Stocks	24,000	Creditors	11,500
	Debtors	18,000	Overdraft	12,000

   Profit and Loss Account

Sales	104,000
Cost of goods sold	65,000
Purchases	61,000

   a. Calculate the working capital.

   b. On these figures creditors average payment time is:

   $$\frac{11,500}{61,000} \times 365 = 69 \text{ days}$$

   Calculate the creditors average payment time if all the figures (including the net working capital) remained the same except as stated with the following independent events:

   i. Stocks increase to £30,000

   ii. Debtors increased to 90 days average collection time

   iii. The bank overdraft was reduced to £8,000

   iv. Sales increased by 20% (but debtors collection time remained the same)

   v. Stock turnover changed to 160 days

   vi. Purchases increased by 20%

2. Some extracts from the annual accounts of RP Trading are:

   Balance sheet at 31.12.19x2:

		£			£
	Stocks	50,000	Creditors	31,500
	Debtors	45,000	Overdraft	12,000

   Profit and Loss Account

Sales	270,000
Cost of goods sold	189,000
Purchases	189,000

   a. Calculate the working capital.

   b. Calculate the creditors average payment time if all the figures (including the net working capital) remained the same except as stated with the following independent events:

   i. Stocks increase by 15%

   ii. Debtors increased to 90 days average collection time

   iii. The bank overdraft was reduced to £10,000

   iv. Sales increased by 15% (but debtors collection time remained the same)

   v. Stock turnover changed to 200 days

   vi. Purchases increased by 1/9

   c. All figures except the bank overdraft rose by 10% as a result of inflation and stock, debtors and creditors ratios remained the same. Calculate the increase in working capital required.

3. The balance sheet of AB Ltd at 31.12.19x2:

Share Capital	20,000	Fixed Assets	35,000
Profit and Loss	32,000	Stock	18,000
Creditors	13,000	Debtors	23,000
Overdraft	11,000		
	76,000		76,000

The Profit and Loss Account for 19x2 showed:

Sales (all credit)	92,000
Cost of sales	56,000
Gross Profit	36,000
Overheads	20,000
Net Profit	16,000

At the beginning of 19x3 the directors are planning:

❏   to spend £8,000 on fixed assets

❏   to increase sales by 20%

a.   Explore the consequences of this on cash requirements assuming stock remains at £18,000 and gross profit ratio, debtors payment time, creditors payment time and overheads all remain the same.

b.   Suggest some possible sources of finance.

*4.   The balance sheet of CD Ltd at 31.12.19x2:

Share Capital	30,000	Fixed Assets	64,000
Profit and Loss	31,000	Stock	24,000
Creditors	28,000	Debtors	56,000
Overdraft	55,000		
	144,000		144,000

The Profit and Loss Account for 19x2 showed:

Sales (all credit)	168,000
Cost of sales	104,000
Gross Profit	64,000
Overheads	20,000
Net Profit	44,000

a.   Stock at 1.1.19x2 was £20,000. Calculate:

Debtors average payment time
Stock turnover
Creditors average payment time

b.   Discuss the company's apparent good points and its apparent problems

At the beginning of 19x3 the directors are planning:

❏   to spend £10,000 on fixed assets
❏   to increase sales by 20%

c.   Explore the consequences of this on cash requirements assuming stock increases by 20% and gross profit ratio, debtors payment time, creditors payment time and overheads all remain the same. Note that profits will bring in £15,000 of additional working capital in 19x3.

5.   The working capital sections of the accounts of Swetblud Ltd and Easy Ltd showed:

	Swetblud	£	Easy	£
Current Assets				
Stock		40,000		76,000
Debtors		54,000		45,000
		94,000		121,000
Current Liabilities				
Creditors	43,000		26,000	
Overdraft	18,000	61,000	2,500	28,500
		33,000		92,500

Other relevant data:

Debtors average credit time		70 days		60 days
Stock turnover		102 days		52 days
Creditors average credit time		91 days		38 days
Bank Overdraft Facility		£16,000		£30,000

Both companies are wholesalers in the same line of business

Required

a. Review all the figures and identify any problems that each company may have.

b. What action would you recommend to each company to remedy any problem?

c. Swetblud has a bill for £10,000 corporation tax to pay. How will this cause difficulty?

d. Easy has a dividend to pay of £15,000. Will this cause any problem?

e. Both companies are looking for an increase in turnover. Discuss the effect this might have on the balance sheet extracts above.

6. The working capital of two companies is:

	A	£	B	£
Current Assets				
Stock		230,000		360,000
Debtors		23,000		417,000
		253,000		777,000
Current Liabilities				
Creditors	186,000		172,000	
Overdraft	64,000	250,000	213,000	385,000
		3,000		392,000
Other data:				
Annual Sales		1,100,000		1,375,000
Annual Purchases		745,000		923,000
Bank Overdraft Facility		100,000		200,000

A   Ltd is a warehouse retailing garden things to the public.

B   Ltd is a wholesaler of garden furniture. One third of the company's purchases are imported and the whole cost of imports is paid when the goods are released from the docks.

Required:

a. Review these figures, calculate any useful ratios and comment on them.

b. Identify any problems that may be worrying each company.

c. Suggest some solutions to the problems.

d. Do you think that the figures above would change if the year end was changed in each case?

e. Explore the effects of i. an increase and ii a decrease in turnover.

7. EF Ltd have large stocks of an imported widget for which they have exclusive importation rights. They are considering the size of orders to make. Data collected includes:

- ❑ The costs of making one order (including clerical costs, banking charges and transport) is £240
- ❑ Throughput is 10,000 units a year
- ❑ Holding costs are £2.00 a unit a year
- ❑ The supplier will only ship in multiples of 200 items.

Calculate the economic order quantity.

The supplier takes twelve weeks from the order to delivery. There are 50 weeks in the year. Calculate the re-order level.

8. GH Publishers Ltd have large stocks of a guidebook for which they receive regular orders. They are considering the size of print orders to make. Data collected includes:
   - ❑ The costs of making one order is £80
   - ❑ Throughput is 8,000 units a year
   - ❑ Holding costs are 50p a unit a year
   - ❑ The printer will only print in multiples of 500 items.
   a. Calculate the economic order quantity.
   b. Discuss the difficulties and imperfections of this model in the real world.

   The supplier takes six weeks from the order to delivery. There are 50 weeks in the year.
   c. Calculate the re-order level.
   d. Discuss the consequences of a stock-out.

*9. LM Ltd have a difficulty in collecting in their debts from customers and are considering offering a settlement discount of 5% for payment on invoice. Data about their sales and collection times includes:

Annual Sales £	Average collection time
48,000	1 month
60,000	2 months
120,000	3 months
84,000	4 months

If all the customers took the discount:
a. What would the annual cost be?
b. What would be the reduction in credit granted?
c. Calculate a./b. x100. This gives the effective cost as an interest rate.
d. Discuss how the discount idea would work out in practice.

10. JK Ltd have a problem in collecting debts from their customers and are considering offering a settlement discount. Data about their sales and collection times includes:

Annual Sales £	Average collection time
30,000	1 month
60,000	2 months
90,000	3 months
50,000	4 months or more

The company estimate that if 3,4 or 5% were offered for immediate settlement, all the 1 month payers would take it, 60% of the 2 month payers would take it at 5%, 50% at 4% and 40% at 3%, only 20% of the 3 month payers would take it at 5% and none at 3% or 4%. The 4 month payers would never take the discount.

The company can borrow at 14%. What should they do?

Further development

Operating Cycle

The problem of working capital is largely one of the operating cycle. Suppose the trade cycle consists of:

> buying a good
>
> holding it in stock
>
> selling it

So far as cash is concerned this can be stated as

> Paying for the good
>
> Receiving payment after sale

The further apart these two events are the more the need for working capital. It can be measured as:

Average days held in stock	50
Less: Average creditors period	(45)
Add Average debtors period	72
Conversion cycle	77

The aim should be to shorten this period as much as possible.

In manufacturing, this is more complicated and the conversion cycle is generally longer.

11. Some extracts from the annual accounts of Chad Trading are:

    Balance sheet at 31.12.19x2:

	£		£
Stocks	44,000	Creditors	21,500
Debtors	38,000	Overdraft	32,000

    Profit and Loss Account

Sales	154,000
Cost of goods sold	105,000
Purchases	102,000

    Required:

    a. Calculate the conversion cycle in days.

    b. Calculate the overdraft if the cycle could be shortened by 10 days.

    c. How might this shortening be achieved?

Case Study

The directors of Harbridge Manufacturing PLC are meeting to discuss a cash crisis which is afflicting their profitable company. The problem is that the company is taking an average of 90 days to pay their suppliers and some of the suppliers are threatening to cut off supplies unless the period is shortened. In addition the company wish to pay an interim dividend. The bank have said that the overdraft facility is already larger than the bank would like. The views of the directors are:

Alec, the Chairman: I think we should borrow more money by the issue of some debentures. Of course, the interest rate will be high and we shall have to offer convertibility to attract investors but such an issue should solve our cash problem permanently.

Beryl, the works director: the problem lies in debtors. I see these are now £1,440,000 on annual sales of £6,600,000. If they paid more quickly we would solve the problem. We may have to pay to have a better computer system as I know that invoices take a week to process and statements do not go off until the 8th of the month.

Charles, the finance person: we could make the debtors pay more quickly if we offered 5% discount for quick payment. But my opinion is that the problem lies in the stock levels. We have a raw material stock of £400,000 and that is 15 weeks supplies. If that were reduced we would have no cash problem to worry about. Further the work in progress of £300,000 is absurdly large.

Donna, the sales director: we sell as much as we can but do we really need to hold more than 5 weeks supply of finished goods we have in stock? I think we should stop making some of our lines and buy them from Korea.

Required:

Write a report to the Board commenting on each of the director's remarks and recommending actions which would alleviate the cash problem. You may make assumptions but should then state them.

19 The stock exchange

Exercises

1. David is a manager with a major company and his wife is a primary school head. They have a house with an endowment mortgage and both have life assurance. Both are averse to gambling and would not dream of investing in the stock exchange which they see as a casino.

   Comment on this scenario.

2. Freda invested some £10,000 in 5,000 units of Infinite Life's Smaller Companies Unit Trust. She notices that these have a bid price of 154.7p and an offer price of 166.2p. She reads in the paper that this is one of the best performing unit trusts in the sector.

   Explain this statement to Freda and also to Joan who is thinking of buying some units.

*3. Lee is considering putting all his savings which he has in a building society into an investment trust. He has selected the Pacific and Oriental Trust PLC which specialises in Pacific Basin companies. In the Telegraph he finds that the company is quoted at 192 and has net assets per share of 217. Yield is 0.9 and high and low in the past year are 221 and 158.

   Required:

   a. Explain all this.

   b. Do you think this is a suitable investment for Lee if:

      i. He is married and 61 and retires soon with a very small pension

      or

      ii. He is unemployed, disabled and has a wife and three children.

      iii. He is married with no children, aged 52 and has a very large salary with a brewery.

4. Louie invested £50,000 in £46,000 nominal of Treasury 12 3/4% 19x6 three years ago. It is now 19x1.

   She sees in the Times that the stock has an entry as:

19x0/19x1 High Low	Price	+/–	Interest yield %	Gross Redemption yield
111 105	109 3/16	+ 1/32	11.68	9.54

   Explain all this to her. Has this been a good investment?

5. Doddery inherited some £12,000 of 3 1/2 % War loan from his grandfather. This has a high/low of 38 and 33, a quotation of 37 5/8, and a yield of 9.3% There is no gross redemption yield given.

   Explain all this. Do you consider this to be a great fraud on the part of the British Government?

6. Tweed has some shares in a building company and a supermarket group. Data are

19x1/19x2 High Low	Company	Price (p)	+/–	Net Div	Yield %	P/E
256 123	AB Constr	123	...	11.2	12.2	14.1
280 200	CD Stores	245	+ 2	5.2	2.9	14.4

   Explain all this to Tweed.

   Can you explain the disparity in statistics given that at the time he read these statistics there was a very deep depression especially in the building trade. Supermarkets were doing comparatively well.

*7. Judy has £2,000 Nominal of 8% convertible loan stock 19x9 in EF PLC. The stock is convertible into 20p ordinary shares of the company at the rate of 50 shares per £100 of stock. Conversion

dates are all of August in all years 19x3 to 19x7 The current price (19x2) of a 20p share is 120p. The stock is quoted at 86.

Comment on:

a.   the future possibilities of this investment.

b.   the price of 86.

8.   Tell has £100,000 in cash which he has inherited from his mother. He is considering investing it in one of:

> a seaside cottage
>
> a building society
>
> shares in ICI
>
> antiques.

Discuss what are the benefits and drawbacks of each.

Flotation

Assignment 1

Cringe Ltd make and supply a range of widgets from their freehold factory on a trading estate in Walsall. They also have a number of warehouses round the country. Most of these are also freehold or on long leases. The company is very profitable but most of the profits have been retained in the company for expansion. Current profits are in the region of £4 million a year before tax but dividends are only £10 a share.

The share capital is held by a small number of people:

Jack Cringe (56)	3,000
Mrs Cringe (54)	2,000
Albert Cringe (Jack's father)	2,000
The Cringe Foundation	3,000

Jack is still very ambitious and wants to expand much further, including building a new factory and moving into Europe. He also wants to buy a country estate as his hobby is pheasant shooting.

Mrs Cringe wishes to support her husband but she also wants some money to finance her son-in-law's new venture into film production.

Albert is a life long Methodist and has an ambition to donate a very large sum to build a replacement for his crumbling local Church.

The Cringe foundation was set up with the shares left by Jack's son who died of Ping's disease. The ultimate aim is to finance research into the disease.

Jack has seen an opportunity to acquire three companies:

Pierre Widgettes – a French company which has a widget distribution chain throughout Europe. The owners will sell but require cash.

Flounce Ltd – a local company which provides a complementary range of widgets. The owners would like to throw in their lot with Cringe and Jack is willing to make Phil Flounce a director of a combined group. However Flounce is advised by his accountants not to accept shares in a private company as consideration for his company.

Rhubarb Widgets PLC – this is an old established company which has made losses in recent years. To stem the losses the company has sold properties and now is cash rich but is still making losses. The shares are quoted in the penny share category. It needs new blood in the management team.

Required:

Write a report to Jack explaining how the ambitions of all the parties mentioned might be met if Cringe Ltd were to obtain a listing on the stock exchange. You should include a section on how the issue price should be calculated and any alternative way of seeking quoted status they may be possible.

Assignment 2

Note this assignment is best done by a number of students but can be written up individually for personal assessment.

Each student is given a paper sum of £10,000 and asked to "invest" it a portfolio of shares. Possible portfolios are:

i.   A single blue chip company.

ii.   12 companies with low PEs

iii.   12 companies with high PEs

iv.   12 companies with low dividend yields

v.   12 companies with high dividend yields

vi.   12 companies with low dividend cover

vii.   12 companies with high dividend cover

viii. 12 investment trusts

ix.   a single investment trust

x.   a single unit trust

xi.   12 unit trusts

xii   12 companies recommended in the financial press

xiii. 12 USM companies

No doubt other possible portfolios will occur to teachers and students.

Record the progress of the portfolio over a period of time. Dividends will need to be included in gains as these will vary from portfolio to portfolio. Contrast the progress of each portfolio with the indeces.

Write a report on findings and put forward any theory that may suggest itself from the figures.

Real Investment

Students of finance are strongly advised to become real investors. Investing involves the student in the real world of investment and with the mechanisms and paperwork of the stock exchange. There is of course a risk of loss but also a chance of gain. Many people seek out companies which give concessions to shareholders. I myself have enjoyed many years of half price channel crossings thanks to a modest investment in P and O.

Further development

Personal Equity Plans

Every person who is resident in the UK is entitled to make investments through personal equity plans known as PEPs. Any dividends and capital gains on PEP investments are entirely free of tax providing the investments remain within the plan. The rules as to how much may invested each year and what investments are eligible change in each Finance Act. However investors are strongly advised to take up the maximum they can afford and are allowed in PEPs.

Assignment 3

Find out the rules as to how much can be invested in PEPs and critically review a number of PEPs advertised.

Tax Exempt Special Savings Accounts

Tax Exempt Special Savings Accounts (TESSAs) are another attempt to persuade the people to save rather than to spend. However these are bank and building society deposits and not stock exchange investments. They should perhaps be in every investors portfolio.

Assignment 4

Find out the rules for TESSAs and suggest which investors might invest in them.

A world wide market

Investment in shares and other company securities by UK investors was at one time more or less confined to UK companies. The stock exchange was a fair market with a wide variety of companies and substantial activity. Uk investors have been well served by the Stock Exchange and few shares have such a thin market that buying or selling is difficult. A similar situation has prevailed in many foreign stock exchanges notably those in the USA. As a result many sophisticated investors have spread their portfolios across the world. This is both more exciting and probably safer as a wide spread of geographical investment will mean that while one area droops others will prosper.

Investment in non UK securities is now open to all through Unit Trusts and Investment Trusts and direct investment is possible. New stock exchanges are opening in the former Eastern Bloc countries and my readers may care to watch the future of stock exchange investment with wonder and perhaps profit.

Exercise

9. Examine the city pages of the serious newspapers and see their coverage of overseas stock exchanges. Note details of any indeces given for these markets and note how they change over time and in relation to the UK and other market indeces.

Share prices

Share prices change frequently, even minute by minute. I noted that Tesco shares had a low in a period of twelve months of 207p and high of 299p. What causes a share price to change? The first reason is that the market in general changes. An announcement is made that the trade gap is twice as bad as expected and all shares tend to move down. This tendency of the whole market to move can be seen in the indeces such as the Financial Times Ordinary Share Index. In addition an individual share may change price due to factors intrinsic to the share. This may be a change of market sentiment about the share or its sector. For example the announcement of a road building programme may push up the shares of construction companies. The change may also come about as a result of new information. For example the announcement that profits were less than expected will depress a share price.

Is it possible to predict share price changes? There is a theory called the *efficient market hypothesis* which suggests not. This theory states that the market is efficient in setting prices. The implication of this is that shares are neither underpriced nor overpriced. In effect the price of a share is the market consensus of what its price should be. In practice the market is not perfectly efficient and academic argument usually centres around the degree of efficiency. Another form of the hypothesis is that a share price reflects all available, relevant information. The implication of this is that any new information which bears on the firm will be instantly incorporated into the price of the share. For example the price will change if the firm announces it is negotiating to buy a competitor or if the half year's profits are less than expected. The hypothesis has three levels of efficiency:

a. The *weak* form – this implies that any information which might be contained in past price movements is already reflected in security prices. This strange idea comes as a refutation of the ideas of chartists. Chartists draw charts of the price of a share over time and might produce something like this.

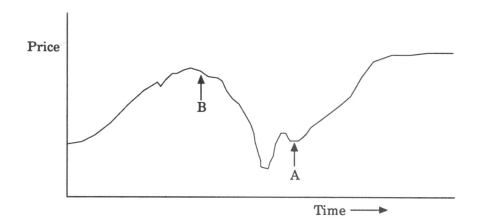

They then predict that in the future there will be similar patterns of movement, allowing perhaps the share to be bought when it is at a similar position to A and sold when it is in a similar position to B and thus making a profit. The logic of this idea is easily refuted and statistical tests show that movements in share prices are randomly distributed and cannot be predicted. Punters always tell you of their gains and never of their losses!

b. The *semi-strong* form – this implies that all publicly available information is encompassed in the share price. So it is pointless looking through endless annual reports and accounts looking for undervalued shares. Despite this most intelligent investors believe with all their hearts that they can find undervalued shares but doubt with all their minds! Stock exchange firms employ researchers to look into companies and assess their worth as investment. In effect this research process is aimed at finding undervalued shares but by so doing ensures that shares are not undervalued.

c. The *strong* form – if this is true then all information, publicly available or not, would be incorporated in the share price. Insiders who are privilege to information not made available to the public (for example knowledge of the intention to make a takeover bid or of the results before they are announced) could not make a profit if this form is true. The general feeling is that insiders can make a profit although to do so is illegal. However an interesting piece of logical thinking is that if several *insiders* have secret information they will buy or sell and thus incorporate the information in the price by creating demand or supply.

10. Danielle is drinking in the Pub one Sunday morning and expresses a need for advice on which shares to buy:

Len works for a major PLC and has seen in his horoscope that he will prosper in his work. This seems a good reason to him to buy shares in his employer.

Den subscribes to a journal which recommends penny shares. They never fail he says and suggests she buys shares in this month's recommendation.

Ken has seen a chart which suggests that Wen PLC's share price is at the same position on the chart that it was in two years ago before it rose 20%.

Penny operates a system where she buys and sells Mega PLC. She buys when the price is 10% below her "norm price". She sells when it is 10% above. Made a fortune she says. She bought some yesterday.

Xen says that his broker recommends MacroBig PLC which the firm's researchers find to be undervalued.

Yen suggests buying Whopper Construction PLC as he notes that they have just landed a big contract to build the new motorway.

Ben who works for a merchant bank and has drunk too much whispers that he has heard in his office that F.M.Errall PLC are going to be subject to a takeover bid that week.

Hen advises her to invest her money in equal amounts in twelve different companies and hold for the long term.

Comment on all these ideas.

11. Kate has 10,000 shares in Mediocre PLC which she bought for 96p each. She has seen the share price rise over the last three months from 120 to 160. Then the company receive a takeover bid from Superior PLC. Superior are offering four shares in Superior for 6 shares in Mediocre.

    She notes in the FT that the news has caused Mediocre's price to rise to 180 and Superior's to fall from 250p to 235p.

    Explain what might be happening.

Capital asset pricing model

If an investor wishes to invest in equities what should he do? Try and follow the following bit of logic:

a. an investor, in investing in a particular share takes two risks:

   ❐ the risk intrinsic to that share, for example, that profits will fall more than expected or that the managing director will have an aeroplane accident. Such events will probably change the share price but are unpredictable.

   ❐ the risk that the market as a whole will rise or fall due to unpredictable events such as the election of a liberal democrat government or an increase in interest rates. All shares tend to move to a greater or less extent with the market.

b. The intrinsic risk can be avoided by investing in a range of shares. Ideally the whole market should be invested in but as this is impossible about a dozen shares is considered reasonable.

c. The market risk cannot be avoided. However each share has a unique reaction to movements of the whole market. Some move more than the market because they are especially prone to changes in the whole economy (eg housebuilders) and some move less because they deal in necessities (eg food processors). It is possible to use statistical means to find the degree of *correlation* of a share with the market movements. The degree of correlation is called the *Beta* and Betas for all quoted companies are published by the London Business School.

d. An investor can thus avoid intrinsic risk by *diversifying* and select the degree of exposure to market risk he requires by selecting companies with the appropriate Betas. Risk averse investors will select low Betas and risk seekers will choose high Beta companies.

   The use of Betas is part of a theory called the Capital Asset Pricing model.

12. Eric and Paul are partners in a firm of insurance brokers. They have done well and both now have some funds that they wish to invest in shares for the long term. Eric is a very solid, cautious person. Paul is a born gambler. How might information on company betas be useful to them?

Answers to selected questions in Section 3

Topic 1

1. C   Gross profit = £100,200. A is the supermarket (cash sales!). B is the fish wholesaler (low stock!)

2. F   Cost of goods sold £540,000. Gross Profit £440,000

6. £15,000 + £1,200 + (10.4% of £16,200) = £17,884.8

7. Alpha. Gross profit £463,000. Wages £207,000. Rates £13,200. Net Profit £23,050.

Topic 2

1. B   Fixed Assets £148. Current Assets £311. Curent Liabilities £250. Net Assets £209. Capital £188 + £51 − £30 = £209.

2. Alan. Gross Profit £750. Rent etc £35. Net Profit £20. Fixed Assets £206. Current Assets £259. Current Liabilities £42. Net Assets £423. Capital £438 + £20 − £35 = £423.

Topic 3

1. c.   Straight Line £1,167 a year. Written down values: 1992 £4,833, 1993 £3,666, 1994 £2,500.

1. e.   i.   Depreciation £4,833 − £1,500 = £3,333. Not on Balance Sheet at end of 1993!

1. g.   Depreciation will be charged in the years 1994 through 1996. But no depreciation after that with straight line. Generally reducing balance would however continue.

3. a.   Lorry £7,000 a year. Copier 1992: £667, 1993: £1,333, 1994: £1,333 1995: £1,333, 1996: £667.

3. b.   Fax Machine 1992 £200, 1993 £150, 1994 £112. Written down values: 1992 £600, 1993: £450, 1994: £338.

5. At the end of 19x9 the old Warehouse will have a written down value of Land £ 10,000 + Buildings £38,750 = £48,750. As it was sold for £100,000 the gain is £51,250. The depreciation on the new warehouse in 19x9 is £3,000. Clearly the gain has a large impact on profit!

   It might be shown as:

	£
Net Profit before exceptional item	31,000
Exceptional item:	
Profit on sale of warehouse	51,250
Profit after exceptional item	82,250

Topic 4

2. c.   Value at £6 + £4 = £10 Prime cost + Overheads £15 = £25.

3. b.   Cost = £40,000 but net realisable value = £38,000 − £4,000 − £1,000 = £33,000 so value at £33,000.

5. FIFO 10 × £15 + 3 × £12 = £186. LIFO 13 × £10 = £130. AVCO 13 × £11.57 = £150.40

Topic 5

1. a.   1993: Raw Materials £528. Prime Cost £1,326. Works Overheads £954. Gross Profit £746. Admin £425. Selling £627. Net Loss £386.

1. b.   ii.   Decrease 19x3 loss by £38,000 and decrease 1994 profit by same amount

1. d.   Factory Direct Wages: Remained relatively stable (gone slightly down in 19x4) despite inflation and increased turnover. Conclusion labour force reduced. Perhaps big increase in Plant and Machinery in 19x3 is connected.

   Royalties: big increase in 19x4. Possibly new products being made under licence, perhaps with the new machinery.

Topic 6

1. Cain: Gross Profit £2,500. Profit after Interest £720. Dividends £210. Retained Profits £330. Fixed Assets £4,668. Current Assets £1,399. Current Liabilities £1,755. Net Assets £1,912. Profit and Loss Account £693. Capital and Reserves £1,912.

4. a. Balance Sheet at end: Net Assets £17,800. Share Capital £3,750. Share Premium £2,850. Revaluation Reserve £6,000. Profit and Loss Account £5,200.

Topic 7

3. The contract for importing the US product has no effect on the Profit and Loss Account or Balance Sheet as it had no cost. When profits are earned later as a consequence of having the contract, the financial statements will show these profits but not until then. The effect of full order books will also not be shown as they had no cost. Again profits will eventually affect the financial statements when the orders are translated into profits. The possibility of making 20 workers redundant would have been to pay a large sum of redundancy pay but the removal of the threat would not affect the profits. The old factory owned by the company has within it the possibility of substantial payments to right environmental wrongs. Such possible payments would not appear in the accounts as a consequence of the going concern convention.

7. If liquidation values were to be substituted then:

   ❏ Fixed Assets would be at net realisable value

   ❏ Stock would be at net realisable value

   ❏ Approved current contract work awaiting payment would probably not be paid and, if sued, the debtors would countersue for losses incurred as they would have to employ other contractors to finish the jobs.

   ❏ Retentions would likely not be paid as Cowboy would not be able to continue to guarantee their work.

   ❏ Current contract work – as contract debtors

   ❏ Prepayments – most likely lost

   ❏ add redundancy pay to creditors

   ❏ add to creditors future rent payments on leased properties until the ends of leases

   ❏ Any corporation tax included in taxation would probably not be payable because of terminal losses

   ❏ Dividend would probably not be paid

   ❏ Debenture becomes a current liability

   ❏ Profit and Loss Account would have to reflect all the losses envisaged above!

Topic 8

4. a.

		K	L	M
i	ROCE $\left(K \text{ is} \frac{2,400}{6,350}\right)$	38%	19%	6.6%
ii	AUR $\left(L \text{ is} \frac{21,000}{6,340}\right)$	5.6	3.3	1.45
iii	DPP $\left(M \text{ is} \frac{4,200}{34,000} \times 365\right)$	–	55 days	45 days
iv	NPTS $\left(K \text{ is} \frac{2,400}{35,800}\right)$	6.7%	5.7%	4.5%
v	Stock $\left(K \text{ is} \frac{1,100}{27,100}\right)$	15 days	40 days	82 days

K is the Supermarket. L is the textile company and M is the process plant manufacturer.

ROCE is not really meaningful for supermarkets but is for the other two. However valuation differences are important. AUR is also less meaningful for supermarkets (especially those with high spare cash) and in any case must be considered in relation to similar companies.

Supermarkets sell for cash! The other DPPs are relevant. NPTS must be compared only with **similar** companies. Stock turnover (against cost of sales!) is the relevant bit. In the case of the **manufacturers** separate figures for raw materials, work in progresss and finished goods are needed.

9. B   Gearing $\dfrac{170}{170 + 200 + 480}$ = 20%

        ROCE $\dfrac{240}{170 + 200 + 480}$ = 28% (before tax)

        ROSF $\dfrac{240 - 25 - 62}{200 + 480}$ = 22.5% (after tax)

Topic 9

2. Micah

Operations (27 + 22 − 3 + 2 − 4 − 8)	36
Dividend paid	(13)
Tax Paid	(12)
Fixed Assets (66 − 8)	(58)
Debenture	10
Share Issue (6 + 6)	12
Net Outflow (21 + 4)	25

Topic 10

3. a. £294,000   b. £14.70   c. £394,000   d. £19.70   e. £56,000

7.

	Cut	Make	Finish
Rates	4,348	8,696	6,956
Machinery Depeciation	8,400	4,200	1,400
Electric Power	18,000	9,000	3,000
Supervision	4,000	8,000	10,000
Total	34,748	29,896	21,356
Machine hour rates	£57.91	£99.65	£213.56

d.

Materials	300
Labour (78 × £6)	468
OHDs Cutting	695
Making	598
Finishing	4,698
	6,759
Profit	1,690
Sales Price	8,449

Clearly, finishing overheads on this basis are nonsense and a labour hour rate would seem to be more appropriate!

Topic 11

3. a.   At 600,000, cloth is 54p a metre + 10p + $\dfrac{200,000}{600,000}$ = 97.3p

At 1,200,000 cost is 74.7p.

3. b.   Material costs are non-linear. Fixed overheads are spread over more output thus lowering unit costs.

6.   Ken: Breakeven − 2,000 batches. Relevant range − 2,000(?) to 4,000.

Margin of Safety 20%. Statistic is : number of batches sold must exceed BE point or sales (BE sales are £100,000). Period is not specified but if figures are annual then sales of £8,333 a month.

Topic 12

4. a. She has to pay out on overheads before cash is received from customers. Also she pays her friend 20% up front.

    b. Fixed costs are £6,000 + interest £2,000 = £8,000. This means turnover (of which 20% goes to her friend) will need to be £10,000.

        Viability means making more than £8,000 a year as that is the opportunity cost of going on her own. Turnover would need to be £20,000 a year.

    c. Risk, fear, excitement, upside possibilities, personal satisfaction.

7.

Profit and Loss Accounts (all figures in £'000)	£300SP Make	£300SP Buy	£320SP Make	£320SP Buy
Sales	1,500	1,500	1,440	1,440
Variable	650	1,000	585	900
Fixed	600	200	600	200
Profit	250	300	255	340

Best is to Buy in and sell at £320.

Problems of control over production, supply, quality, stability of pricing etc. Desire to give employment in the UK.

14.

	A	B	C
Contribution	5	6	7
Contribution per minute	1	3	1.17
Rank	3	1	2
Make	2,760	3,000	2,700
Usage (max 600)	230	100	270

Topic 13

2. a. Reduce staff by one and work overtime if necessary.

        Reduce training, reduce Margaret's management and training time.

        Keep the old vans.

        You can visualise the consequences of these measures in reduced efficiency, stress and sickness.

        An alternative may be to improve efficiency by more preventive maintenance or scheduling client visits more scientifically to reduce travelling time and costs.

6. On conventional approaches: as last year + %age for inflation + extra for new initiatives.

    Zero-based: Do we need any PR? If yes, how much? Do we have the right approach, cost structure, people? Can we get it more efficiently by using outside firms?

Topic 14

3. a. Cloth – Total variance

	Std	$300 \times 12 \times £2$ =	£7,200
	Actual	$4,000 \times £1.89$ =	£7,560
	Variance		£360 ADV
Price		$4,000 \times 11p$ =	£440 FAV
Usage		$400 \times £2$ =	£800 ADV

3. b. Price: Price change, lower quality, special deal, bulk purchase.

        Quantity: Natural variation, wastage, damage to cloth, poorer quality cloth, poor supervision or labour practice.

3. c. Low price and high usage may both be a function of quality.

3   d. Consider quality of cloth, labour practices, supervision.

6. a. Total Variance is Actual £23,900 compared with $13,100 \times \frac{£20,400}{13,500}$ = £4,104 ADV.

Efficiency: 13,100 should require $\frac{13,100}{3}$ = 4,367 labour hours but actually took 4,650.

So 283 extra hours were worked. They would drive $\frac{£20,400}{4,500}$ = £4.533 per hour overheads.

Ergo variance is £4.533 × 283 = £1,283 ADV.

Expenditure. 4,650 labour hours should drive $4,650 \times \frac{£20,400}{4,500}$ = £21,080 but actual was £23,900 so variance is £2,820 ADV

Note that £1 is lost in rounding.

6. b. Variable overheads are thought to be driven by labour hours. Too many labour hours were used. Possibly due to breakdowns, sickness, accidents, poor supervision, use of lower grade/inexperienced labour.

Actual were more than expected from labour hours. Possible causes are natural variation (eg repairs, lubricants), price rises, inefficiencies (low grade labour?), price rises.

8. a. Standard Overhead recovery is $\frac{£10,000}{4,000}$ = £2.50 per unit.

Actual cost	£11,050
Recovered 3,870 × £2.50	£9,675
Total Variance	£1,375 ADV

Expenditure variance is simply £11,050 −£10,000 = £1,050 ADV

Volume variance is volume shortage 130 units × £2.50 = £325 ADV

8. b. Expenditure may be price rises or natural variation (eg preventive maintenance)

Volume may be inability to produce for reasosn such as accidents, breakdowns, need for maintenance downtime, inefficiencies in the labour force etc. Volume may also be deliberate underproduction due to lack of sales.

Topic 15

2. Receipts: Capital £2,500. From Sales £31,500

Payments: Farmers £30,000. Wages £5,230. Drawings and expenses £10,200

Balances Overdrawn: £2,427, £7,117, £10,080, £11,880, £11,800, £11,430

b. Say £15,000 to be safe.

c. Evidence of willingness of farmers to deliver and sell to him, evidence that supermarkets will buy, evidence of acceptabilty of price differences.

d. Not at all if Giles personally guarantees the overdraft.

e. Profit of £3,420 less bank interest in first six months. Contrast with drawings of £4,200. But at £9,000 a month business would be profitable.

f. Rising then falling. The usual pattern unless expansion continues for ever.

Topic 16

1. Project B: Payback 3 years. NPV at 12% £20,770. Profitability index £20,770/£20,000 = 1.0385. Internal rate of return 14% gives £19,950 so that is the IRR as near as can be calculated with tables.

4. a. NPV at 14% is £46,656 – viable. at 22% £38,004 – not viable

b. Approximately 20%

c. If new machine is purchased then £50,000/6 = £8,333 a year + loss on sale of old machine in first year.

If not purchased then £8,333 for next 5 years on the old machine.

d. £4,288 a year.

8. B + E would give NPV of 130, but B + C + D + F would give 131.

Topic 17

3. a. Positive balance on Profit and Loss Account. This is not conclusive – losses may be have been incurred in recent years. Better evidence is that Corporation Tax (payable on profits) is payable.

    b. It has a large overdarft and has to repay the Unsecured loan stock in the near future.

    c. Lack of cash and (b) above.

    d. Mortgage of premises, rights issue, issue of more loan stock (perhaps convertible to make it attractive), factoring debts.

    e. Net Assets value is Net Assets/number of shares ie $\frac{£992,000}{1,000,000}$ = 99.2p. The actual quote is way below this. The cash crisis seems to have scared investors!.

Topic 18

4. a. Debtors average payment time 121 days. Stock Turnover 84 days. Creditors average payment time 94 days.

    b. Seems to have a high ROCE. Problems are a very long debtors payment period and a dangerously long time taken to pay creditors.

    c. Working Capital will rise by £15,000 and fall by £10,000. Components will change as:

    debtors + £11,200, stocks + £4,800 and creditors – £5,600.

    Consequently overdraft may increase by £5,400.

9. a. £15,600.   b.   £72,000.   c.   21.7%

    d. The one and two month people would mostly take the discount. The 3 and 4 months people would mostly not. So the cost would actually be much more than 21% and would not reduce the debtors much.

Topic 19

3. a. Each share is priced at £1.92. If the assets were realised at their book value(unlikely!) and the liabilities paid off £2.17 would be available for each share. Dividends will be received and in the past the annual dividends paid represent only 0.9% of the Share price. The share price has been fairly volatile in the last year so unless care is taken over the time of disposal a capital loss could be sustained. Current price is at the higher end.

    b. i.   No, as he needs income and, at his age, a capital gain is not so essential.

        ii. No, as he also needs income.

        iii Yes, he needs no income, needs a capital gain to maintain his capital on eventual retirement. He would also probably like the risk.

7. a. If the share price stays at or near 120p, then conversion will change an investment valued at 86 into one valued at 60. So conversion will depend on a substantial rise in the share price. There are five years in which this can happen. If conversion does not take place then redemption (presumably at par, giving Judy a capital gain over curent price) will be in 19x9 and, in the meantime, Judy will receive annual interest of £160.

    b. The price of convertibles is a complex function of several variables and one of these is prevailing interest rates. If rates fall the value of the convertible will rise.

Glossary of accounting terms

Absorption: the sharing out of the costs of a cost centre among the products which use the cost centre.

Account: a record in a double entry system that is kept for each (or each class) of asset, liability, revenue and expense.

Accounting equation: an expression of the equivalence, in total, of assets = liabilities + equity.

Accounting period: that time period, typically one year, to which financial statements are related.

Accounting policies: the specific accounting bases selected and followed by a business enterprise (eg straight line or reducing balance depreciation).

Accounting rate of return: a ratio sometimes used in investment appraisal but based on profits not cash flows. Not recommended.

Accounting Standards Board: a quasi-statutory subsidiary of the Financial Reporting Council which makes, amends and withdraws accounting standards.

Accounting standards: Prescribed methods of accounting. The original set (Statements of Standard Accounting Practice – SSAPs) were issued by the Accounting Standards Committee and adopted by the professional bodies. Currently Financial Reporting Standards are issued by the Accounting Standards Board.

Accruals: (that which has accrued, accumulated, grown) expenses which have been consumed or enjoyed but which have not been paid for at the accounting date

Accruals convention: the convention that revenues and costs are matched with one the other and dealt with in the Profit and Loss Account of the period to which they relate irrespective of the period of receipt or payment.

Accumulated depreciation: that part of the original cost of a fixed asset which has been regarded as a depreciation expense in successive Profit and Loss Accounts: cost less accumulated depreciation = net book value.

Acid test: the ratio of current assets (excluding stock) to current liabilities.

Activity based costing: cost attribution to cost units on the basis of benefit received from indirect activities. The idea is that overhead costs are driven by activities (eg setting up a machine) not products.

Allocation: the charging of discrete, identifiable costs to cost centres or cost units. A cost is allocated when it is unique to a particular cost centre.

Amortisation: another word for depreciation: commonly used for depreciation of the capital cost of acquiring leasehold property

Apportionment: the division of costs among two or more cost centres in proportion to estimated benefit on some sensible basis. Apportionment is for shared costs.

Assets: resources of value owned by a business entity

Assets utilisation ratio: a ratio which purports to measure the intensity of use of business assets. Calculated as sales over net operating assets. Can be expressed as sales as a percentage of net operating assets.

Asset value: a term which expresses the money amount of assets less liabilities of a company attributable to one ordinary share.

Avoidable costs: the specific costs of an activity or sector of a business which would be avoided if that activity or sector did not exist.

Auditing: the independent examination of, and expression of an opinion on, the financial statements of an enterprise by an appointed auditor in pursuance of that appointment and in compliance with any relevant statutory obligation.

AVCO (average cost): a method of valuing fungible assets (notably stock) at average (simple or weighted) input prices.

Bad debts: debts known to be irrecoverable and therefore treated as losses by inclusion in the Profit and Loss Account as an expense

Balance sheet: a financial statement showing the financial position of a business entity in terms of assets, liabilities and capital at a specified date.

Bankruptcy: a legal status imposed by a court. Usually a trustee is appointed to receive and realise the assets of the bankrupt and to distribute the proceeds to his creditors according to the law.

Benefits in kind: things or services supplied by a company to its directors and others in addition to cash remuneration. The best known is the provision of and free use of a motor car. The value of benefits in kind are taxable.

Bond: a formal written document that provides evidence of a loan. Bond has mainly American usage. Its UK equivalent is debenture.

Bonus issue: a free issue of new shares to existing shareholders. No payment is made for the shares. Its main effect is to divide the substance of the company (assets less liabilities) into a larger number of shares.

Book value: the amount at which an asset is carried on the accounting records and Balance Sheet. The usual book value for fixed assets is cost less accumulated depreciation. Alternative words include written down value, net book value and carrying value. Book value rarely if ever corresponds to saleable value.

Breakeven chart: a chart which illustrates costs, revenues, profit and loss at various levels of activity within a relevant range.

Breakeven point: the level of activity (eg level of sales) at which the business makes neither a profit nor a loss ie where total revenues exactly equal total costs.

Budget: a formal quantitative expression of management's plans or expectations. Master budgets are the forecast or planned Profit and Loss Account and Balance Sheet. Subsidiary budgets include those for sales, output, purchases, labour, cash etc.

Capital: an imprecise term meaning the whole quantity of assets less liabilities owned by a person or a business.

Capital allowances: deductions from profit for fixed asset purchases. In effect capital allowances is a standard system of depreciation used instead of depreciation for tax purposes only

Capital budgeting: the process of planning or appraising possible fixed asset acquisitions.

Capital employed: a term describing the total net assets employed in a business. Various definitions are used, so beware talking at cross purposes.

Capital expenditure: expenditure on fixed assets

Cash: strictly coins and notes but used also to mean all forms of ready money including bank balances.

Cash discount: a reduction in the amount payable by a debtor to induce prompt payment (equivalent to settlement discount)

Cash flow: a vague term (compare cash flow difficulties) used for the difference between total cash in and total cash out in a period.

Cash flow forecast: a document detailing expected or planned cash receipts and outgoings for a future period

Cash flow statement: a formal financial statement required by Financial Reporting Standard (FRS) 1 and showing a summary of cash inflows and outflows under certain required headings.

Committed costs: those fixed costs which cannot be eliminated or even cut back without having a major effect on the enterprise's activities (eg rent)

Common stock: the US equivalent of ordinary shares.

Companies Act 1985: the major Act of Parliament which regulates companies. Was modified and extended by the Companies Act 1989.

Company: a body corporate regulated by the Companies Act 1985.

Conservatism: (also known as prudence) the convention whereby revenue and profits are not anticipated, but provision is made for all known liabilities (expenses and losses) whether the amount of these is known with certainty or is a best estimate. Essentially – future profit, wait until it happens – future loss, count it now.

Consideration: the amount to be paid for anything sold including businesses. May be cash, shares or other securities.

Consistency: convention that there is consistency of accounting treatment of like items within each year and from year to year.

Consolidation: the aggregation of the financial statements of the separate companies of a group as if they were a single entity.

Contribution: a term used in marginal costing – the difference between sale price and associated variable costs.

Controllable costs (also known as managed costs): costs, chargeable to a budget or cost centre, which can be influenced by the actions of the persons in whom control is vested.

Conversion cost: the cost of bringing a product or service into its present location or condition. may include a share of production overheads

Convertible loan stock: loans where, at the option of the lender, the loan can be converted into ordinary shares at specified times and specified rates of conversion.

Cost behaviour: the change in a cost when the level of output changes

Cost centre: a location, function, or item of equipment in respect of which costs may be ascertained and related to cost units.

Cost convention: the accounting convention whereby balance sheet assets are mostly valued at input cost or by reference to input cost.

Cost-volume-profit (CVP) analysis: the study of the relationships between variable costs, total fixed costs, levels of output and price and mix of units sold and profit.

Credit: commonly used to refer to a benefit or gain also the practice of selling goods and expecting payment at a later date.

Credit control: those measures and procedures adopted by a firm to ensure that its credit customers pay their accounts.

Creditors: those persons, firms or organisations to whom the enterprise owes money.

Creditors payment or settlement period: a ratio (usually creditors/ inputs on credit in a year × 365) which measures how long it takes the firm to pay its creditors.

Cumulative preference shares: preference shares where the rights to dividends omitted in a given year accumulate. These dividends must be paid before a dividend can be paid on the ordinary shares.

Current assets: cash + those assets (stock, debtors, prepayments, bank accounts) which the management intend to convert into cash or consume in the normal course of business within one year or within the operating cycle.

Current cost accounting (CCA): a system of accounting which recognises the fluctuating value of money by measuring current value by applying specific indices and other devices to historical costs. A valid method which is complex and difficult to understand intuitively.

Current liabilities: debts or obligations that will be paid within one year of the accounting date. The Companies Act prefers the expression – Creditors: amount falling due within one year.

Current ratio: the ratio of current assets to current liabilities.

Cut-off: the difficulties encountered by accountants in ensuring all items of income and expense are correctly ascribed to the right annual profit statement.

Debenture: a document which creates or acknowledges a debt. Commonly used for the debt itself.

Debt: a sum due by a debtor to his creditor. Commonly used also as a generic term for borrowings.

Debtors: those who owe money.

Debtors payment (settlement) period: a calculation of the average time taken by credit customers to pay for their goods. Calculated by Debtors/credit sales in a year × 365.

Depletion method: a method of depreciation applicable to wasting assets such as mines and quarries. The amount of depreciation in a year is a function of the quantity extracted in the year compared to the total resource.

Depreciation: a measure of the wearing out, consumption or other loss of value whether arising from use, effluxion of time or obsolescence through technology and market changes. Depreciation should be allocated to accounting period so as to charge a fair proportion to each accounting period during the expected useful life of the asset.

Direct costs: those costs comprising direct materials, direct labour and direct expenses which can be traced directly to specific jobs, products or services.

Discount: a monetary deduction or reduction. Settlement discount (also known as cash discount) is given for early settlement of debts. Debentures can be redeemed at a discount. Trade discount is a simple reduction in price given to favoured customers for reasons such as status or bulk purchase.

Discounted cash flow: an evaluation of the future cash flows generated by a capital investment project, by discounting them to their present value.

Dividend: a distribution of earnings to its shareholders by a company.

Dividend cover: a measure of the extent to which the dividend paid by a company is covered by its earnings (profits).

Dividend yield: a measure of the revenue earning capacity of an ordinary share to its holder. It is calculated by dividend per share as a percentage of the quoted share price.

Drawings: cash or goods withdrawn from the business by a proprietor for his private use.

Earnings: another word for profits, particularly for company profits.

Earnings per share: an investor ratio, calculated as after tax profits from ordinary activities/ number of shares.

Economic order quantity (EOQ): that purchasing order size which takes into account the optimum combination of stockholding costs and ordering costs.

Entity convention; the convention that a business can be viewed as a unit that is a separate entity and apart from its owners and from other firms.

Equity: the ordinary shares or risk capital of an enterprise. Also a system of law and a Trade Union for actors.

Exceptional items: items of expense in the Profit and Loss Account which are abnormal as to size or incidence but are not extraordinary items. They include abnormal charges for bad debts, write offs of stocks and abnormal provisions for losses on long term contracts. They should be disclosed.

Expense: a cost which will be in the Profit and Loss Account of a year.

Exposure draft: a document issue on a specific accounting topic by the Accounting Standards Board for discussion.

Extraordinary items: items which derive from events or transactions outside the ordinary activities of the business and which are both large and expected not to recur frequently or regularly. They may include profits or losses arising from discontinuance of a significant part of a business. Extraordinary items are shown "below the line" after the results derived from the ordinary activities have been computed.

Factoring: the sale of debtors to a factoring company to improve cash flow. Factoring is a method of obtaining finance tailored to the amount of business done but factoring companies also offer services such as credit worthiness checks, sales and debtor recording, and debt collection.

FIFO: first in first out – a method of recording and valuation of fungible assets, especially stocks, which values items on the assumption that the oldest stock is used first. FIFO stocks are valued at most recent input prices.

Finance lease: a leasing contract which transfers substantially all the risks and rewards of ownership of an asset to the lessee. In effect the lessee is really buying the assets with the aid of a loan and the lease instalments are really payments of interest and repayments of capital. They are accounted for as such in accordance with the accounting convention of substance over form.

Financial Reporting Council: quasi government body which encourages good financial reporting. This is done through the Accounting Standards Board, the Financial Reporting Review Panel and the Urgent Issues task Force.

Financial Reporting Review panel: a subsidiary of the Financial Reporting Council which reviews accounts of companies and seeks to ensure compliance with the requirements of the Companies Act and the Accounting Standards Board.

Financial statements: Balance Sheets, Profit and Loss Account, Income and Expenditure Accounts, Cash Flow Statements and other documents which formally convey information of a financial nature to interested parties concerning an enterprise. In companies, the financial statements are subject to audit opinion.

Fixed assets: business assets which have a useful life extending over more than one year. Examples are land and buildings, plant and machinery, vehicles.

Fixed cost: a cost which in the short term, remains the same at different levels of activity. An example is rent.

Flexible budget: a budget which is flexed to recognise the difference in behaviour of fixed and variable costs in relation to levels of output. Total budgeted costs changed to accord with changed levels of activity.

Floating charge: an arrangement whereby a lender to a company has a floating charge over the assets generally of the company gives the lender priority of repayment from the proceeds of sale of the assets in the event of insolvency. Banks frequently take a floating charge when lending.

Format: a specific layout for a financial statement. Several alternatives are prescribed by the Companies Act 1985.

Funds flow statement: a financial statement which links balance sheets at the beginning and end of a period with the Profit and Loss Account for that period. Now replaced by the cash flow statement.

Fungible assets: assets which are substantially indistinguishable from each other. Used for stocks which can then be valued on FIFO or AVCO principles. LIFO is also possible but not usually in the UK for tax reasons.

Gearing: also known as leverage, the relationship between debt and equity in the financing structure of a company.

Gilt-edged securities: securities and investments which offer a negligible risk of default. Principally government securities.

Goal congruence: the situation in which each individual, in satisfying his (her) own interests, is also making the best possible contribution to the objectives of the enterprise.

Going concern: the accounting convention which assumes that the enterprise will continue in operational existence for the foreseeable future. This means in particular that the Profit and Loss Account and Balance Sheet assume no intention or necessity to liquidate or curtail significantly the scale of operation.

Goodwill: an intangible asset which appears on the Balance Sheet of some businesses. It is valued at (or below) the difference between the price paid for a whole business and the fair value of the net assets acquired.

Gross: usually means before or without deductions. For example Gross Pay or Gross Profit.

Gross profit: sales revenue less cost of sales but before deduction of overhead expenses. In a manufacturing company it is sales revenue less cost of sales but before deduction of non-manufacturing overheads.

Gross margin: (or gross profit ratio), gross profit expressed as a percentage of sales.

Group: a set of interrelated companies usually consisting of a holding company and its subsidiary and sub-subsidiary companies.

Group accounts: the financial statements of a group wherein the separate financial statements of the member companies of a group are combined into consolidated financial statements.

HIFO: highest in highest out, a pricing policy where costs are collected for a job on the basis that the cost of materials and components is the highest recent input price.

Historical cost: the accounting convention whereby goods, resources and services are recorded at cost. Cost is defined as the exchange or transaction price. Under this convention, realisable values are generally ignored. Inflation is also ignored. The almost universal adoption of this convention makes accounting harder to understand and lessens the credibility of financial statements.

Hurdle: a criterion that a proposed capital investment must pass before it is accepted. It may be a certain interest rate, a positive NPV or a maximum payback period.

Income and expenditure account: the equivalent to Profit and Loss Accounts in non-profit organisations such as clubs, societies and charities.

Indirect costs: costs which cannot be traced to particular products. An example is rent or management salaries. They are usually shared by more than one product and are called overheads.

Insolvency: the state of being unable to pay debts as they fall due. Also used to describe the activities of practitioners in the fields of bankruptcy, receivership and liquidations.

Intangible assets: assets which have long term value but no physical identity. Examples are goodwill, patents, trade marks and brands.

Interim dividend: a dividend paid during a financial year, generally after the issue of unaudited profit figures half way through the year.

Internal rate of return: the rate of discount which will just discount the future cash flows of a proposed capital investment back to the initial outlay.

Inventory: a detailed list of things. Used by accountants as another word for stock.

Investment appraisal: the use of accounting and mathematical methods to determine the likely returns for a proposed investment or capital project.

Key factor: a factor of production which is in limited supply and therefore constrains production.

Labour hour rate: a method of absorption where the costs of a cost centre are shared out amongst products on the basis of the number of hours of direct labour used on each product.

Leverage: an American word for gearing.

LIFO: Last in first out – a valuation method for fungible items where the newest items are assumed to be used first. Means stocks will be valued at old prices. Not used much in the UK for tax reasons.

Limiting or key factor: a factor of production which is in limited supply and therefore constrains output.

Liquidation: the procedure whereby a company is wound up, its assets realised and the proceeds divided up amongst the creditors and shareholders.

Liquidity: the ease with which funds can be raised by the sale of assets.

Liquidity ratios: ratios which purport to indicate the liquidity of a business. They include the current ratio and the acid test ratio.

Listed companies: companies whose shares are traded on the stock exchange.

Machine hour rate: a method of absorption of the costs of a cost centre where the costs are shared out among the products which use the centre in proportion to the use of machine hours by the relevant products.

Management accounting: the provision and interpretation of information which assists management in planning, controlling, decision making, and appraising performance.

Management by exception: control and management of costs and revenues by concentrating on those instances where significant variances by actual from budgets have occurred.

Manufacturing accounts: financial statements which measure and demonstrate the total costs of manufacturing in a period. They are followed by Trading and Profit and Loss Accounts.

Marginal costing: a system of cost analysis which distinguishes fixed costs from variable costs.

Marginal cost: the additional cost incurred by the production of one extra unit.

Margin of safety: the excess of budgeted activity over breakeven activity. Usually expressed as a percentage of budgeted activity.

Mark-up: gross profit expressed as a percentage of cost of goods sold.

Matching convention: the idea that revenues and costs are accrued, matched with one another as far as possible so far as their relationship can be established or justifiably assumed, and dealt with in the Profit and Loss Account of the period in which they relate. An example is the matching of sales of a product with the development costs of that product. The appropriate periods would be when the sales occur.

Master budgets: the overall budgets of an enterprise comprising cash budget, forecast Profit and Loss Account and forecast Balance Sheet. They are made up from subsidiary budgets.

Materiality: the accounting convention that recognises that accounting is a summarising process. Some items and transactions are large (= material) enough to merit separate disclosure rather than inclusion with others in a lump sum. Examples are an exceptionally large bad debt or an exceptionally large loss on sale of a fixed asset.

Minority interest: the interests in the assets of a Group relating to shares in group companies not held by the holding company or other members of the group.

Modified accounts: financial statements which are shortened versions of full accounts. Small and medium sized companies can file these with the Registrar of Companies instead of full accounts.

Money measurement: the convention that requires that all assets, liabilities, revenues and expenses shall be expressed in money terms.

Net: usually means after deductions. For example net current assets = current assets less current liabilities and net cash flow means cash inflows less cash outflows. Contrast gross.

Net book value: the valuation on the Balance Sheet of an asset. Also known as the carrying value or written down value.

Net present value: the value obtained by discounting all cash inflows and outflows attributable to a proposed capital investment project by a selected discount rate.

Net realisable value: the actual or estimated selling price of an asset less all further costs to completion (eg cost of a repair if it needs to be repaired before sale) and all costs to be incurred before and on sale (eg commission).

NIFO: Next in first out – a pricing policy where costs are collected on the basis that the cost of materials and components is the next input price.

Nominal value: the face value of a share or debenture as stated in the official documents. Will not usually be the same as the issue price which may be at a premium and which will almost never correspond to actual value.

Objectivity: the convention of using reliable and verifiable facts (eg the input cost of an asset) rather than estimates of "value" even if the latter is more realistic.

Operating cycle: the period of time it takes a firm to buy inputs, make or market a product and sell to and collect the cash from a customer.

Opportunity cost: the value of a benefit sacrificed in favour of an alternative course of action.

Ordinary shares: the equity capital of a company.

Overheads: indirect costs

Overtrading: a paradoxical situation when a firm does so much business that stocks and debtors rise leading to working capital and liquidity difficulties.

Par value: the nominal sum imprinted on a share certificate and which appears in the Balance Sheet of a company as share capital. It has no significance as a value.

Payback: the number of years which will elapse before the total incoming cash receipts of a proposed project are forecast to exceed the initial outlays.

Periodicity: the convention that financial statements are produced at regular intervals usually at least annually.

Preference shares: shares in which holders are entitled to a fixed rate of dividend (if one is declared) in priority to the ordinary shareholders and to priority over ordinary shareholders in a winding up.

Planning variance: a variance arising because the budgeted cost is now seen as out of date. Examples are wage or price rises.

Premium: an amount paid in excess of par or nominal. Premiums can be on issues and redemptions of shares or debentures.

Prepayments: expenditure already made on goods or services but where the benefit will be felt after the Balance Sheet date. Examples are rent or rates or insurances paid in advance.

Price earnings ratio: an investor ratio calculated as – share price/ earnings per share.

Prime cost: the direct costs of production.

Private company: any company that is not a public company.

Profitability index: in investment appraisal, the Net Present Value of cash inflows/ the initial outlays

Profit and loss account: a financial statement which measures and reports the profit earned over a period of time.

Pro Rata: in proportion to.

Prospectus: a document being an advertisement offering shares for sale to the public. Must comply with the rules of the Companies Act and the Stock Exchange.

Provision: a charge in the Profit and Loss Account of a business for an expense which arose in the past but which will only give rise to a payment in the future. To be a provision the amount payable must be uncertain as to amount or as to payability or both. An examples is possible damages awardable by a court in a future action over a past incident (eg a libel).

Prudence (or conservatism): the convention whereby revenue and profits are not anticipated, but provision is made for all known liabilities (expenses and losses) whether the amount of these is known with certainty or is a best estimate. Essentially – future profit, wait until it happens – future loss, count it now.

Public company: a company which states that it is a public company, ends its name with the designation Public Limited Company (PLC) and has a minimum share capital of £50,000. All listed companies are PLCs but not all PLCs are listed.

Quick ratio: also known as acid test ratio, current assets (except stock)/ current liabilities.

Quoted company: also known as a listed company, a company whose shares are traded on the stock exchange.

Realisable value: the amount that an asset can be sold for.

Realisation: to sell an asset and hence turn it into cash.

Realisation convention: the concept that a profit is accounted for when a good is sold and not when the cash is received.

Receiver: an insolvency practitioner who is appointed by a debentureholder with a fixed or floating charge when a company defaults.

Redemption: repayment of shares, debentures or loans.

Redemption yield: the yield given by an investment expressed as a percentage and taking into account both income and capital gain or loss.

Reducing balance: a method of depreciation whereby the asset is expensed to the Profit and Loss Account over its useful life by applying a fixed percentage to the written down value.

Registrar of companies: a civil service agency situated in Cardiff where files are maintained on all companies. These are open to view by the public.

Relevant costs: costs that will only be incurred if a proposed course of action is actually taken. The only ones relevant to an actual decision.

Relevant range: the range of activity which is likely. Within it variable costs are expected to be linearly variable with output and fixed costs are expected to be unchanged.

Reporting: the process whereby a company or other institution seeks to inform shareholders and other interested parties of the results and position of the entity by means of financial statements.

Reserves: a technical term indicating that a company has total assets which exceed in amount the sum of liabilities and share capital. This excess arises from retained profits or from revaluations of assets.

Retained profits: also known as retentions, the excess of profits over dividends.

Return on capital employed: a profitability ratio being income expressed as a percentage of the capital which produced the income. A difficult idea because of the problems of defining income and capital.

Return on sales: the ratio of profit to sales expressed as a percentage.

Returns: the income flowing from the ownership of assets. May include capital gains.

Revenue: amounts charged to customers for goods or services rendered.

Revenue expenditure: expenditure that benefits only the current period and which will therefore be charged in the Profit and Loss Account.

Rights issue: an invitation to existing shareholders to subscribe cash for new shares in the company in proportion to their holdings.

Salvage value: also known as residual value, the amount estimated to be recoverable from the sale of a fixed assets at the end of its useful life.

Secured liabilities: liabilities secured by a fixed or floating charge or by other operation of law such as hire purchase commitments.

Securities: financial assets such as shares, debentures and loan stocks.

Segmental reporting: the practice of breaking down turnover, profits and capital employed into sections to show the separate contributions of each to the overall picture. Segments can be distinct products, geographical areas, classes of customer etc.

Semi-variable costs: costs which have a fixed element and a variable element. Repairs to machinery and telephone are examples.

Settlement discount: a reduction in the amount payable given to a customer to induce rapid payment.

Shares: the division of a company into numerous equal parts. A shareholder may have one or many shares.

SSAPs (Statements of Standard Accounting Practice): accounting practices which are now mandatory in the UK. There are 22 SSAPs covering numerous subjects including depreciation, stock valuation, extraordinary items, segmental reporting.

Standard cost: a predetermined cost that management establishes with great care and uses as a basis for comparison with actual to measure variances.

Stepped fixed costs: fixed costs which are fixed within a specific range of outputs but which step up to a new level if the range is exceeded.

Stock turnover: a ratio which purports to measure the speed at which raw materials or stocks for sale are used up or sold. It is expressed as average time in which the relevant stocks are actually in stock.

Straight line: a depreciation method which allocates the cost of a depreciable asset(less salvage value) over the estimated useful life of the asset in equal instalments.

Subsidiary company: a company of which more than half of the equity capital is owned by another company.

Substance over form: an accounting convention whereby a transaction is accounted for in accordance with its substance or commercial reality in preference to its legal form. Examples are finance leases, hire purchase and group accounts.

Sum of digits: a depreciation method that allocates the cost (less salvage value) of a depreciable asset over its useful life by steadily diminishing instalments.

Sunk costs: costs which have already been incurred and therefore are irrelevant and are not considered in making a decision.

Total absorption cost: a system of costing where all costs (or just production costs) are ascribed to products. Thus the total absorption cost of a product is its direct cost + its fair share of shared overheads.

Trade discount: a reduction in invoiced price of a good given to favoured customers, special classes of customer or for bulk purchase.

Trading account: a financial statement which measures and demonstrates the gross profit earned in a period.

Transaction: any event or activity in a firm requiring an entry in the double entry bookkeeping system. Examples are sales and purchases of goods and services and the receipts and payments of cash.

Trial balance: a listing in two columns (debit and credit) of all the balances in a double entry bookkeeping system.

True and fair view: the view that the Companies Act requires all financial statements to give. It is a difficult concept which is usually discussed in auditing texts.

Turnover: another term for total sales in a period.

Unsecured creditors: those creditors, short or long term, who do not have the benefit of a fixed, floating or other charge over any assets.

Value: the difficult concept in accounting. There are values in use, book values, values to the firm, going concern values, realisable values, nominal values, par values, written down values and many others.

Variable cost: a cost which in the short term and over a relevant range tends to vary linearly following the level of activity.

Variance: the difference between a planned, budgeted or standard cost and the actual cost. Variances are generally referred to as adverse (= unfavourable) or favourable.

Wasting assets: assets which are used up in producing goods. Can be applied to all fixed assets but usually confined to mines, quarries, and mineral rights.

Winding up: the liquidation of a company by realising the assets and distributing the proceeds to the parties entitled.

Working capital: the excess of current assets over current liabilities.

Work in progress: the inventory of goods started but not completed at a Balance Sheet date.

Write-off: to write something off is to charge it to Profit and Loss Account as an expense.

Written down value: the cost of an asset less accumulated depreciation. Also known as net book value or carrying value.

Yield: the return on an investment usually expressed as a percentage.

Index

Cost and
Management Accounting
An Active-Learning Approach

T Lucey

ISBN: **1 873981 09 0** • Date: **August 1992** • Edition: **1st**
Extent: **400 pp (approx)** • Size: **275 x 215 mm**
Lecturers' Supplement ISBN: 1 873981 75 9

Courses on which this book is expected to be used
BTEC Higher National Business and Finance and other business studies courses. In conjunction with a text such as *Costing* by the same author, accountancy courses (ACCA, CIMA, AAT etc)

This book provides a complete teaching course in cost and management accounting. The three-part structure of the text ensures that first students identify problems in realistic contexts (Section1) and then are directed to the appropriate information on principles and practices to solve them (Section 2). Case exercises, assignments and examination questions (with and without answers) develop knowledge and skills (Section 3).

Contents:

Section 1 – Scenarios and Related Tasks An ongoing scenario of a management trainee joining a large group of diverse companies; the accounting problems he encounters form the tasks and assignments.

Section 2 – Student Information Bank The Basics of Cost and Management Accounting • Materials and Labour • Overheads • Costing Methods: Job, Batch and Contract Costing • Costing Methods: Service, Process and Joint-product Costing • Planning, Control and Cost Behaviour • Budgeting • Cash Budgeting • Standard Costing • Decision Making and Marginal Costing • Break-even Analysis • Investment Appraisal.

Section 3 – Developing Knowledge and Skills Assignments and examination questions develop the skills of the student.

"Promoting Active Learning"

Accounting and Finance for Business Students
M Bendrey, R Hussey & C West

An Active-Learning Approach

ISBN: **1 873981 05 8** • Date: **July 1992** • Edition: **2nd**
Extent: **450 pp (approx)** • Size: **275 x 215 mm**
Lecturers' Supplement ISBN: **1 873981 34 1**

Courses on which this book is known to be used
BTEC National and HNC/D Business and Finance; BA Business Studies; CMS/DMS; IPM; ICM; HND Business Information Technology; A Level Business Studies; BSc Engineering; BSc Computing; BEd in Business Studies; BA in Modern Languages and other management development courses.

On reading lists of IAM and ICM

This book provides a comprehensive introduction to accounting and finance. It includes numerous examples, with solutions in the text, to assist the student in understanding each topic. Also, for directed private study, there are student activities (assignments, objective tests, etc).

The opportunity has been taken in the second edition to improve the layout and presentation of the book. There is a new chapter on Manufacturing Organisations, and every chapter has been thoroughly reviewed and updated where necessary. The index has been expanded and the number of tasks, questions and assignments increased.

Contents:
Sources & Uses of Finance • Personal Finance • Business Finance • **Financial Accounting** • Sole Traders • Concepts & Control • Limited Liability Companies • Other Organisations • **Management Accounting** • Using Costs for Planning and Control • Using Costs for Total Costing • Using Costs for Decision Making • Project Appraisal.

Review Comments:
'Best textbook at this level [HNC Business & Finance].' 'Price and coverage are excellent.' 'Easily referenced sections – good, clear layout' 'Perfect for the course! [HNC Business & Finance]' 'Concise and easy for students to follow.' 'Gives a good introduction at an excellent price.' 'Assignments are excellent for classroom activities.' – Lecturers

Free Lecturers' Supplement